CITIZENS' MEDIA AGAINST ARMED CONFLICT

CITIZENS' MEDIA
AGAINST ARMED CONFLICT

Disrupting Violence in Colombia

CLEMENCIA RODRÍGUEZ

University of Minnesota Press
Minneapolis
London

Portions of chapter 3 were published as "Knowledges in Dialogue: A Participatory Evaluation Study of Citizens' Radio Stations in Magdalena Medio, Colombia," in *Making Our Media: Global Initiatives toward a Democratic Public Sphere,* vol. 1, *Creating New Communication Spaces,* ed. Clemencia Rodríguez, Dorothy Kidd, and Laura Stein, 131–54 (Cresskill, N.J.: Hampton Press, 2010). Portions of chapter 3 were also published as Clemencia Rodríguez and Amparo Cadavid, "From Violence to Discourse: Conflict and Citizens' Radio in Colombia," in *Conflicts and Tensions,* vol. 1 of the Cultures and Globalization series, ed. Raj Isar and Helmut Anheier, 313–27 (Thousand Oaks, Calif.: Sage, 2007); published by the UCLA Center for Civil Society.

Lyrics from the song "Anthem" copyright Sony/ATV Music Publishing LLC. All rights administered by Sony/ATV Music Publishing LLC, 8 Music Square West, Nashville, TN 37203. All rights reserved. Used by permission.

Published by the University of Minnesota Press
111 Third Avenue South, Suite 290
Minneapolis, MN 55401-2520
http://www.upress.umn.edu

Printed in the United States of America on acid-free paper

Library of Congress Cataloging-in-Publication Data

Rodríguez, Clemencia.
    Citizens' media against armed conflict : disrupting violence in Colombia / Clemencia Rodríguez.
        p. cm.
    Includes bibliographical references and index.
    ISBN 978-0-8166-6583-9 (hc : alk. paper) — ISBN 978-0-8166-6584-6 (pb : alk. paper)
    1. Citizen journalism—Colombia. 2. Local mass media—Political aspects—Colombia. 3. Mass media—Political aspects—Colombia. 4. Political violence—Press coverage—Colombia. 5. Insurgency—Press coverage—Colombia. I. Title.
    PN5052.R53 2011
    079 .861—dc22

                                        2010048760

17 16 15 14 13 12 11   10 9 8 7 6 5 4 3 2 1

Para Antonia, Mariana y Leonarda.
Ojalá a ellas el país no les duela tanto como a nosotros.

The use of language is all we have to pit against death and silence.

—Joyce Carol Oates

CONTENTS

LIFE AT THE CROSSFIRE

An Introduction to Colombia's Violence
and Its Context

Se percibía el miedo, pero aun así la vida parecía ser más fuerte.

—Santiago Gamboa, *Necrópolis*

ARMED GUERRILLAS, PARAMILITARIES, and other groups storm and terrorize small towns isolated by Colombia's impossible geography with a frequency that has granted a perverse everyday-life feeling to such violence over the course of the country's forty-year armed conflict. The scene is well known in Colombia. The armed ones (*los armados*) cut off the electricity and dozens, sometimes hundreds, of armed men and women invade a town. In the case of guerrilla assaults, sparsely staffed police stations attempt to repel the attacks. Paramilitary groups operate differently; they enter civilian communities, list in hand, privileging selective assassinations over military attacks.

How do isolated communities react when harassed by armed groups? Is there any type of agency in their response? Do media play a role when communities try to galvanize a response? As the guerrilla-driven conflict worsened in southern Colombia during the mid-2000s, the Fuerzas Armadas Revolucionarias de Colombia (FARC) [Revolutionary Armed Forces of Colombia], the main guerrilla group operating in the country, attacked the town of Belén de los Andaquíes in southern Colombia. Gunfire, explosives, and the presence of hundreds of armed guerrillas in the small downtown terrified residents. People locked their doors, hid under their beds, and surrendered to the fear and isolation war imposes. In the midst of this chaos, the local community radio station opened a new communication space, where an alternative to the reigning terror could be felt and shared.

By transmitting traditional Colombian Christmas carols (known in Colombia as *Villancicos*) and asking people to open their windows and turn up the volume, the radio station created a way out of terror. Soon, dozens of unarmed civilians, waving white flags, came out onto the central plaza. The Colombian Christmas music, transmitted by the station and amplified by the church's loudspeakers and home radios, created a "symbolic shield," allowing people to overcome the terrifying effects of violence. The radio station opened a communication space and triggered a sense of togetherness and collective agency in the community, successfully, albeit momentarily, countering the fear and isolation wrought by violence. In moments of crisis, when victimized by armed groups, local citizen-controlled media can help their communities overcome feelings of collective terror, helping people to find crucial information about food, shelter, medicine, and other logistical support. In crisis situations, these media also serve as impromptu forums where citizens can discuss responses to the crisis and make collective decisions. During my fieldwork in Colombia, however, I heard citizens' media producers insist that their long-term peacebuilding efforts have greater impact than their media responses in moments of crisis. This book explores how Colombian communities cornered by armed groups use communication and media to buffer, answer, and in some cases resist the impact of armed violence.

War's impact on civilian communities goes far beyond the immediate devastation of direct attacks. War gradually erodes the social, democratic, and cultural fabric of communities when civilians are forced to live side-by-side with armed groups for years. The groups recruit the children of these communities and inject massive doses of mistrust, individualism, fear, and uncertainty into the lives of regular citizens. The rule of law is replaced by the use of force, and local democratic institutions are weakened. Armed groups corrupt, co-opt, or threaten local government officials. Levels of impunity increase, and governance and accountability are subsumed by corruption and bribery. Local elections are bought out or boycotted by the occupying groups, and warring factions impose friend/foe ideologies that diminish citizen participation in local decision-making processes. Tanks invade public spaces, soldiers dig sand trenches, and military platoons patrol parks and plazas, severely restricting freedom, mobility, and use of public spaces to create and maintain social bonds. The presence of armed groups and their practice of recruiting informants and supporters among local civilians deteriorate traditional bonds of solidarity, togetherness, and trust in communities. Individuals and families learn to mistrust neighbors, friends, and distant relatives, leaving them severely isolated. As isolation and terror mount, feelings of impotence and victimization take over, and the use of weapons and aggression becomes normalized. Resolving everyday conflicts with violence and force is perceived as acceptable and effective. Intolerance of difference increases extremist and sectarian ideologies.

Here I examine how media and information and communication technologies (ICTs) can act as powerful tools to help civilian communities survive conflict and war. When grassroots communication media are deeply embedded in their communities, truly open to collective participation, and responsive to immediate and long-term local communication needs, they strengthen the agency of the community as it responds to armed violence.

As tools explicitly designed to craft symbolic products and processes, media and ICTs occupy a privileged position in helping communities reconstitute symbolic universes that have been disrupted by violence. Through production of their own radio, video, or television programming, civilian communities can begin reconstituting webs of meaning, allowing them to make sense of their experience of war. When communities are able to access their own media and develop their own communication competencies as media producers, they can use citizens' media to narrate, interpret, remember, and share the lived experience of violence. Citizens' media facilitate communication processes in which civilians recreate traditional solidarities and form new ones, return to public places that have been abandoned in terror, and organize collective actions. ICTs trigger communal processes to bring civilians, one step at a time, out of the isolation and terror imposed by armed violence and back into the public sphere.

During my fieldwork in Colombian armed-conflict regions, I witnessed the phenomenon of citizens' media "stealing" children and youth from war to cultivate ideologies of peaceful coexistence grounded in local cultures. When citizens' media are genuinely open to community participation and situated in local knowledges, languages, and aesthetics, they help keep children and youth away from armed groups. These media cultivate alternative understandings of difference, encourage nonaggressive ways of being and interacting, and model nonviolent conflict management.

Media can become powerful tools for empowering civilian communities to strengthen processes of good governance, transparency, and accountability. A local election overseen by a community radio station, or a public budget scrutinized by civic groups in front of community television cameras, increases the legitimacy of public institutions. These media technologies have the potential to transform private political and institutional processes into public sphere events, thereby solidifying people's trust in democratic institutions and the rule of law.

Perverse Economies, Social Movements, and War

Armed conflict in Colombia is not a black or white proposition. Political actions, economic interests, illegal economies, class alliances, and social movements in Colombia create complex scenarios of armed conflict that overlap, intersect, and diverge, resulting in outcomes that can change from moment to moment and region to region. Illegal armed groups, including guerrillas, paramilitary organizations, self-defense militias, drug, emerald, gold, and gasoline mafias, along with legal armies, such as the Colombian army and other security institutions, saturate local and regional social, political, economic, and cultural processes with the logic of war, the normalization of violence and weapons, and authoritarian ideologies.

In the following pages I attempt to describe some of the contexts foregrounding Colombia's armed conflict and the impact they have on the everyday lives of civilian communities in the places where I conducted fieldwork on citizens' media. Instead of attempting to create a complete reconstruction of the history of Colombia's armed conflict, my goal is to paint the scene in rough strokes to provide readers with some background for understanding the social and political contexts of my fieldwork. The following pages are written from the point of view of the civilian communities under siege in regions far from the country's centers of economic and political power. My main sources are the scholarship of Colombian and Colombianist historians, political scientists, anthropologists, sociologists, and economists. I attempt to be comprehensive in my search for regional studies of Montes de María, Magdalena Medio, and Caquetá, the three regions where I conducted fieldwork.

In Colombia, grassroots social movements, armed groups, economic and political elites, and illegal economies interact in complex, ambiguous, and sometimes even contradictory ways that shape regional realities of armed conflict and social/political unrest. The interactions between these disparate actors change over time, creating what French sociologist Daniel Pécaut has called "a kaleidoscopic perception of violence" (Pécaut 2001, 93)[1] in the viewpoint of local communities. As varied armed groups, economic elites, and state actors establish and break alliances in their battles for military power and control of wealth, local communities living in regions of armed conflict experience war's impact as a constant shifting in the shape of their everyday lives. Based on decades of historical research in Colombia, Pécaut states that, against their will, Colombia's "population finds itself inscribed in the logics of war" (Pécaut 2001, 18). The recognition of this involuntary conscription of the daily lives of civilians in a war that is not their own is perhaps the most significant lesson to be learned from recent regional scholarship by Colombian social scientists. In the words of anthropologist of violence Carolyn Nordstrom, unarmed civilians experience the terrorizing comings and goings of antagonistic armed groups in their communities as "a time of trial, terror, deprivation, and bereavement" (Nordstrom 1992, 265), and not in politicomilitary or ideological terms. What follows is an analysis of the main elements shaping the armed conflict as experienced by unarmed civilians in the three regions I studied.

Land Tenure and Social Violence

In Colombia, disputes around land tenure emerged at the end of the nineteenth century as a pivotal historical process, a significant cause of social unrest, and an instigator of social movements. Each of the three regions studied in this book have been home to instances of large-scale land appropriation, due to such factors as illegitimate allocation of land titles to landowners guilty of bribing corrupt government officials; abusive use of barbed wire; the use of force or threats to expel landowners from small farms close to large haciendas; the use of generalized terror by large hacienda owners to push small landowners from their plots, and then buy their land at bargain prices; and the central government's lax attitudes toward the regulation of assigning public lands to hacienda owners (Legrand 1986; Reyes 1999; Zamosc 1986, 1997). (In chapter 1, I describe in detail land tenure problems in Caquetá; in chapter 2, I cover Montes de María; and in chapter 3, I describe these problems in Magdalena Medio.) These corrupt and often violent land appropriation practices can be seen in the examples of the Larandia hacienda in Caquetá and the Bellacruz hacienda in Magdalena Medio, both existing in regions where I conducted field-work for this book.

In the early 1930s Larandia, one of the largest cattle haciendas in Latin America, began expanding in Montañita, a municipality neigh-boring Belén de los Andaquíes, home of Radio Andaquí, a community radio station I examine in chapter 1. The hacienda was started in 1933, when more than twelve thousand acres were allocated to Josefa de Perdomo; in 1935 she sold her land to the Lara family (Arcila Niño et al. 2000, 117). Between 1935 and 1950 Larandia grew by one thou-sand acres annually; between 1955 and 1965 the hacienda was grow-ing at a rate of six thousand acres every year (Arcila Niño et al. 2000, 57). The hacienda's name honors the Lara family, who maintained it for several generations. At its peak, Larandia covered ninety-nine thousand acres and held fifty thousand head of cattle; the hacienda included ports and piers on the Orteguaza River, bridges, an airport, and forty kilometers of road on which the Laras charged a toll to any-one passing through (Jaramillo, Mora, and Cubides 1986, 11). Twelve hundred people lived and worked in Larandia. The hacienda grew so large an entire Huitoto community was forcefully displaced from their land to accommodate the hacienda's need to expand (Arcila Niño et al. 2000, 117).[2] Today, one of the two main military bases in the region is housed at Larandia.

The Bellacruz hacienda, in the department of Cesar, has been a site of conflict and struggle since 1934, when the Marulanda family, who bought seventeen thousand acres of land from the Canadian Royal Bank, began pressuring neighboring small landowners to sell their land. "By 1950, news stories about conflict between the Marulanda family and agricultural unions could already be found in the national press" (Madariaga 2006, 59). By 1956 the hacienda had accumulated more than a hundred thousand acres "full of cattle" (Madariaga 2006, 59). In 1994 the government allocated nearly five thousand acres of what had been the Bellacruz hacienda to the 170 agricultural families that held claims to the land before being forced out by the Marulandas. In 1996 280 of the families who had received parcels of the Bellacruz hacienda in restitution left their lands due to violent persecution and harassment by drug lord Victor Carranza's paramilitary forces. The paramilitaries "stole our money, electrical goods and household items, and set fire to our houses. They beat adults and children with sticks, rifles and *rejos* (knotted whips). They used machetes to cut short the hair of those who wore it long. They set fire to and destroyed the schools and their furniture and teaching materials" (Amnesty International 1997, 1). Those expelled said they had received threats and "a deadline of five days to leave the hacienda and stay more than a hundred kilometers from it, otherwise they would be assassinated" (Madariaga 2006, 61). Between 1998 and 1999 two members of the Marulanda family and managers of the Bellacruz hacienda were tried on charges of terrorism and the formation of illegal armed groups (Madariaga 2006, 64). In 2004, after years of unfulfilled agreements with the government, 578 peasants fleeing the Bellacruz area were relocated to La Miel, in the department of Tolima, thousands of miles from their homeland.

Processes of land accumulation have only worsened. According to a recent study, twenty years ago land estates of more than twelve thousand acres occupied 32 percent of the useful land in the country; today, these large land holdings occupy 62 percent of the land and belong to only 4 percent of the landowners. Also, according to the same study, one in four small landowners has been displaced from his or her land (Semana 2010).

Parallel Realities: Community Activism and
Radicalized Armed Movements

In response these kinds of illegitimate land appropriations, Colombian peasant communities formed their own grassroots organizations to resist the actions of large landowners and demand rights from the central government. Although it is generally believed that these peasant organizations are leftist, the groups began organizing years before the spread of leftist ideologies in Latin America in the 1960s and 1970s. For example Ligas Campesinas [Peasant Leagues], Sindicatos de Obreros Rurales [Rural Workers' Unions], and Unidades de Acción Rural [Rural Action Units] date back to the 1930s, decades before the proliferation of strong leftist ideologies in Latin American social movements. Later, in the 1960s, Juntas de Acción Comunal (JACs) [Community Action Boards], county-based elected citizens' committees, played a central role in strengthening peasant social movements.[3] In some cases, a grassroots organization emerged from the status quo before it evolved into a social justice movement. The Asociación

Nacional de Usuarios Campesinos (ANUC) [National Association of Peasants], for example, was created by government mandate in 1966 to address land tenure issues. From its official origin, ANUC evolved into one of the primary leaders of peasant movements for social justice and against land appropriation; in 1971, only five years after its creation, ANUC had almost a million members and more than thirteen thousand trained leaders (Grupo de Memoria Histórica 2009, 80).

Other grassroots social movements, such as a strong labor movement led by unions of oil workers, palm workers, and cement workers; urban movements; youth movements; and a more recent women's movement emerged in Colombia during the 1960s and 1970s (A. Delgado 2006; Madariaga 2006; Vásquez 2006).

Without a doubt, grassroots social movements express the agency of Colombian communities. Beginning in the 1930s and continuing through the 1960s and on to today, these community-based movements have organized, marched, spoken out, protested, proposed, met with consecutive governments, signed agreements, complained about the government's lack of accountability in realizing the agreed actions, organized again, marched again, and so on. Social movements commonly go beyond just demanding land, improved conditions, and social justice for their own constituencies. Magdalena Medio's oil worker unions, for example, are known for demanding (and obtaining) improvements in the educational, health, and transportation infrastructure for their entire region (A. Delgado 2006, 155–57).

Although in some cases and points in history the boundaries may blur, armed social struggles and nonviolent social movements have coexisted as distinct realities in Colombia for decades. However, armed groups tend to make so much noise that social movements are drowned out in the landscape of social justice struggles. Tatiana Duplat, a young historian working with citizens' media, and one of my key contacts during my fieldwork, explained:

> One of the main conclusions of my dissertation is that the reconciliation initiative in Ariari was successful on account of a very strong legacy of agrarian organizational culture in the region. Guerrilla organizations emerged and grew in the region very early on, but civilian peasant organizations did not succumb to them; in other words, the agrarian movement in the region during the 1920s was very strong. . . . [Later] persecuted by the Conservative regime, this agrarian movement split in two; one faction remained organized around agrarian unions and the other faction opted for armed

struggle. The faction that opted for armed struggle was the beginning of FARC in the area. Many scholars have studied the armed peasant movements, but they are forgetting or not giving enough visibility to the other reality, that of peasant organizations that continue to this day, with different names, but still very strong; these organizations coexisted with armed groups. Sometimes they confronted armed groups, and sometimes they didn't, but they were not afraid of armed groups, and they were not entirely cornered. For example, Ariari farmers told me that during the 1960s, even though FARC had influence in the entire region, the guerrillas still had to consult with the directors of Juntas de Acción Comunal [Community Action Boards], Juntas Agrarias [Agrarian Boards], and Sindicatos Campesinos [Peasant Unions]. The director of each group would convene a meeting with the entire board or union and a dialogue and consultation followed. Guerrillas were not permitted to just arrive in a community and impose what they wanted on these communities. This was the state of affairs until the late 1970s. Today it's a different story, because what you have today is a crossfire. Now it's no longer about a dialogue with one interlocutor, instead it's a question of hiding while different armed opponents shoot each other to extinction . . . it's about waiting to see what happens. But in any case, all those other organizational processes still exist and are strong and vibrant; they are our hope for the future, not tomorrow's future or next year's future, but a long-term future. (Duplat 2004)

In many cases, radicalized factions, willing to realize social change via the use of force and armed violence, broke away from social movements to form armed groups. This was true in the case of several guerrilla organizations that emerged in the 1960s and 1970s; for example, several of ANUC's leaders resurfaced as M-19 *guerrilleros* in Caquetá in the 1970s (see chapter 1).

The main guerrilla organizations in Colombia's recent history include Movimiento 19 de abril (M-19) [April 19 Movement], Ejército Popular de Liberación (EPL) [Popular Liberation Army], Ejército de Liberación Nacional (ELN) [National Liberation Army], and FARC. Born from a radicalized traditional party (the Alianza Nacional Popular, or ANAPO [National Popular Alliance]) and supported by radical students and young professionals, M-19 was the only guerrilla group with a strong presence in Colombia's urban centers. M-19 negotiated a peace process with then-president Virgilio Barco in 1989. Today, several former M-19 leaders are dynamic political figures in the Colombian Congress and other political spheres.

EPL and ELN emerged from radicalized peasant movements formed to resist land expropriation; one of the main claims these two groups made to the Colombian state, and maintained for decades, is the need for agrarian reform. EPL was never able to recruit more than a thousand combatants; in 1991 this organization agreed to demobilize under the administration of President César Gaviria. Since demobilizing, the organization has become a political movement known as Esperanza, Paz y Libertad [Hope, Peace, and Freedom]; however, small, radicalized factions that never agreed to demobilize still operate in some areas (OPPDHDIH 2002, 33). ELN is a 1960s reincarnation of the earlier Liberal guerrillas, led by Rafael Rangel in the Chucurí area in Magdalena Medio. In 2003 ELN had five thousand combatants (seventeen hundred women) (González, Bolívar, and Vásquez 2003).

FARC is a leftist reincarnation of the Liberal guerrillas. It emerged out of the bipartisan political violence between the Liberal and Conservative parties in the 1950s and 1960s. Radicalized factions of the Liberal Party took up arms after the period of social unrest following the assassination of Liberal leader Jorge Eliécer Gaitán in 1948. Over the next twenty years, some of these radicalized Liberal guerrillas became depoliticized and formed gangs of bandits that terrorized farmers (large and small landowners) in rural areas where state institutions are weak.[4] Some other Liberal guerrillas incorporated leftist ideologies and resurfaced years later as Marxist, Maoist, and Trotskyist guerrillas. This incorporation of leftist ideology was the case for FARC, which by 2003 had more than sixteen thousand combatants (fifty-eight hundred women) (González, Bolívar, and Vásquez 2003).[5]

Colombia's political violence has to be examined from a framework of social inequality. In contrast with many other intrastate conflicts that spiral around ethnic or religious differences in other parts of the world, the Colombian conflict is deeply embedded in the extremely unequal distribution of resources and power in Colombian society (Rappaport 2005, 16). Despite all of its legal and illegal social justice struggles, Colombia "is one of the most unequal countries on the most unequal continent in the world" (García Villegas and de Sousa dos Santos 2004, 34). In 1999 the wealthiest 10 percent of the Colombian population received 45 percent of the country's total income (García Villegas and de Sousa dos Santos 2004, 35). Colombian economic elites play crucial roles in the escalation of armed conflict; elites maintain control over the country's natural resources, have the political power to uphold exclusionary policies, and sponsor and support private armies and vigilante-type justice, among other actions.

Complicating Circumstances: Guerrilla Organizations and Social Movements

The 1970s and 1980s are characterized by the growth of guerrilla organizations and the increasingly complex interactions between guerrillas, civilian communities, and social movements. Guerrilla organizations, such as FARC and ELN, took hold of larger and larger territories, forcing more and more unarmed civilian families to learn to coexist with the presence of armed guerrillas. In rural areas, given the absence of police or other state security, this meant that if a group of *guerrilleros* came to one's farm, the best practice was to accommodate them; farmers fed *guerrilleros,* allowed them access to trails, and roads, etc. Families who were new homesteaders in agricultural frontier regions cultivated a social fabric of solidarity and mutual help; in the words of a Magdalena Medio farmer: "In those days solidarity was common; if someone needed something you had, you shared what you had; if a new homesteader came, we fed them until they could grow their own food" (Arenas Obregón 1998, 39). As newcomers to this type of homesteader society, guerrillas were embraced, and benefitted from the same type of solidarity. In some areas, the guerrillas were widely accepted by the larger communities. As an example of the contradictions and ironies so common to Colombia's contemporary history of armed conflict: until 1977, FARC enjoyed wide acceptance even among large hacienda owners in Magdalena Medio, because *guerrilleros* were the only ones persecuting and punishing the cattle robbers and bandits terrorizing agricultural families in the area (Vásquez 2006). This early acceptance allowed guerrilla organizations to grow and become stronger.

As early as the 1950s, guerrilla organizations were supporting civilian communities in their struggle for better life conditions. There are multiple instances of early guerrilla organizations "accompanying" massive caravans of civilian families venturing beyond the agricultural frontier in search for new land to homestead. Known as *colonización armada* (armed colonization), these caravans present an accurate symbol of Colombia's historical complexity, with grassroots initiatives and armed struggles journeying together as two sides of the same coin—a coin spiraling on a scenario of urgent search for land.

During the 1960s and 1970s, guerrilla organizations supported peasant and labor organizations, as well as urban social movements that, by that time, had demonstrated clear leftist inclinations. To illustrate the symbiotic interaction between social movements and guerrilla organizations, I quote a testimony from a participant in the peasant movement in Magdalena Medio:

> A year after we came here, we were beginning to organize in order to start the legalization of land titles. We built a shelter to have our meetings. Once, we were having a meeting in our shelter, when we saw two men in civilian clothes, coming with one of the land takeover leaders. They waited until we finished our meeting and then they identified themselves as members of the ELN. They gave us a lecture [about the process of legalization of land titles] and because we didn't have any money to travel to the capital to start the paperwork, they gave it to us. Then they came every week, or every month. (Arenas Obregón 1998, 53)[6]

However, there is abundant evidence demonstrating that guerrilla organizations and social movements are autonomous and independent social processes, despite the mass media trend to conflate them. In some cases, individuals can belong to both, but the idea that a Colombian union is a social movement by day and an armed militia—with uniforms, military training, and so forth—by night cannot be sustained (Bolívar 2006; A. Delgado 2006; Madariaga 2006; García Villegas and de Sousa dos Santos 2004; Ramírez 2001).

The complex interaction between social justice movements and guerrilla organizations continues to this day (Archila and Bolívar 2006; de Sousa Santos and García Villegas 2004; Duplat 2003; Ramírez 2001). Although guerrilla organizations play significant, if variable roles in the actions of social movements, we need to remember that grassroots organizations and social movements have their own agency, their own ideals, their own leaders, and their own reasons for accepting or rejecting guerrilla support. In some cases they accept guerrilla help for utilitarian purposes, in other cases because they are terrified, and in other cases because they cannot say no. During the 1980s and 1990s, guerrilla organizations made supporting social movements' actions one of their priorities. Thus, marches, demonstrations, and strikes were "supported" with weapons and force provided by guerrilla organizations (F. González 2006, 522). Some Colombian analysts state that in certain regions at certain points in history, due to their alignment with guerrilla organizations, social movements were manipulated by the guerrillas, criminalized by the state, and lost the support of their local communities (Alvaro Delgado cited by F. González 2006, 520). In regions where guerrillas and social justice movements were too closely allied, such as in the case of the alliance between the palm oil unions and FARC in Magdalena Medio, the negotiations between the company and the workers were greatly permeated by armed violence. While guerrilla organizations murdered and/or kidnapped company executives and professionals and destroyed company infrastructure, right-wing paramilitaries were murdering and disappearing union leaders (F. González 2006, 523). In the words of Colombian historian Fernán González, "the abuse of citizens by the guerrillas, and dirty wars fought by militaries and paramilitaries against the leaders of social movements blurs the lines between social justice actions and violent actions" (F. González 2006, 533).

According to Pécaut, Colombian regions in which patron–client relationships are historically normal and legitimate easily transition to submitting to guerrillas, seeing them as just a new type of patron (Pécaut 1999, 17). It is important to keep in mind that communities are frequently alone in their dealings with guerrilla organizations. In the daily lives of agricultural families living in regions far from national centers of power, where the central government, international organizations, nongovernmental organizations (NGOs), and human rights organizations are known only for their absence, these families have to find their own ways to survive.

Drug Mafias and Paramilitaries

In the early 1980s, guerrilla organizations, emboldened by their increasing numbers and strength, shifted goals. Before this time, the guerrillas' goal was to disseminate leftist ideologies in poor farming communities (what these organizations called "a political/ideological line of action"). After the shift in the early 1980s, however, guerrilla organizations began to prioritize military and financial goals (De Roux 1996, 98). FARC and ELN attempted to extend their military power throughout their regions of influence, and to gain control over alternate sources of income, including illicit drug economies, kidnapping, and "safety taxes,"[7] known in Colombia as *vacunas* (vaccines). Guerrilla organizations devised a new form of demonstration known as the *paro armado* (armed strike), in which the FARC and ELN ordered people to stay home, thus stopping all local social and economic activities and paralyzing local economies. In order to finance their military infrastructure, FARC and ELN began taxing not only large hacienda owners, but also small farmers, shop owners, and even market vendors. As a result of this shift, there is abundant evidence of the general population's escalating rejection of *guerrilleros* and increased negative attitudes toward the guerrilla organizations (González, Bolívar, and Vásquez 2003; Vásquez 2006, 319).

Illicit drug economies grew parallel to the growth of guerrilla organizations in different regions of the country. In 1981 coca and marijuana plantations covered 62,000 acres; by 1998 coca, marijuana, and poppy plantations covered 272,000 acres (Tokatlián 2000, 37). In the two decades from 1980 to 2000, the illicit drug economy brought 40 billion dollars into Colombia. The impact of illicit drug economies on the armed conflict in the country is overwhelming. Drug economies and organized crime permeated and corrupted state institutions, including the armed forces and the police, the judicial system, and also legal economies, sports, and even beauty pageants. Yet, even more devastating, drug traffickers made enormous quantities of money available. This liquid cash flowed into armed groups, allowing them to multiply their armaments, recruit more combatants, and intensify the violence. Tokatlián describes how "the bourgeoisie, the guerrillas, and the paramilitaries established marriages of convenience with organized crime to meet their tactical needs" (Tokatlián 2000, 40). Colombian drug traffickers' "functional polygamy" (Tokatlián 2000, 40) provides the war with a never-ending source of income. Illicit drug economies, according to Pécaut, alter and influence all social sectors and dimensions of war (Pécaut 2001, 116).

At the same time that public opinion turned against the guerrillas, drug traffickers began buying large landholdings in territories with strong guerrilla presence. By 2000 drug traffickers owned 15 million acres of farmland in 40 percent of the country's municipalities (Tokatlián 2000, 37). These new landowners were unwilling to accept the type of guerrilla bullying that communities had learned to live with. In response, they formed their own militias to exterminate the guerrillas in their territories. Many traditional hacienda owners supported these new ways of resisting guerrilla harassment by hiring their own private armies and imposing weapons-backed regional regimes.[8] These landowner militias are the birthplace of many radical right-wing paramilitary militias that sought to exterminate not just guerrillas, but anything and anyone with leftist leanings (Cadavid 1996, 39). These "anticommunist" vigilante groups evolved into right-wing paramilitary organizations intolerant of any type of dissent or even difference. The massacre of Mapiripán carried out by paramilitary forces in the department of Meta on July 15, 1997, marks the beginning of a paramilitary national expansion (Grupo de Memoria Histórica 2009, 202). Anyone not perfectly aligned with their conservative, capitalist, Catholic, and heterosexual values (i.e., gay people, hip youth, feminists, human rights activists, social movement leaders, among many others) became a military target (Martha Cecilia García 2006; F. González 2006; Vásquez 2006).

Paramilitary Violence

While guerrillas made the Colombian armed forces and state institutions their military targets, the paramilitary organizations targeted civilians. Using the argument that farming families "support" the guerrillas, paramilitary groups assassinated, massacred, disappeared, and generally terrorized people in entire regions of farming communities. Between 1990 and 2000 the paramilitary were responsible for 4,757 violent actions against civilians (35 percent of the nation's total), while they only engaged in 176 combat actions against other armed groups (González, Bolívar, and Vásquez 2003, 102). Guerrilla organizations followed the lead of the paramilitary groups, with ELN and FARC each being responsible for 22 percent of all attacks against civilians between 1990 and 2000 (González, Bolívar, and Vásquez 2003, 103). During the same years, the Colombian armed forces were responsible for 13 percent of all attacks against civilians (González, Bolívar, and Vásquez 2003, 103).

Leaders of grassroots organizations have been singled out as targets by paramilitaries, weakening social movements and unarmed dissent. On the other hand, given the popular exhaustion with trying to meet guerrilla demands, paramilitary organizations began to enjoy popular support (in some regions, and at some times more than others). In 1980, before the emergence of paramilitary and self-defense groups, there were twenty-one homicides per hundred thousand inhabitants in Colombia, three times higher than the homicide rate for the rest of Latin America. Paramilitary violence in the 1980s and after multiplied that figure by four, until it reached a rate of eighty homicides per hundred thousand inhabitants (Romero 2003, 27).[9]

The emergence of radical right-wing paramilitary groups brought devastating consequences for unarmed civilian communities (González, Bolívar, and Vásquez 2003). Caught between the guerrillas, the paramilitaries, the Colombian armed forces, and the mafias, unarmed civilians experienced increased paralysis and less freedom of action. According to De Roux, in Magdalena Medio "the conflicting camps demand that [unarmed] people declare their allegiance to one or the other [of the armed groups]" (De Roux 1996, 99). In Colombia today, rather than battling over ideological differences, armed groups are fighting for the control of territories, civilian communities, and sources of wealth, and "terror is the most frequently used tactic to secure territorial control" (García Villegas and de Sousa dos Santos 2004, 51).

Armed groups regulate everything about the daily lives of citizens in the communities they control. They control comings and going, how many groceries and medicines are bought at the market and kept at home, interactions with neighbors and friends (in some cases armed groups monitor even the flirting of young women [Meertens 2001, 139; Pécaut 1999, 20]), parties and drinking, and even love-making.[10] Guerrilla organizations solidified their position in civilian communities by acting as a parallel state, mediating everyday conflicts between locals, regulating land tenure disputes, and taxing legal and illegal economic operations. Paramilitary occupation is accompanied by the imposition of a set of cultural values that are based on conservative Catholicism, "family values," and heteronormative morality. In regions controlled by paramilitaries, miniskirts on young women are prohibited, as is long hair on young men; piercings and tattoos are not allowed; families are forced to decorate their houses with lights at Christmas time; youth are not allowed after dusk in traditional meeting places, like parks and plazas; even certain musical genres are prohibited (salsa is banned due to its social justice lyrics) while other musical styles, such as *Norteño* and *vallenato* music,[11] are privileged; and gay bars are forced to close down (Martha Cecilia García 2006, 298; Madariaga 2006, 69).[12]

Paramilitary monopolization of power in certain regions (including Magdalena Medio and the Colombian Caribbean, two of the three case studies in this book) is rooted in collective fear and intimidation. Colombian anthropologist Maria Victoria Uribe describes the feeling of "shifty and slimy terror that builds on a foundation of rumors about what people living in the rural places of terror see and hear, and what they believe they see and hear" (Maria Victoria Uribe 2007, 118). The other side of this coin is that becoming a member of the paramilitary becomes an attractive option for young Colombians who seek validation and social recognition (Cadavid 1996, 39; Vásquez 2006, 341). Colombian sociologist Mauricio Romero called the paramilitary "entrepreneurs of coercion" and defined them as "individuals specializing in the administration, implementation, and use of organized violence, offered as a commodity in exchange for money or another type of value" (Romero 2003, 17, cited in Vásquez 2006, 333). Originally created exclusively as a response to guerrilla abuse, paramilitary organizations later evolved into a "morality police" taking on the responsibility of countering what they see as "excessive concessions and privilege given to ethnic, cultural, and gender minorities" (F. González 2006, 547).

Weapons of the Weak

All these players—the guerrillas, paramilitaries, drug mafias, and local traditional economic elites—are engaged in endless disputes over sources of wealth. Access to legal and illegal economies and control of their operations is constantly in flux. Traditional economic elites, mafias, and armed groups repeatedly form and break alliances, go to war, and sign truces in their continuous attempts to profit from gold and emerald mines, oil processing, coca and poppy cultivation, cocaine and heroin production and distribution, gasoline (stolen from gas pipes and refineries),[13] cattle ranching, and palm oil and tobacco plantations. The presence of significant sources of wealth, in the form of legal or illegal economies tied to extraction and/or processing of natural resources, is a significant factor in most Colombian contexts of war (Pécaut 1999). According to Tony Hodges, "resource rich countries are four times more likely to be embroiled in severe political violence" (quoted in Nordstrom 2003, 223), and Colombia fits the bill. In their ethnographic work on numerous war fronts, from Mozambique to Sri Lanka, Carolyn Nordstrom and Kay Warren document how the instability, dislocation, and reduced legal restraints armed conflict produces create an excellent breeding ground for shady economies to grow and thrive (Nordstrom 2003, 2004; Warren 2002).

In Colombia, coca and poppy cultivation, and cocaine and heroin production and trafficking provide the primary sources of wealth for guerrillas and paramilitaries in several regions, including the south (Caquetá, Putumayo, Nariño, Guaviare, Meta), the southeast (Vichada,

Vaupés), the northeast (Arauca), and the northwest (Antioquia, Córdoba, Santander, Cesar, and Bolívar) (see map on page 62 of United Nations Office of Drugs and Crime 2007). The gold mines of Bolívar and the emerald mines of Boyacá are magnets for armed groups that battle for their control. Via "safety taxes," extortion, and kidnapping, guerrillas and paramilitaries profit from coal and oil extraction ventures in Cesar, Arauca, Casanare, and Santanderes; from banana extraction companies in Urabá and Antioquia; and from large cattle estates in Magdalena Medio and Córdoba (Pécaut 2001, 101–2). In Colombia, war and wealth are two sides of the same coin. The economic resources distributed throughout the national territory function as magnets, attracting warring factions. Armed groups know that military control of a wealthy region means significant income in the form of kidnap ransom, bribes, extortion, and taxes imposed on national and international corporations, landowners, cattle barons, illicit drug farmers, laboratories, and traffickers. A recent report on human rights violations in the country states, "the financial resources that feed the war seem endless" (OPPDHDIH 2002, 21). Whether armed groups seek to win the war or whether they are merely trying to keep profits coming into their coffers is a question always in Colombians' minds. The relationship between war and wealth is complex. War creates opportunities for profit making in wealthy regions. Citing Christian Dietrich's work on the diamond trade, Nordstrom explains these complex linkages between war and wealth: "These aren't wars over resources per se. Instead, war facilitates the looting of resources" (Nordstrom 2004, 192). Thus, war itself is a stimulant of shady economies linked to natural resources. Colombian unarmed civilians watch traditional elites, guerrillas, paramilitaries, and mafias profit and become wealthier from these corrupt economies, while their own conditions of life worsen.

It's easy to see civilians as passively accepting the controls imposed by guerrillas, paramilitaries, drug traffickers, and armed forces. However, domination does not necessarily mean hegemony. As Colombian historian Mauricio Archila says, "in the apparent acceptance of armed actors by the people, there is not only fear, but also hidden codes of survival that at any moment can become public discourses of open opposition. . . . These survival codes become the way people preserve the fabric of their societies, build invisible solidarities, and allow for the sudden emergence of multiple quotidian acts and small claims of resistance" (Archila 2006, 504).

Colombian unarmed civilians experience armed conflict as a complex mesh created by armed actors who impose their military logic, use of force, and cultural values on civilian communities. Power relations between guerrillas, paramilitary groups, mafias, and the armed forces are constantly shifting from region to region and from one moment to the next. Allen Feldman observes that chronic violence in Northern Ireland produced its own ideological and material formations and thus the conditions of reproduction of antagonism. Feldman's analysis is applicable to the Colombian case, where one form of violence triggers other forms of violence (Feldman 1991, 5, 20).

From the work of anthropologists and ethnographers of violence, we can learn that the lived experience of violence pushes people to the edge of their emotional and psychic strength (Nordstrom and Robben 1995). Extreme experiences of chaos, uncertainty, and powerlessness produced by war parallel extreme experiences of empathy, courage, and agency (Nordstrom 2004). I draw from Feldman's idea that extreme and chronic violence becomes its own formation to suggest that specific forms of individual and collective agency emerge in communities cornered by armed groups, precisely because the community has been pushed to the edge (Feldman 1991). In Feldman's analysis of Northern Ireland, as Republican activists became progressively disempowered, they found new ways to express political agency; when they were deprived of the street as a political space, imprisoned activists politicized the prison cell; when they were deprived of this space, they politicized their own bodies; subsequently, they politicized their own feces and urine, then their body orifices, and finally their own deaths: "Political agency is relational—it has no fixed ground—it is the effect of situated practices" (Feldman 1991, 1). In the words of anthropologists of violence Carolyn Nordstrom and JoAnn Martin: "Resistance may thus be encoded in a wide range of cultural practices that are meaningful by virtue of their opposition to a dominant culture" (Nordstrom and Martin 1992, 7).

In Colombia, around the blatantly visible realities of armed conflict, other less visible, yet equally or perhaps more significant realities of political agency, in the forms of social movements, grassroots initiatives, and collective actions of resistance, shape the experiences of Colombian communities.[14] Pécaut writes of Colombia, "I see everywhere, even in combat zones, all kinds of efforts and initiatives to escape war and try to build, despite the violence, new forms of solidarity and of citizen participation" (Pécaut 2001). The communication initiatives featured in this book are a case in point.

War, Peace, and Media

Every year, many academic monographs, journalists' accounts, assessment reports, and research studies are published about the interactions between mass media and war. These publications cover crucial subjects, such as media coverage of armed conflict and refugee crises (Allen and Seaton 1999; Greenberg and Gantz 1993; Hudson and Stanier 1998; Jeffords and Rabinovitz 1994; Magnusson 1996; Moeller 1999; Rotberg and Weiss 1996; Smith 1992; Thumber and Palmer 2004); media framing of war, armed violence, and terrorism (Bennett, Lawrence, and Livingston 2007; Hess and Kalb 2003; Kavoori and Fraley 2006; Moeller 1999; Norris, Kern, and Just 2003); peace journalism (Lynch and McGoldrick 2005); conflict-sensitive journalism (Howard 2002, 2003, 2005); and the media's role in intensifying or de-escalating armed conflict (Allen and Seaton 1999; Balabanova 2007; Frohardt and Temin 2003; Kamalipour and Snow 2004; Manoff 1996; Melone, Terzis, and Ozsel 2002; Myers, Adam, and Lalanne 1995; Rolston and Miller 1996).

Academic literature on media and armed violence is plentiful, and yet most of it focuses on the mass media, while only a handful of studies explore the role(s) of local, community, and citizens' media in contexts of armed conflict (Department for International Development 2000; Hiebert 2001; Howard 2002; Loewenberg and Bonde 2008; Ndong'a 2005; Radio Netherlands 2008; Rodríguez 2004, 2008; Rodríguez and Cadavid 2007; Shamas 2011; Spitulnik 2002). My goal in this writing is to help fill this gap. I want to explore what community radio stations are doing in places where unarmed civilians are trapped in the crossfire of warring groups; how local community television stations represent their communities when they are engulfed in armed violence; how grassroots video-production collectives respond to the impact of armed conflict.

Based on an analysis of forty projects in eighteen countries, a recent initiative of the U.S. Institute of Peace (USIP) mapped the field of media and peacebuilding.[15] This study found six main uses of media and communication in peacebuilding: (1) conflict-sensitive journalism; (2) peace journalism; (3) edutainment; (4) social marketing for peace; (5) regulation of media inciting conflict; and (6) citizens' media and peacebuilding. Both "conflict-sensitive journalism" and "peace journalism" attempt to produce accurate and responsible journalism in which journalists operate with an awareness of the role that news coverage can have in polarizing societies or de-escalating conflict. They differ in that conflict-sensitive journalism strives to maintain journalistic impartiality, while peace journalism is overtly peace and solution oriented. In "edutainment for peace," media producers use entertainment media in the form of soap operas, songs, dramas, and so forth to persuade audiences to support peacebuilding goals.[16] "Social marketing for peace" uses mass media campaigns to "sell" peace to audiences; the recent "It's your decision" campaign, developed by a well-known public relations firm to promote the peace accords in Northern Ireland is a good example. In the phenomenon of "media regulation for peacebuilding," governments and regulatory agencies attempt to prohibit inflammatory language and images that could incite violence. "Citizens' media for peacebuilding" refers to the use of community/alternative/citizens' media to restore social fabrics and relationships torn by armed conflict. The first five categories reported on the USIP map emphasize mass media, while only the last category focuses on local, community media, such as those featured in this book. Except for this last category, most media recorded on the USIP map involve communication processes in which senders attempt to persuade massive numbers of listeners, viewers, or readers with peacebuilding messages. These approaches, informed by media effects theories, are framed by narrow views of media technologies as persuasive tools. Seeing media exclusively as tools for mass persuasion obscures the rich potential of media as technologies that can be embedded in communities, creating tremendous opportunities for networking, reaching, communicating, and connecting in all directions. Placing media technology in the hands of local communities multiplies communication spaces, loci of interaction, and sites in which meaning can be produced, exchanged, reinterpreted, hybridized, and so on.

It is all too evident that technology in general, and communication technologies in particular, are regularly used to inflict injury on human bodies and terrorize communities (Chalk 1999; Kabanda 2005; Radio Netherlands 2008). Allen Feldman's work on Belfast residents' experiences of visual technologies (cameras, videos, photographs) as terrorizing weapons (Feldman 2000, 59), and Jeffrey Sluka's analysis of instances in which art and media are used to justify violence (Sluka

1992) reveal how communication technologies can reinforce war machines. However, we know less about ways unarmed communities use communication technologies to resist war and terror. Using layered media ethnography and in-depth interviews, I document the uses of media technologies (community radio, television, video, and digital photography) by unarmed Colombian communities in regions engulfed by armed violence. This book is the product of several years of fieldwork with citizens' media producers, conducted between 2004 and 2006, in regions of Colombia occupied by leftist guerrillas, right-wing paramilitary groups, the armed forces, and drug trafficking mafias.

My findings were contrary to common perceptions of the dominant role of local media in contexts of war. I did not find journalism and news to be a priority among Colombian citizens' media; instead, media are used to open communication spaces where cultural processes, art production, and storytelling can repair torn social fabrics, reconstruct eroded social bonds, reappropriate public spaces, and strengthen strategies of nonviolent conflict resolution. In the following chapters I explore the ways people whose lives and communities are eroded by armed violence use citizens' media to resist and overcome the negative impacts of war.

The end of the cold war left a geopolitical landscape in which armed conflict predominately happens within national borders. In recent years, interstate conflicts have largely been supplanted by conflicts between states and armed antagonist groups, such as extreme leftist or rightist guerrillas, ethnic and/or religious factions, or resource-based mafias (e.g., cocaine, heroin, and diamonds) (Wallensteen and Sollenberg 2000). From 1989 to 2005 ninety intrastate conflicts were recorded worldwide, while there were only seven interstate conflicts and wars on record (Harbom, Högbladh, and Wallensteen 2006). Traditional interstate wars are generally waged among official armies, while these new intrastate conflicts increasingly target civilians (Appadurai 2006). Current conflicts involve issues of identity (e.g., ethnicity and religion), politics, and resources. The effects of armed violence from these conflicts are increasingly felt in civilians' everyday lives and the cultural and social fabric of their communities (Rothman and Olson 2001). "Civilians accounted for fifty-two percent of all war related deaths in the 1960s, but eighty-five percent in the 1980s" (Colson 1992, 280). Colombia's armed conflict follows this trend; out of 21,355 violent actions occurring between 1990 and 2000, only approximately 40 percent were combat actions, while 60 percent were attacks on civilians (including assassinations, disappearances, sexual assault, torture, uses of civilians as human shields, kidnapping of civilians, use of weapons such as mines, and recruitment of minors) (González, Bolívar, and Vásquez 2003, 100). In intrastate conflict, terrorizing unarmed civilians becomes the goal of armed groups; in Nordstrom's words, "The victims themselves become the template on which power-loaded scripts are inscribed" (Nordstrom 1992, 266).

My work here is driven by the urgency of cultural analyses of armed violence and conflict resolution in these new contexts of intrastate conflict and violence. We must recognize the impact armed violence has on the cultural fabric of civilian communities caught in the crossfire, and how civilians use culture, communication, and art to disrupt this violence.

From Alternative Media to Citizens' Media

Many different terms are used to label media technologies appropriated and used by citizens' groups and grassroots collectives, including alternative media, participatory media, community media, radical media, grassroots media, autonomous media, the French term *médias libres,* the Spanish term *medios populares,* alterative media (a term meaning media that alter, coined by Peruvian communication scholar Rafael Roncagliolo), and citizens' media (Kidd and Rodríguez 2010).[17] Each term emphasizes a different aspect of these media and connects with specific theories of media democracy. For example, the term "autonomous media" emphasizes that these media generally try to maintain their independence from political and economic powers, and additionally, the term connects with political economy of media approaches. In contrast, the term "alterative media" emphasizes processes of individual and collective empowerment, and connects with communication and social change theories.

In my 2001 book, *Fissures in the Mediascape* (Rodríguez 2001), I coined the term "citizens' media." Drawing from the work of Belgian political scientist Chantal Mouffe's theories of radical democracy and citizenship, I proposed "citizens' media" as a term more appropriate than alternative or community media. Mouffe argues the necessity of reconceptualizing the term "citizen" as foundational to democratic life. In her argument, Mouffe breaks away from theories of liberal democracy that define citizenship as a status granted by the state, and proposes that a "citizen" should be defined by daily political action and engagement:

> The radical democratic concept of citizenship "implies seeing citizenship not as a legal status but as a form of identification, a type of political identity: something to be constructed, not empirically given." . . . Thus, citizens are not born as such; citizenship is not a status granted on the basis of some *essential* characteristic. Citizens have to enact their citizenship on a day-to-day basis, through their participation in everyday political practices: "The citizen is not, as in liberalism, someone who is the passive recipient of specific rights and who enjoys the protection of the law." (Rodríguez 2001, 18–19, quoting Mouffe 1992, 231, 235)

Mouffe's "citizen" is a creature drawing political power from his or her daily participation in democratic processes, not simply someone whom the state has granted the required status to engage in political actions (Mouffe 1988, 1992). Mouffe understands citizens as individuals in permanent interaction with their contexts, gaining and generating power from social relations in their neighborhoods, workplaces, families, churches, and so forth. Citizens combine this fragmentary power to enact everyday political actions that shape their communities to reflect their personal and collective visions of utopia. For Mouffe, a citizen is a person who uses his or her quotidian power to activate social and cultural processes, which in turn move the citizen's community toward the future he or she envisions.

I then defined "citizens' media" as those media that facilitate the transformation of individuals into "citizens," as understood in Mouffe's redefinition of citizenship. Citizens' media are communication spaces where citizens can learn to manipulate their own languages, codes, signs, and symbols, empowering them to name the world in their own terms. Citizens' media trigger processes that allow citizens to recodify their contexts and selves. These processes ultimately give citizens the opportunity to restructure their identities into empowered subjectivities strongly connected to local cultures and driven by well-defined, achievable utopias. Citizens' media are the media citizens use to activate communication processes that shape their local communities.

Throughout this book I use the term "community media" to refer to radio and television initiatives that have been granted a community broadcasting license by the state. I reserve the term "citizens' media" to refer to community media that purposely cultivate processes of transformation and empowerment in their producers and audiences.

The Colombian Mediascape

Commercial radio in Colombia was born in 1929 (Ferreira and Straubhaar 1988); by 1941 Colombia had seventy-one commercial radio stations. From the start, Colombian commercial radio replicated corporate media models imported from the United States, using a system based on media advertising to boost sales. According to Ferreira and Straubhaar, these early commercial radio entrepreneurs, "generally ham radio aficionados, some having been educated abroad, imported not only new technology, but also a mercantile spirit, organizational style, programming patterns, and even [their corporations'] names from the United States" (Ferreira and Straubhaar 1988, 288). For example, in 1930 a company with the anglicized name Colombian Radio and Electric Corporation owned HKF, Bogotá's first commercial radio station; in 1932 a second commercial radio company continued the trend of anglicized names by calling themselves Colombian Broadcasting, and in 1936 a company started with the name Santander Broadcasting (Ferreira and Straubhaar 1988, 289).

Caracol, Todelar, and RCN, today's main Colombian commercial radio networks, began developing in the 1950s. These networks, plus the public Radiodifusora Nacional, reach a vast majority of the country's broken geography, making radio the main information and communication technology in the country.

Since the early decades of the twentieth century, Colombian mass media have been saturated with social and political conflict. By the 1920s a significant number of national and regional newspapers had appeared on the Colombian mediascape; these newspapers, along with the commercial radio ventures of the 1930s, were owned by wealthy Colombians deeply entrenched in traditional politics. Each Colombian newspaper and commercial radio station had a known political leaning, either with the Liberal Party or with its legendary opponent, the Conservative Party. During La Violencia, a period of political violence between Liberals and Conservatives that lasted from 1948 to 1953 and left two hundred thousand Colombians dead, Conservative newspapers and radio stations not only supported Conservative leaders with selective information and news, but also fueled

violent conflict among their readers and listeners. Liberal radio stations and newspapers followed suit. Colombian media scholar Mario
Murillo describes the ways party leaders used the airwaves to intensify the country's political polarization:

> Such was especially the case with the famous *Radio-periódicos,* or "radio-
> newspapers," the news programs developed by the radio programmers of
> the mid-1930s. The Liberal leader and President, Alfonso López Pumarejo,
> a reformist behind the so-called *Revolución en Marcha,* or Revolution on
> the March, launched the first of these *Radio-periódicos* in 1934 with his
> program, "La República Liberal." He was quickly answered by his Con-
> servative nemesis, Laureano Gómez, in 1936, when the future President
> launched his own radio station, "La Voz de Colombia." The intense air wars
> that resulted from these and other politically driven broadcasts led to a 1936
> decree prohibiting the transmission of political news over the airwaves.
> (M. Murillo in press)

Mainstream commercial radio and newspapers have a long history of
being used as loudspeakers for political elites.

Today, Colombia's radio sector includes a variety of radio broadcasting licenses: commercial radio, public interest radio, and community radio.[18] Public interest radio licenses can only be assigned to
public institutions, such as public universities and schools, police and
the armed forces, local governments, and indigenous *cabildos.*[19] Community broadcasting licenses are assigned to nonprofit community
organizations.[20] At the time of writing, Colombia had 656 commercial
radio stations, 167 public interest stations,[21] and 651 community radio
stations. Although radio signals reach the entire national territory,
almost five hundred Colombian municipalities (approximately 50 percent) still do not have their own radio station.

Radio Sutatenza, commonly known as the first alternative radio
station in Latin America, belongs to the category of public interest
radio. Founded in 1947 by Colombian priest José Joaquín Salcedo,
Radio Sutatenza disappeared in 1990 after a forty-three-year run
(Ferreira and Straubhaar 1988, 296). Radio Sutatenza's main goal was
to create a radio school for illiterate adults in rural areas. To accomplish this, unschooled peasants were organized into what Sutatenza
called "radio schools"; these literacy groups gathered around a radio
receiver to listen to lessons on writing and reading and to complete
work booklets and homework. Radio Sutatenza did not encourage

peasant voices to participate in radio production and was therefore limited to one-way, vertical communication. In my view, to maintain the notion that Radio Sutatenza was a pioneer in Latin America's powerful tradition of alternative/participatory media is inaccurate, and worse, unfair to the true participatory media pioneers of Latin America, like the Bolivian miners' radio stations born in 1949 (Gumucio Dagron 2001; O'Connor 2004).

Colombian television maintains its own ties to armed conflict. La Violencia, the near-civil-war period mentioned above, came to an end in 1953 when General Gustavo Rojas Pinilla overthrew the Conservative regime and installed a military junta. Initially, Conservative and Liberal leaders acquiesced to the imposition of Rojas Pinilla's military regime as a way to put an end to the bloody conflict. However, the increasingly populist policies introduced by Rojas Pinilla began to alienate the leadership of the traditional parties. Little by little, Conservative and Liberal newspapers and radio networks isolated the general by refusing to give him airtime or journalistic coverage. Silenced by the traditional Colombian media outlets, without a mass medium with which to communicate with his constituents, General Rojas Pinilla decided to create his own mass medium, and in 1954 brought television to Colombia.

Brought to the country to serve as the general's loudspeaker, television took hold and remains a public medium to this day. In the early days, the general's speeches were the main programming component, but the rest of the programming grid had to be filled somehow. Interestingly, some of the day's most creative stage directors, scriptwriters, and actors were brought in to help fill the rest of the programming slots. Left on their own with almost complete creative license, these intellectuals and artists took their new roles to heart and filled the early days of Colombian television with fascinating productions, including original scripts as well as adaptations of everything under the sun, from Kafka and Marguerite Jourcenar to Latin American writers. This explains in part the idiosyncratic identity of Colombian television drama and particularly of today's Colombian *telenovelas* (Rodríguez and Téllez 1989).

The fact that Colombian television began as a government initiative, and not a corporate profit–driven venture as in most other Latin American countries, left an imprint on the development of the medium. The origins of Colombian television can be traced back to the country's only military government, and as a result, it has never been entirely privatized. For decades, up until the late 1990s, television was controlled by the state, which rented slots of time to commercial television producers. In 1998 the Comisión Nacional de Televisión [National Television Commission], an autonomous public entity formed by commissioners to represent a wide diversity of Colombian society, assigned commercial television broadcasting licenses to several media corporations. By 2008 only Caracol and RCN had survived, providing the only national commercial television channels. At the time of this writing, Colombian public television includes three national channels (Señal Colombia, Canal Uno, and Señal Institucional), eight regional channels, and forty-one nonprofit local channels (seven of which are university channels). Commercial television includes the two national channels mentioned above, one satellite television provider, and sixty-nine cable television providers (Comisión Nacional de Televisión 2006, 7). The two commercial channels and three public national channels reach almost the entire national territory. In 2005 close to 91 percent of all Colombian households had at least one color television set (Comisión Nacional de Televisión 2006, 8).

In addition to the broadcasting of public and commercial television stations, community television comprises an important component of the Colombian mediascape. By 2008 the National Television Commission had assigned 553 community television broadcasting licenses (Comisión Nacional de Televisión 2006, 7).

Community Media

In 2008 the Colombian mediascape included 651 community radio stations, 553 community televisions, and 26 indigenous radio stations. These incredible numbers can only be explained by the tenacious efforts to democratize the airwaves made by Colombian media activists. The initiatives of media activists seeking to consolidate a strong base of community media began during the early 1980s, led by several communication and media NGOs with strong connections to national and regional social movements.[22] During the two previous decades, these NGOs worked closely with labor, peasant, youth, women's, and indigenous movements, helping them set up and run their own media. They employed a variety of communication strategies, including newsletters, newspapers, comic books and *fotonovelas,* loudspeakers, theater, and video, among others.

In 1985 these NGOs formed the Colectivo de Comunicación Popular [Popular Communication Collective], an umbrella association of loosely affiliated groups that organized annual community communication festivals until 1989. These festivals opened a space where media activists from every corner of the country could meet and share their experiences (frequently for the first time) in Bogotá, the capital city.[23] Even though no community radio or television projects existed in the country at that time, the main theme of the second festival, held in Bogotá in 1987, was community radio. During the previous festival, many participants had expressed an interest in community radio; thus, the second festival was organized around two tracks in response. The first track included a theoretical discussion of community radio and its relationship to participatory media, political power, and social movements. The second track consisted of a series of community radio production workshops (Colectivo de Comunicación Popular 1988, 16).

By 1989 media activists had coalesced to form a strong group that organized the First National Encounter of Community and Cultural Radio, "where participants agreed on the urgency of pushing forward a legal framework for community radio" (Salazar Arenas 1988). From 1989 to 1994 media activists maintained the early momentum with annual national meetings and regional events, where discussions centered on sustainability and management of community radio stations, media production training, and the need to develop stronger community radio organizations and networks (Osses Rivera 2002; Salazar Arenas 1988, 11). Some of the key media activists behind these initiatives worked from within the walls of state institutions, in entities such as the Ministry of Communications' ENLACE project, and the Servicio Nacional de Aprendizaje (SENA) [National Learning Service].[24]

Although no community radio legislation existed in the country at the time, community radio pioneers were beginning to experiment. Aires del Pacífico [Airs of the Pacific],[25] a community radio station in Guapi in the Colombian western Pacific region, began broadcasting in 1993. Around the same time, media activists launched La Voz del Barrio [The Neighborhood's Voice],[26] a radio program produced by popular reporters in Santander, eastern Colombia. In several of Bogotá's working class neighborhoods, media activists launched La Fiesta de la Palabra [The Word's Party],[27] a series of audio productions distributed on cassette tapes and played on city buses. These pioneering

media activists were strongly influenced by Latin American communication scholars, including Jesús Martín Barbero, José López Vigil,
Rosa María Alfaro, and Mario Kaplún. Latin American community
media organizations such as ERBOL (Bolivian community radio network), ALER (Asociación Latinoamericana de Educación Radiofónica [Latin American Association of Radio Education]), CIESPAL
(Centro Internacional de Estudios Superiores de Comunicación para
América Latina [International Center for Higher Studies of Communication in Latin America]), and CALANDRIA (a Peruvian community communication NGO) also lent a helping hand (Colectivo de
Comunicación Popular 1988).

Since these early days, Colombian media activists have prioritized
the development of regional activist networks in order to create a
national media democratization movement powerful enough to make
demands of the Colombian state. Thus, the meetings and experiments
above germinated regional networks in Santander, Bogotá, and the
Pacific region. To this day, regional community radio and television
networks make up the backbone of the Colombian media democratization movement.

In the early 1990s, during the same time period that activists were
experimenting with community media, Colombian social movements
achieved the most important transformation in the Colombian legal
and political framework in recent times: the signing of the new Colombian Constitution of 1991. A turning point in Colombia's contemporary
history, the new constitution brought to fruition years of grassroots
organizing and mobilizing that began in the 1960s and 1970s. Colombia's new social contract, as articulated by the Constitution of 1991,
embraced the idea of the Colombian nation as a complex dialogue
between multiple and diverse identities, eschewing the idea of "nation"
as a monolithic entity founded on one language, one religion, one identity, and one culture (Wills Obregón 2000). Among the many constitutional articles guaranteeing rights and access, Article 20 guarantees
the right of every Colombian to "establish their own mass media."[28]

Article 20 of the 1991 Constitution provided the crucial legal lever-
age media activists needed to demand that the Colombian state establish and sanction legal frameworks for community radio and television.
Using Article 20 as their main argument, media activists pressured
the government to implement measures to support the constitutional
right of every Colombian to found their own media. Four years later,

President Ernesto Samper's administration passed Decree 1447 of 1995, giving the green light for the Ministry of Communications to begin assigning community radio licenses. In 1999, under President Andrés Pastrana's administration, Acuerdo 006 was approved, legalizing community television (Téllez 2003). These two legal reforms are at least partially behind the explosion of community radio and television in the last twelve years. Given the proliferation of community media in Colombia, heterogeneity is the norm. Community radios and television stations come in every style and form, from banal replicas of commercial radio and television, to fascinating experiments in citizens' media and participatory communication. As is common in countries with multiple community media outlets, many of Colombia's so-called community radio and television stations are nothing more than loudspeakers for a local priest or political lord.[29] However, among the more than one thousand legal community radio and television stations operating in Colombia today, I have found some of the most creative, courageous, and wise citizens' media I have seen since I started doing research on this topic in 1984. Documenting and analyzing a few among these many exceptional examples of citizens' media is the main purpose of this book.

A note about the celebratory tone of this book: my goal is to convey to the reader my own experiences as I discovered that, in the midst of situations in which armed groups impose silence, terrorize civilians, and make entire communities feel hopeless, a handful of exceptional Colombian men and women figured out how to use radio, television, video, and photography to overcome the impact of war on their communities. In this sense, when I am responding to the things I witnessed in my fieldwork, this book is shamelessly celebratory. My enthusiasm, however, does not blind me to the vulnerabilities and weaknesses in Colombian community media.

All Colombian community media, even those I deem worthy of the label "citizens' media," face multiple challenges and limitations. A great number of stations granted a community broadcasting license do not even come close to understanding what community communication is all about; their founders simply saw a good opportunity to make a buck or get their hands on an effective persuasion tool.[30] Even those media that understand the value of community media have multiple Achilles' heels. No one in Colombia has figured out how to make community media financially sustainable. To generate enough revenue to finance their operations, community media leaders sell local advertisements; form paid membership clubs among listeners and viewers; organize community events such as raffles, contests, and concerts; form alliances with NGOs and social movements exchanging public relations and media services for money; sell media services (e.g., production of video, photography, print materials, and institutional campaigns; or media training for employees) to state institutions and community organizations. Despite all these entrepreneurial strategies, Colombian community media are constantly on the brink of going bankrupt.

As a result, community media are run by a continuous revolving door of volunteers and/or badly paid staff members who, in part due to their precarious situation, are commonly co-opted by political and economic interests. Continuity is one of the major challenges in the Colombian world of community media. Highly trained volunteers leave for better-paying jobs, forcing the medium to go back to the drawing board and carry on with mediocre programming. Media with intensely creative producers frequently establish chaotic accounting and administrative practices, and conversely, media with efficient administrators sometimes scare away those with creative and artistic souls.

In regions of armed conflict, the vulnerabilities of community media multiply. Frequently, these media are permanently testing the boundaries of what armed groups will allow; at times they are silenced, paralyzed, attacked, or co-opted. On occasion, crossing invisible boundaries brings fatal consequences, and several community media producers in different parts of the country have been assassinated. Although I try to touch on more specific weaknesses and vulnerabilities in the chapters that follow, these weaknesses are not the focus of this book. I did not want to write a book about yet another thing that doesn't work in Colombia. I wanted to write a book about the few things that do work; about something that succeeds, despite all the challenges, limitations, vulnerabilities, and risks. As Pécaut says, many more Colombians are involved in building peace than in waging war (Pécaut 2001, 19). Among those building peace, and working against all sorts of obstacles and limitations, are the Colombian citizens' media producers, artists, and activists featured in this book.

The first chapter takes us to southern Colombia, where the Andean mountains fade into the Amazonian plateau. Nestled between frigid and pristine mountain rivers and the border of the Amazonian rain forest, the municipality of Belén de los Andaquíes is surrounded by natural beauty. This chapter traces the history of this southern Colombian region and documents how, since colonial times, extractive economies and consecutive waves of immigrants have encoded the region in the popular imagination as an empty frontier without an identity of its own. Since the mid-1970s, the region has seen the arrival of coca economies, drug traffickers, and left-wing guerrilla organizations. In this complex scene of warring factions, state neglect, drug economies, and stunning natural wonder, a community radio station and children's audiovisual school create communication spaces that are able to counter the impact of armed violence on civilians.

Chapter 2 moves to the opposite side of the national geography: the northern Colombian Caribbean. Here, at the end of the 1990s, the region known as Montes de María had some of the worst levels of social and political violence in the country. The chapter recounts the arrival of left-wing guerrilla organizations and right-wing paramilitary militias in this rich agricultural area surrounded by wealthy cattle estates. The presence of these two illegal armed groups disrupted everyday life and eroded the traditional Caribbean culture of exuberant expressiveness and strong collective solidarities. The presence of armed groups in this territory imposed a culture of fear, isolation, and distrust in the agricultural areas and urban centers of Montes de María. Thousands of farming families were displaced from their land by force, fleeing in terror from the crossfire of army, guerrilla, and paramilitaries. The chapter analyzes how, in this context where war has saturated much of the social fabric and social relations, a local media initiative known as the Communications Collective of Montes de María constitutes a parallel cultural milieu. In order to serve as an alternative to a cultural environment that sanctions sectarian sensibilities, intolerance of difference, and the use of force, the Communications Collective operates a media school, allowing students to learn radio, television, and video production, and more importantly, a different ethos of peace.

In chapter 3 we continue the journey toward the center of Colombia, where we discover a water world in which amphibious human communities have developed a symbiotic relationship with the overpowering Magdalena River. The chapter documents Magdalena Medio's location at the very center of the country and its status as one of the country's most marginalized regions. While the exploitation of natural resources (such as oil, gold, and African palm) in the region yields profits that merit standards of living equivalent to those in European countries, most residents of Magdalena Medio live in extremely impoverished conditions. Since the 1960s, leftist guerrillas, right-wing paramilitaries, and drug and oil mafias have ravaged the region, which is home to one of the strongest networks of citizens' radio stations in Latin America. The chapter analyzes how a network of nineteen citizens' radio stations is used to strengthen good governance, government transparency and accountability, citizen participation in local decision-making processes, strong public spheres, and the art of mediation in this neglected region.

Chapter 4 articulates views, experiences, and ideas gathered from the testimonies of dozens of Colombian citizens' media pioneers from all reaches of the Colombian geography. Here, these brave media producers tell us how they have learned to use community radio, the Internet, and television in contexts of armed conflict. Although the first three chapters illuminate some of the most salient initiatives, three case studies do not exhaust what citizens' media pioneers have to say. In this chapter I document how Colombian citizens' media have dealt with the pressures imposed by armed groups and how citizens' media leaders are able to articulate their goals and objectives in efforts to disrupt the normalization of the use of force.

In the concluding chapter, I develop a theory of citizens' media in contexts of armed conflict based on the evidence and analyses of the previous chapters. Here I present a dialogue with two very different bodies of research and theory. First, I draw from anthropological studies of war to understand how unarmed civilians under siege experience armed conflict by armed groups. The lived experience of terror imposed by war is complex and felt in many different ways, as it erodes social and cultural fabrics and imposes isolation, fear, and mistrust on the communities in its throes. Citizens' media can play equally complex and varied roles in these contexts of armed violence, as they disrupt violence and terror and help unarmed civilians overcome the impositions of war.

Second, I draw from theories of communication as performance to suggest that efficacious citizens' media in war zones are those that help trigger lived experiences alternative to terror, isolation, and fear. Here I privilege citizens' media that make it possible for people to feel, share, and experience an alternative to the terror imposed by war over community media used to inform, persuade, or disseminate pre-designed messages to their audiences. Citizens' media that regard communication as performance, rather than as information dissemination or persuasion, are better positioned to disrupt violence in contexts where unarmed civilians are cornered by war.

1 DRUGS, VIOLENCE, AND THE MEDIA OF THE PEOPLE IN THE COLOMBIAN AMAZON

Para recalcar que estoy vivo en medio de tantos muertos
To emphasize that I am still alive among so many dead
—Victor Heredia, Razón *de Vivir*

IT IS JUNE 1976. I am sixteen years old and a school friend invites me to come along on her family's holiday trip to Caquetá, in southern Colombia. On a warm afternoon, visiting the municipality of Montañita, we walk along a wide pasture, behind a guy who's showing us around. We visit the ruins of what used to be a huge hacienda mansion called Larandia. The house, or what remains of it, is a very large, typical Spanish white adobe building with a beautiful red clay tile roof overgrown with lichen and moss. The terracotta forms intricate patterns and landscapes as the tiles overlap with the plants' greens and grays. The house must have once been an amazing place, three stories high and enclosed with wooden-railed balconies.

We walk about five hundred meters behind the house, where the guide shows us a huge tree where the last heir of the hacienda family was hanged by his own employees.

Almost thirty years later, in August of 2005, I returned to Caquetá to visit Radio Andaquí, a community radio station located in a small town with the charming name of Belén de los Andaquíes. I traveled with a young Colombian writing her master's thesis on Radio Andaquí. Alirio González, one of the founders of the station, came to meet us at the airport in Florencia, the state capital. As we drove the forty-three kilometers from Florencia to Belén, the beauty of the landscape took my breath away. This is the place where the Andes end and the

Colombian Amazon begins. To the north I could see rolling hills backed by magnificent mountains. To the south were vast plains, formerly tropical forests, but used now as pastures cleared for cattle and dotted by *morichales,* the local name for oasis-like water holes surrounded by palm trees. Hundreds of egrets peppered the *morichales.* Here and there, we crossed rivers so clear that I was able to see the rocks of the riverbeds, even from the road.

Suddenly a large bullfighting arena appeared on our left. Alirio and the taxi driver explained that we were passing the hacienda of a local cocaine trafficker who loved bullfighting so much he built his own arena.

The huge tree that witnessed the hacienda heir's hanging and the bullfighting arena are both key icons of a region where perverse economies mark the landscape. Since the 1800s, Caquetá has seen diverse waves of immigrants coming from other parts of the country, seeking opportunities to exploit the region's natural resources. In the last decades of the 1800s, new arrivals came attracted by rubber and other forest products; later, during the 1950s and 1960s, the vast "wastelands" of Caquetá became ideal for agricultural homesteaders and cattle ranchers. In the 1980s and 1990s, the isolation of the region, and its climate and agricultural know-how, made it ideal for coca cultivation and processing. Each wave of newcomers, and their thirst for extracting from the land, left behind a trail of environmental degradation and social violence that spiraled into armed conflict. Cattle ranchers pushed small farmers from their land; homesteaders kept pushing the agricultural frontier, burning down the forest looking for new land. Coca plantations were built on the labor of indentured coca leaf pickers. All of this happened in the context of a society of immigrants, where "no one is from here." In such a context the sense of belonging is fragile, and a homogenous cultural identity is vulnerable. This complex place became the home of Radio Andaquí, one of the first community radio stations to be granted a community broadcasting license by the Colombian government in 1997.

Belén de los Andaquíes is located in the foothills of the southern Colombian Andes, in the department of Caquetá. This 1,095-square kilometer municipality is home to about twelve thousand people (Arcila Niño et al. 2000, 168) and sits at the point of intersection between the higher altitudes of the Andes and the Amazon lowlands (60 percent of the municipality sits on Amazon lowlands and 40 percent on Andean foothills). The municipality includes a wide array of altitudes, ranging from two hundred to three thousand meters above sea level (García Montes and Santanilla 1994, 33). This "terraced" topography offers different climates; cool and warm weather can be experienced without crossing municipal boundaries. As a result, Belén de los Andaquíes produces a wide variety of agricultural products such as corn, rice, sugarcane, coffee, cacao, and palm. Several large cattle ranches produce dairy products and meat. The main urban settlement, a town by the same name of Belén de los Andaquíes, is home to about half the population (approximately six thousand). Growing around a central park and a large church, Belén de los Andaquíes is marked by the militarization of the area: heavily armed army platoons frequently patrol the town and its vicinity; gunfire can be heard as military personnel practice in the nearby base; and the small bridges on the town's outskirts are protected by sandbag barricades designed to deter car bombs.[1] In the following pages, I explain the historical processes that originated Caquetá's armed violence and how two local citizens' media initiatives have learned to play key roles in helping the community of Belén resist, overcome, or buffer the impact of armed violence in its daily life and social fabric.

An Unseen Region

Since colonial times, Caquetá has been linked to global scapes, in the Appadurainian sense of the term (Appadurai 1996). When the Spanish ceased military subjugation of the Amazonian indigenous peoples in the Gran Caquetá, Jesuit and Franciscan missionaries were encouraged to enter the region and "civilize" the savages (Arcila Niño et al. 2000, 27). Toward the late seventeenth century, Caquetá began to integrate into world markets with extractive economies centered on rubber, the cinchona tree (source of quinine), tagua, hardwoods, beeswax, and furs (Arcila Niño et al. 2000, 30), which brought the first wave of immigrants during the rubber boom of the late 1800s. Poor agricultural families, mostly from Huila, came to the region hoping to be hired as laborers in rubber and cinchona tree extraction and processing ventures (Arcila Niño et al. 2000, 35).[2] When international markets lost interest in these products in the 1920s, many of the laborers' families settled in the region, beginning a process of homesteading in the Amazon lowlands (García Montes and Santanilla 1994, 45).

A second wave of migrants came into Caquetá on the heels of the Colombian army. The 1932 war with Peru forced the central government to open two roads (Altamira to Florencia and Pasto to Mocoa) connecting the center of the country to the Peruvian border so that troops and armaments could be sent to defend national sovereignty (Jaramillo, Mora, and Cubides 1986, 10). These roads became major travel arteries for agricultural families from neighboring regions who came looking for new land to homestead. In addition to migrant farmers, many of the troops sent to fight in the Peruvian war decided to settle in the region once the war was over.

A third wave of migration to Caquetá and Belén de los Andaquíes took place when people from the higher Andes were forced from their land by political violence between the Liberal and Conservative parties. This conflict tore the country apart between the late 1940s and the 1960s. Peasant families came to Belén de los Andaquíes seeking land and fleeing the bipartisan violence that was plaguing the interior of the country (García Montes and Santanilla 1994, 46). From 1932 to 1951 the population of Caquetá grew from 15,000 to 46,588 (Jaramillo, Mora, and Cubides 1986, 12).[3]

During this time the central government developed a colonization initiative that encouraged peasant families displaced by political violence to migrate to Caquetá, where they were offered land and subsidies to support their families during the initial phases of homesteading. The government promoted the cultivation of rubber and palm (for palm oil) among these newcomers.[4] Attracted by the government-sponsored colonization programs, thousands of farmers came to Caquetá, but the programs only had the capacity to serve a small percentage.[5] Thus, homesteading families were left on their own in meeting the challenges of domesticating the forest to make room for agricultural plots. Often the only equipment available to these families was a dog, a rifle, an ax, a machete, salt, and *panela* (Jaramillo, Mora, and Cubides 1986, 35).[6] Between 1938 and 1951 the population of Caquetá grew by 122 percent, and this rate of growth continued until 1966 (Jaramillo, Mora, and Cubides 1986, 12–13).

The migrant farmers' desire to be isolated from the state can be seen as a direct reaction to the violence they experienced in their homeland. Not only did the Colombian government allow this violence to happen, it also actively participated in violating citizens' basic human rights. Contrary to the general view that social and political violence in Colombia are the result of an absent state, Colombian political scientist Mauricio Romero asserts that peoples' trust in the rule of law and public institutions was eroded by the presence of a state that violates precisely the rights it is supposed to guarantee (Romero 1998, 2003). At the same time, public institutions providing basic infrastructure for education, health, transportation, and other public services are weak or nonexistent. For these migrant farmers, leaving behind their homelands meant not only abandoning "land and scarce properties, but also their social and cultural environment, and with them their institutional links, however scarce, and their alliance to a legitimate power source" (García Villegas and de Sousa dos Santos 2004, 55).

Partly caused by government negligence, the lack of roads or other effective transportation infrastructure originated a cycle of rural poverty that left peasants cut off from markets for their agricultural products. Caquetá's ingenious *colonos* began raising pigs,[7] and instead of marketing their produce, they fed it to the pigs. Once fattened, pigs could walk themselves to the market, which allowed farmers to transport goods to market in a way that was far easier and cheaper than carrying sacks of corn, cassava, or plantains down a mountain trail all the way to those markets (García Montes and Santanilla 1994, 127).

In surviving the precarious conditions of the early days, homesteading families formed strong bonds of solidarity and communal labor. Colombian historians mention how neighbors developed collective initiatives to work the land and build bridges, schools, and roads (Jaramillo, Mora, and Cubides 1986, 45–46). Families exchanged seeds and borrowed food, medicine, and tools from one another, maintaining strong relationships of mutual aid as a survival strategy. Today, the families that came in these migration waves from Huila, Tolima, Valle del Cauca, Cundinamarca, Caldas, and Quindío constitute Belén de los Andaquíes's social fabric.

The cultural profile of the people of Belén de los Andaquíes is a hybrid of many different regional idiosyncrasies brought by migrants from the late 1800s (García Montes and Santanilla 1994, 104).[8] To this day, annual cultural celebrations in Belén de los Andaquíes include a "parade of the homelands," in which different immigrant communities display folk dances, songs, and outfits from their places of origin.[9]

Exploring the history of Caquetá leaves one with the sense that few have been able to truly see this region for the past two hundred years. At different points in history, waves of immigrants from other parts of the country have come to Caquetá looking for a place where they could replicate what they left behind. They saw Caquetá as a blank slate where they could have a second chance to realize what they had left or had not achieved in their places of origin. These migrants dedicated their lives to making Caquetá look like Huila, Antioquia, or Tolima. In the words of Alirio González, "here, everything comes from somewhere else" (A. González 2006). A good example is the cattle economy, established in Caquetá, despite the land's unsuitable conditions for livestock.

Larandia, one of the largest cattle estates in Latin America and the site of the hanging tree described above, is located in Montañita, just a few miles from Belén de los Andaquíes. At its peak in the late 1960s, Larandia expanded to over ninety-six thousand acres and supported fifty thousand heads of cattle (Jaramillo, Mora, and Cubides 1986, 11). Larandia's influence on the region was significant not only because the hacienda determined the type of infrastructure that would be privileged, but also because it introduced the notion that Caquetá was "good for cattle," an idea that came to be known as "the Larandia effect." Seeing Larandia's success, state institutions, including the Instituto Colombiano de Reforma Agraria (INCORA) [Colombian Institute of Agrarian Reform] and the Caja Agraria, responsible for shaping the nascent homesteading economies in the region, began granting homesteaders who opened pastures and introduced cattle special privileges in the form of land titles and loans (Arcila Niño et al. 2000, 57–58).[10] Between 1962 and 1965, 61,052 heads of cattle were brought to the region. The land area dedicated to pasture grew from 12,523 acres to 22,400 acres in three years (Arcila Niño et al. 2000, 118). Between 1984 and 1997, the land dedicated to cattle grew by 50 percent, at the cost of 134,800 acres of forest each year (Arcila Niño et al. 2000, 118). In 1997 only 2.9 percent of all land in Caquetá was used for legal agriculture, while 97.11 percent was used for cattle ranching (Arcila Niño et al. 2000, 119).

In the 1980s the Swiss transnational dairy producer Nestlé came to the region, further solidifying the "cattle disposition" of Caquetá (Arcila Niño et al. 2000, 118). Nestlé not only bought most of the milk in the region, it also offered technical support to cattle farmers in the form of advice about cattle breeds and types of pastures (SINCHI 2000, 49).[11] Years later, it became clear how unsustainable this economic model was for the region.[12]

In Foucault's terms, Larandia imposed a cattle discourse on Caquetá (Foucault 1972, 1980). Larandia determined the type of infrastructure that would be privileged by government and corporate institutions, and by elites. Parallel to economic policies, cultural notions emerged around images of Caquetá as "a land of cattle, cowboys, and *rancheras*."[13] Larandia triggered a series of cultural meanings, economic policies, and institutions that shaped the emerging local culture deeply rooted in a cattle economy.

Also, immigrants who came to Caquetá to escape the political violence of the 1950s brought the idea of replicating their homelands' cattle economies. Normalized notions of "success" became closely tied to images of cattle ranchers, their barbed-wired pastures, heads of cattle, and taste for *ranchera* music.

Colombia's central government discourse, originating in Bogotá, the distant capital city perched on the Andes, made its own contribution to the taken-for-granted idea that Caquetá is good for cattle. Founded on plain ignorance or dubious evidence (Ramírez 2001 cites cases in which official government documents designated populated lands as wastelands, producing official maps on which well-established Caquetá communities didn't exist), Bogotá confused Caquetá with Los Llanos Orientales [the Eastern Plains], a well-known cattle region. In its ignorance, Bogotá assigned all of the stereotypes of the *llanero* and cattle economies to Caquetá in one fell swoop (A. González 2006).

The idea that Caquetá is good for cattle gradually and insidiously solidified, until it became the "truth," while alternative economic models and cultural identities became subjugated knowledges as only cattle and its corresponding cultural practices became normalized, part of the region's common sense. By 1994, 30 percent of the forest areas in the municipality of Belén de los Andaquíes had already been opened for cattle pastures (García Montes and Santanilla 1994, 73).

There is plenty of evidence to call into question Caquetá's "cattle disposition." According to a study by the Ministry of Agriculture, only 14.6 percent of Caquetá's soil is appropriate for agriculture, and 0 percent is appropriate for cattle ranching, due to its high acidity and low nutrient concentration (Arcila Niño et al. 2000, 151). The cattle economy established in the region since the 1930s has had tremendous negative social and environmental impact. First, notions of success are tied to cattle and pastures, thus homesteaders and newcomers see the forest as something to get rid of in order to open pastures for cattle, dramatically degrading forests and waterways. Second, cattle economies produce a stratified society with a class system based on access to land. Cattle haciendas need a pool of landless peasants willing to work for low wages. As ranchers expand their haciendas, they simultaneously secure a pool of cheap labor by forcing small landowners from their properties and creating a class of dependent laborers.

In sum, Caquetá is a region of immigrants with very little confidence in the rule of law and the central government, and a strong sense of cultural connection with their places of origin. These newcomers seem not to see a real Caquetá and instead insist on replicating what they left behind and importing economic models and cultural imaginaries from other regions. Sometimes, as in the case of imported cattle-based economies, these models come with highly detrimental social and environmental effects. Eroding this collective imaginary and pushing new generations to create new, more authentic and sustainable visions of Caquetá and to develop a sense of belonging is one of Radio Andaquí's main goals, as I will explain later.

Armed Conflict in Caquetá

During the early 1970s, social unrest in Caquetá moved from a phase of mobilization and dissent led by peasant social movements to guerrilla warfare and armed violence. Despite its origin as a government initiative, the ANUC mobilized peasant communities to pressure the government to implement land redistribution policies.[14] In 1972 ANUC protesters paralyzed Florencia with demands for such things as basic infrastructure and services such as schools and health centers (these same demands reappeared, almost identically, twenty-four years later during the *cocalero* movement of 1996). In all of Caquetá, and perhaps particularly in Belén de los Andaquíes, some ANUC groups and collectives began a process of political and ideological education which led to the transformation of many ANUC leaders into followers of the then young M-19 guerrilla movement.[15] By 1977 Caquetá had become a stronghold of the Southern Front of the M-19, and the escalation of violent conflict between guerrillas and the army resulted in what is known as the War of Caquetá, between 1978 and 1982 (Arcila Niño et al. 2000, 67).

Between 1979 and 1982 the M-19 attacked Belén de los Andaquíes, killed a policeman and a judge, established checkpoints, and bombed

the bridge over El Saladito creek just as an army truck was crossing it, killing several soldiers. These years saw some of the highest
guerrilla concentration in the area, culminating in 1983 with the
"Malvinas invasion," a takeover of the Larandia hacienda by peasant
families supported by the M-19 (Arcila Niño et al. 2000, 98; García
Montes and Santanilla 1994, 176).

As early as 1979 the army began defining Belén de los Andaquíes
as guerrilla territory. After the attacks of 1979 the army publicly
declared that "there is at least one M-19 *guerrillero* in each family"
(García Montes and Santanilla 1994, 141). To counter the alleged influence of the M-19 on the general population, the army set up a "psychological operation" in Belén, consisting of a team of army personnel
charged with infiltrating the civilian population in order to identify
guerrilla sympathizers.[16] To support the psychological operation, the
army created a radio station called Voz de los Héroes, Radio Belén
[The Heroes' Voice, Radio Belén] in an attempt to persuade listeners to collaborate with the military by denouncing guerrilla activity
(García Montes and Santanilla 1994, 141).

Agricultural families, caught in the middle of the conflict between
the army and the M-19, began experiencing pressure from both armed
groups. Each guerrilla incursion triggered a response from the army.
Soldiers stormed farmers' homes, interrogating family members about
guerrillero sightings. Peasant families were caught between a rock
and a hard place. If they collaborated with the army, they were victimized by the M-19; if they didn't, the army labeled them "friends of
the guerrilla." Local testimonials collected by García Montes and Santanilla describe instances of torture, rape, and even murder of civilians
at the hands of both the army and the guerrillas during these years
(García Montes and Santanilla 1994, 142–47). In an attempt to control the civilian population and simultaneously deplete the resources
reaching the M-19; the army established four checkpoints on the main
roads of the municipality. Agricultural families were given identity
cards, and census data was kept on each family. The army decided how
much food the family was allowed to have.[17] At checkpoints, families
were searched and any excess food, medicine, or clothes were confis-
cated. In the town of Belén, the army also established a curfew. Citizens were not allowed outside between the hours of 6 P.M. and 6 A.M.

These were the same families that, just a few decades earlier, had
escaped the political violence of the 1950s. They left their land, their

extended families, and their cultures in search of an opportunity to work this far-away land in peace. As a result of mounting harassment from the army and the guerrillas, many of these families decided to migrate yet again in order to homestead deeper in the Amazon, beyond the agricultural frontier. Terrified farmers displaced by armed conflict migrated deeper into Caquetá's forest; this wave of migration has been dubbed the "neo-colonization of Caquetá." By 1982 Belén de los Andaquíes began to experience its first waves of forced displacement from rural areas to urban centers or to places deeper into the Amazon (García Montes and Santanilla 1994, 142).

During the 1970s a second guerrilla movement, FARC, made its first appearance in Belén de los Andaquíes. The Fourteenth Front of the FARC settled in the lower altitudes of the municipality, leaving mountainous areas for the M-19. FARC presence in Caquetá dates back to the 1950s and '60s, when the Conservative Party persecuted thousands of peasant families aligned with the Liberal Party and expelled them from the northern regions of Huila and Tolima. In an attempt to protect civilians, the Liberal guerrillas (which later evolved into FARC) organized expeditions in which hundreds of Liberal families marched, sometimes for months, across steep mountain ranges in search of a place beyond the agricultural frontier, where they could work the land and live in peace. Several of these convoys of civilian families protected by armed guerrillas settled in Caquetá, in a process known as "armed colonization" (Arcila Niño et al. 2000, 199). Since this time of migration and armed colonization, FARC has had a strong presence in Caquetá, though not in Belén de los Andaquíes.

In 1989 the M-19 signed a demobilization agreement with then-president Virgilio Barco. As M-19 *guerrilleros* demobilized and left the area, a vacuum of power was created in Belén de los Andaquíes. This vacuum was rapidly filled by the Fourteenth and Fifteenth fronts of FARC, which began moving up from southern Caquetá (Jaramillo, Mora, and Cubides 1986, 249). In 1996, sixteen hundred FARC *guerrilleros* roamed the region, and Caquetá experienced an unprecedented number of guerrilla attacks. By the mid-1990s, FARC had begun to profit from coca economies through *gramaje,* a system of taxes on coca cultivation and processing activities.[18] Two years later, in 1998, FARC staged a boycott of municipal elections, resulting in the all-time lowest participation in electoral politics in the region. That same year, as part of a peace agreement, FARC negotiated a *zona de despeje* (an army-free zone where FARC had complete control) with then-president Andrés Pastrana. This free zone was known as "Farclandia" and included the municipalities of San Vicente del Caguán in Caquetá and three other municipalities in the neighboring department of Meta (Arcila Niño et al. 2000, 203–4).

Legacy of this long history of armed conflict is a popularly held notion that Caquetá is a land of *guerrilleros,* and a place beyond order and civilization, which must be brought under control by the state through the use of military force. A retired army official sent to Caquetá in 1979, during one of the worst years of armed confrontations between the army and FARC forces, recounts how he "saw" the region: "[In the army] we had been taught that whoever wore Croydon rubber boots was a *guerrillero;*[19] if a person wore a T-shirt with blue and white stripes on the shoulders (such as those used by the Millonarios soccer team), he was a *guerrillero.* To my surprise, when I arrived to Belén de los Andaquíes I saw that they all dressed that way, so I believed they were all *guerrilleros"* (interview by García Montes and Santanilla 1994, 249).

Drug Economies and Community Life in Caquetá

In Caquetá, illicit drug economies permeate everything from local politics to armed conflict and the social fabric of farming communities. Between 1998 and 1999 Colombia grew 53 percent of the world's total coca (Ramírez 2001, 60), reaching 62 percent in 2006 (United Nations Office of Drugs and Crime 2007, 1). In 1999 Caquetá contributed 32 percent of the total coca cultivated in Colombia at the time (58,000 acres) (Ramírez 2001, 61). In thirty years, the world markets made the price of coca leaf skyrocket in the Colombian countryside. The price of one kilo of coca paste increased from US$70 in 1978 to US$395 in 1981 (Arango and Child, cited by Jaramillo, Mora, and Cubides 1986, 101) and US$879 in 2006 (United Nations Office of Drugs and Crime 2007, 88). Between 1979 and 1981, a time known as the coca boom years, "the profit of 2.5 acres of coca fluctuated between US$76,000 to $118,000 per year" (Jaramillo, Mora, and Cubides 1986, 144); the same plot planted with corn produced a profit-per-crop of US$5, and US$31 if planted with cassava (Jaramillo, Mora, and Cubides 1986, 150). In 2000 a recently opened plot produced between 5.4 and 6.7 kilos of coca paste per year, at a value of between US$17,700 and US$26,700.[20]

In 2006 the potential annual gross income of 2.5 acres of coca pro-cessed into coca paste was $8,966 (United Nations Office of Drugs and Crime 2007, 91). Even though coca cultivation in Caquetá has de-creased in recent years, coca plots increased steadily from 20,700 acres in 1992 to 53,300 in 1996 (Arcila Niño et al. 2000, 208).

Coca economies bring with them a complex and diverse set of neg-ative social and economic processes with tremendous impact on local communities' social fabric. Coca economies are magnets for chaotic waves of immigrants to the region. During coca booms, a coca region generally sees a 30 to 40 percent increase in its population with the arrival of leaf pickers, drug traffickers, people with coca-processing know-how, peddlers, laborers, prostitutes, and fortune seekers.[21] While coca economies can generate new labor and trade relationships, these are mostly short-term contracts. Coca cultivation monopolizes avail-able paid labor, because salaries paid by coca entrepreneurs are much higher than usual laborers' salaries in the region. Thus, other agri-cultural ventures are unable to find workers (Jaramillo, Mora, and Cubides 1986, 58–62). Coca brings new forms of faster transportation, with motorboats replacing canoes on the rivers. Coca also stimulates price inflation of agricultural products such as fertilizers and pesticides, as coca growers are able to pay much higher prices than farmers cul-tivating legal crops. Basic commodities like sugar, salt, oil, and soap experience price hikes that make them prohibitively expensive for agricultural families who are not growing coca and thus do not have access to the capital generated by illegal crops (García Montes and Santanilla 1994, 135). Coca economies make a region dependent on other regions for basic food products like corn, cassava, rice, and veg-etables, as coca becomes the privileged crop.

Coca trade produces new styles of capital accumulation based on instant gratification. As a result, traditional peasant values such as frugality and saving are replaced by overspending and boasting. Boys and young men commonly drop out of school during coca harvests, because they are paid enormous amounts of money to help pick coca leafs (García Montes and Santanilla 1994, 165). The *coquero,* a young man who enjoys fast money, disposable capital, mobility, and the admiration of women, has become an icon and a strong influence on younger generations (Arcila Niño et al. 2000, 149–60; Jaramillo, Mora, and Cubides 1986, 71). Local testimonies, gathered by García Montes and Santanilla in Belén, describe how one of the first commodities coca growers purchase with their excess capital is a gun (García Montes and Santanilla 1994, 137). Many quarrels, especially those induced by heavy alcohol drinking, would have been resolved with fistfights in the past but now result in gunshot victims.

Each acre of coca cultivation or coca processing originates at least two tons of chemicals, including pesticides, fertilizers, and processing substances such as gasoline, sulfuric acid, chlorhydric acid, ammonia, caustic soda, sodium permanganate, and thinner being dumped into waterways and soil (Arcila Niño et al. 2000, 214).

On the other hand, as opposed to other extraction economies, such as rubber and cinchona, coca cultivation actually allows homesteaders to improve their quality of life. Drug traffickers pay homesteaders on site, directly in cash. Coca money does not end up in the hands of intermediaries. Instead, the money goes directly into the pockets of local farmers, who are able to access markets and buy clothes and medicine (Ramírez 2001, 80). Cocaine producers buy the harvest directly from the growers. By way of contrast, in 1984 a harvest of corn with a local market value of 300 Colombian pesos had to be transported by mule from the farm to the river at a cost of 250 pesos, and from the river to the town by canoe at a cost of 100 pesos (Jaramillo, Mora, and Cubides 1986, 138). However, due in part to fluctuating cocaine prices in world markets, coca growers hardly get rich. In 1998, 7.5 acres of coca gave a family 240 dollars of profit per month, only twice the minimum wage in Colombia at the time (Ramírez 2001, 85).

In sum, Belén de los Andaquíes is a good example of complex Colombian contexts of armed conflict and social violence. In the case of Belén, a long history of perverse extractive and unsustainable economies (cattle and coca) converges with fragmented cultural imaginaries brought in by different waves of immigrants, with a long tradition of social justice struggles led by social movements, and with armed confrontations between guerrilla organizations, the Colombian armed forces, drug traffickers, and, more recently, right-wing paramilitary organizations.

Media in Belén de los Andaquíes

I came to Belén de los Andaquíes because I was attracted by the uniqueness of a community radio station by the name of Radio

Andaquí. I heard many stories from media activists and scholars in Bogotá about Radio Andaquí. These stories told of a station that would interrupt its programming at any time if a kid asked to speak on the air, just to say hello to her mom. The station has a mobile transmission unit set on a bicycle, "the radiocycle," they called it. The first set of equipment obtained by the station was rapidly damaged because everyone was allowed "to play with it."

What I found is much more impressive than anything anyone had told me. Belén de los Andaquíes, a municipality of twelve thousand people, isolated in the Colombian Amazon and with a complex history of social and political violence, is the birthplace of not just one but two pioneer citizens' media initiatives: Radio Andaquí and the Escuela Audiovisual Infantil de Belén de los Andaquíes (EAIBA) [Belén de los Andaquíes Children's Audiovisual School].

Born twelve years apart, Radio Andaquí and EAIBA both have the creator's signature of Alirio González. Although González intended both initiatives to be profoundly committed to collective ownership, his idiosyncratic genius makes them particularly interesting and complex in terms of citizens' communication. In 2005, on a cold October

Radio Andaquí. Photograph by Clemencia Rodríguez, 2005.

Escuela Audiovisual Infantil de Belén de los Andaquíes. Photograph courtesy of EAIBA, 2010.

day in Montreal, as I tried to articulate how González designed these citizens' communication projects weaving information and communication technologies with the community's everyday lives and social fabric, my good friend and filmmaker Liz Miller responded saying that it sounded like "citizens' media d'auteur"; since then, as I will explain, I have grabbed onto this notion as I try to understand the case of citizens' media in Belén de los Andaquíes.

Eased by a few shots of rum to reduce the anxiety of talking on the air for the first time, Radio Andaquí's founders began broadcasting on April 21, 1996. Three years earlier, in 1993, they began envisioning how to use a local community radio station; in their mid-twenties this group of friends shared the same leaning toward cultural production—musicians and music aficionados, teachers, amateur poets. Led by Alirio González, who at the time was director of the Casa de la Cultura [Home of Culture],[22] they submitted a successful application to the Ministry of Communications for a community broadcasting license. In contrast with most other Colombian community radio stations where the license is granted to a local nonprofit organization, Radio Andaquí's license belongs to the people of Belén de los Andaquíes. The station's license is literally owned by the municipality's entire population. From 1996 to 2003 González was director of Radio Andaquí, and during those years he cultivated a group of radio producers with enough ideas, creativity, and energy to transform Radio Andaquí into one of Latin America's citizens' media best practices.

Together with Raúl Sotelo, Canario, Mariana García, Stella, Luisa Fernanda, Don Anselmo, and Blanco Alirio, González developed a fascinating series of citizens' communication initiatives, such as *La Cantaleta,* a daily program conducted by self-designated municipal ombudswoman Marta Calderón. In her show, Calderón literally yells at anyone not meeting their civic responsibilities, be it the mayor's neglect of streetlights and garbage collection, or mule cart owners who do not pick up their animals' droppings, or people raising pigs in their backyards and defaulting in cleaning standards, allowing bad odors to affect everyone in town. *La Cantaleta's* origin illustrates well González's way of folding communication technologies into everyday life. When Marta Calderón approached Radio Andaquí and asked González to complain publicly about the park's broken lights, González responded: "Doña Marta, why don't you come and have your own program and do it yourself?" (Calderón 2005).

Similarly, González tapped into local tailor Raúl Sotelo's hidden talent as a journalist; Canario's passion for environmental issues; Mariana, Stella, and Luisa's abilities to produce radio shows for and by children; Don Anselmo's ability to compose rhymes about all kinds of farming issues; and Blanco Alirio's skills to monitor local authorities and probe into shady local government actions (or inactions).

Exploring ways to bring "radio technology to wherever people are, not the other way around" (A. González 2005), González developed a "radiocycle," a mobile radio unit installed on a tandem bicycle. Trying to figure out how to bring Radio Andaquí to every corner of the municipality, to the river where so many local fishermen work, to a farm perched on the Andean foothills, or to a faraway elementary school only accessible by mountain trails, González thought of bicycles. Knowing that bicycles are privileged as vehicles appropriate for local conditions, González designed one that could carry a radio transmitter and two radio producers to the municipality's most isolated corners. He told me it took months of local design and technology trial and error until finally he obtained a bicycle strong enough to deal with local roads and trails. Trying specifically to respond to local conditions, González and the local mechanics collectively designed a radio-cycle, a sturdy tandem bicycle able to carry a thirty-watt transmitter. The radiocycle is made up of motorcycle, farm equipment, and bicycle parts. Every year, a different shop asks to have the radiocycle in for a few days to give it a fresh coat of paint. Radio Andaquí's radiocycle sports a new design and new colors every year, all done for free by a different local body shop.

Elsewhere, González and I have documented Radio Andaquí's first decade, from 1996 to 2005 (González and Rodríguez 2008). We emphasized the station's achievements, in terms of strengthening local public spheres; cultivating local appropriation of technology; and empowering the voices of children, farmers, and women. As in the case of the community radio stations of the Asociación Red de Emisoras Comunitarias del Magdalena Medio (AREDMAG) [Magdalena Medio's Community Radio Stations' Network], which I will discuss in chapter 3, we stressed the key role Radio Andaquí plays in pushing people to participate in local decision-making processes, monitor local governments, demand accountability, and stay well informed

Radio Andaquí's radiocycle. Photograph by Clemencia Rodríguez, 2005.

The radiocycle in action. Photograph courtesy of EAIBA, 2010.

on issues and news that affect the municipality. We also delved into Radio Andaquí's vulnerabilities, the lack of continuity of its volunteers, difficulties maintaining enough income sources to stay alive, and lack of support from its community in times of crises. As of 2008, Radio Andaquí's director was twenty-six-year-old Mariana García, a station participant since she was ten; at the time of writing, Mariana is finishing her undergraduate thesis to obtain a communication degree from Universidad Surcolombiana in the nearby city of Neiva. As is the case of most citizens' media in Colombia, Mariana, Alirio, Marta Calderón, and all other Radio Andaquí producers scramble writing grant proposals, participating in development projects funded by national and international donors, and engaging in myriad other ways such as contests, raffles, and fundraisers to secure an income for the station and to make their own living.[23]

EAIBA, Belén's audiovisual school for children, is González's most recent citizens' communication project. Singlehandedly, González developed a child-driven method to train Belén's children in audiovisual production and storytelling. González began experimenting with kids and digital photography in December of 2005, and in the following year the kids produced close to sixty digital stories. Thirteen-year-old Maira Juliana Silva chronicled the impact of the arrival of cellular phones on her community (Silva 2008); Fabián, Juan Carlos, Luis Alfredo, and Yeison explored the daily life of a coca leaf–picking family (Cuéllar et al.

2007); and twelve-year-old Jordan Alejandro Moreno reported on how the carcass of a poisoned dog caused the death of thirteen vultures and numerous fish, with serious consequences for the local environment (Moreno 2007b). All stories originate with the kids and are kid-driven, thus many focus on issues significant in their kid-world, such as a handmade toy boat (M. González 2007); a day in the life of a grandmother (Moreno 2007a); a grandfather's farm (Silva 2007); or the foreign accent of a Swiss visitor (Acosta 2007).

Any boy or girl from the municipality, eight or older, can approach the school with a story he or she wants to tell. To develop the narrative, the child works closely with González, and together they develop a digital soundtrack that—in a second step—the child illustrates with digital photographs edited and animated using Flash. The child produces her or his own images and sounds by taking a digital photography camera and a digital minidisk recorder to the local scenarios of her or his story. González insists in pushing the kids to explore their ordinary daily places—their streets, homes, playgrounds—through audiovisual technologies. The final product is a digital visual narrative of up to two minutes, animated and layered with a sound track; they have baptized this format *"fotovideo."*

The school's *fotovideos* are premiered at a public street presentation. In my experience, citizens' media producers tend to pay close attention to how videos, television shows, and radio programs are produced, but very little is done about how audiences will access those media products; that is not the case with González. He carefully designs how each new *fotovideo* will be viewed in the community; he cultivates media audiences as much as he cultivates media producers. Each *fotovideo* is projected on a big screen placed on the street in front of the home of the producer or the protagonist, thus transforming the street into a public sphere where the people of Belén can see themselves through their children' eyes. Subsequent presentations of each *fotovideo* are done through the local cable television channel and in local schools' classrooms. Radio Andaquí disseminates information about times and places of each of these public presentations. Finally, all *fotovideos* are uploaded in the school's blog using YouTube. The children themselves maintain the blog with comments and entries about their work (see http://escuelaaudiovisualinfantil.blogspot.com). According to González,

> the school operates under the following principles: first, without a story, there's no camera; the number one condition to begin the process is for the child to approach the school with a local story he or she wants to tell—the school does not teach anything that the child does not demand for the completion of her or his storytelling project. Second, we believe in the power of technologies to create strong bonds between child and place; I've seen a child observing his or her world through a digital camera, falling in love with it, interrogating his or her place in the community, and realizing his or her role in the construction of a collective future. Third, we narrate what we do and who we are, so that we can discover where we want to go. And fourth, the school "steals" children from the war; we offer local children and youth an alternative to a life in the ranks of armed groups and/or drug trafficking. (A. González 2007)

On August 16, 2008, Pildorito, one of the school's youngest, received the keys of EAIBA's new building; the children left behind the crammed two-room small house that served as the school's facility since 2005 and quickly appropriated their new school, a large building filled with natural light and covered floor to ceiling with colorful murals where every space is especially designed to nurture individual creativity and self-confidence and at the same time encourage collective action.[24] Characteristic of González's commitment to collective ownership of the citizens' communication projects he designs, during the construction process he privileged contracting the parents of the kids already involved with the school as painters, bricklayers, and laborers in the construction crews.

In the following pages I explain how Radio Andaquí and EAIBA contend with armed conflict in Belén. When asked if these citizens' communication initiatives were born to counter armed conflict in the region, González, Marta Calderón, Mariana García, and all others respond adamantly with a negative. In their view, war is not the main reason behind their local citizens' media; however, their community lives side by side with armed conflict; in the same way that municipal elections, local governments, police, families, and local businesses are affected by the presence of armed groups, so are the children producing radio programs at the station or *fotovideos* at the audiovisual school. In this sense, Radio Andaquí and EAIBA have developed

Without a story, there's no camera. Photograph courtesy of EAIBA, 2010.

sophisticated communication skills to support unarmed civilians' attempts to buffer war's impact on their daily lives and social fabric. Since EAIBA was just beginning when I was doing my fieldwork in Belén, I focus almost exclusively on Radio Andaquí.

Citizens and Their Media Respond to War

From Isolation and Fear to Agency and Voice

In Colombia, armed conflict takes a different shape in each region of the country. Based on research into the decades-old social and political armed conflict, Colombian scholars explain how and why each Colombian region produces its own version of war. During my fieldwork with different citizens' media initiatives in Magdalena Medio, Montes de María, and Caquetá, I was able to see how main characters, war strategies, and targets shift from place to place, sometimes even within the same region. In these contexts, citizens' media have learned to tailor their strategies of resistance to the specific shape that armed conflict takes in their territory. What follows articulates Radio Andaquí's strategies.

During one of my visits to Belén de los Andaquíes in 2005, I found myself in the house of Doña Marta Calderón, the producer, director, and anchor of La Cantaleta. Torrential rain was pouring down; we sat in Doña Marta's living room, talking and waiting for the rain to stop. I said that I liked the noise of the water as it hit her tin roof, and she responded that she did not, explaining that "it reminds me of the last guerrilla attack . . . the noise of shooting was similar" (Calderón 2005). Doña Marta then gave me details of the guerrilla attack. Her narrative was a collection of fragments about terrified neighbors, people running for cover, disconnected phone lines, electricity outages, and an intense feeling of fear overtaking everyone in town.

At a different moment in my fieldwork, in 2006, I was sitting with my notebook computer on my lap, busy with something. In the same room were Mariana, the young Radio Andaquí producer who would later become the station's director, and Alirio González. We were all lost in concentration, working on our own projects. Mariana and I worked on my computer and Alirio wrote on his desktop. Suddenly, we heard loud gunfire coming from behind the house, and I saw the faces of my two companions immediately distort in expressions of fear. At that point, I could not identify what the noise was, but they certainly did. In an instant, Alirio jumped from his chair and was outside asking questions. Five minutes later he came back and reassured us, explaining that it was just the army battalion discarding old ammunition.

These vignettes are important because they remind us that people living in contexts of armed conflict experience life in the form of parallel and fragmented realities. The notion that people "get used to" armed conflict and war in regions such as Caquetá is as common as it is wrong. The idea that people in violent contexts somehow habituate to their conditions is problematic, because it causes us to lose sight of the intense fear, dislocation, and just plain rejection of armed conflict experienced by local communities. We are also prone to lose sight of the "parallel realities" armed conflict creates, which citizens experience as everyday life. One minute life is normal in Belén, and the next minute it is total chaos (Das 2000, 2001, 2007; Nordstrom and Martin 1992; Nordstrom and Robben 1995). Lewin notes how in contexts of war "a weird encounter between 'ordinary' and 'common' factors . . . allows people to live in a chronic state of fear with a facade of normalcy, while terror, at the same time, permeates and shreds the social fabric" (Lewin 2002, 52–53).

In all my interactions in Magdalena Medio, Montes de María, and Caquetá, I have never encountered one single person who experiences the presence of armed groups in their territory as normal. In Caquetá, people commonly express pain, bitterness, resentment, and sadness over the impact of armed conflict in their region. They note how their landscape has changed to include military checkpoints and barricades, camouflage-patterned uniforms drying in people's backyards, war planes flying over, and the presence of heavily armed platoons patrolling roads, trails, and downtown streets. Based on her fieldwork on war zones in Sri Lanka and Mozambique, Carolyn Nordstrom wrote: "Probably the most destructive aspect of dirty war tactics is the creation of the culturally destabilized space" (Nordstrom 1992, 268), a landscape that bears visible markings of terror through which people have to walk every day.

What role does a community radio station play in this context? Radio Andaquí taught me an important lesson: using communication and media to help civilians resist the negative impact of armed conflict is complex, multifaceted, and multidimensional. It is an endeavor that involves developing immediate, sometimes ad hoc or improvised, communication strategies in moments of crisis, when armed conflict engulfs the community in a state of collective terror. It also involves, however, more long-term strategies of resistance to the lasting impact of armed conflict on people's collective imaginaries, their notions of themselves, and their territory. In some cases, the work of community radio even involves "stealing" from war, in the sense of not allowing war to define the purpose of the medium and reminding the community that there's much in their lives and landscapes that still exists beyond the reach of war. The following pages attempt to articulate these uses of a citizens' radio station in a difficult context of armed violence.

On December 31, 2001, at seven in the evening, Radio Andaquí played New Year's music. The station was busy preparing for the live transmission of the town's Old Year parade, until the sound of machine gun fire took everyone by surprise. Alirio González, recounts,

I remember thinking, "Fuck! The guerrillas once again!" and then the phone rang and I put the call through. It was a listener who called to say "turn [the station] off, turn it off, the guerrilla is in town." All I was able to say on the microphone was: "There's fighting in the streets. Stay inside, lock all doors, and let's be cautious." The radio station shook, and because we had previous experience with guerrilla attacks, we sought cover under desks and tables in case a wall collapsed. Callers kept the phone ringing, asking for advice on what to do. I was engulfed by fear and the only thing I could think of was to put in a CD and play *villancicos*.[25] We began telling callers to turn the radio on and turn up the volume to amplify the *villancicos* in their homes. We called Father Ignacio Trujillo and came up with the idea of transmitting the *villancicos* through the church's loudspeaker system and ringing the bell calling the people to New Year's Mass. An hour later we heard screaming coming from the central plaza, so I took the radiocycle and went downtown to see what was going on. Waving white T-shirts, sheets, or any other white cloth at hand, about a dozen people had gathered downtown screaming, "We are civilians! Stop shooting! All we want is peace!" It started with a few people who had just arrived in town on a bus. Terrified by the combat, they took off their shirts and began screaming. Thinking that it was an organized demonstration, others began to join in. I joined the people and we began transmitting people's voices using the radiocycle, with the *villancicos* in the background. There was no need for speeches or slogans for or against anyone. If someone wanted to use the mics at that moment to speak for or against any of the armed groups, we told them it was not the moment for that. If a police officer wanted to speak, we did not allow them; telling them it was not the moment for that. We only opened the mics for citizens asking for peace and rejecting all armed actions. The priest was there too, singing *villancicos* with the people. The people, accompanied by the radiocycle, went around the town. We do not use the station to narrate combat. What would that do? It would only intensify the feeling of fear, nothing else; absolutely nothing else. Instead of narrating combat, we used the station to amplify the voices of unarmed civilians. [After the guerrilla left] the local disco made its sound system available so the New Year's Mass could be held on the central plaza. (A. González 2004)

The above narrative demonstrates how Radio Andaquí positions the technology on the side of civilians, privileging the point of view and lived experiences of unarmed civilians and their voices over those of armed actors. Radio Andaquí intervenes to try to erode the state of collective terror that overtakes civilians coping with armed conflict in a moment of crisis. In the case of this guerrilla attack, the station joined the people left in the street by an ill-timed bus arrival waving white flags and transformed an event of a few people into a public forum that many others could join. Initially, Radio Andaquí served as an amplifier of a local response. As participation increased, this emerging public sphere began taking shape. The presence of the local priest, the *villancicos,* and the white flags helped create a public statement in which the community clearly rejected the takeover of armed groups, the destructive impact on their town, and their lives. No names were mentioned, so *all* armed groups were rejected. As more and more people joined in, feelings of fear receded, giving way to an experience of togetherness and collective agency. Here, this citizens' medium opened a public sphere allowing feelings of togetherness to materialize, which in turn eroded the isolation and loneliness that had been imposed by fear. The symbolic power of *villancicos* unified the collective resistance as these songs are shared and cherished by all Colombians, regardless of ideological or political difference. In this moment of crisis, Radio Andaquí succeeded in creating a shield that symbolically protected an act of citizens' resistance.

Anthropological studies of war show that survivors of armed violence experience chaos, uncertainty, and terror (Das 2000, 2001, 2007; Nordstrom and Martin 1992; Nordstrom and Robben 1995; Warren 2002). Armed violence shatters webs of meaning, leaving individuals and communities without the necessary language to make sense of their situations. Experiencing extreme violence unmakes the symbolic universe of survivors. In the Colombian case, "armed groups are aware of the political advantages they gain when they use terror to destroy collective conscience. . . . [V]iolence is used against not only people and groups but also against collective conscience, as the source of collective action" (García Villegas and de Sousa dos Santos 2004, 51).

However, in the case of this small town coping with a guerrilla attack, we can see how, in the hands of the people, citizens' media can become a powerful force, enabling unarmed civilian communities to resist and overcome the terror of armed violence by recreating a web of meaning well grounded in powerful symbolic codes—such as the *villancicos,* in this case.

Radio Andaquí's spur-of-the-moment decision to accompany civilians' response to the attack allowed this Colombian community, victimized by FARC, to confront feelings of fear and isolation and engage in a collective action of resistance through communication processes. People in Belén frequently recounted how, during guerrilla attacks, families lock doors and windows and hide under beds; this is also how González's narrative of the events that night begins; however, the narrative evolves from individuals hiding under desks to a collective action with a unified voice. Mediating cultural and communication processes, such as the amplification of unarmed civilians and the *villancicos,* Radio Andaquí contributed to transform the white flag–waving group into a media event; from being the target of armed groups' victimization, the community emerged as a collective of active agents with a voice.

In his work about Argentina's dirty war, Suárez-Orozco described terror as a centrifugal force that thrusts unarmed civilians into silence and isolation—two processes that feed off each other; in this context, the Mothers of Plaza de Mayo "subverted the silence and the centrifugal isolationism" (Suárez-Orozco 1992, 242) by merely coming together and walking around a plaza every week. Similarly, Radio Andaquí triggered a communication space where unarmed civilians could move out of isolation and toward togetherness.

Over time, Radio Andaquí has learned how to use information and communication technologies to counter the effects of armed conflict on the people of Belén. How has this citizens' medium developed these communication competencies? "We learn from people. They have learned to cope with these kinds of crisis situations, so they provide the clues. The radio station learns from them" (A. González 2004).

Carolyn Nordstrom articulates well the significance of these acts of resistance on the part of civilians cornered by the fear imposed by armed actors:

Conventional wisdom posits that war must first be ended, and then the developments of peace can be attended to, as people are able to turn their energies to creating a future. But my data does not support this conclusion. It would seem peace begins—indeed must begin—in the thick of battle, among those least armed and often most violated. . . . War depends on fear of oppression, a belief in force, and a willingness to use violence. Soldiers fight wars and civilians support them because they fear losing what they have and hope to gain something they don't. War also depends on placing these fears and beliefs in a framework that specifies friend and foe, political alliance and alienation. When citizens hold these fears and support these beliefs, and when they are willing to use force in their name, war remains paramount. So peace begins when people find violence the worst threat of all. With this, the fears and beliefs in force wane and support for violent solutions withers as a search for creative non-aggressive solutions waxes. This isn't merely a political process. It is forged in the center of daily life. It is carried through simple conversations and philosophical debates; crafted in art and reproduced in music; relayed in folk tales and honed in literature. (Nordstrom 2004, 180–81)

Despite the intensity and drama, the leaders of Radio Andaquí do not see this type of action as the most significant work they do. On the contrary, they take more pride in the long-term, ant-like work of trying to erode the collective imaginaries and cultural codes both inherited from and feeding armed conflict in the region.

Recovering Public Places and Repairing Social Fabric

In December of 2005, González and I walked to a part of town where he said he wanted to show me "the reindeer." I had no clue what he meant. We reached a neighborhood where people seemed extremely busy, going in and out of houses. We were told which house held the reindeer, and were invited to go and look. We entered a small house and asked the owners if we could see the reindeer. I was introduced as a "friend of Radio Andaquí" wanting to see the reindeer. The hosts, a couple in their thirties, welcomed us warmly and asked us to wait in the small living room. They proceeded to go in and out of rooms, each time bringing out a white reindeer the size of a large dog. Little by little the living room filled with reindeer, and as I looked around the house, into the hall and other rooms, I realized every room was overflowing with reindeer. The couple arranged them in order, explaining that some were in the finishing stages while others were just beginning to take shape. As I took hundreds of photos, the husband insisted that praise should go to his wife, as she and her women neighbors were the true reindeer artists. Word of my presence as the "foreign visitor" went around, and other women came in. These women made the reindeer entirely by hand. Their "skeletons" were perfectly shaped out of some kind of sturdy white wire, and once the structure of the skeleton was complete, the women explained, they carefully wrapped it in a type of white industrial gauze-like fabric. In the final stage, each reindeer was wrapped in hundreds of tiny white Christmas lights.

A neighbor told me the whole story behind the reindeer. In 1996, after a difficult time of social unrest, armed violence, and guerrilla attacks, the entire town plunged into a state of collective fear. Families locked themselves in their houses as the sun went down and downtown businesses closed early. In those days, they told me, Belén looked like a ghost town by six in the evening.

In Belén, this movement toward the private sphere had a negative impact on a community of people accustomed to enjoying warm evenings in one anothers' company, where adults would have a couple of beers at one of the central plaza *tiendas,* teens would stroll around the park, and kids would run around in packs. The practice of locking doors and spending evenings in isolation is foreign and frightening. Others have documented how the presence of armed groups "clears" public places traditionally shared by civilians to interact, have dialogue, and form and maintain friendships, bonds of solidarity, trust, and, in sum, sustain social cohesion. According to Lechner, "fear depoliticizes citizens as it makes people feel incapable of defending themselves against the source of threat. People's last recourse is to find refuge in the private sphere" (cited in Ramírez 2001, 276). Hannah Arendt identified this type of isolation as an element of terror that provokes a feeling of "not belonging to the world at all" (Arendt 1966, 474).

Historical accounts in Magdalena Medio in central Colombia describe how it feels to lose the social fabric of friends and neighbors talking and socializing:

> In those days we lived out there in the countryside, and at night, seeing a flashlight coming toward your house was a source of joy, 'cause you knew a friend or neighbor was coming; today, you see someone coming and you feel fear. Back then there was trust, solidarity, friendship among people; we all lived in harmony. In today's situation, where everything is fear and distrust, you may believe that was impossible, you may think I'm a liar. We don't trust anyone, and no one trusts us. (Arenas Obregón 1998, 38)

Sluka documents how instructions imparted through a pamphlet distributed in Catholic neighborhoods in Northern Ireland spiraled into collective isolation. Warning people of behaviors to avoid, the pamphlet told them that most murder victims are those who "open their door at night; those who accept lifts from strangers; those who accept a joint taxi ride" and advised people to "never travel in a cab that has already got passengers; never accept an invitation to a party which may be extended in a pub; DISCUSS NOTHING WITH YOUR WORKMATES no matter how long you have worked with them" (Sluka 2000a, 138–39). Similar processes are experienced by civilians in Colombian contexts where guerrillas, paramilitaries, the Colombian armed forces, and drug traffickers compete for control of territories, people, and resources; such was the case of Belén de los Andaquíes in the late 1990s.

In December of 1996, using the Christmas spirit as a pretext, Radio Andaquí began encouraging people to decorate their street blocks. Day after day the station would use microphones and the airwaves to let everyone know that a certain block had started painting the sidewalk, or that another neighborhood was using egg cartons to construct small houses shining with Christmas lights. Little by little, people began coming out of their isolation to decorate their blocks. Individual decorations were not encouraged, as the station wanted people to get together to talk and interact, leaving front doors open to allow for the comings and goings necessary to fetch tools and materials, and to discuss new ideas. Almost a decade later, the custom of collectively decorating the entire town, block by block, at Christmastime has become a tradition in Belén's collective imaginary. Year after year, Radio Andaquí announces and applauds the town's decorations. This annual event, initiated by the radio station years ago, is still a media event today.

The reindeer block is known as one of the most creative. Neighbors begin planning months in advance, coming up with an entirely new idea every year. Throughout the year the neighbors organize several fundraising events, and each family contributes five thousand Colombian pesos each month (about US$2.50). The block accumulates fairly large amounts of money, and everything is spent on the Christmas installation, "entirely counter to all market rules; that's the idea" (A. González 2005).

December 16, the first Christmas day in the Catholic calendar, marks the beginning of intense decorating, and from that day on, every spare moment is spent cutting, painting, hanging. Neighbors stay up late at night, until eleven or twelve, all kinds of conversations taking place as they work. Night by night, the street landscapes begin taking shape. Using the radiocycle, Radio Andaquí narrates what this or that block has accomplished, encouraging people to go see for themselves. Everything comes together on the night of December 24. That night, the reindeer block throws a major party, with hot chocolate and pastries for everyone wandering by to admire their art. Their street has been transformed into an arctic landscape—in the middle of the Amazon—with every inch, including the pavement, painted white. The reindeer float in the air, suspended by a complex system of cables and pulleys, descending for the first time ever on Belén de los Andaquíes, as if history and geography do not matter.

As in the case of the Purple Rose of Cairo film project in Montes de María (see chapter 2), Radio Andaquí designs media events that trigger collective conversations and interactions in public places where the war had imposed silence and isolation. The streets, the sidewalks, peoples' front porches come back to life with the pretext of neighbors joining efforts to decorate their block during Christmas time. One conversation at a time, Radio Andaquí reappropriates public places colonized by fear and individual entrapment and repositions them at the service of the community, so that they can be repopulated and used for collective interaction, to weave bonds of friendship and solidarity, to flirt, play, or just plain get to know one another.

Navigating Armed Violence and Peaceful Dissent

In the book's introduction and in the analyses of regional armed conflict in the next two chapters I have tried to convey the perplexing complexity of social movements' interactions with armed groups such as guerrilla organizations and paramilitaries. In Belén de los Andaquíes I found a clear case of a citizens' medium trying to navigate such complexity when Radio Andaquí dealt with the *cocalero* demonstrations of 1996. In order to understand this case, though, I need to explain thoroughly the complex *cocalero* mobilization of the late 1990s.

During the early 1990s, with the support of and under pressure from the United States,[26] the Colombian government initiated a policy attempting to end the cultivation of illicit crops in southern Colombia by fumigating the crops with the pesticide Roundup (fosfonometil, or ghyphosate). After four decades of being invisible to the central government, the homesteaders now growing coca began to experience another, more perverse form of exclusion and rejection coming from Bogotá: fumigation. The Colombian central government that did not listen, did not see, and had a thin presence at the local level, had now initiated a new type of interaction with these southern communities through a poisonous chemical dropped from the sky.

On November 18, 1994, the city of Puerto Asís, in the neighboring department of Putumayo, was paralyzed by a *paro cívico* (civic strike).[27] The strike was led by local peasant organizations protesting the fumigation of illicit crops with Roundup. They outlined the health and environmental impacts of this chemical on communities affected. A local newspaper wrote, "Fumigating and repressing peasants is the only way the Colombian state remembers that peasants exist" (*Diario del Sur*, November 17, 1994, 10A, cited by Ramírez 2001, 106). Rejection of the fumigation was so strong that in 1996, local peasant organizations in Putumayo said they would not allow "one single acre to be fumigated" (Ramírez 2001, 116).

Two opposing versions of the situation in the region emerged from this mobilization known as the *cocalero* movement. On one hand, local civil society, under the leadership of peasant organizations, was trying to send a message to the central government, insisting that fumigation and repression were not the appropriate solutions to a problem that ultimately had its roots in social injustice and official neglect. The following demands motivated the civic strike: better roads to facilitate access to agricultural markets, and improved access to electricity, health services, and basic public education. In terms of illicit crops, the demands included that only plots of two or more hectares, planted *only* with coca, be fumigated (manual eradication was proposed for smaller plots and plots that combined coca with other crops), and that crop substitution and alternative development projects be implemented in the region simultaneously with fumigation (Ramírez 2001, 110–11).

On the other hand, local military leaders and more importantly, the national media, presented a very different version of the civic strike. According to this version, guerrillas and drug traffickers had taken complete control of the local population. The media reported that the strikes and demonstrations were massive because guerrillas and drug traffickers were forcing people to demonstrate, and that the chaos of the region was not exceptional, but rather a normal expression of this savage, violent part of the country where "people have become used to these barbarian ways" (Ramírez 2001, 108–9). According to this official version, the region, marginal and savage, had to be recolonized with culture, civilization, and military might brought in from Bogotá (Ramírez 2001, 149).

According to Colombian anthropologist María Clemencia Ramírez, the *cocalero* movement was determined to contest the identity imposed upon the communities of the Colombian Amazon region by the government, the military, and the media. The movement was a response to the notion of the "*cocalero* peasant" as a delinquent, antisocial anticitizen controlled by FARC and only interested in fast profit. Led mainly by traditional civic organizations in the form of JACs,[28] the movement claimed that first, local peasants were homesteaders and farmers and not drug traffickers; second, that local peasants plant coca only because government neglect and poverty do not leave them any other option; third, that eradication of illicit crops should be concomitant with government provision of solutions to basic infrastructure, health, and education needs in the region. The central government's deafness toward this Amazonian peasant movement can be explained in part by the Samper administration's (1994–98) need to "prove" to the United States its willingness to fight the war on drugs. In order to maximize the image of battling an "evil" enemy, the Samper administration needed to maintain the delinquent and antisocial image of *cocaleros* (Ramírez 2001, chap. 4).[29]

The Samper administration portrayed *cocaleros* as puppets of the guerrillas, but Ramírez thoroughly demonstrates that this peasant mobilization was actually asking for a stronger state presence in the region. *Cocaleros* sought the government's help in gaining access to roads, health care, and education. They wanted the presence of state institutions capable of maintaining the rule of law. What they rejected was the presence of a state in the form of military control and chemical fumigations.

In May of 1996, the central government made two moves in its "war on drugs" that set off angry responses in the Amazon region. First, authorities drastically restricted the circulation of cement in the region, paralyzing all construction, and especially public works.[30] Second, the army declared the regions of Guaviare, Vaupés, Meta, Vichada, and Caquetá a "*zona especial de orden público*"[31] (region of social unrest) because, in the words of the army, "criminal and terrorist organizations have concentrated in the region" (Decreto 0871 of May 13, 1996, cited in Ramírez 2001, 135).

On July 22, 1996, Operación Conquista, a major fumigation operation led by the army and the police, sprayed the municipality of Remolinos del Caguán, in Caquetá. In public statements to the media, military leaders explained that the operation would lead to "conquering the region from the hands of the *narcoguerrilla.*"[32] Seven days later, on July 29, thousands of coca growers began to mobilize from far away communities in Caquetá and Putumayo toward the main urban centers (Florencia and Mocoa, respectively).[33] Military leaders delegitimized this mobilization, saying that the peasants were "nothing but herds of cattle enslaved and driven by FARC terrorists" (General Bedoya's declaration to *Cambio,* cited in Ramírez 2001, 140). In declarations to the national media, another general stated that the demonstrators "do not know why they are demonstrating" (General Galán Rodríguez to *La Nación,* cited in Ramírez 2001, 144). According to Arcila Niño and his colleagues, between fifty and seventy thousand peasants marched in Caquetá alone (Arcila Niño et al. 2000, 204). Confrontations erupted in different places between demonstrators and armed forces. With a series of agreements between coca growers and a governmental delegation, the peasant mobilization ended on September 12, 1996, after forty-seven demonstrations, six deaths, and more than seventy wounded (Arcila Niño et al. 2000, 206).

Were the peasants demonstrating because they were forced to do so by FARC? Ramírez explains that the relationship between FARC, homesteaders, and coca growers is complex and multilayered. As one farmer and demonstrator explained, "we came out, voluntarily forced" *(salimos voluntariamente obligados)* (Ramírez 2001, 153). Saying that the *cocalero* demonstrations of 1996 were exclusively the result of FARC domination denies clear evidence of strong, autonomous peasant organizations with their own agency. On the other hand, FARC "not only supported the demonstrations, but also pressured communities to join" (Ramírez 2001, 153). This ambiguity surrounding FARC's influence is a direct result of the complex system of negotiations that have evolved over the years between FARC and local communities. This is a complexity with which local citizens' media have to contend. In a context where armed organizations have such entangled relationships with civil society, citizens' media have to learn to navigate an environment without clear good guys and bad guys.

In regions such as Caquetá, FARC legitimates and supports JACs that are public institutions. Many local communities recognize FARC as a form of local government that fills the vacuum left by the absence of state institutions. In these communities, FARC acts as the police and legal authority, mediating land disputes and even domestic conflicts.[34] FARC forbids minors to enter billiard joints and discos, prohibits alcohol consumption and disco partying during weekdays, regulates all land sales, and collects taxes. FARC even supported local organizations in their demand for stronger presence of the central state in the region, rather than attempting to replace the central state with a guerrilla state. Ramírez describes the ways her fieldwork in the region allowed her to see how FARC, far from rejecting the central state, frequently utilized its institutions. In one example, FARC demanded that every local citizen be a member of a JAC. Membership in JACs requires a citizenship identity card, thus forcing everyone in the region to get official identification. Through forced JAC membership, FARC achieved the only accurate census in the region (Ramírez 2001, 157–61).

According to Ramírez, FARC supported the *cocalero* mobilization with its financial and organizational know-how. FARC established a tax system in which all the monies collected went into a mobilization fund, which later fed and supported thousands of peasants marching toward urban centers. The money was allocated by the JACs' financial committees. FARC also organized a system to decide who would join the demonstrations and who would stay behind to take care of valuables, crops, and cattle.[35] The food logistics were so well organized that, according to testimonies collected by Ramírez, in some cases demonstrators were feeding the soldiers charged with repressing the demonstrations (Ramírez 2001, 163). FARC had an undeniable presence in the demonstrations of 1996, but the peasants and their JACs' leaders were the genuine authors of the proposals and demands presented to the central government. Key to the peasant demands was the proposal that the region be declared a "region of social investment" *(zona especial de inversión social)* instead of a "region of social unrest" (Ramírez 2001, 181). The Samper administration focused on the criminal nature of the problem in the region, considering only illicit crop cultivation. In contrast, the peasant movement focused on the social nature of the problem, explaining that desperate poverty had driven local peasants to grow coca. While government representatives insisted that only radical eradication of illicit crops via fumigation was acceptable, the peasant movement advocated a gradual,[36] voluntary, and environmentally friendly eradication program. In the end, both camps negotiated a series of signed agreements.

As Ramírez points out, the success of the *cocalero* movement should not be measured only in terms of whether or not specific objectives were reached. The value of the movement can be seen in terms of strengthening a political culture of grassroots participation in democratic decision-making. Citing Cohen and Arato, Ramírez states that in places where the rule of law and the state are absent, and where armed conflict permeates all spheres of communal life, one of the most significant accomplishments of social movements is the "democratization of values, norms, and institutions" (Ramírez 2001, 297). The *cocalero* movement went beyond demanding the development of basic infrastructure and services to issue a plea for the recognition of coca farmers as Colombian citizens in crisis, rather than as delinquents.[37] The movement also functioned as a demand for "the right to have rights" (Hannah Arendt, cited in Ramírez 2001, 300), understood as the right to belong to a political community where rights and responsibilities are regulated peacefully according to the rule of law. Finally, the *cocalero* movement clearly articulated the paradoxical conception of the state shared by so many Colombian social movements. In some ways, the state is feared and rejected for its repressive measures and its neglect, while in other ways, the state is perceived as a deliverer of rights, resources, and services needed by communities (Ramírez 2001, 310).

The intricate interaction of coca economies, guerrilla presence, and active peasant resistance set the stage for Radio Andaquí's response to the arrival of the *cocalero* march in Belén de los Andaquíes. How do citizens' media deal with this kind of complexity?

In September of 1996, the *cocalero* demonstrators arrived in Belén de los Andaquíes. Twenty thousand people camped in Belén for a few days, regrouping and gaining strength before continuing on toward the capital city of Florencia, their final destination. Thousands of marchers set up tents on the shores of the Sarabando River, a few blocks from the downtown. Belén's local disco, Radio Andaquí's conference room, and all local schools were designated as shelters for the demonstrators. At the time, Radio Andaquí did not yet have its license, so it was not on the air. The *cocalero* march was too significant to miss, however, so Radio Andaquí's leaders spontaneously decided to bring the station to life. González remembers how this decision was made: "The first impulse is to say 'let's remain silent!' but on the other hand, we felt we had to serve our citizens; we decided to open the mics. Instead of a narrow focus on the reasons behind the march, or if the demonstrators were right or not, which at that point was quite confusing, we opened the focus to anyone who wanted to sing, recite poems, etc." (A. González 2004). A few rules were agreed upon. The station would avoid any type of discourse for or against the *cocalero* mobilization, maintaining instead dynamic programming in support of the people marching, calling people to meetings, disseminating safety information (especially in regard to the well-being of the children camping on the shores of the fast-moving river), and transmitting messages from the demonstrators to their families and communities back home; in the words of González: "The key is to align the medium with the needs of unarmed civilians" (A. González 2004).

Radio Andaquí's agenda was driven by the information and communication needs of unarmed civilians at that moment. During the *cocalero* mobilization, Radio Andaquí served the needs of both local citizens and the *cocalero* demonstrators coming from far away communities. Soon, the station was filled with marchers transmitting their messages to those who had stayed back home. *Cocaleros* sent messages such as: "Sell the calf, because we ran out of money and nothing has been defined yet"; "Give corn to the chickens and sell a few hens because we have no money"; "We are fine, in Belén, and God willing we will reach our goal"; and "*M'hija* [my daughter], take good care of the animals, because we don't know how long this will take" (González and Rodríguez 2008, 114).

Apart from meeting the information needs of the demonstrators, Radio Andaquí invited both demonstrators and the people of Belén to come to the station and share their music, poetry, and songs. So many people came to play music, sing, and recite that the station had to improvise an outdoor stage in front of its studio. Soon, the new transmission site was baptized La Tarima del Sol [The Sun's Stage] because it sat under a canopy of trees that filtered the sunlight into beautiful shadows reflected on the artists. For eight days, the Sun's Stage was witness to what Alirio González calls "the most significant festival of music, poetry, and song we have ever transmitted in ten years":

Quisiera que Samper
se fuera a los infiernos
con toda su fumiga
para no volverlo a ver

se levantaron en marcha
los campesinos en contra del gobierno
protestan por la fumiga
que con nosotros acabará

I wish Samper
Went to hell
With all his fumigation
So that I never have to see him again

They rose and marched
The peasants against the government
They protest the fumigation
That will ultimately finish us (González and Rodríguez 2008, 115)

Although some of the song lyrics were clearly political (as the one above), not all of them focused solely on the *cocalero* mobilization. On the Sun's Stage, *cocaleros* and locals could learn about one another, and appreciate one another's creative abilities and identities as human beings, beyond any political agenda. Radio Andaquí provided *cocalero* demonstrators and their local hosts with a communication space for recognizing one another as multidimensional, complex subjects with a lot in common. Belén's radio audiences saw that the demonstrators were not the terrorists, delinquents, drug traffickers, or guerrillas that the national media had portrayed. Instead, audiences saw and heard families of farmers, very much like themselves, struggling to have their rights recognized by the central government. Locals were able to see the demonstrators as members of loving families like their own, whose lives were disrupted by the need to join this effort to have their voices heard. González recounts:

> One afternoon don Pedro Vargas came to the Sun's Stage. He had walked all the way from Albania and once he was positioned in front of the microphone, he gave the following instructions: "*M'hija,* kneel down, you and the kids, because here goes dad's blessing." With his right hand he made the sign of the cross over the microphone, recited the blessing, and finished by saying, "Stop worrying. God is with us, I am fine, and we will make it to Florencia." (González and Rodríguez 2008, 115)

Radio Andaquí's role in the *cocalero* demonstration can be interpreted as that of what Chantal Mouffe calls the "democratic mobilization of affection in order to weave communal identities" (Mouffe 2006). According to Mouffe, we need to reinstate the centrality of affection in politics. Mouffe states that "democratic politics need to have a real influence on people's desires and fantasies" so that, despite tremendous differences, people can see the "other" not as an enemy or antagonist to be eliminated, but as an "agonist" whose demands, although not shared, have a legitimate place in the public sphere (Mouffe 2006). Radio Andaquí carefully designed an open communication space where locals and demonstrators could see one another as poets, singers, fathers, mothers, husbands, and farmers. With the Sun's Stage, Radio Andaquí helped deflate the potential antagonism between locals and *cocaleros,* and simultaneously fueled "agonist identities," as Mouffe conceives of the term.

The Sun's Stage helped defuse conflict between the demonstrators and the people of Belén, who may have felt threatened by the "invasion" of thousands of "terrorist criminals manipulated by FARC." Although violence erupted in many places where the demonstrators stopped on their way to Florencia, the people of Belén supported their guests until they left town a week later. The only violent incidents in Belén originated with the local armed forces, which attacked the demonstrators minutes before they left. The lone victim was a local man who, like many others, sided with the demonstrators and against the soldiers, and was injured by a soldier's gunshot as he was trying to shield the *cocalero* families.

To end this section I would like to emphasize what I believe is Radio Andaquí's most admirable achievement: to maintain, in such a complex mesh of interactions among social movements, legal and illegal armed groups, and communities, its purpose of serving the people, meaning unarmed civilians. Radio Andaquí triggers, facilitates, cultivates, and maintains communication processes that strengthen whatever threads remain of a nonmilitarized social fabric in a militarized context.

Transforming Collective Imaginaries

As I noted before, Belén's citizens' media producers do not attach much importance to how they use radio and audiovisual technologies in times of crisis brought about by armed conflict and/or social unrest.

In fact, only when I began asking questions did they articulate how they have used the station and the school in difficult and complex crisis situations. What holds a central place in their minds is more the long-term purpose of citizens' media in a context such as Belén de los Andaquíes. In their view, transforming the collective imaginaries is Radio Andaquí and EAIBA's most significant contribution to long-term peacebuilding. Transforming collective imaginaries is, I found, a common concern in all my case studies; as with Radio Andaquí and EAIBA, the leaders behind the Montes de María Communications Collective and those behind AREDMAG's community radios (see chapters 2 and 3), stress the potential of using citizens' media to resist armed conflict's erosion of social fabrics.

What do these citizens' media pioneers mean by "collective imaginary"? "Collective imaginary" refers to the set of cultural codes and symbolic webs of meaning shared by a collectivity; these codes and meanings form a collective sense of identity, a notion of "us" closely tied to space and place (sense of belonging to a territory, or sense of place), to "a relationship to the past, which is expressed in a collective memory, and a relationship to the future, which is expressed in utopias" (Bouchard 2005). A community's collective imaginary is shaped by versions of a shared past (a collective memory) and shapes a collective vision for the future. A collective imaginary is permanently fed by collective experience (such as a long history of armed conflict) but also by images, visions, and versions of "who we are" tied to the natural environment, local lifestyles, local aesthetics, languages, and narratives. In this sense, Colombian citizens' media leaders share similar diagnosis about the collective imaginaries of their respective regions: the decade-long presence of armed groups and violent conflict has intensely permeated collective imaginaries; notions of "who we are" are tied to violence; collective memories are grounded on a violent past; lifestyles privilege violence and aggression as efficient ways to resolve mundane conflict. Based on such diagnosis, these media pioneers seek to use communication processes to intervene in local collective imaginaries with alternative images, visions, and stories of "who we are."

I cannot stress enough the fact that citizens' media such as Radio Andaquí and EAIBA do not expect to stop or even diminish armed conflict in Caquetá. Instead, citizens' media are used to resist the negative impact of armed groups (legal and illegal) on their communities' social and cultural fabric. These media target the tenuous boundary between armed groups and unarmed communities. While armed groups colonize public spaces, social dynamics, cultural expressions, ways to solve daily disputes, and children's games, Radio Andaquí and EAIBA aim all their communication know-how to counter such colonization.

The long-term effort of Radio Andaquí to counter the militaristic logics of war and armed conflict is driven by the need to question and problematize the meanings ascribed to the region and its people. Decades of armed conflict in Caquetá have cultivated certain notions of self and place that define the region, both for its people and also for the rest of the nation. Years of built-up symbolic codes portray Caquetá as a region of violent people and "savage" communities, and this portrayal suffocates any alternative version of place and people. Ascribed identities of "violent" and "savage" converge with immigrants' collective imaginary of indifference toward local natural environments, mistrust of the rule of law, and apathy toward participation in local democratic processes. A recent analysis of this type of erosion of Colombian social fabric in regions like Caquetá explains that "what is new in the last twenty years is the collapse of society itself, of those mental connections that people make with their peers in family, local, regional, and national environments, and which should create a feeling of belonging that provides meaning to one's destiny, to social practices and to society in general" (García Villegas and de Sousa dos Santos 2004, 50).

This is Radio Andaquí's and EAIBA's most difficult challenge. González states:

> What we need is for this territory to rethink itself as a subject, as an actor. The people here need to rethink their identities, their goals, and who they want to be. One can already see the beginning of this, a new generation with a different type of life project here in Belén. Those whose participation in Radio Andaquí began ten years ago when they were small children, today, as young adults, want to start productive ventures here in Caquetá, but from a completely different perspective. They are the ones who have begun to internalize the need to rethink this place and the need to redesign economies appropriate for this territory. (A. González 2006)

Radio Andaquí responds with a series of communicative and cultural practices insisting that armed conflict and social unrest do not exhaust the character of Caquetá and its people. Radio Andaquí

Learning to see one's territory. Photograph by Clemencia Rodríguez, 2006.

coined the term Territorio Andaquí [Andaquí Territory] as a signifier to recodify the municipality and its people in terms radically different from those imposed by national media and other outside voices during the long history of armed conflict. Territorio Andaquí represents a series of meanings that express the heterogeneity, diversity, and potential of the place and its people. Radio Andaquí functions as a public communication space (a public sphere) where local environmental groups have programs about their ecological park, about their community organic gardens and how to manage pests naturally (such as eliminating slugs with beer); it is also a place where teenage librarians read children's stories on the air; and a place where local farmers and fishermen produce a daily morning show about farming and local music.

In an effort to create cultural practices to affirm the notion that there are lives and identities in Belén beyond war and social or political violence, Radio Andaquí insists on incorporating communication technologies into people's everyday lives. Technology is molded, redesigned, and reinvented so that it can truly "be there," with the community of Belén in its unique natural and cultural context, capturing and expressing life in all its daily detail. Perhaps the best example of merging technology and local cultural identities is Radio Andaquí's radiocycle, which roams the municipality from one everyday-life scenario to the next, capturing the sounds of people as they live, work, love, learn, party, and play in ways not determined by armed conflict. González insists that the role of Radio Andaquí is to become one with the people of Belén: "If it were up to me, Radio Andaquí would be just the radiocycle. Why have a station?" (A. González 2005).

Undeniably, there is an urgent need to study and understand the immediate responses of citizens' media in moments of collective terror caused by armed violence. I am sure numerous community radio and television stations (as well as other media) are figuring out ways to help protect civilians, coordinate collective actions against armed violence, redistribute scarce resources, de-escalate conflict, and create cultural and communication buffers against collective terror. As scholars, we need to conduct ethnographic studies focused on these functions of citizens' media so that we can share them with others and profit from the knowledge and wisdom of citizens' media practitioners in war zones. When it comes to citizens' media best practice, I have never believed in formulas; however, perhaps such studies can help to strengthen the potential of these media to protect unarmed communities.

However, it is the long-term, inch-by-inch performative role of citizens' media in contexts of war that I find rich with potential toward the construction of peaceful communities. More than *affirming* or explaining that war does not exhaust the identities and the lived experiences of people in Belén, Radio Andaquí and EAIBA *perform* the local everyday lives and identities that exist beyond armed conflict. Radio Andaquí and EAIBA resist the negative impact of armed conflict on the local social fabric by amplifying and giving visibility to every inch of everyday life that has not been permeated by war and its militaristic, exclusionary logics and values. Belén's citizens' media motto seems to be "peace does not have to be brought to Belén de los Andaquíes; it already exists here; not everything has been colonized by armed conflict; and we'll make every effort to not allow further colonization."

Colombian citizens' media activists have taught me that the best antidote to armed conflict's negative impact is a community deeply committed to maintaining a strong participatory democracy, a community with a clear sense of itself, well grounded in local knowledges and cultures. In simple words, armed conflict is best resisted by a collective of people connected to their past, shaping their own futures on their own terms, with resources from their strong identities. However, this is easier said than done. With the idea that children's collective imaginaries are more malleable, they are the main target of Belén's citizens' media. Radio Andaquí and EAIBA perceive boys and particularly girls not as listeners to be persuaded with media messages, but instead, as subjects with the potential and talent to reinvent themselves and to create alternative versions of Caquetá. Radio Andaquí and EAIBA invite children to relearn how they see their local environment. Children are encouraged to use communication and information technologies as tools to detect and capture the images and sounds that make up their local environment, their place in the world. During my fieldwork in Belén I frequently participated in excursions to the river, where I saw children "playing" with digital recorders and microphones, trying to capture the sound of a pebble falling in the water or the quality of a bird song. Mariana García, who began participating in Radio Andaquí at ten years of age and now, at twenty-six, is the latest station director, remembers how Caquetá entered her field of vision: "Every time I hear the clear sounds of the river I remember how we used the songs of the birds, a rooster's crow, a dog barking, or the sounds of my neighbor's pigs to color our radio productions" (Mariana García 2006).

The following two testimonies illustrate well how Radio Andaquí nurtures emerging collective imaginaries. First, we hear the voice of the traditional homesteader who sees the forest as an obstacle to agriculture and ranching:

> We found trees thirty and forty meters high. . . . I gave them the ax from six in the morning, and by noon they were still standing. You had to brace yourself when one of those trees fell! They knocked down half a hectare of smaller trees I had already punctured. You've never seen anything like it. To see one of those trees falling is terrifying! Animals scamper away, birds scream, the land shakes. It is scary if one is not used to it. I am talking about the year [19]83. (Arcila Niño et al. 2000, 136–37)

Then we hear Radio Andaquí's attempt to codify the territory in different terms in a thirty-second promo:

> Blue tanager: feeds on fruit.
> Woodpecker: with its beak pricks trees to make its nest.
> Oropendola: weaver of hanging baskets, so that we can have Christmas
>   year 'round.

Thrush: seeker of earthworms, artisan of the mud.
Different colors, various sizes, distinct voices; all struggling for life in one
   single tree. Bárbara Charanga, a radio series about how to use our differences to find common ground. (Radio Andaquí 2003)

Both discourses mention the forest and its trees; the first one
regards the forest as something to be annihilated. The second one sees
the forest as a home for life. Radio Andaquí uses radio to cultivate a
collective imaginary strongly grounded in the beauty and value of
local environments. This citizens' medium gambles on the belief that
a community with a strong cultural identity, deeply rooted in a solid
sense of place, will be able to produce its own sustainable economic
models and a robust local participatory democracy. If a child grows up
with these images of his or her local environments, will she or he
embrace economic models such as cattle ranching? Will she or he cut
the tree with the tanager and the oropendola? Radio Andaquí believes
that these sounds and images strengthen collective imaginaries that
will prompt these children to resist the negative impact of war on the
social fabric, and to design sustainable economies for their community
when they grow up.

With EAIBA's new introduction of digital cameras, children
explore not only sounds but also images. Instead of trying to capture
the taken-for-granted meaning of reality, children use the cameras to
explore new possibilities of what their reality can signify (see Arango
Rendón et al. 2008 for similar uses of video and film). The aesthetic
qualities of their everyday lives serve as scenarios where the children
explore and express who they are and begin trying to articulate who
they want to be.

Conclusion

Formulaic responses are not an option for citizens' media operating
in difficult contexts of armed conflict. Instead, these media have to
develop their own expertise, their own communication strategies to
counteract the negative impact of armed conflict on civilians' everyday lives and the social fabric of communities. Strong citizens' media
emerge organically from within local communities. They are deeply
rooted in local languages and aesthetics, and respond to the unique
shape that armed conflict takes in each locality (Gumucio Dagron
2003). Citizens' media must continuously develop creative ways to

Cameras capture place. Photograph courtesy of EAIBA, 2010.

meet the challenges of civilian communities under siege by armed groups. Caquetá's Radio Andaquí and EAIBA are true pioneers in terms of understanding the roles of a community radio station and an audiovisual school in a context of guerrilla warfare and illicit drug economies. Based on my fieldwork, I can articulate two main lines of action developed by these citizens' media.

On one hand, Radio Andaquí implements immediate, ad hoc responses in moments when the community is under attack. In this type of situation, communication helps civilians overcome collective terror and coordinate collective actions. Communication also helps to protect people and de-escalate conflict. These actions are generally designed on the go, according to how each crisis situation evolves; thus, rather than definite plans or guidelines, *communication competence* is a crucial resource for a community radio station in moments of crisis. The skills and creativity to generate immediate communication strategies using whatever elements a crisis provides is a valuable asset for a citizens' medium when trying to support civilians under attack.

On the other hand, Radio Andaquí and EAIBA insist that their contribution to peacebuilding in the region is to open public spheres for the expression of everyday life in Belén. I will call this the *performative function* of citizens' media in contexts of war. Here, the goal is not to communicate, express, or inform, but instead *to perform* all those local identities, values, ways of life, cultural practices, and forms of interaction that have not been permeated by militaristic, war-driven logics (in chapter 5 I theorize the notion of communication as performance).

Anchored in Marxist and Gramscian ideas of collective agency, citizens' (or alternative, or community) media scholarship and praxis have considered these communication initiatives to be products of collective authorship. Our writings and case studies on citizens' media tend to erase individual agency and emphasize collective signatures (see for example Atton 2002; Downing et al. 2001; Rennie 2006; Rodríguez 2001; Rodríguez, Kidd, and Stein 2010). I found, however, that these assumptions do not provide an adequate framework in the case of Radio Andaquí and EAIBA. The exceptionally creative role of Alirio González as the main architect behind Radio Andaquí and EAIBA is explicit, I believe, in the pages above. I learned to appreciate González, not as a community media leader, but as an artist passionately designing community communication projects in the same way a poet designs each word of a poem, or a painter deliberates over each stroke of the brush. His art is not writing or painting, but a series of media happenings and installations that capture and reveal the identity and aesthetic qualities concealed in Belén's everyday life. It is in this sense that I began using the term "citizens' media d'auteur."

González's art consists of threading invisible links between media technologies and everyday-life local aesthetics. In August 2005 I witnessed the prelude of what would later become the Children's Audiovisual School. That afternoon I came to Radio Andaquí to find Alirio in the station's wooded backyard, surrounded by a group of kids; they were all playing with my small Canon digital camera, which sat on a tripod; the kids ran around, climbing trees, trying to catch a cat; Alirio told me that they wanted to recreate in a photo a scene from one of the station's children's books; the scene had a cat, thus one of the kids went home to retrieve her cat; but when she came back carrying the animal, all the other kids made such a ruckus that the cat was startled and ran away; after much running around, the kids finally succeeded producing their photo. I wrote in my field diary:

The kids embody their new roles of media storytellers with ease. I can see how this could be the beginning of their future profiles: a film director, a set designer, a camera person, an actor. Alirio lets them play with the camera, he gives them a few ideas, but more than anything, he legitimizes the kids' own ideas. He joins their games and in the midst of those games, girls and boys develop entirely new visions of who they could be and what they could accomplish. He addresses the kids, pushes them to revise their versions of themselves, invites them to be someone they have never considered, to cross boundaries, to inhabit spaces that have always been beyond reach, to believe in those threads of identity they have never listened to because the social environment has told them that is not who they are. These kids have been told they are nothing but poor kids in a poor town in a savage region in a poor country; that they are not film directors, or photographers. Alirio is the first person in their nine years who believes in them when not even they believe in themselves. His gaze, the revised way he looks at those elements of their identity they have learned to despise, makes them question what they have always believed about who they are. His gaze prompts them to open doors to new options of who they are and who they want to be. (Rodríguez 2005b)

Alirio succeeds when the rhymes and compositions of Don Anselmo, a local senior farmer, become part of the radio programming. When the sounds of local birds, rivers, cows, and peddlers become part of Radio Andaquí's sound library. He merges training, technological convergence, and participatory communication to create communication spaces where the texture of Belén's everyday life is expressed as part of this community's cultural capital. González knows the political power of art. He has gambled his life on the belief that when people witness their lives transformed into art they are able to access new levels of appreciation for self and environment. These are the building blocks of a new future for the region, a vision born out of local needs and talents. This, according to González, is the best antidote to war and violence.

2 NATION BUILDING, ONE VOICE AT A TIME

Citizens' Communication in Montes de María

You never see artists painting with machine guns!
—Johnny Vergara, *La Calle theater group, Zambrano, Colombia*

AS MY PLANE DESCENDS from the Andean city of Bogotá (the capital of Colombia) I can see the geography change below me. The steep mountains and narrow canyons become the vast savannas of the Colombian Caribbean. I am flying to Cartagena, and from there I will travel to the region known as Montes de María.[1] It's 2004, and for months I have attempted this field trip, but the situation of unrest kept me from making the trip until now. Things seem to have calmed down, at least for a while. My destination is the Colectivo de Comunicaciones de Montes de María Línea 21 [Communications Collective of Montes de María: 21st Line], a participatory radio, video, and television initiative that won the National Peace Award in 2003.[2] My colleagues in Bogotá frequently mention this initiative, but no one seems to be able to explain clearly why the Collective won the peace award. Few Colombian communication academics, even those who specialize in citizens' media or communication for social change, have visited Montes de María. The region is too far away from the capital and the situation of unrest too intense to make it an easy destination.

Soraya Bayuelo, one of the founding members of the Collective, picks me up at the airport. One of her friends has offered to drive us to Montes de María, so we board his taxi and take off, looking for the road that will take us to El Carmen de Bolívar, the main urban center in Montes de María.

We leave Cartagena behind and travel for about an hour on a straight and unexciting road. Flat lands covered with low shrubs on the right and the same on the left. I could be in Oklahoma, except that sometimes we border the ocean. Although Cartagena is a common tourist destination and I have visited it on countless occasions, I've never been in this part of the country; in fact, I don't think I ever heard of Montes de María while growing up in Colombia. I began hearing about the region in the mid-1990s, when it was frequently mentioned in the news as a site of guerrilla activity, paramilitary massacres: the usual war zone. In my mind, Montes de María exists as another of Colombia's *"zonas calientes"* (violent regions).

About an hour into our trip we cross a large waterway, and Soraya tells me this is the Canal del Dique, which marks the beginning of what is known as Montes de María. The landscape changes almost immediately. A mountain chain comes into view. These are the Montes de María.

As the road begins zigzagging and swerving up and down, the landscape becomes lush, with thick forests packed with vines, wildflowers of incredible beauty, and green in all imaginable shades. But something else changes with the new landscape: the extent of militarization is hard to believe. I have never seen such a concentration of weapons, barricades, and heavily armed men. Every mile and a half

Video production in San Basillio de Palenque. Photograph courtesy of Soraya Bayuelo, 2010.

small army platoons weighed down by machine guns and all kinds of heavy military gear patrol the road.[3] In the next hour we will be stopped at ten military checkpoints. In some places Soraya tells me that just a year ago driving past this or that curve had become a terrifying experience, as these had become preferred sites for the guerrillas to stop traffic, kidnap travelers, and burn vehicles.

It is hard to imagine what the people of Montes de María endured in the last ten years. People here used to talk about their region as a *"zona bendita"* (a blessed region). The broken topography offers access to many different climactic zones, making it an ideal setting for agriculture. You could plant almost anything in Montes de María. It stands green and proud in the middle of the flat, almost barren lowlands covering most of Colombia's northern Caribbean region. The last two decades, however, brought many changes to the region, including increasing guerrilla attacks, paramilitary massacres, and permanent army bases. Now Montes de María occupies a place of terror, massacres, destruction, and broken community in the Colombian imaginary.

The History and Geography of War in Montes de María

During the late nineteenth and early twentieth centuries, as the country began its integration into international markets for agricultural products, Colombians from the highlands came to Montes de María looking for the more favorable climates of the lowlands. Catherine Legrand, a historian of agricultural expansion in Colombia, explains:

> Because the Colombian highlands are cool, the crops that can be raised there are potatoes, corn, barley, and wheat, crops also produced in Europe and North America. What the industrial nations wanted and could not provide themselves were tropical products that, in Colombia, can only be raised in the middle altitudes and lowlands. [Coffee, cinchona bark, and] Colombia's other exports, such as bananas, tobacco, cotton, rubber, are all products of the steamy lowlands. Thus, during the period of export growth the intensification of commercial production occurred primarily in the midlands and lowlands in the western part of the country and along the Caribbean coast, areas comprised mainly of public lands. (Legrand 1986, 9–10)

This period of migration and frontier expansion initiated one of the most violent processes in the history of Colombia. Wealthier Colombians, with their government connections, resources to bribe local officials, and immense greed, began appropriating huge expansions of public lands in the Caribbean savannas. On the low flatlands, they established large cattle estates. On the higher altitudes of Montes de María, they established tobacco haciendas.[4] As they appropriated more and more land, hacienda owners expropriated small landowners, thus securing a pool of landless labor for their intense agricultural and cattle ventures. Debt peonage and indentured labor helped landowners secure cheap pools of labor among landless peasants (Escobar 1998).

The greed with which landowners accumulated land and dispossessed peasants in the Caribbean coast was saturated with social violence. In their studies of frontier expansion and peasant resistance, Catherine Legrand (1986) and Leon Zamosc (1986) document how landowners accumulated extensions of land impossible to exploit in a lifetime, simply in hope of selling it at some point in the future. Many estates just passed from one generation to the next completely uncultivated. Landowners used barbed wire to extend legal estates into illegal invasions: "In Río de Oro (Bolívar), for example, one man granted 100 hectares in 1907 proceeded to fence in an additional 4,900 hectares of public lands" (Legrand 1986, 52).

Landowners frequently filed fraudulent claims stating that the land they were appropriating was uninhabited and idle, and therefore available. Legrand describes how one morning the inhabitants of a town awoke to find that "the whole village had been granted to one man" (Legrand 1986, 58). Neither government authorities nor elite politicians in Bogotá seemed to care about the usurpation of public lands by local elites on the Caribbean coast. Legrand says that "the records suggest that the Colombian government was either unaware of or indifferent to the widespread usurpation of public lands" (Legrand 1986, 56).

This land appropriation and expropriation translated into deep inequalities for the people of the region. By 1936 Montes de María and the surrounding Caribbean coast had become a region in which a small number of families owned huge estates, enjoyed the benefits of being recognized and protected by the central government, and profited from national and international markets. By 1971, 0.05 percent of the land properties in Sucre covered 26.2 percent of the land and in Bolívar 0.3 percent of the land properties covered 16 percent of the total land (PNUD, Corporación Territorios, and Universidad de Cartagena 2004, 67). In Sucre 75 percent of the land and in Bolívar 67 percent of the land belonged to estates of one hundred hectares or more, while only 3.8 percent of the land in Sucre and 4 percent in Bolívar was in the hands of small landholders (five to ten hectares) (PNUD, Corporación Territorios, and Universidad de Cartagena 2004, 67–68). At the same time, the great majority of citizens became dependent on the landowners for employment, political power, and civil rights. These were delivered by patrons as "favors," which eventually solidified a patron–client system that to this day is poisonous to any attempts at developing a civic culture and ensuring a democratic process based on rights and responsibilities. Montes de María became fertile ground for guerrillas and paramilitary, partly because the people have no faith in the rule of law and the ability of the state institutions to guarantee their rights. What started as an issue of land distribution became fertile ground for armed factions at war. During the 1960s and 1970s, dispossessed agricultural families organized into peasant social movements. Later, during the second half of the twentieth century, radicalized factions of these social movements lost hope in the ability of the movement to bring about social change and took up arms. In the words of Colombian sociologist Alejandro Reyes,

> All the regions where the peasant movement confronted landowners around issues of access to land during the 1970s have been occupied by guerrillas and paramilitaries and have been site of army operations at some point in the last two decades [1980–2000]. The war has displaced a large portion of the rural population and has broken the neighbor relations that are the foundation of agricultural societies. These facts have entirely changed the nature of the agrarian problem in Colombia, because the new situation puts security as the most important need, over land distribution. (Reyes 1999, 206–7)

During most of the second half of the twentieth century, the region of Montes de María experienced various phases of intense peasant mobilization in a struggle for access to land and against the consolidation of patron–client structures.[5] Still, until about 1994, the social and political violence levels in the region remained some of the lowest in the country; for example, the number of paramilitary actions in the region jumps from about one or two from 1988 to 1995 to twenty-six in 1996 (Grupo de Memoria Histórica 2009, 190).[6]

The 1990s brought more major changes to Montes de María. The radical factions of the peasant movements of the 1960s and 1970s transformed into guerrilla organizations such as the EPL and the Corriente de Renovación Socialista (CRS) [Socialist Renovation Line].

During the first half of the 1990s, the EPL and the CRS negotiated disarmament agreements with the Colombian government. The resulting power vacuum in the region would soon be filled by another guerrilla organization, FARC. Thanks to its exploitation of drug economies, FARC became the fastest growing guerrilla organization in the country during the 1980s and 1990s. Since 1990, expanding west from the neighboring department of Córdoba, the Thirty-fifth Front of the FARC began operating in the mountainous region of Montes de María, while the Thirty-seventh Front settled in the southern lowlands (Escobar 1998, chap. 6).

At the same time, during the early 1990s the ELN, the second largest guerrilla organization, continued in a northward expansion from the region known as Magdalena Medio. Guerrilla organizations arrived in Montes de María, drawn by the wealth of cattle ranchers and tobacco hacienda owners. Twenty-two percent of guerrillas' income comes from ransom money paid by families to ensure the recovery of kidnap victims. A region full of rich landowners is likely to attract a guerrilla presence, and the higher altitudes and mountainous topography of Montes de María provide guerrillas with strategic staging grounds and hiding terrain for their kidnap victims.

During our drive into Montes de María, Soraya tells me that many of the military bases we are passing by used to be tobacco-processing plants. Some of the owners were kidnapped by the guerrillas, others were taxed and blackmailed, and still others were threatened. Many left the region, abandoning their land and tobacco ventures. When the army came to Montes de María it found that the processing plants were perfect facilities for their operations, and transformed them into bases. The former tobacco processing plants are now painted in camouflage and surrounded by sandbag barricades. Not finding enough abandoned tobacco plants for their purposes, the army also took over hospitals, schools, and in one case, a building that now operates as half–military base and half–nursing home.

The expansion of drug economies in other parts of the country generated a new class of rich drug lords hungry for large land estates. Traditional landowning families in the Colombian Caribbean, tired of dealing with guerrilla incursions in the region, were more than happy to sell their land to these newcomers. The new rich drug lord landowners had their own ideas about handling the guerrillas. Following their logic of vigilante justice, the landowners hired, trained, and armed their own self-defense militias. By the mid-1990s these self-defense militias gained autonomy and became right-wing paramilitary illegal armies. Beginning in the 1990s, a phase of escalating dirty war between guerrillas and paramilitaries emerged throughout the region. These two dynamics of leftist guerrilla and right-wing paramilitary violence produced what has been called the "hall of mirrors of violence," in which the actions and reactions of guerrillas and paramilitaries result in increased attacks on civilians (González, Bolívar, and Vásquez 2003; Maria Victoria Uribe 2007). Montes de María became a region in which guerrillas and paramilitaries are constantly competing for territorial control (including a strategic route for the transportation of cocaine paste from the south of the country to the Caribbean [González, Bolívar, and Vásquez 2003, 88; Wilson 2001a]) and access to resources and wealth. But perhaps most significantly, in order to cut off civilian support for their adversary, guerrillas and paramilitaries battle for control of civilian populations (González, Bolívar, and Vásquez 2003, 120). According to the report by the Colombian National Commission of Reparation and Reconciliation [Comisión Nacional de Reparación y Reconciliación], forty-two massacres took place in Montes de María between 1999 and 2000 with 354 deaths (Grupo de Memoria Histórica 2009, 9).

Between 1988 and 2007, 692 military actions were perpetuated by different guerrilla groups in Montes de María (Grupo de Memoria Histórica 2009, 186). At the turn of the century, in only two years, 27 violent actions by FARC terrified civilians in El Carmen de Bolívar, the municipality at the heart of Montes de María.[7] This made El Carmen de Bolívar the fifth most violent municipality in the country in terms of guerrilla attacks by the FARC (OPPDHDIH 2002, 31).

As a response to the heavy guerrilla presence in the region, on March 9, 1999, a group of eighty paramilitaries from the Autodefensas Campesinas de Córdoba y Urabá (ACCU) [Peasant Self-Defense Forces of Córdoba and Urabá] came to the small town of San Isidro in the municipality of El Carmen de Bolívar. They cut off the electricity, leaving the people in darkness, and then proceeded to surround the town. With a list of names in hand, the paramilitaries executed eleven men. This type of paramilitary incursion continued in Montes de María throughout the late 1990s (OPPDHDIH 2002, 56). The worst paramilitary massacres, however, took place at the dawn of the new millennium. In 2000, between the night of February 16 and the afternoon of

February 17, paramilitaries from ACCU murdered forty-two peasants in the municipality of Ovejas (Sucre) (OPPDHDIH 2002, 57). Less than a year later, on January 17, 2001, the same illegal army returned to the municipality of Ovejas, where they executed twenty-seven people and burned down the town of Chengue—one of the main local urban centers (OPPDHDIH 2002, 58). A *Washington Post* reporter describes the devastating events: "They assembled them into two groups above the main square and across from the rudimentary health center. Then, one by one, they killed the men by crushing their heads with heavy stones and a sledgehammer. When it was over, 24 men lay dead in pools of blood" (Wilson 2001b). Each of these massacres resulted in a wave of survivors fleeing their hometown in terror and in search of safety in the nearest urban center. For example, the town of Ovejas, two hours away from Chengue, saw its population swell by 10 percent in the wake of the massacre (Wilson 2001a).

On February 16, 2000, in a blood bath that lasted six days, 450 paramilitaries from the paramilitary fronts led by Salvatore Mancuso, Jorge 40, and Carlos Castaño entered the small town of El Salado in the municipality of El Carmen de Bolívar (Grupo de Memoria Histórica 2009, 24). After announcing that they came "to clean the area of guerrillas" (Grupo de Memoria Histórica 2009, 30), they tortured and decapitated sixty people and sexually abused several women (Grupo de Memoria Histórica 2009, 8–9; OPPDHDIH 2002, 57). This is known as the second massacre of El Salado, as this same village suffered a similar paramilitary attack on March 23, 1997 (Mesa de Trabajo 2004, 21). As a result of the 2000 massacre, seven thousand people, or three hundred families, from El Salado fled to the municipal urban center of El Carmen de Bolívar (Cadavid 2005, 13; Mesa de Trabajo 2004, 21).[8] The two massacres and resulting exodus of the terrified citizens resulted in El Salado losing 76 percent of its total population in seven years (Mesa de Trabajo 2004, 21).[9] When the National Commission of Reparation and Reconciliation made public its report on El Salado in July of 2009, only seven hundred people had returned to their land (Grupo de Memoria Histórica 2009, 14). Montes de María is one of the main originators of forcefully displaced population in the country. In 2009 the region had forty-two completely empty parishes; in the municipality of El Carmen de Bolívar, where close to one-third of the population left expelled by armed conflict, only seven out of the seventeen counties are inhabited (Grupo de Memoria Histórica 2009, 83).

Evidence of the effects of the escalation of violence between guerrillas and paramilitaries on the region, and especially the civilian population, is visible everywhere. During the years I did fieldwork in Montes de María (2004–8), the main roads connecting El Carmen de Bolívar to the rest of the country were closed by the army every day as the sun went down; anyone driving after closure could be shot without warning. At night, a general feeling of isolation seemed to descend and overtake us all; we knew we were cut off from the rest of the country with all the roads closed. In El Carmen proper, the city hall and police headquarters were barricaded, and adjacent streets were closed to traffic to prevent car bombings. On every other block, bombed buildings lay in ruins. Their owners were dead, or left after a guerrilla attack. Very few cars were visible. The empty streets are evidence of the flight of the middle class to Cartagena or Bogotá. This is the home of the communications collective that won the National Peace Award for its contribution to peace and reconciliation in the region.

The Communications Collective of Montes de María

Interestingly, the birth date of the Communications Collective of Montes de María coincides with the eruption of armed violence in the region. The Collective was formed in 1994 by a small group of young intellectuals from El Carmen de Bolívar who made it their habit to spend their evenings in the park talking politics and poetry or just shooting the breeze. They came from different professional backgrounds: schoolteachers, law students, poets, and so forth. During an interview conducted in the park, sitting on the very same broken bench, Soraya Bayuelo, one of the youngest at the time, recalled those bygone years:

> Napoleón Garrido read his poems; Rafael Gallo, who wanted to become a lawyer, argued; Beatriz Ochoa, also a poet, shared her poems with Napo; Eduardo wrote a play called *The Man Who Became a Dog*—he rehearsed it right here, in the park, with Miguelito, and El Capo, and El Pilo; I believe he was inspired by Kafka. We could say it was our adaptation of Kafka. A cockroach there, a dog here. And Soraya Bayuelo . . . not having something to perform, I grabbed a mic and interviewed all my friends, as a way to display and admire their work. Dawn would find us here, *mamando gallo y jodiendo la vida* [joking and passing the time]. (Bayuelo 2005)

The broken park bench in El Carmen de Bolívar where it all began. Photograph by Clemencia Rodríguez, 2005.

At the time, Bayuelo was pursuing an undergraduate degree in communications in Barranquilla and loved radio production. Beatriz Ochoa had studied philosophy and loved art, music, and literature. The group fervently discussed how to invigorate their city with a communication and culture project. In Soraya's words, "I feel that what Beatriz and I share is our love for music, for literature, and for film; and the Collective is like a mix of all those dreams brought together" (Bayuelo 2005).

Someone obtained a video camera and the group began exploring video as a new language to create cultural products. Also, the group used the video camera to generate income in what Bayuelo calls "the BBC—*bodas, bautizos, cumpleaños,*" meaning that they sold their services videotaping weddings, baptisms, and birthdays. Soon the group began to explore the use of this new technology as a tool for citizens' journalism.

The group had made an alliance with the owner of Centro de Educación Comunitario Las Flores, a crafts academy, where they were given space to set up a community journalism school. Students in the school chose among baking, embroidering, and community journalism courses. With their first class, Soraya and Beatriz began a frenzied effort to produce twenty hours of television news per week with two video cameras. Thanks to hundreds of feet of cable, the cameras were moved to the town hall, schools, and other nearby locations from which events were transmitted live. In 2000 the Collective "transmitted fourteen weekly television shows entirely produced—from the original idea to postproduction—by children and youth; themes include environmental issues, sports, cooking shows, youth programs, local characters, daily life, children's programs, and in sum everything that shapes our existence" (Bayuelo 2000).

A local entrepreneur convinced the group to take out a loan to purchase a satellite dish that would allow them to download commercial television programming. The Collective operates in what used to be Beatriz's family home on the central plaza. A huge satellite dish sits on the back patio, downloading satellite television programming.[10] The Collective installed cable throughout the city, and subscribers pay seven thousand pesos per month (about US$2.50), which allows them to view commercial television programming downloaded by the dish, as well as twenty hours a week of programs locally produced by the Collective.[11] Bayuelo notes, "as you can imagine, we are permanently evaluating what we do, 'cause we are competing with ourselves; what we produce is always competing with the Peruvian and Venezuelan channels we download" (Bayuelo 2000). Ten years later, the Collective has evolved from an attempt to publish a cultural periodical that never took off to a full-blown citizens' communication NGO. Today the Collective encompasses several avenues of endeavor, including radio production training for children and teens, television and video production training for teens and young adults, radio and television production training for displaced women, an itinerant street-film project, and a cable television channel. Although the Collective's headquarters are located in the main urban center of El Carmen de Bolívar, its projects and initiatives spread throughout the entire region of Montes de María.

On paper, the Collective defines its goals in the following terms: "First, to position boys and girls as active protagonists of community development projects; second, to strengthen the roles of women in community development; third, to recover local identities and cultures in the form of oral traditions, myths, legends, and awareness of local environments; and fourth, to develop and legitimize alternative media such as print, radio, loudspeakers, or television" (Bayuelo 2004). The Collective articulates two goals for their work. First, developing a pedagogy for peaceful coexistence, and second, strengthening a culture of citizenship—understood as empowered citizens committed to solidifying a local participatory democracy founded on rights and responsibilities (Red de Gestores Sociales 2004, 2).[12] Since 1994 approximately 3,600 boys and girls, 1,000 teens, 150 parents, and 80 teachers have participated in the Collective's projects (Cadavid 2005, 41; FESCOL 2003). The Collective also trained eighteen facilitators, some of whom still work for the Collective, some have gone to work in other media outlets, and others have formed their own citizens' media initiatives in different cities and small towns throughout the country.

The Collective operates in a large house built in the 1920s in the traditional Caribbean style of high ceilings, mosaic floors, thick white adobe walls, and Moorish arches. The house is packed with communication technology. Television production equipment is stored on one side, radio production equipment on the other. A video projector and a wide collection of locally produced and commercially distributed programs, films, and documentaries line the walls. The most striking feature is the beehive of movement inside the building. At all times of

Strenghtening local identities and cultures. Photograph courtesy of Soraya Bayuelo, 2010.

the day and night swarms of little boys, little girls, teens, and women come in and out with video cameras, recorders, cables, monitors, lights, and microphones. Some of the training and production happens here in the house on the plaza, but most of it does not. People come in to pick up equipment to be taken to workshops and production sites far away in neighborhoods, local schools, and nearby towns and counties, and in communities of displaced families.

Communication as Pretext

Soraya and Beatriz insist that communication is just a pretext for the Collective. The ultimate goal of the Collective is not to produce media, but to transform collective imaginaries. They happened to find a way to accomplish this goal by involving children, young people, and women in radio, video, and television production, but it is very clear in their minds that their target is to offset the erosion of the local social fabric caused by violence, including both social violence and also the violence brought into the region by armed conflict. In the words of Wilgen Peñaloza, one of the oldest participants, the Collective operates as "a school without walls, where children, teens, and women from the region are encouraged to reinvent themselves, to become different human beings" (Peñaloza 2004).

According to Daniel Pécaut, Colombia entered a new era of generalized terror in the early 1990s (Pécaut 2001). Previous to this transition, each region had to deal with the presence of the right-wing paramilitary or that of the leftist guerrilla, but rarely both. Civilians learned to cope with these armed groups in their territory using survival mechanisms that today prove fatal. For example, offering a cup of coffee to a guerrilla patrol that enters one's farm used to be a common action to stay in good terms with them. Today, in regions such as Montes de María, where guerrilla groups and paramilitaries compete for control of the civilian population, to do so is to ensure a death sentence as a "friend of the guerrilla." In this generalized state of terror, civilians "become afraid to travel on the roads, to talk and to maintain relationships with friends and neighbors, to establish romantic relationships, to stray far from urban centers, to go to far away parcels [of land] to cultivate, to go fishing, to create collective organizations, in one word, to live" (Mesa de Trabajo 2004, 42). The presence of adversarial armed groups in a region creates concentric circles of civilian informants, vigilantes, and collaborators from the guerrilla and paramilitary groups: "Everybody feels they are being watched by everyone;

A school without walls. Photograph courtesy of Soraya Bayuelo, 2010.

these places are characterized by total distrust, the weakening of all solidarity relationships, and the retreat into isolated life and individual action: one has to be suspicious not only of the armed groups trying to control the territory, but also of neighbors and even of relatives, who could have become informants of one group or another" (González, Bolívar, and Vásquez 2003, 214).

Because paramilitaries and guerrillas depend on local contacts for information about who "the enemy" is, personal and communal conflicts become entangled with armed groups; locals use armed groups to annihilate antagonists in land conflicts and love triangles, and to avenge past offenses (Ramírez 2001, 269). Also, rumors begin circulating about people who leave their civilian clothes at home at night and change into their paramilitary uniforms; others talk about farmers who are also guerrillas; thus, the boundaries between civilian and armed groups become blurred and nobody knows anymore who is who (Ramírez 2001, 276). What Colombian sociologist Iván Orozco (Orozco 2002) calls "gray zones" emerge, in which the boundaries between civilians and combatants blur.

It is important to emphasize the contribution of traditional patron–client systems to the erosion of the social fabric in Montes de María. Within the patron–client system, families compete for the favors of rich patrons. Only a close relationship with a patron can guarantee that one's rights will be respected. Patrons then will expect families to support them (or their friends) at election time, or exchange votes for money. The patron–client system is so strong in the Colombian Caribbean that in her study of the region, Escobar found that "people believe that selling their vote is a right" (Escobar 1998, 92).

For decades, the region of Montes de María has been severely neglected by central government administrations. For example, El Carmen de Bolívar, a city of about ninety thousand and the main urban center in the area, lacks running water. Each household has to design and finance its own strategies for obtaining water, including collecting rainwater or, in the worst of cases, purchasing expensive commercial water from water trucks.

As a result of a weak state that cannot guarantee the rule of law or citizens' rights, of the consolidation of patron–client systems, and of the strong presence of armed groups, the people of Montes de María have become increasingly individualistic, fearful, suspicious of one another, isolated, and aggressive in their interactions. In her fieldwork in war zones, Carolyn Nordstrom recorded testimonies that resonate with the situation in Montes de María. One of Nordstrom's informants told her:

> If you are exposed to violence, you become violent. It is a learned response. And this is a fact of life, not a fact solely of war. The war may come to a formal end, but all those people who have learned violence—learned to solve their problems, and conflicts, and confusions with violence—will continue to use it. They will be more violent with their families, with their friends, in their work. They will see violence as the appropriate response to any political contest.
>
> So is the war really over? Is the violence of war gone suddenly with declarations of peace? No, violence lives in the belly of the person and ruins society, unless peace is taught to the violent. And peace must be taught just like violence is, by subjecting people to it, by showing them peaceful ways to respond to life and living, to daily needs and necessities, to political and personal challenges. (Nordstrom 2004, 179–80)

A parent and Collective participant describes how the presence of armed violence erodes family life in Montes de María:

> Many of us here at the Collective have experienced the impact of armed conflict in our own lives. And this affects our everyday life very much. For example, we stop communicating with our families; in the home, no one talks to one another, or parents begin treating their children in a very rough manner, and children develop very nasty responses to parents. This is what we need to change; we cannot allow armed conflict to destroy our family relationships. My own changes have had a positive impact on my family; I have brought home what I learned here [at the Collective]; for example to talk things out, to understand each other's differences; to trust myself much more, and to trust my own ability to solve our problems. (Cadavid 2005, 51)

Similarly, a father describes the changes he perceives in his children as they began participating in the Collective: "When they talk to their brothers and sisters, to my wife or to me, it's no longer the usual rude way, these kids are now less condescending, more respectful" (Sr. Rafael, focus group cited in Sarmiento 2005, 101).

These types of transformations are precisely what the Collective is trying to trigger and cultivate. The Collective's leaders believe that using radio and television production to reach this goal is nothing more than a pretext. What is more important in their view is the interpersonal communication space created by the Collective, a space

Dialogue replaces the use of force as children are subjected to peace. Photograph courtesy of Soraya Bayuelo, 2010.

where people can be "subjected to peace," to use the terms of Nordstrom's informant. A space in which peaceful interpersonal interaction is normalized, where difference is not only respected but appreciated, and where the experience of living in a peaceful environment can be felt and embodied in everyday life. In chapter 5, drawing from communication as performance theories, I analyze this type of citizens' media initiative that uses media to subject people to an experience, instead of trying to persuade them with a message.

Diminishing Collective Fear

The cool breeze of the night is a relief to the ninety-something degrees in which we sweat all day long. A group of about four teens begins coming in and out of rooms inside the Collective, carrying out different pieces of equipment. Soraya asks them what they are doing, and they tell her that they have decided to show a movie that night. By seven the setup is ready. The kids have placed a long table on one side of the street, right in front of the Collective's building; on the table sit a DVD player connected to a sound console and a projector. That night hundreds of people congregate on the plaza to see the film *Spirit* projected on the white adobe wall of the Collective, for free.

Months earlier I heard about the Collective's street-film project. Wilgen Peñaloza, sixteen years old at the time he began participating in the Collective, told me the project's history. He explained that evenings used to be lively and intensely social in El Carmen de Bolívar. Neighbors brought their rocking chairs to the front porches; kids and teens congregated in the central plaza around street vendors offering hot dogs, kebabs, *arepas,* and soda; people walked to friends' houses just to shoot the breeze for a couple of hours before calling it a night. However, in 1995 things changed dramatically. After sunset, at around six o'clock, people locked themselves away in their houses. Frequent guerrilla incursions to the downtown made people fearful. Later, when the paramilitaries became a strong presence in town, anyone could easily be labeled as a friend of the *paras* or a friend of the guerrillas if they were seen talking to the wrong person. Neighbors and friends became suspicious of possible connections with armed groups. Even the intercity bus station located on the outskirts of town—on a strip of restaurants, street vendors, and people coming and going on buses and taxis, a place filled with constant activity, trading, shouting, and human movement—became a deserted and dark crossroads in the middle of nowhere. A taxi driver told me that in those years the bus and taxi companies, traditionally open twenty-four hours, decided to close at six P.M. for fear of guerrilla and paramilitary attacks. The bus station had become a target because many of the street vendors had become informants for one camp or the other, keeping track of who came to town. Not aware that activities at the bus station ended before sundown, travelers coming from other regions or towns would get off the bus at the station, located a few miles from downtown. Not finding a single taxi in sight, they had no other option but to walk the dark and deserted road toward the downtown. The first building they would come to was the hospital, and frequently the guard at the door would warn them of the risk of walking in the dark and would invite them to spend the night at the hospital. Frequently newcomers to El Carmen spent their first night sitting in the hospital wait area (Gómez 2005).

In this context, the only safe thing for people to do was to avoid each other. Little by little, El Carmen became a town full of individuals living next to one another, but in complete isolation. Colombian anthropologist Pilar Riaño-Alcalá describes well the invasion of public spaces by war and terror: "The use of popular gathering places such as the plaza, soccer pitch, and streets as sites of massacres, executions, and rapes by various armed factions fragments the basic social elements that nourish community life. The chaos and confusion generated by acts of terror and intimidation corrode the foundations of social cohesion, eroding trust in the community and exacerbating fears" (Riaño-Alcalá 2008, 271).

The members of the Collective found themselves witnessing the social erosion of their town, and they decided to do something about it. In October of 2000 they designed the Purple Rose of Cairo Street-Film Project, which projects films on a wall in the central plaza using a DVD player, a projector, and a sound system. The group conceived ways to draw the people back to the central plaza, where they could repopulate this abandoned public space and effectively challenge their collective fears. Wilgen remembers the opening night of the Purple Rose of Cairo:

> We were supposed to begin on a Saturday evening the first week of October. But then that morning there were five explosions in different parts of town. We didn't know what to do. Should we go on with the idea of showing a film that night? Would anyone come? We met in a kind of last minute editorial committee meeting to decide what to do. The final decision was to go on with the plan. We were all very fearful. And we were convinced that no one would come. We envisioned the five of us sitting in the central plaza watching the film. But we decided to go on, because we wanted to reappropriate this public space, we did not want to be locked away anymore, giving in to fear and the sense of powerlessness. That night's film was *Central Station*. But then people began coming out. We had made the right decision! Approximately three hundred people came that night, which we remember as a gala function lit by the moon, with the stars above as if telling us "we are here with you." I remember the smiling faces of children, entire families sitting together watching the film, moms with their babies, teens on their bicycles, men on their motorcycles, couples in love sharing a broken bench on the plaza. This was like a human fusion of shared smiles, as if trying to say, "We are all still here." That night was a turning point for many of us, myself included. I never imagined that in the middle of the terror of war you could find ways to reach out to each other, so that you do not end up all alone in the middle of the war. That night I learned that we have the necessary skills to build peace, we are not entirely powerless in the face of war, and that we can transform public spaces from sites of fear and isolation to scenes for sharing experiences and life. (Peñaloza 2004)

Wilgen's words illustrate well one of the main findings of my field-work in Colombia. Citizens' media do not attempt to end or even decrease armed conflict. Instead, they direct all their energy at recovering and defending civilian spaces that have been colonized by armed conflict and the militaristic logics of armed groups. As they elbowed their way into public spaces and push away the isolation and fear imposed by war, Wilgen and his peers discovered other elements of collective resistance: first, Wilgen described the sense of empowerment as he discovered that war and armed conflict cannot entirely silence him; second, he found that they do have the abilities necessary to resist the pressure of armed groups and to gather as a community; and third, he found that the experience of "human fusion," togetherness, and collective sharing is in itself a source of empowerment to counter fear.

In a coauthored research study about this film initiative, Soraya Bayuelo and Colombian communication scholar Jair Vega explain how the Purple Rose of Cairo Street-Film Project is anchored in local culture (Vega and Bayuelo 2008). Vega and Bayuelo explain how, traditionally, the people of Montes de María have used certain cultural codes to maintain a buffer against pain, suffering, and the fear of death; to illustrate this, Vega and Bayuelo use the case of a local popular folk song that tells the story of a hundred-year-old man who argues with death when she comes to take him away. Explaining that he still has the strength and the wish to live, he makes death postpone the decision to take him with her. At the end of the song death leaves empty-handed:

La muerte me vino a buscá
y yo le dije carajo respeta . . .
yo tengo cien años no má,
por ahí por donde viniste regresa . . .

Ay conmigo, que nadie se meta
Oye conmigo, que nadie se meta

La muerte se puso a escuchá
Y "hombe" me dijo "eso si es fortaleza
no más te vine a saludá
todavía puedes seguí aquí en la tierra"

Ay conmigo, que nadie se meta
Oye conmigo, que nadie se meta

La vejez no sólo es la edá
ay las ganas de viví es lo que cuenta
siento que toavía hay facultá
para medirme a to lo que se venga

mi diente ni asomo a aflojá
pa las mujeres mi alma está dispuesta
yo como lo que haya e tragá
dicen lo que no hace daño aprovecha

Ay conmigo, que nadie se meta
Oye conmigo, que nadie se meta

Death came looking for me
And I told her damn, you better respect me
I am only a hundred years old
Go back the same way you came in

Hey, no one messes with me
Listen, you better not mess with me

Death began listening to me
And told me "Man, that's real strength
I only came to say hello
You can remain here on earth"

Hey, no one messes with me
Listen, you better not mess with me

Old age is not only about years
The desire to live is what counts
I feel I still have the stamina
To deal with whatever comes

My teeth do not show any sign of loosening
For women my soul is at their disposal
I still eat whatever there is to gobble up
They say it's good to enjoy what doesn't hurt you

Hey, no one messes with me
Listen, you better not mess with me (Vega and Bayuelo 2008, 54–55)

The song was composed by Nando Coba, a medical doctor from Montes de María, for his friend Fernando Mosquera. Mosquera, well-known as one of the best drummers in Montes de María, was suffering from a long illness, and Coba composed the song as part of the therapy to improve Mosquera's spirits and help him recover. Once popularized in the region, the song is frequently invoked by the people of Montes de María to overcome pain, illness, and the feeling of being defeated by death. According to Vega and Bayuelo: "Songs such as this one speak of a cultural capital of traditions that express symbolic constructions used against fear of death. However, these traditions deal with natural death, death caused by old age and the body's natural decay typical of aging" (Vega and Bayuelo 2008, 54).

During the mid-1990s, as paramilitaries entered the region of Montes de María, and armed conflict spiraled into the "hall of mirrors" that targeted civilian communities particularly hard, death caused by old age was replaced by death caused by armed conflict. The traditional cultural "arguments" against death and suffering available to the people of Montes de María became obsolete. The traditional cultural capital became ineffective in dealing with life's difficult times. Now death "comes to visit" not hundred-year-old men, but young, healthy men, women, and children: "These new conditions challenge the people of Montes de María to find new cultural codes with which to maintain their resistance against the fear of death; and as they develop new cultural traditions to deal with death, they take advantage of the new technological options available, such as film; this is the cultural and technological backdrop of the Purple Rose of Cairo Street-Film Project" (Vega and Bayuelo 2008, 56). This type of agency used by a community to resist injury and violence by invading forces resonates with the work of Patricia Lawrence among Sri Lankan communities in war zones. Lawrence reveals how oracles reconfigure traditional Hindu goddess cults to help people deal with systematic trauma, silenced families, broken kin relationships, terror, and confusion imposed by armed groups (Lawrence 2000). If in prewar times oracles dealt with issues such as lost articles, missing cattle or poultry, sickness, and wife–husband problems, during war times Lawrence found that "through oracles' embodiment and witnessing of the injury of war, unshielded truth is expressed, pain is acknowledged, and relationship with death is restored into its process" (Lawrence 2000, 200).

More recently, the Collective's film project expanded outside of El Carmen, bringing films to streets and plazas in nearby towns and villages; thus, the project has been renamed the Purple Rose of Cairo Itinerant Street-Film Project. As the itinerant project reaches municipalities recently consumed by the chaos of war imposed by armed groups, its healing qualities begin to show. Vega and Bayuelo's ethnographic observation of the film project's impact on survivors of violence is testimony:

> The itinerant film project, and with it the reappropriation of public spaces, of the evening time for conversation among neighbors and friends in the street and the plazas begins weaving new certainties. The day after a film was shown in a new community center recently built over the ruins of a building demolished by a bomb in the municipality of Chalán, a man who had attended the show the night before expressed this well: "and to think that this same place brings such conflicted memories. Ever since the bomb [exploded], people were afraid to come here; or worse, people ran for cover in their houses if they heard the noise of a car they did not recognize. With the film and the music I felt that people recovered not only trust, but also joy. We had lost the joy in this town. [This project] is so that life can be reborn here in Chalán." (Vega and Bayuelo 2008, 60)

In 2006 the film project received enough funding from international donors to incorporate film production workshops parallel to the itinerant film showings. The film production component of the project intends to offer training and access to technology for local collectives to produce their own short films; the project is called Cinta de Sueños: Proyecto de Cine Rosa Púrpura del Cairo [Ribbon of Dreams: A Purple Rose of Cairo Film Project].[13] Bayuelo explains: "As you know, *The Purple Rose of Cairo* is a film about a story in which the characters come out of the film to join the people. In *Ribbon of Dreams* it's the opposite, where the people of Montes de María jump into the film" (Colectivo de Comunicaciones 2006b).

The Collective uses media technologies to repair the broken social links caused by isolation, fear, and distrust brought to Montes de María by armed groups. While paramilitaries, guerrillas, and even the Colombian armed forces progressively invade quotidian spaces and pressure civilians to become entangled in their wars as informants and supporters, the Communications Collective uses film and video to reappropriate spaces that once were public, collective, and used to knit the local social fabric.

The Icotea: Language to Speak the Unspeakable

Icoteas are turtles found in the region of Montes de María and are known for their skill at blending in with the mud at the first sign of a predator. *Icoteas* are capable of hiding quietly for a long time until the threat has passed. In my interviews with people from the Collective, the sentence "we are like the *icotea*" was frequently repeated.[14] The Collective does not deal directly with the actions of armed groups on these communities of unarmed civilians; the Collective does not denounce human rights or international humanitarian rights (Geneva Convention) violations, or the atrocities committed by legal and illegal armed groups against civilians. The Collective is aware that any of these actions could easily make it a military target of any of the armed groups present in the region. The Collective is deeply committed to peacebuilding, but its leaders know well what they can and cannot do; doing or saying anything that directly refers to the actions of armed groups is clearly outside the confines of the Collective's safe sphere of action. In other words, the Collective acknowledges that there are some peacebuilding processes within its reach while others are entirely out of it. The Collective engages in peacebuilding processes that purposely bypass direct references to any of the armed groups active in the region.

In 1995 the Collective had a television program and a series of radio programs focused on human rights. In recent years, however, human rights discourses have become perilously loaded in Colombia. In their anticommunist and antiguerrilla discourses, paramilitaries demonize human rights organizations and activists as "auxiliaries of the guerrilla" (Romero 2003, 107). The Colombian armed forces have also contributed to the demonization of human rights; when these organizations question paramilitary attacks against civilians, and particularly leaders of grassroots organizations, armed forces respond in what sociologist Mauricio Romero explains as "the enemies of my enemies are my friends" (Romero 2003, 107), thus attacking human rights organizations and discourses as "subversive."

Even the Colombian central government has made its own contribution to the demonization of human rights. On September 9, 2003, on Human Rights Day, in response to *El Embrujo Autoritario*,[15] a recently published report that denounced hundreds of human rights violations, many carried out by state institutions, then-president Alvaro Uribe referred to human rights organizations as "human rights traffickers who should once and for all take off their masks, show their political ideas and end such cowardly acts of hiding political ideas behind human rights," and called human rights defenders "ideologues at the service of terrorism" and "prophets of disaster" (Semana 2003). On

February 3, 2007, Uribe compared human rights activists working in Colombia with "terrorists dressed as civilians" (Semana 2008). President Uribe's attacks have fueled the fire that stigmatizes international and Colombian human rights organizations and activists. In the ensuing atmosphere, including the terms "human rights" as part of one's vocabulary can easily connote "radical" or "guerrilla allied." In this context, the Collective decided to realign its work. Instead of talking about human rights, the programs now focus on children's rights and women's rights. By avoiding issues and discourses that can prove lethal, Collective members found various discursive strategies that allow them to speak about human rights violations and how civilians experience the negative impact of armed conflict in their lives.

One example is that of a weekly television cooking show produced by a group of internally displaced women. This form provides plenty of opportunities to express the pain and alienation provoked by the experience of forced displacement. As a case in point, in the cooking show *La Sartén por el Mango* [Holding the Pan by the Handle], a woman lists the ingredients she uses to prepare a traditional local dish. She describes how she has had to change the recipe after she had to leave her hometown because she cannot find this particular herb in El Carmen, so she replaced it with a different spice. In this subtle reference to the experience of forced displacement, she is connecting with other women and their experiences of alienation in their new environments. Beatriz Ochoa, founding member of the Collective explains:

> We stay away from any type of news or information programming; but people find a way to talk in our programs about the impact of violence on their lives. Around here it is rare that a person has not suffered the direct consequences of violence on their lives or on their loved ones. You can ask people the most trivial question, "when was the last time that you dyed your hair?" for example, and when you allow people to speak, people who have been directly touched by violence sooner or later will talk about it. In one of the programs, a woman was talking about her job of smashing rocks here in El Carmen, she is narrating her daily life and she says: "I've never really done this, I've always lived on my land, cultivating; but with this situation of violence; my husband was killed and I became afraid of what could happen to me, so I had to come here to El Carmen." We have the camera in front of her but we don't say anything, just let her narrate her life, and we know that people are drawing their own conclusions. We call this "low profile denunciation." (Ochoa 2004)

The Collective's *icotea* discursive strategies, their "low profile de-nunciation," their "camera as a silent witness," and their "say it with-out saying it," provide the threads with which these women can weave sophisticated communication spaces of subtlety, connotation, indirect talk, and indirect references. These spaces allow the communities of Montes de María to name what is not mentionable, to express what is inexpressible, to remember what did not happen, and to leave a record of what cannot be stated. In her ethnographic research in war zones, Carolyn Nordstrom describes communication processes that resonate with the Collective's response to the militarization of everyday life in Montes de María: "When truth is too dangerous to tell, people don't stop talking. Instead, they shape truth into stories. People who might be arrested for talking openly of arms transfers and corruption are far less likely to come to harm for telling parables about brothers and birds. But anyone with sharp ears 'knows' who the brothers and the birds are, and in this way people gain the information they need to survive" (Nordstrom 2004, 143).

The report about one of the worst paramilitary massacres perpetu-ated in Montes de María, released in 2009 by the Grupo de Memoria Histórica [National Commission of Memory], documents how sur-vivors use "oblique language" to refer to the atrocities experienced. In attempts to navigate the horror of reliving the experience and at the same time the need to narrate the massacre, survivors find language formulas to talk about the massacre without mentioning it; for exam-ple, they say "when what happened here happened," or "when what took place here happened" (Grupo de Memoria Histórica 2009, 17).

With its *icotea* politics, the Collective has opened a communica-tion space for what James Scott calls "hidden transcripts" (Scott 1992, 61), defined as gestures, ways of talking, discourses that exist out of the field of vision of those who terrorize civilians (Ramírez 2001, 103). According to Scott, "the practice of domination then creates the hid-den transcript" (Scott 1992, 61). Hidden transcripts "guard those expressions and statements that—if openly expressed—would be dan-gerous" (Ramírez 2001, 103). Hidden transcripts are an organic form of resistance for civilians in regions where armed groups impose a regime of terror. In contrast with most hidden transcripts, which remain in private spheres, in Montes de María unarmed civilians' hidden tran-scripts move toward public spheres thanks to the Collective's commu-nication technologies.

To Give the Key to the Thief: Ownership and Belonging

Perhaps the Collective's most impressive achievement in terms of citizens' communication is the sense of ownership participants feel for this communication initiative. As soon as kids come through the door, off go their shoes and socks, their demeanor relaxes, and they all get to work. During an evaluation workshop, we asked a group of about fifty kids, ages six to ten, to remember their first day at the Collective and what they felt, and to express this visually. Many of them drew the building where the Collective operates as a home. The sense of belonging is so strong among Collective members that old-timers, young adults who have participated in Collective activities for more than ten years now, feel that their identity is inseparable from the Collective. Wilgen Peñaloza, who was sixteen when he joined the Collective in the mid-1990s, says, "to tell you about the Collective is to tell you about my personal life. . . . *I am* the work we do with communication and media at the Collective" (Peñaloza 2004).

Inside the Collective, doors are not locked and expensive television and radio technologies are not secured. These are brave decisions, if we take into consideration that the Collective has minimal access to resources and that repairing one piece of equipment may suck up an immense portion of the Collective's budget for an entire month. Soraya calls this *"darle la llave al ladrón"* (to give the key to the thief). In other words, the Collective is deeply committed to the principle of trusting those who, outside the Collective, are widely believed to be untrustworthy. The Collective operates by leaving office and storage room doors opened with sixty "wild" kids in the building, allowing teens who lack training to use expensive and delicate video equipment, relinquishing control of entire projects to a fifteen-year-old whose failure could cause the organization to lose important grant money, or appointing a fourteen-year-old to coordinate an entire radio production training program at a local school. Soraya Bayuelo recalls: "Around 1998 we bought two brand new Panasonic 9000 cameras—how did we do it? Beatriz and I borrowed money from Mercedes's sister; we had to pay it all back with interest, and we gave them to the kids, brand new, and told them: 'You are going to produce the programs; whatever new ideas you have, go for it!' there . . . in freedom" (Bayuelo 2005). These are the building blocks on which kids and youth begin to develop a strong sense of ownership and self-confidence.

As the founders of the project, Beatriz and Soraya insist that all relationships inside the Collective should be built on trust. Trust permeates everything and is frequently mentioned in interviews as the main reason first-time participants realize that they will keep coming. One Collective participant remembers:

> Carnival was going full blast, and we were supposed to produce a program about it. It was my first day and I was with Soraya in the street. We had two video cameras and Soraya told me to take one of the cameras. If we went in two different directions, each with a camera, she said, we would cover many more activities. I said I had never used a video camera before, and she proceeded to give me a ten-minute lesson on how to operate the camera, and then sent me my own way. She trusted me. (Collective Participant 2004)

Even though this had happened years ago, this participant still remembers the day as a moment that made him realize he would keep coming back to the Collective.

These levels of trust, which are rare even in "normal" settings, are even more exceptional in communities where armed violence and generalized terror have debilitated most trust-based social relationships. Younger members, who years ago were age eight or nine when they began participating in Collective projects, are now the coordinators of their own production projects. Now they are able to continue to propagate the legacy of developing equally trusting relationships with the newcomers with whom they work.

Construir País desde lo Pequeñito
(Nation Building from the Ground Up)

For many women, children, and youth in Montes de María, the Collective opened a social and cultural space in which alternative ways of interaction can become "normal." Cultivating a different ethos among participants is perhaps the most taxing challenge of the Collective. Operating in the middle of a region where the social fabric is largely shaped by an absent state, patron–client systems, great inequality, and armed conflict, the Collective attempts to foster an inclusive set of principles, applicable to anyone and everyone who wants to be a member. As soon as you enter the doors of the Collective, you enter a different collective imaginary, a different set of values, an alternative ethos. Within its walls, things are done differently and people are treated differently. The Collective's common sense is not the same as that of the outside world. Wilgen Peñaloza describes the Collective in the following terms:

> It's a space, a different space that helps you to wake up. Soon you realize that there is a different way of seeing in here, a different way of doing, a different way of feeling, so the Collective is like an alternative family, it allows you things that many times not even your own home offers . . . so in the middle of all these difficult situations [of violence] the Collective is like a lighthouse that allows you to be who you are, that recognizes you for who you are, and where you can recognize others for who they are . . . that's what we do here, we are building a nation one thread at a time. (Peñaloza 2004)

This alternative ethos is founded on the principles outlined in the following sections.

Moving from the Margin to the Center

In Montes de María, as in most armed conflict contexts, people become invisible as their humanity is reduced to their position vis-à-vis the war. People lose their names and their individual persona, becoming only "a friend of the guerrilla," "a supporter of the paramilitary," "a friend of the army," "a victim of violence," or "a displaced person."

People who participate in Collective activities are not labeled "participants" or "stakeholders" or even "community members." Each person is perceived as unique, with a name, an individual history, with her or his own potential to contribute to the group and their own barriers to overcome. In an interview I asked Modesta, one of the founding members, where she saw evidence of the Collective's accomplishments. She recounted the story of a woman involved with a group producing a weekly television program about local cuisine. In one of the programs, the introductory segment had to be filmed several times because the woman in question could not say a word correctly. Instead of saying "*y hoy haremos dulce de papaya*" (and today we will make papaya compote) she would say "*y hoy aldremos dulce de papaya*" (a common mistake of Spanish-speakers with low literacy levels; *aldremos* is not actually a word in Spanish). After several takes and much support from her teammates and program coordinators, the woman was finally able to say "*y hoy haremos dulce de papaya.*" The scene was taped, the woman was beaming with pride, and the entire production team broke out in applause. For Modesta, this moment is a good example of how the Collective realizes its mission. The woman's sense of empowerment and accomplishment means that the Collective has succeeded. This is its raison d'être. Each person's empowerment takes a different form, precisely because each person is understood as an individual with his or her own idiosyncrasies. Each participant is unique, and in honoring this uniqueness the Collective pays close attention to each case, listens to each story, and responds to individual needs.

Within this mandate of individual development, it is very important for the Collective to have the ability to perceive the ways each person is changing in their individual ways. In her ethnographic study of one of the children's production groups, Joyce Sarmiento found that there are no predefined guidelines to run a production workshop (Sarmiento 2005). There are no formulas to detect what the children want, what interests them at a given time, or what they want to work on. At the Collective, the entire relationship between the children and the Collective's workshop coordinators is based on interaction. Coordinators are encouraged to detect kids' behaviors, nonverbal signs, gestures, looks, and facial expressions and to shape the workshop accordingly. The coordinators have learned to read and decode verbal and nonverbal communication in order to detect every child's needs and the group's needs. Interaction is the basis on which decisions are made on what the children want and what interests them. In the words of one of the coordinators, "there's no better communication channel than what the children express Saturday to Saturday with a word, an action, or a look" (Eva Maria, children's collective coordinator, interview, February 2005, cited in Sarmiento 2005, 105).

Processes of social change are not to be understood as formulas, but rather as products of unique sets of interactions among the changing individuals. Each person's process is affected by his or her own features, history, traumas, talents, and interactions with other Collective participants. Social change happens as each participant explores new ways of being, facilitated by the new ethos they are able to inhabit and embody once they pass through the Collective's doors.

Within the Collective, members are perceived as multidimensional, complex, and unique creatures. In an evaluation of a radio production workshop, for example, a young boy, participating in a project for the first time, was asked what he liked most about his first day being part of a Collective project. He told the evaluators that what he liked most was being called by his name; he said that the time he spent working on the project had been the first time ever he was called by his name (Ochoa 2004). The Collective helps counter the negative impact of a culture of violence that reduces human beings to war-related categories. The Collective responds with a series of communication processes that restore human interactions in which people are addressed in all their complexity and uniqueness. The Collective does not simply send messages about a culture of peace; instead, it opens a communication space *to perform* such culture of peace, a communication space where participants can embody peace, experience what peace feels like, and discover how peace can be learned and appreciated.

Building a Culture of Democratic Citizenship

Violent societies produce contexts of unequal access to power. As has been widely documented by scholars investigating violence in Colombia, the social fabric of societies engulfed in armed conflict normalizes hierarchical relationships, and equal relationships become scarce (González, Bolívar, and Vásquez 2003; Pécaut 2001; Steiner 2005). The combined effects of patron client relationships, a state unable to guarantee civil rights, widespread bribery and corruption, and the presence of armed groups and their territorial control create and normalize a culture in which grabbing as much power as possible (with the help of money, political connections, or weapons) becomes common sense. Cultural anthropologist Claudia Steiner says that in Colombia the case is not that you have a gun because you are somebody, but that you are somebody *because* you have a gun (Steiner 2000). As a result, when interacting with one another, the immediate impulse of people living under these conditions is to demonstrate one's access to power. People are automatically classified as friend or enemy, and the drive is to demonstrate (or perform) enough force to threaten the other— perceived as a potential antagonist. Thus, hierarchical relationships become the norm.

This is the social fabric in which the Collective operates. Each month hundreds of children, youths, and women, some of the most vulnerable and disempowered groups in the region, enter the Collective to experience a different possible reality. Entrance into the Collective grants each person exactly the same rights and access to power as the directors and coordinators. Soraya describes the Collective in the following terms: "The Collective is like a beehive, with adults and kids coming and going, all working together, like a beehive except that we don't have a queen; here we are all queens and kings" (Bayuelo 2004). Under this paradigm, an eight-year-old has the same decision-making power as a fifty-year-old. Knowing how to operate a television camera becomes much more important than age, education, gender, or status. Soraya Bayuelo explains: "When we talk about the rights of children, we want children to realize, and we want parents to realize, and we want teachers to realize that children's rights cannot stay at the level of discourse. These rights have to be embodied in daily life, in mundane interactions; they cannot remain at the level of discourse. It is in this sense that we feel we are building a culture of peace and citizenship" (Bayuelo 2004).[16] A document about the history of the Collective explains: "In a world where people are classified according to gender, age, profession, or handicaps, what our participants value the most is the level of integration among all of us, from the oldest one, who is close to fifty to the youngest ones, who are no more than eight or nine" (Colectivo de Comunicaciones 1999, 14).

During a personal interview, Soraya described instances in which breaking age hierarchies led to situations normal within the walls of the Collective, but clearly "abnormal" outside. For example, Soraya recounted, a local school asked the Collective to help them initiate a radio production initiative for their students. At the weekly meeting in which tasks were assigned among Collective members, it became obvious that the best candidate to go to the school and work with the principal and teachers was Leonarda, a fourteen-year-old girl who had accumulated much expertise as a radio producer. Soraya came with Leonarda to the school and introduced the work of the Collective to the principal and teachers. Then, she introduced Leonarda as the would-be coordinator of the nascent project. The teachers and the principal looked on in dismay at first, as Leonarda took the stand and began explaining how the school radio production initiative should be set up. However, she spoke with such confidence and authority that the adults in the school quickly became accustomed to receiving instructions from a fourteen-year-old.

Self-discipline and Negotiated Rules

Violence in Colombia is often explained as the result of a state that is, at best weak, and at worst absent, in large portions of the national territory (Acevedo 1995; Pécaut 2001, 2003; Perea 1996; Maria Teresa

Uribe 1991). Levels of impunity in Colombia reach 99 percent in some years (García and Uprimny 1999, 40).[17] This lack of institutional presence causes the erosion of the social fabric; not able to count on state institutions to guarantee the rule of law, individuals engage in struggles to maintain their privileges while bypassing their responsibilities. Malcom Deas states that violence in Colombia is triggered by the thirst for power in those social spheres where the state cannot maintain the exclusive use of force (Deas 1995). The precarious presence of state institutions "leaves communities abandoned to their own dynamics, without being able to count on state apparatuses to resolve their tensions . . . with the result of generalized impunity and inefficiency of justice" (González, Bolívar, and Vásquez 2003, 31). The notion of a collective responsibility to maintain the common good is weak. Private usurpation of public resources becomes the norm. Any available resource, such as municipal budgets, public spaces, public property, and even natural resources are perceived as loot to be appropriated by individual interests as quickly as possible.

According to Colombian economist Jorge Luis Garay Salamanca, in Colombia

> the profound absence of the sense of a public sphere permeates the behavior and conduct of citizens, privileging individual interests over the so-called common good. . . . [T]he resulting precariousness of social relations increasingly invades multiple instances of social interactions in the country, from the level of individual relations with other individuals to groups' relations with other groups and with the state. . . . [T]his erosion of citizens' coexistence fortifies, cultivates a culture where violence is king, where individuals and groups use force, coercion, powerful influences, or dominance of some groups over others in order to achieve their own individualistic—even self-centered interests. (Garay Salamanca 1999, 404–5)

García Villegas and de Sousa dos Santos present an excellent description of the social fabric's erosion in contexts of armed conflict in Colombia; in their view, the result of such erosion is "violence, corruption, social conflicts, the state's weakness, the privatization of justice, marginality, the vulnerability of social identities, individuals' vulnerability, the uncertainty of life, and the collapse of social expectations" (García Villegas and de Sousa dos Santos 2004, 55). In this context, where democratic institutions are perceived as inaccessible or ineffective in guaranteeing one's rights, to mediate and manage any type of social conflict, or to combat impunity, "the construction of citizenship projects is something difficult, that demands exceptional levels of courage and solidarity" (García Villegas and de Sousa dos Santos 2004, 52).

This is the context in which the Collective embarks on the daily exercise of civic education. Kids are not told what to do when they come into the Collective. Instead, a discussion is activated each time there is a need for collective rule-making. Commonly, when a group of new kids begins a radio production workshop, the entire place is littered with paper wraps and juice boxes discarded after their snack break. Kids replicate what they see on the streets, where they see parents and other adults throwing trash on the ground in complete disregard for public spaces. However, inside the Collective this type of behavior does not go unquestioned. A plenary is quickly organized in which the question is posed: "Do we prefer to work in a littered environment, or would it be better to work in a clean environment?" A discussion follows and most times, kids decide that they prefer a clean environment. This is followed by a session of collective rule-making. The rules are written on a big sheet of paper and posted on the wall. Quickly, the rules become common sense and are passed on from the old-timers to the new kids. One day, the sheet of paper disappears from the wall; it is not needed anymore.

Parents see their children begin to internalize alternative ways of interacting with each other and their environments, without the need for authoritarian discipline:

> My younger kid is now a member of the Collective, and I am really happy about that, because he is so hyperactive—he is the kind of kid that walks past his mother and has to pull her hair; he walks by me and has to hit me in the head—his way of playing around—but now he's changed, he used to be like that, rude, with everybody, his brothers, but now he sees that it is not right to treat others like that, he sees that the other kids do not do that, and I believe that is what has changed him. (Sr. Rafael, focus group cited in Sarmiento 2005, 104)

The Collective does not use authoritarian discipline. Rules are established for a reason and negotiated collectively. Adults emphasize that rules exist for collective well-being. Children in the Collective rarely experience rules imposed for the sake of propriety or to entertain adults' privilege. Kids are encouraged to be comfortable while they work. Most take this to heart and shed shoes and socks as soon as they come in. Although this type of behavior in a public place breaks the most basic rules of decorum imposed on children by Colombian culture, it is behavior legitimate inside the Collective because it does not negatively affect collective well-being.

Nonviolent Conflict Resolution

A culture permeated by violence and aggression fosters the idea that difference is the primary axle around which power is distributed. Class, gender, and age differences organize subjects into rigid power structures. In social contexts where individual power (in the form of use of force, money to bribe, or powerful influences to get things done) is key to securing the most basic rights, encountering any type of difference in everyday interactions triggers the impulse to overpower the other simply because they are different and thus threatening. Difference—any difference—is perceived as an opportunity to gain (or lose) power. According to Colombian sociologist Mauricio Romero, the Colombian state and regional elites disseminate distorted and derogatory perceptions of anyone with an identity different from those sanctioned by the status quo (Romero 2003); this has normalized the notion that difference is something to mock, stay away from, and ultimately snub.

The Collective proposes and implements a different way to understand difference and to manage conflict. Inside the Collective, difference is perceived as that which makes each participant unique, and thus it becomes an asset for the group. For example, during a video shoot, production teams are encouraged to explore different perspectives and points of view to tell a story, as well as different camera angles and movements. Individual participants are valued for what makes them different and for their unique ideas, not for conforming to the norm. Difference is articulated as an asset, a source of potential, and a well of resources, not as a source of vulnerabilities for individuals and/or groups. Radio, video, and television producers learn that media are excellent tools to recognize and celebrate difference. A television camera becomes a means to discover different cultures, experiences, and stories that circulate in the region. The Collective produces media content in order to capture those differences and to bring them to a public sphere where they can become part of the cultural capital of the community (Bayuelo 2004).

Colombia has been in a state of near-war and armed conflict for more than fifty years now. One of the most devastating effects of the persistent presence of war is the normalization of the use of force to solve conflict, any type of conflict (Pécaut 2003). During the 1980s, for example, drug lords recruited and trained small armies of young thugs to use force and violence against individuals and groups. These *sicarios,* or paid killers, were commonly employed by drug lords to kill competitors, solve deals gone bad, and settle debts. Eventually, the use of *sicarios* spilled over into other scenarios of communal life. People began using *sicarios* to evict unwanted tenants or even to seek revenge in romantic triangles. Executions appearing to be political assassinations when in reality they are the result of people solving conflicts by violent means are a well-documented effect of the incursion of armed groups into a region (Ramírez 2001; Riaño-Alcalá 2006).

The use of force and violence to solve common, everyday-life conflicts permeates the social fabric and becomes part of people's common sense. Nordstrom's findings in the war zones of Sri Lanka and Mozambique resonate with the Colombian case: "Terrorized civilians thus may increasingly come to absorb and, more dangerously, accept fundamental knowledge constructs that are based on force. The average citizen then comes to 'know' that politics, force, and might (and possibly even justice and right) are equal. Violence parallels power" (Nordstrom 1992, 269).

Inside the Collective an alternative common sense circulates. Collective ethos states that difference and conflict are not only normal but to be cherished, and that learning to appreciate and use difference will make the group stronger. Conflict is not something to be afraid of, but an element of everyday life manageable through dialogue and mediation.

In one of the workshops I attended at the Collective, I had the opportunity to witness firsthand how conflicts are resolved. Approximately thirty kids, ages ten to sixteen, came on a Saturday morning to attend the workshop. Soon, Soraya perceived that two twelve-year-old girls who have been best friends for years were hardly talking to each other. Usually the girls would work together, but now they made great efforts to avoid each other. During the course of the morning, Soraya took each one away from the group and asked her what was going on. She later told me that the girls had a major falling out, and one of them had behaved in a strongly questionable way toward her friend (she did not tell me more, not wanting to betray the girls' trust). Soraya heard both versions of the conflict. She told both girls that it was important for them, as well as for the well-being of the group as a whole, that they be able to solve their conflict on their own. She told them they were the only ones who could solve the conflict: no one else could do it for them. She proposed to the girl who had behaved in a questionable manner that she examine and reflect on her past behavior and decide if her friend deserved an apology.

The workshop ended with a plenary in which each child talked about what they learned since they began coming to the Collective. When it was the turn of one of the friends in conflict, the girl took the microphone and said that one of the things she had learned in the Collective was that you can resolve conflict by thinking and talking about it. She said she had thought about her recent behavior toward her best friend and found it reproachable, and she wanted to apologize. She was visibly shaken and burst out crying with such force I thought she was on the verge of collapsing. Soraya quickly approached her and embraced her. Then her friend came too, and the two girls embraced, crying.

More than to recount a sappy story with messages about nonviolent conflict management or reconciliation techniques, I want to emphasize how the Collective opens a communication space in which a culture of peace is *performed*, becoming lived experience for participants. The Collective's approach to communication for peace is in sharp contrast with traditional media peacebuilding initiatives, which have historically involved designing and developing communication campaigns with the intention of *persuading* people to resolve conflicts peacefully (Rodríguez 2004). In contrast, the Collective carefully designs a communication space in which people are able *to perform* nonviolent conflict resolution. Here, participants experience the process of shifting how they interact with others, and how they move from dealing with conflict violently to dealing with conflict discursively.[18]

The Collective emerges as a community in which everyday-life practices and relationships are knit together using as threads "respect, pluralism, trust, solidarity, freedom, friendship, joy, love, belonging, and creativity" (Colectivo de Comunicaciones 2003).

All We Do Is to Facilitate People's Dreams

"All we do is to facilitate people's deams," says Alvaro Salgado expressing his view of the Collective (Salgado 2004). According to Gumucio Dagron, forms of community media become sustainable only when local communities feel a profound connection with these information and communication technologies (ICTs). Gumucio Dagron argues that such sense of connection is grounded in local culture, local languages, and most of all, local needs (Gumucio Dagron 2003). In other words, community media become relevant for citizens only when their use is driven by local imaginaries, culture, language, and communication needs. The Communications Collective of Montes de María has learned this well, as it tailors its initiatives to the various needs of different communities in the region.

The Collective is an exceptionally flexible institution. The leaders, Beatriz and Soraya, do not have preconceived ideas about how radio, video, television, or film should be used by the people in Montes de María's diverse communities. Instead, they are very aware that each community is different, and their task as leaders is to help each community articulate how community media can address their needs and dreams. Thus, their mode of operation is as follows: the leaders approach or are first approached by a community leader or a grassroots collective. Beatriz, Soraya, as well as other Collective old-timers immerse themselves in the community, and it is in this immersion that the idea for a new project emerges. For example, the Collective began working with the Benkos Biohó School in Palenque, a community with very unique cultural features.

Palenque de San Basilio came into existence in the early seventeenth century as a community formed by fleeing slaves from the nearby colonial city of Cartagena. For decades, the people of Palenque made a great effort to isolate themselves from the rest of the region and the nation. Maintaining their freedom required a low profile. As a result, Palenque was able to preserve a very strong African cultural identity, such that African music, art, burial rituals, family relations, and even language survived more than three centuries of colonization and westernization. On November 25, 2005, UNESCO (the United Nations Educational, Scientific, and Cultural Organization) declared the cultural space of San Basilio de Palenque one of forty-three Masterpieces of the Oral and Intangible Heritages of Humanity. Being a tight community proved crucial when, during the paramilitary offensive of the late 1990s, San Basilio de Palenque made loud and clear its zero tolerance of the presence of armed groups within the community's confines. In 2002 a group of paramilitaries entered Palenque and killed four high-school age young men with the argument that they belonged to a guerrilla organization. The paramilitaries intended to stay in

Palenque and told the community they wanted to "protect them against the guerrillas." But the community had its own response:

> They said the police and the army would soon come to help protect us, but we've seen how those towns where the army or the police have a strong presence always have problems with the paramilitaries and the guerrillas. The entire community got together and we all decided that here the only leaders with authority have always been the elders, and we want to keep it that way. So we went to Cartagena, and we talked to the state governor, and told him we did not want any of those entities here, from the right or the left—no one. And since then, they left us alone. (S. Delgado 2009)

Soraya Bayuelo explains: "while the armed groups cornered civil society in all the other municipalities here in Montes de María, Palenque resisted; maybe the force of Benkos helped them stay free from these new forms of slavery" (Bayuelo 2009).[19]

However, among young *palenqueros* African culture is becoming extinct. Worried by the erosion of traditional *palenquero* culture and language, community leaders developed a series of curricula about their African traditions for the local school. When the Collective found out about Palenque's cultural curriculum, they proposed a project aimed at strengthening this initiative with a media component. The result is a radio series called *Chaqueros de Paz,* produced by Benkos Biohó, a radio production collective formed by Palenque's school children and their teacher. The series is closely entwined with the curriculum on African culture, giving kids a chance to practice their Bantú (the traditional African language spoken in Palenque) as they interview grandparents and research African myths, stories, and personal histories.[20]

One episode of *Chaqueros de Paz* explores cultural issues such as gender roles in Palenque, where women travel daily to the city to sell agricultural products and homemade candy while men stay home in charge of agricultural plots and children. Another segment of the program features Umbalú, a funeral rite used to recall the dead person's life through song and drumming. In the case of San Basilio de Palenque, the Collective designed a participatory radio production initiative especially tailored to meet the current communication needs of Palenque's community.

Compare this with the Collective's work with a group of internally displaced women in El Carmen.[21] Here, as women began producing their own radio programs, they became aware of their illiteracy, which had never been a problem before forced displacement, when they were agriculturalists. Now, in their work with the Collective, their illiteracy became a handicap. Only those who could read and write were able to use a script, thus making the production process much easier. Also, in their new urban environment, the women began realizing that many job options require literacy. They expressed their desire to address their inability to read and write, and as a result, the Collective now includes literacy as part of radio production workshops for these women. A year later, the first group of displaced women is already reading.

Institutionally, the Collective has developed a series of competencies that allow it to shape media initiatives to the cultural identity and the communication needs of specific communities. In this sense, the Collective is well positioned to succeed in achieving sustainability in the sense Gumucio Dagron defines the term.

Media and Everyday Life

Soraya constantly asks, "if all this is true, this new ethos, this alternative way of being, then we should be able to see all these different values reflected in what the Collective participants produce for radio, video, and television, right? Can we see these values expressed in the ways the kids are using these technologies? In the themes they decide to focus on? In the narratives and the genres? In the type of images they decide to shoot?" (Bayuelo 2004). This is important, says Soraya, because these cultural products are ultimately what have the potential to trigger changes in the cultural imaginary of Montes de María, thus having an impact beyond the walls of the Collective.

Between 1997 and 2004 the Collective produced close to two thousand hours of video, television, and radio content. Currently, Collective participants create twenty hours of television programming weekly. This programming is aired on one of the channels reserved for local programming on the weekends, and rebroadcast as reruns on weekdays. Additionally, eighteen radio production groups operate in local schools spread throughout the region, producing hundreds of hours of radio programming each month.

Although the following paragraphs in no way imply an exhaustive analysis of the Collective's cultural products, I would like to highlight several features.

The focus of much of the programming is on local cultures, lifestyles, stories, characters, and themes. Various television and radio series have titles such as *Lo Nuestro* [What Is Ours], *Fiestas que Unen* [Festivals That Unite], *Así es mi Tierra, San Jacinto* [This Is My Homeland, San Jacinto], *La Historia del Bullerengue* [History of the Bullerengue],[22] and *Vida y Memoria de Montes de María* [Life and Memory in Montes de María]. Examples of themes include a one-hour television program about how to prepare the local *mote de queso* (cheese bisque). In another case, an episode of a radio program titled *Tradición o Conservación* [Either Tradition or Conservation] deals with a dilemma of drum-making and asks if drum-makers should follow their tradition and continue the deforestation required to produce the drums, or if they should instead stop producing drums in the traditional way to protect their forests (the program is part of a radio series produced by the Efectos y Compromisos radio production group in the Nelson Mandela neighborhood) (Cadavid 2005, 31).

In several interviews and testimonies, Collective radio and television producers mention how much research they carry out to prepare for their productions (Cadavid 2005; Sarmiento 2005). The children read books about the subject of their programs, interview elders, citizens, and experts, and search archives in local institutions. All these activities inspire the kids to interact with their surrounding environment in a different, more engaged, and more critical way.

Collective participants recount using microphones and viewfinders to focus their gaze on their environment:

> when I arrived the first day to the Collective, Sora welcomed me, and then she told me: "We need a news story about El Carmen. Take this camera and go look for it." I had never seen, let alone operated, a television camera. She only gave me three instructions and then she sent me on my way. I was terrified, thinking I was going to let them down, but she calmed me down. I went out with the camera and I began looking through the viewfinder. Everything looked different. Looking through the camera I went up and down streets and I recorded things I found interesting. Things that I had never paid attention to. I got to know my town in a different way, as if it was a different, foreign town. I am very grateful to Sora and the others at the Collective for that opportunity. Now I am a different person, and I feel profoundly my belonging to this team. (Leonardo Montes, personal communication cited in Cadavid 2005, 26)

The dynamics of armed conflict and violence surround these kids. Thus, their newfound fascination with exploring their own contexts is permeated by violence and the normalized presence of weapons. For example, the children's magazine *Voces de Colores,* includes the following joke: "Do you know what happens when a hen eats a bullet? Her chicks will come out wrapped in armed conflict!" (Colectivo de Comunicaciones de Montes de María Línea 21 2004). Many of the programs produced for radio and television focus on the experience of forced displacement. *Cuando los Angeles Lloran* [When the Angels Cry], produced by a radio collective, documents the lives of women who arrived to El Carmen after the massacres in El Salado in 2000; *Dos Historias en Conflicto* [Two Histories in Conflict] deals with the displaced community of San José del Peñón; and part of the radio series called *Life and Memory in Montes de María,* a program titled *Se fue la Luz, Vino la Violencia* [The Electricity Left and Violence Came], connects state neglect with armed violence.

In 2007 the Collective reached a more sophisticated level as media producer. This new phase originated when the audiences of Purple Rose of Cairo Itinerant Street-Film Project expressed resentment at their limited role as film viewers. Spread throughout the entire region of Montes de María, and invigorated by the films they saw, these audiences wanted to create their own stories. The Collective sought funds and secured a couple of grants to develop Cinta de Sueños [Ribbon of Dreams],[23] an initiative that allowed the Collective to train and support one hundred people in five video production teams in different localities. By the end of the year, these production teams, formed by people without any experience producing video or film, had finalized five videos of approximately ten minutes each and several shorter audiovisual narratives. Although each of the videos expresses its own unique style, their quality is impressive, with sophisticated camera shots and movements, lighting, and editing techniques. The soundtracks are also exceptional, both in terms of the quality of the sound and the use of local music and musicians, including several songs exclusively composed for the films.

In my view, the most salient feature in all five videos is how they portray Montes de María. Similar to how the *fotovideos* of Belén de los Andaquíes (see chapter 1) focus on local lifestyles and natural environments, the Collective's videos capture the texture of life in Montes de María. Local people, cultures, and places are showcased in all five videos. Seen through the cameras of Cinta de Sueños, Montes de María is a region of beautiful landscapes, populated by friendly and warm people who love music, neighbors who hang out and help each other, and kids on bicycles, urban and rural communities living a fairly good life even amid difficult conditions of poverty and the sly presence of armed groups. The videos insist on the notion that not everything in Montes de María has been permeated by armed conflict. The social fabric left untouched by violence is precisely what the filmmakers focus on. As with Radio Andaquí and EAIBA in Caquetá (see chapter 1) and AREDMAG's community radio stations in Magdalena Medio (chapter 3), the videos of Montes de María cultivate a strong sense of self, a sense of pride and self-esteem deeply rooted in local cultures, art, and life-worlds. The videos serve as "electronic mirrors" where the people of Montes de María can see who they are and appreciate how their social fabric has not been entirely permeated by armed conflict (Rodríguez 2001). The films resist ascribed identities of the region and its people as violent, imposed by the mainstream media's insistence on focusing on armed conflict.

Cinta de Sueños collective video productions include: *De Cochero a Piloto* [From Cart Driver to Pilot], produced and shot in Marialabaja; *El Niño Dios de Bombacho* [The Baby Jesus of Bombacho], produced and shot in Ovejas; *Son del Carángano* [Son of the Carángano], produced and shot in San Antonio de Palmito; *Locuras de Adolecente* [The Foolishness of Adolescents], produced and shot in San Onofre; and *Por el Billete* [For the Ticket], produced and shot in El Carmen de Bolívar.

The opening sequence of *De Cochero a Piloto,* a twenty-minute video drama about a taxi driver with a dream of becoming a pilot, playfully captures a series of everyday-life scenes in Marialabaja, a small town in Montes de María. Positioned on the place of a driver of a *coche-taxi,*[24] the camera sways over typical street scenes, a road lined with homes painted with the traditional pastel colors of Caribbean towns, moving onto the nearby river where someone takes a dip, and then to the front patio of a local shop where three men play Parcheesi. The camera continues to pan over a street fruit vendor, then to a couple of men hanging out on a street corner, to a neighborhood shop, and finally to a moving shot of Marialabaja's central plaza with its yellow church. Layered with intense drumming in the soundtrack, each shot intelligently captures subtle features emblematic of Montes de María's local cultures, such as trees trimmed in the typical Caribbean style where the canopy is made to look like a perfect cube; the inevitable sexy women beer posters exhibited on store fronts; the vivid colors of tropical fruit replicated by the vending cart itself; the primary colors of men's T-shirts commonly seen in the region. The shots reflect a rainbow of colors and people interacting around Parcheesi, a couple of beers, buying and selling fruit, or simply hanging out (Equipo de Producción Audiovisual de Marialabaja 2007).

De Cochero a Piloto tells a story that is profoundly *Montemariana.* The main character is a young man, raised by his grandmother; his mother died when he was a child, and we are told the father joined "those people" (armed groups) thus leaving the son behind. The young man has dreams of becoming a pilot, but feels trapped by poverty and lack of opportunities; he barely makes a living driving a *coche-taxi* he has baptized the Condor (Equipo de Producción Audiovisual de Marialabaja 2007).

Girls in knee-high white socks, bicycles, school uniforms, and book bags pepper *Locuras de Adolecente,* a ten-minute video about a group of five high-school friends who spend an afternoon at a local swimming hole. Suddenly, the teens are chased by guard dogs and men with guns; several shots are fired, and the kids, terrified, hide behind bushes and climbing trees. Finally, one of the armed men recognizes a boy as a friend of the family; he yells at the kids, warning them to never come back to this isolated place as these are "difficult times"; the kids quickly flee on their bikes down a country road. The video ends with the youngsters watching the sunset at a nearby beach, one of them in his underwear, as his clothes were left behind in the rush of the flight (Equipo de Producción Audiovisual de San Onofre 2007).

These two stories capture well the Collective's understanding of its role as local storyteller: on one hand, the Collective is committed to using media to express everyday life and identities in Montes de María as experienced by local unarmed civilian communities. The Collective's videos maintain a fine balance between staying away from portrayals that show the community merely as victims of violence, and, on the other hand, avoiding romanticized versions. In *De Cochero a Piloto* and *Locuras de Adolecente* the main characters' lives are clearly affected by the local presence of armed groups. In *De Cochero a Piloto,* the main character lost his father to one of the armed groups. In *Locuras de Adolecente,* the teens have to deal with their swimming hole's takeover by armed men.

Ciclistas en el Atardecer [Cyclists in the Sunset] is a one-minute moving sequence of two twelve-year-old boys playfully riding their bicycles. The sequence is shot on the soccer field of Las Margaritas, a recently erected neighborhood for internally displaced people in El Carmen de Bolívar. Against the backdrop of the exquisite blues, oranges, and yellows of a Caribbean sunset, the boys enjoy playing with their bicycles as local characters walk by, including a man with his machete, overburdened with a load of feed for his cows or pigs, and a girl followed by a small white dog (Colectivo de Comunicaciones de Montes de María Línea 21 2006a). Here too, the filmmakers opted to capture the parallel realities as experienced by the people of Montes de María, where the impact of armed conflict is felt side-by-side to the joy of everyday life.

Shot in a rural community, *El Niño Dios de Bombacho* tells the folk legend of a miraculous Baby Jesus figurine found by a woman as she fetched water in a nearby creek. The camera captures well life in the countryside: wood houses and thatched roofs, open-fire kitchens, and neighbors passing the afternoons talking on leather chairs balanced on their homes' front wall. When the Baby Jesus figurine heals a very sick boy and a man on crutches, the community realizes its miraculous powers. This nine-minute video ends with a joyful scene of music and dancing, and a band of local musicians playing accordion, *gaitas*,[25] and drums. One of the neighbors explains that clearly, what the Baby Jesus of Bombacho likes best is a good night of music and dancing (Equipo de Producción Audiovisual de Ovejas 2007).

Son del Carángano is an extraordinary visual narrative about the *carángano*, a folk musical instrument used in San Antonio de Palmito, of obscure origins; some people say it is part of African legacies, while others insist it's an indigenous instrument. Played mostly in the month of September, the *carángano* was loved primarily by women. In the old days, women such as Aurorita Mendez and Doña Mercedes Camacho loved their *caránganos*. In the evenings, while sitting at home, a woman would begin playing the instrument. Another woman would respond, then a third one would also join in, each in her own home. The silence of the night was disrupted by a concert of *caránganos* played by women in different parts of this small town. Marcelino Acosta, a local businessman, brought the first radio transmitter to San Antonio back in the 1950s; and that was the beginning of the end for the *carángano*. Invaded by the new sounds of radio, and later television, local *caránganos* were exiled to their owners' attics. The story ends when a grandmother, after seeing the video on her local

television channel, decides to dust off her *carángano* and begins playing it again while her two granddaughters sit by her side, watching
with interest (Equipo de Producción Audiovisual de San Antonio de
Palmito 2007).

Cinta de Sueños: Un Sueño Hecho Realidad, a documentary about
how these media producers lived the experience of filmmaking and
storytelling, states that "these are processes originated by the people of
the region for the region; [the stories] express our experiences, our
moments of joy, our moments of defeat, our people . . . who we were,
who we are, who we want to be . . . we intend to show what Montes
de María really is about, to the rest of the country, to the world, but
especially to its own people" (Colectivo de Comunicaciones de Montes
de María Línea 21 2006b).

Conclusion

I don't want to leave my readers with the idea that the Collective is
an overwhelmingly solid organization with the assurance of a bright
future. That is far from the truth. Challenges abound, ranging from a
precarious legal situation to a constantly revolving cast of volunteers
and staff. The number one challenge, however, is financial sustainability. Each time I travel to El Carmen to visit with Soraya, Beatriz,
and the youth of the Collective, I find a different situation. Sometimes
the Collective seems to be hanging by a thread, barely able to pay the
electric bill at the end of the month. Other times, their budget is robust
enough to hire teams of young communication graduates enthusiastic
about the opportunity to work with local communities. The fluctua-
tions of the Collective's budget depend on organizations and policies
set far from Montes de María. The Collective's financial success is
highly dependent on whether the United Nations, USAID (United
States Agency for International Development), or GTZ (Gesellschaft
für Technische Zusammenarbeit) make it their priority to fund projects
in Colombia, whether armed conflict makes it to the top of the priorities list, and whether communication, media, and culture are perceived
as lines of work worth pursuing.

The Communications Collective of Montes de María has struggled
to develop an alternative to the pervasive state neglect, patron–client
systems, war, and armed conflict in the region. Through its "school
with no walls," the Collective produced a communication space where

younger generations can reinvent themselves as citizens operating under codes different from those of their parents and grandparents. Resisting the erosion of local social fabrics in the form of individual over collective action; the use of force, manipulation, or influence over the rule of law; and terrorizing the other as a legitimate way to protect one's rights, the Collective proposes a different ethos based on inclusion, embracing difference, nonhierarchical relationships, and local collective imaginaries. This ethos is fundamental to sustainable peace. In the words of anthropologist of war Carolyn Nordstrom: "Peace doesn't emerge unless a foundation exists upon which to build. War doesn't end and peace begin in a unilinear process: peace is constructed step by step until war becomes impossible" (Nordstrom 2004, 183).

Beyond simply *proposing* a culture of peace, the Collective allows its members to perform, to experience peaceful coexistence in their everyday life. The Collective operates on the assumption that the first-hand experience of living without fear, experiencing a sense of belonging, and being able to count on clear rules will truly enable participants to understand and appreciate peace and the rule of law. The Collective is committed to facilitating this experience for its members, with the hope that later on, these children and teens from Montes de María will themselves make a personal and professional commitment to maintaining the rule of law, respecting the rules of peaceful coexistence, respecting and appreciating difference, and modeling nonviolent conflict management strategies. A Collective document states: "We learned that, even though we are as small as a grain of sand in the huge land that is Colombia, we, too, are responsible for the future of our country and for our own future" (Colectivo de Comunicaciones de Montes de María Línea 21 1999, 16). Again, Nordstrom's research resonates with the Collective's efforts to build peaceful communities: "Peace begins in the front-line actions of rebuilding the possibility of self (which violence has sought to undermine) and society (which massacres and destruction have sought to undermine)" (Nordstrom 2004, 184).

In 2002 the National Peace Award went to the Asociación de Municipios del Alto Ariari [Association of Municipalities of Alto Ariari]. In this region, municipalities were known as "guerrilla" or "paramilitary" municipalities because of their deep entanglement with guerrilla–paramilitary conflict. Anyone from a guerrilla municipality was assumed to be a guerrilla member, supporter, or informant, and anyone from a paramilitary municipality was likewise assumed to be a member or supporter. In some cases, long detours had to be taken so as not to step on enemy territory to reach one's destination. The Peace Award went to a grassroots association that developed a series of initiatives to erode the power of these labels. Led by two mayors, one from a "guerrilla municipality" and the other one from a "paramilitary municipality," this peacebuilding effort brought neighbors back together. In an extensive interview with Tatiana Duplat (Duplat 2003), one of the mayors remarks that the most important lesson learned through the experience was that civilian communities can build spaces of peace even in regions of intense armed conflict among guerrillas, paramilitaries, and the army. Similar lessons can be learned in the case of the Montes de María Collective.

Instead of allowing armed factions to invade public spaces and everyday-life relations among nonarmed civilians, the people of Alto Ariari and Montes de María reappropriate these social and cultural spaces. And even though armed conflict continues, unarmed civilians can carve out their own public spheres in which difference is respected and valued; conflict is managed in nonviolent ways; and the rule of law is privileged over the use of force. As they gain awareness of their own abilities to build spaces of solidarity and peaceful coexistence, civilians feel a sense of empowerment vis-à-vis armed groups. Civilians realize that, although they can not eliminate armed conflict or expel armed groups from their territory, they are able create a "parallel space" of peace, not peace *between* armed parties or *with* armed parties, but a space where civilians can reach out to one another, play a soccer game or produce a video, even if these spaces have to coexist side by side with armed groups and their logics.

When Wilgen Peñaloza recounts his feeling the first time he saw the central plaza fill with neighbors watching a movie, or when a parent reports his improved self-confidence and newfound abilities to resolve conflicts in his family without violence, the people of Montes de María realize their own competence to build a social fabric of solidarity, closeness, trust, and nonviolence, even in the middle of a region ravaged by armed conflict. Theirs is a gamble for long term peace; not the immediate peace resulting from peace agreements and cease fires signed among leaders and elites, but peace knit "one thread at the time," embodied in quotidian relationships, performed in everyday life, anchored in local cultures.

3 RADIO, RESISTANCE, AND WAR IN MAGDALENA MEDIO

Our way out is in our hands, as long as we are brave enough to go deep inside our own selves and define "the cherished life," the way in which each corner of this land wants to live its own dignity, expressed with determination and courage in the dances of children, the songs of troubadours, the art of our artists, and the orchestras of our towns.

—Francisco de Roux S.J.

I SEEK SHELTER FROM THE SUN under the yellow umbrella of an orange juice vendor in Cerro Burgos, a small river port in Magdalena Medio. It is late 2005, and I wait for a *chalupa* (small passenger motor boat) to take me to Gamarra, where I am about to start my return to Bogotá. The juice vendor has arranged a bench and some plastic chairs around his juice-making cart in order to attract customers. I order a fresh-squeezed orange juice and sit on the bench, surrounded by several other sweaty juice drinkers. I sip on my refreshing drink and eavesdrop on my neighbors commenting on the people disembarking from the numerous *chalupas* that dock for ten minutes to deliver passengers and pick up new ones. *Chalupas* are the main mode of transportation on the Magdalena River; traffic of people and goods up and down the river has been a part of everyday life here since colonial times. Christmas is almost here and *fiestas* are starting in several towns in the vicinity, increasing the number of people coming to Cerro Burgos, the central port in the area.

My neighbors are engaged in a game, the goal of which is to guess the origin of every arriving *chalupa* passenger based on his or her ethnic features, dress style, and nonverbal mannerisms. Passengers with lighter complexions, wearing button-down shirts, dressed in "serious" colors are labeled *cachacos* and assumed to have come from cities and towns on the region's Andean foothills. Those dressed in intense primary colors, with darker complexions, loud voices, and the typical exuberant nonverbals of Caribbeans are labeled *costeños* and said to come from lowland places on the riverbanks. The contestants guess each person's origin and then wait to hear their accent; a Caribbean Spanish accent will confirm a *costeño* background, while an Andean accent is a sure sign of highlands origin. This game is occurring in the heart of Magdalena Medio, a region known as the "hinge" ("*espacio bisagra*") of Colombia. The Magdalena River is the country's main water artery, reaching from the southern regions to the northern Caribbean. The central stretch of the river, flowing between its Andean origin and Caribbean destination in the Atlantic Ocean, is known as Magdalena Medio, or Middle Magdalena. Magdalena Medio is a region in which regional cultures intersect, creating a patchwork quilt of different cultural identities and lifestyles that coexist, hybridize, overlap, and sometimes clash. As a territory of thirty thousand square kilometers, where 750,000 people live in twenty-nine municipalities (De Roux 1999, 18), Magdalena Medio is perhaps one of the most culturally diverse regions in the country. It is a place where the northern Caribbean encounters the southern Andes, the lowlands encounter the highlands, and waves of migrants with varied economies and cultures encounter some of the most radicalized armed organizations on both the left and the right.

Watching the people descending from the *chalupas* in Cerro Burgos made me think that Magdalena Medio represents an imagined community, with an imagined sense of commonality despite all the diversity. The differences highlighted by my gossipy neighbors are blatant; clearly, a *cachaco* from Santa Rosa has very little in common with a *costeño* from Simití, though both towns are in Magdalena Medio, barely twenty minutes apart by road. Indeed, Amparo Murillo, a Colombian historian who has been dedicated for years to documenting and reflecting on the history of the region, states that Magdalena Medio's homogeneity should be understood in terms of the shared experiences of neighboring communities rather than in terms of unifying cultural identities. According to Murillo, the region is a place of convergence for different cultures and ethnic communities. Murillo insists that Magdalena Medio must be seen "in its heterogeneous,

Mics for the people of Magdalena Medio. Photograph courtesy of Daniel León, 2008.

fragmented, changing, and fluid nature, just like the river" (A. Murillo in press).

The twenty-nine municipalities constituting the Magdalena Medio region are located in the political and geographical margins of four different departments. The municipalities, described by Cadavid as "the backyard" of Antioquia, Bolívar, Santander, and César, are isolated and marginalized by distance and neglect from their respective departmental centers of political and economic power (Cadavid 1996, 17). I came to the Magdalena Medio region because of AREDMAG (Asociación Red de Emisoras Comunitarias del Magdalena Medio, or Magdalena Medio Community Radio Stations' Network), one of the most notable community media initiatives in Colombia (see www.are dmag.org.co). AREDMAG is a network of fifteen community radio stations spread throughout the region. In the following pages I attempt to describe the historical context of AREDMAG within the region of Magdalena Medio. I will discuss the birth and evolution of the network and analyze the role these brave community radio stations play in a region where political assassinations, kidnappings, and disappearances have reached some of the highest rates in the world.[1]

The Convergence of Migrants, Economies, and Cultural Identities in Magdalena Medio

Considered a wasteland of impenetrable swamps and forests, the region known today as Magdalena Medio remained beyond the agricultural frontier until the mid-1900s. Historically, while other Colombian areas such as Antioquia; the coffee departments of Quindío, Risaralda and Caldas; Santander; the Andean departments; and the Caribbean savannas developed agricultural and cattle economies well connected to national and international markets, Magdalena Medio became a "frontier territory," existing beyond the margins of economic and political powers (A. Murillo in press). Today, however, Magdalena Medio has come to occupy a central place in the nation: first, as an intersection of major transportation routes connecting the South with the North and the East with the West; and second, as a region with abundant natural resources.

In the last forty years, new economies, waves of immigrants, social movements, and armed groups have been attracted to the region for reasons of both transportation and natural resources, coming together to form an intricate social and cultural landscape framed by magnificent cultural diversity.

For centuries, the Magdalena River was the main route in and out of Colombia. European conquistadors, immigrants, ideas, the slave trade, goods, and natural resources traveled up and down the river from colonial times until the mid-1960s, when highways and planes replaced fluvial transportation. Traditionally, the river was seen as a divider and a boundary,[2] but more recent historiography shows the river to be one of few elements of shared meaning for people living in the region. "No one agrees on a definition of what Magdalena Medio is, but at least they all agree on the centrality of the river; the river and its valley is central in the region's collective imaginary" (A. Murillo in press). Historian Mauricio Archila writes, "in the everyday life of the people of Magdalena Medio, the river is a thread that connects, not a gulf that separates" (cited in Bolívar 2006, 473).

The heavy traffic of steamships transporting cargo and people up and down the river during the first half of the 1900s brought one of the first waves of migrants attracted to the region by economic opportunities. Migrants came to work on the river ports, selling wood for the ships and setting up canoe and small boat transportation ventures to feed the large ships. As these migrants settled in the region, they formed what is known today as Magdalena Medio's "amphibian culture," a string of communities on the river's banks, profoundly dependent on the river financially and culturally. Fugitive slave communities also came to the region, contributing a strong Afro-Colombian influence to Magdalena Medio's amphibian culture (Murillo et al. 1994, 22). The close connection between these communities and the Magdalena River became apparent to me during one of my field trips to Magdalena Medio in 2005, when I found the river swollen due to winter rains. The negative effects of the river flooding were on the tips of everyone's tongues. As I was going down the river in a *chalupa,* my neighbor, who worked for an organization that was helping victims of the flood, told me that a few days ago he had found an elderly couple stranded in their isolated house, which was now surrounded by water. In response to the knee-high water invading their home, patio, and farm, the husband and wife had hung a couple of hammocks from where they could watch the river. The aid worker offered to take them to a shelter but they refused, saying they would rather stay home, close to their river, on their hammocks. Instead of going to the shelter, they told him, they would be grateful if he could bring them some food. My neighbor returned to the isolated farm with food and provisions to find the couple still swaying on their hammocks: "They are so tied to the river that they would rather stay than go, even on a hammock hanging over water!" Amparo Cadavid says that "the people of the river, with significant levels of social cohesion, identity and roots, constitute the only strong cultural axis in the region" (cited in A. Delgado 2006, 88). The amphibian culture of the river is made of extended family networks that have occupied the region since colonial times. These families share a set of *costeño* cultural values, political affinities, kinship, trade, and dynamic communication up and down the river. These communities make their livelihoods from the river in varied ways, fishing, farming, boating, selling sand from the river, and trading (Murillo 1999, 47; Murillo et al. 1994, 32 and 93).

Over the past one hundred years, a number of foreign oil companies established oil extraction and processing operations in Magdalena Medio's central city of Barrancabermeja (Cadavid 1996, 19). A second wave of migrants began arriving in Magdalena Medio, attracted by the possibility of a good salaried job at one of the oil companies (Murillo et al. 1994, 23). Today, the region extracts and processes the majority of Colombia's oil.[3] In response to abusive exploitation of labor by the oil companies (Cadavid refers to bad working conditions, low salaries, extended work schedules, and exploitation of minors [1996, 25]), oil workers came together to form a strong labor movement marked by a radical culture of dissent (Murillo et al. 1994). The main oil workers union, Unión Sindical Obrera (USO) [Workers' Union], was created in 1923 and by 2004 included forty-five thousand members (A. Delgado 2006). USO stands today as a major leader of Colombia's labor movement. Partially as a result of pressure from the USO, oil extraction and processing was nationalized and allocated to ECOPETROL, a government-controlled company, in 1965.[4] In 1995 Magdalena Medio's oil industry produced 2 billion dollars and 90 million dollars net value in oil (De Roux 1996, 71). Oil extraction and processing generated then 70 percent of Magdalena Medio's GDP, of which only 4.5 percent stayed in the region; the rest went to national and international economies (De Roux 1996, 33). In 2008 Magdalena Medio produced 1.7 million barrels of oil every month (Centro de Estudios Regionales 2008, 1). A Regional Economic Atlas produced by the Centro de Estudios Regionales del Magdalena Medio jointly with the Programa de Desarrollo y Paz del Magdalena Medio (PDPMM) [Peace and Development Program for Magdalena Medio] revealed that in 2005 oil extraction and processing had increased to 90 percent of the region's GDP (Sandoval Merchan 2009).[5]

La Violencia, the period of intense political violence in the 1950s and 1960s between the Liberal and Conservative parties, provoked an avalanche of agricultural families to flee their traditional land in terror. These refugees from La Violencia constituted a third wave of migration into the Magdalena Medio region, where they came hoping to homestead a piece of land beyond the agricultural frontier. These newcomers brought the cultural values and symbolic worlds of their places of origin, contributing to the cultural patchwork quilt of the region. By the end of the twentieth century, 32 percent of Magdalena Medio's total population (or forty-six thousand families) was involved in subsistence agriculture as small farmers producing corn, cacao, manioc, plantain, cotton, coffee, sorghum, and rice, or were fishermen (De Roux 1996, 35). In 1995 Magdalena Medio's small farmers produced 142 million dollars worth of food (De Roux 1996, 71). Although this food did not reach markets or produce financial profits, it kept a great majority of the region's population well fed. According to economist Francisco De Roux: "The peasant agriculture does not generate much of a financial profit but it guarantees the precarious subsistence of the majority of the population" (De Roux 1996, 69).

When these poor farmers came during the 1950s and 1960s, the land they settled was generally forgotten and leftover. Today, however, the Magdalena valley and neighboring territories have become highly desirable as a result of their immense potential to generate profit as cattle ranches or as used by the African palm agro-industry.

During the second half of the 1900s, cattle ranchers in Magdalena Medio annexed large parcels of land using force to expel small farmers from their land. Historical accounts describe how landowners "bought" land but assassinated the seller before payment was due (Murillo et al. 1994, 158). In an unarmed but equally violent method of land acquisition, landlords would claim empty public forestlands; once they had obtained the claim, the landlords allowed poor agricultural families to clear the land and plant corn. The first year, these families lived off the lumber extracted from the forests, and the second and third years, the families were entitled to one third of their yield, while the landowner kept two thirds. The fourth year, the families had to plant feed grasses and then the deal was over. After the fourth year, the families were forced to leave the land, and the owner had his pastures ready to introduce cattle (Murillo et al. 1994, 155).

By 1995 cattle ranching had taken over 60 percent of the land in Magdalena Medio (80 percent in the municipalities of Puerto Berrío, Sabana de Torres, and Cimitarra) (De Roux 1996, 37). The irony is that today, cattle ranching uses twelve times more land than small farming (60 percent versus 5 percent), while it produces 20 percent less profit than the value produced by small farms (36.8 percent versus 57.4 percent) (A. Delgado 2006, 106). According to De Roux, ranchers would like to see Magdalena Medio converted into "an immense savanna of large cattle ranches with all the land in the hands of three to four hundred cattle ranchers and the disappearance of small farmers" (De Roux 1999, 29).

In 1961 several large haciendas (more than thirty-seven thousand acres) introduced African palm to Magdalena Medio, pioneering one of the most profitable land uses in the region (Murillo et al. 1994, 125). By 1994, 23 percent of the total palm oil produced in Colombia came from Magdalena Medio (A. Delgado 2006, 105); and by 1995 the region produced 45 million dollars of palm oil and 22 million dollars in net value (De Roux 1996, 71). Today, "the region is one of the main producers of palm oil in Colombia, 'the world's fourth biggest exporter of palm oil and other oil palm products after Malaysia, Indonesia and Nigeria'" (Rodríguez and Cadavid 2007, 315).

Despite the immense wealth generated by the oil, palm, and cattle ranching economies, 70 percent of Magdalena Medio's population lives in poverty because only a very small percentage of the wealth produced stays in the region (De Roux 1999, 20; 1996, 60). Seventy-nine percent of the profits from the oil, palm, and cattle-ranching economies based in Magdalena Medio end up outside of the region (De Roux 1996, 69), nourishing national and international markets, while only 21 percent benefits the local economy (De Roux 1999, 20). Conversely, all the nonmonetary value produced by small farmers in the form of agricultural food products stays in Magdalena Medio. Known as "perverse economies," oil, cattle, and palm production processes extract wealth from the region and produce riches that feed distant economic circuits. This type of economic model has created a staggering 72.84 percent unemployment and underemployment rate in the region, meaning that only 27.16 percent of the working-age population has access to a decent income (De Roux 1996, 62).[6] The resulting conditions of poverty and marginality have become "normal" in the eyes of the people who do not realize "that this normalization is a catalyst of hopelessness and violence" (De Roux 1996, 106).

The pattern has remained the same even as the industries have changed. During the 1800s poor families came looking for work in the construction of the railways,[7] good trading opportunities around the river's ports, and access to unused land. At the turn of the century, migrants arrived chasing a salary in the oil industry; in the 1960s it was work on the African palm plantations that drew the poor to the region. They also came during the 1950s and 1960s trying to flee the political violence ravaging their homeland (Murillo 1999, 51); in contrast with the consolidated and more or less homogenous cultures of the coffee region to the west, the Andean regions to the south, or the Caribbean savannas to the north, Magdalena Medio is a patchwork of diverse cultures brought by migrants (Cadavid 1996, 11, 21; Cubides, Olaya, and Ortiz 1998, 79).

The stunning beauty of the river and the kaleidoscopic scenario of human activity, phenotypes, and accents make Magdalena Medio one of those places that steals your heart. In the words of Francisco De Roux, Magdalena Medio is

People and place in Magdalena Medio. Photograph courtesy of Daniel León, 2008.

where you walk to work and spend hours at dusk chatting with neighbors on the rocking chairs that invade the sidewalk in front of your house. It is the people of Barranca, the big city, where the daily routines are marked by the sirens that establish the oil workers' shifts; where the central market comes to life before sunrise and the refinery's buses cross the new morning before six. It is the people of the great country, thousands of peasant families getting up every morning to milk the farm's two cows, bring the milk to the road, and continue their day scrutinizing corn and manioc plots every day. It is the early morning fishermen of the silent water. It is the *chalupas'* travelers on the rivers. It is the caretakers of the haciendas herding, branding, vaccinating, observing, and preparing cattle for the market. It is the loggers coming down the Magdalena's tributaries, pushing trains of logs. It is the miners of San Pedro Frío, looking like robots as they return back from the mine as the sun goes down, covered in mud from head to toe. It is the coca-leaf pickers, visiting the nearby town on Sundays to spend part of their weekly salary on beer and girlfriends. (De Roux 1999, 14)

Dissent and Activism

Since the early 1900s, the collective actions organized by the strong unions of oil workers in Magdalena Medio have had a ripple effect in the region (Romero 1998, 67). Typically, Magdalena Medio's established social movements take smaller initiatives formed in response to oppressive actions from powerful actors (the government, foreign companies, large landowners) under their wings and support and mentor them in their development. For example, in the late 1960s a small committee of local fishermen organized to protest a recent environmental law forbidding certain types of fishing in the river (Arenas Obregón 1998, 45). This group evolved, with the support and guidance of regional peasant and oil workers' unions, into the Colombian Union of Fishermen.

During the first half of the twentieth century, Magdalena Medio became known as a place "of revolutionaries," and as the epicenter of resistance in the country.[8] Powerful social justice movements in the region include organizations of peasant/farmers resisting appropriation of their land by large landowners; unions of oil, cement, and oil palm workers fighting for better working conditions for themselves and better health, education, and transportation infrastructures for everyone in the region; and urban associations seeking better public services (F. González 2006, 513; OPPDHDIH 2001, 243; Vásquez 2006, 317). In addition to these more traditional collectives, in 1996 Cadavid found dozens of women's organizations operating in Magdalena Medio (Cadavid 1996, 52). All these grassroots organizations, with their imposing size and power, have great capacities to disrupt regional and national economies by calling strikes. Strikes of the region's palm workers, train employees, cement workers, peasant organizations,[9] and oil workers are feared throughout the country. Strikers of any kind could block the main highways connecting the south and the north of the country (Murillo 1999, 52), and more troublesome still, striking oil workers could paralyze the nation because of the country's dependence on oil processed in the region's refineries in Barrancabermeja. The politically mobilized nature of the region reaches even the *desplazados,* one of the most vulnerable populations. These agricultural families displaced by armed violence in rural areas have been well organized since 1987 under an association known as ASOCIPAZ (Asociación Cívica para la Paz [Civic Association for Peace]) (Arenas Obregón 1998, 62; Vásquez 2006, 318).

The expansive character of political dissent in the region is not unique to secular concerns. The primary Catholic institution in the region is the heavily Liberation Theology–influenced Diocese of Barrancabermeja. The diocese reinforces the atmosphere of collective political action in the region by focusing its mission on strengthening grassroots organizations and networks, and empowering communities through consciousness raising, autonomy, and economic options based on solidarity (Angulo Novoa and Arboleda 2003; Cadavid 1996, 37). All of the conditions combine to make Magdalena Medio into the definitive cradle of dissent and the legal left in the country (OPPDHDIH 2001, 242). Since the 1920s, Magdalena Medio has been a tremendous guiding influence on all of Colombia's social justice organizations and movements. In dissent and organized collective actions, Magdalena Medio leads the way.

Trapped between the Guerrilla and the Paramilitary: The Lived Experience of War

According to De Roux, armed conflict in Magdalena Medio can only be understood within the historical frame of "rural development and expansion of cattle ranching and coca farming, the consolidation of the oil industry enclave, the history of migration, and the specific manner in which political actors shaped local state institutions" (De Roux 1999, 19).

The year 1965 marked the birth of the ELN in San Vicente de Chucurí, the heart of Magdalena Medio (Madariaga 2006, 49). Mutating from Rafael Rangel's Liberal guerrillas of the 1950s to a leftist guerrilla movement, the ELN made Magdalena Medio its base. Also in 1965, the Forth Front of the FARC began operating in Magdalena Medio. Guerrilla presence in the region was initially, from 1965 to about 1979, welcomed by almost everyone, because the guerrillas were the only structures keeping cattle robbers and other terrorizing bandits in line. Cattle ranchers even offered money, food, medicine, and heads of cattle to support these emerging guerrilla groups because of their stabilizing effect on the region (Madariaga 2006, 49–52; Murillo et al. 1994, 163; OPPDHDIH 2002, 87). During the 1970s and 1980s, FARC and ELN approached unions, peasant organizations, and other local social movements to offer logistical support, political education, and ad hoc alliances during key strikes (F. González 2006). Between 1980 and 1995, the memberships of ELN and FARC experienced tremendous growth. The ELN expanded from one to ten fronts (OPPDHDIH 2002, 88) and the FARC from two fronts to five (OPPDHDIH 2001, 245).

Around 1980, emboldened by their growth, massive appeal, and close alliances with social justice movements, ELN and FARC shifted their goals from cultivating ideological support to achieving military control. ELN and FARC focused on gaining influence over territories and civilians, amassing fortunes from kidnap ransom (cattle ranchers were favorite kidnap targets), taxing coca cultivation and processing operations, and demanding a cut from municipal budgets. Although both FARC and ELN have strong presence in Magdalena Medio, the latter was responsible for 63.2 percent of all guerrilla actions between 1990 and 2000, while FARC was responsible for a smaller 25 percent (OPPDHDIH 2002, 89).

During the 1980s Magdalena Medio's civilian communities witnessed their lives spiraling down into a state of generalized terror brought on by increasing political violence between the left and the right. In the early years of the decade, many cattle ranchers, tired of dealing with guerrilla kidnappings, taxes, and bribes, sold their land to millionaire drug traffickers looking for laundering strategies (Cadavid 1996, 33, 38; A. Murillo in press). Certain areas such as the Serranía de San Lucas and the south of Bolívar began growing coca and processing cocaine. Drug traffickers began infiltrating the regional social spheres of Magdalena Medio "by purchasing land, financing illegal militias, and influencing local politics" (Madariaga 2006, 43). Born as a response to leftist guerrillas, the first known paramilitary groups known in the country emerged in Puerto Boyacá (Vásquez 2006, 335) and Puerto Berrío (Cubides, Olaya, and Ortiz 1998, 81), both located in Magdalena Medio, around 1982.

Different organizations closely allied with drug lords and/or cattle barons, such as Muerte a Secuestradores (MAS) [Death to Kidnappers] and Movimiento de Restauración Nacional (MORENA) [National Restoration Movement], began subsidizing extreme right-wing militias to combat the leftist guerrillas (Murillo et al. 1994, 167; Vásquez 2006, 335). There is plenty of evidence to demonstrate that the Colombian armed forces and police frequently supported these private armies (Madariaga 2006, 50; Vásquez 2006, 331).[10] One of Murillo's interviewees recounts that "drug traffickers formed alliances with cattle hacienda owners and the army to annihilate communists. The alliances made contributions of two hundred thousand pesos each to hire local young men, who were paid a sixty thousand peso monthly salary and given a Toyota SUV and machine guns, and offered training at the paramilitary school called 081 in Puerto Boyacá" (Murillo et al. 1994, 170).

The paramilitary organizations and self-defense organizations are made up of many different small private armies, groups and militias, but they all maintain basically unified military goals driven by radical conservative values and antiguerrilla agendas. Initially these groups sought to destroy the existing social fabric of the region. After this was accomplished, they focused on gaining complete control over the general population, and most recently they have been trying to gain social and political legitimacy by imposing a new social fabric shaped by their own values (CREDHOS 2002, 11). The paramilitaries believed the existing social structure was leftist and in support of guerrilla organizations. In their attempts to destroy this allegedly leftist social fabric that supposedly supported guerrilla organizations, the paramilitaries broadly targeted any and all people and organizations they suspected of leftist leanings. Newspaper kiosks were monitored to identify readers of the Colombian Communist Party weekly *Voz Proletaria* [Proletariat Voice], and the party offices in Barrancabermeja were observed to identify frequent visitors (Murillo et al. 1994, 167).[11]

During the 1990s, paramilitary groups took control of significant resources in the region including coca cultivation as well as gold mining in the south of Bolívar, gasoline black markets (known as gasoline cartels) (Vásquez 2006, 335), and extortion of oil and palm industries (OPPDHDIH 2001, 248; 2002, 94). Some analysts believe the wealth of resources in Magdalena Medio has made the region a magnet for armed groups (OPPDHDIH 2002, 86). During the 1990s, as paramilitary groups gained strength, the guerrillas began to retreat into isolated wilderness areas, leaving social movements, grassroots organizations, local governments,[12] and civilians at the mercy of the paramilitaries' brutal violence (OPPDHDIH 2001, 243; Vásquez 2006, 323). Madariaga explains, "Civilians felt that the guerrillas left them in the hands of the *paras;* the civilians were the ones getting killed, not the guerrillas; they felt the guerrilla had used them as cover" (Madariaga 2006, 69). The leaders of social movements in the region were particularly targeted by the paramilitaries. In 1995, during negotiations between palm oil union leaders and the palm oil companies, union leaders received recurrent threats and harassment, and eleven workers were assassinated. Three years later, in October 1998, the palm oil workers' union president was assassinated and seven members of the board had to leave the region after receiving death threats. In March of 1999 the new union president was also assassinated, and the remaining board members were forced out of the region. This assassination was the effective end of any real activity in the union at Indupalma, a large palm oil company (Madariaga 2006, 77–78).

Paramilitary groups in Magdalena Medio promoted a sectarian, rightist ideology that intersected with some of the most radical conservative movements in the country. An example of these extremist views can be found in an early pamphlet authored by a paramilitary group allied with Tradición, Familia y Propiedad [Tradition, Family, and Property]. The pamphlet states that "to purchase arms for collective self-defense, and to shoot and kill someone who is supposedly an unarmed guerrilla is not just philosophically correct and legal, but also virtuous in religious terms" (Madariaga 2006, 55).

The phenomenon of paramilitary groups imposing orthodox Catholicism and patriarchal and authoritarian ideologies onto civilian communities is repeated in many regions of Colombia. This pattern was painfully evident in the Magdalena Medio region. In the late 1990s paramilitary groups distributed a fifteen-point pamphlet in the city of Barrancabermeja regulating when minors could be on the street, how late bars could stay open, who could be armed, who could gamble, who could wear military uniforms, and how people should maintain their homes, garbage, yards, pets, and farm animals. The document made school obligatory for minors and stressed respect for private property. The pamphlet specified penalties for the violation of each prohibition and rule. The punishments ranged from fines and sanctions to exile from the region (see the entire document in Martha Cecilia García 2006, 310–11). Cases of spouses being beaten publicly as punishment for infidelity or domestic violence were reported as one instance of the penalties doled out by the paramilitary leaders for infractions of the code detailed in the pamphlet (CREDHOS 2002, 12).

During my fieldwork between 2004 and 2007, the extensive paramilitary control of social and cultural life was very obvious. One December evening in 2005, I was at a café on the river in the magnificent colonial city of Mompox. I was meeting with a group of citizens' media leaders from the region, including several from the community radio stations in Magdalena Medio. As is common among community radio producers, they carried a selection of their favorite music on

CDs. They asked the café's owner to let them play their music and she acquiesced. They began to play classic salsa on the café's stereo. This kind of music is known in Colombia for its politicized lyrics and connotations of dissent, leftover from the 1970s when salsa became the favorite music of Colombian progressives and intellectuals. As we listened, a loud SUV with tinted windows arrived suddenly outside. Three men with military haircuts and sunglasses came into the café and sat at a table close by, immediately demanding that the owner change the music, back to the usual *vallenato* music.[13] My friends simply said, "it's time to go."

The decade between 1990 and 2000 was a time of extreme brutality, terror, and uncertainty in Magdalena Medio. By the end of the 1990s, the northern section of the region was controlled by the ELN and the FARC, while the south had become one of the main paramilitary strongholds in the country. The city of Barrancabermeja straddles the boundary between the north and the south (Cubides, Olaya, and Ortiz 1998, 82), which made it a prime military goal, resulting in barbaric violence for civilians living in the city, trapped between guerrillas and paramilitary forces. On May 16, 1998, the paramilitary group known as Autodefensas de Santander y del Sur del Cesar (AUSAC) [Self-Defense Forces of Santander and the South of Cesar] assassinated eleven people and kidnapped twenty-five more in the city's western district (Madariaga 2006, 66; Romero 1999, 69; Vásquez 2006, 338); days later, AUSAC distributed a communiqué stating that those detained had been tried and killed, their bodies incinerated and thrown to the Magdalena River. This violent attack on civilians, known as the "Barranca massacre," sent shock waves through the region (Vásquez 2006, 338–39) and marked the beginning of a cycle of spiraling violence. Paramilitary groups began a three-year military campaign of brutality. They terrorized civilians and assassinated, tortured, disappeared, and threatened dozens of community leaders, members of unions, and grassroots organizations in an effort to take control of the city's neighborhoods away from guerrilla organizations. As each neighborhood or municipality was occupied by paramilitary or guerrilla groups, the civilians living in the area became stigmatized as *guerrilleros* or *paras*. These identities are rarely voluntarily adopted but ascribed by others outside the community (Archila 2006, 501). Between January 1999 and September 2001, 550 incidents of political armed violence were recorded in the city (OPPDHDIH 2001, 245). In 2000, 403 assassinations took place in Barrancabermeja alone (a 55 percent increase from the 260 committed on 1999), bringing the homicide rate to 206 homicides per 100,000 inhabitants (OPPDHDIH 2001, 248; 2002, 99).[14] Between 1996 and 2000 the kidnapping rate reached 36 per 100,000 inhabitants in the region, while the kidnapping rate for the entire country (one of the highest in the world) was 8.8 kidnappings per 100,000 inhabitants (OPPDHDIH 2002, 95). By March 2001, only one and a half out of seven city districts were not under paramilitary control (Martha Cecilia García 2006, 303). The region was being occupied and overtaken by the war between paramilitaries, guerrillas, and the armed forces. Between 2002 and 2004, the Centro de Investigación y Educación Popular (CINEP) [Center for Popular Research and Education], a well-known Colombian NGO, documented 162 political assassinations in the region, of which the paramilitaries were responsible for 141 (Observatorio de Paz Integral 2005, 11–13).

Testimonies gathered by historian Amparo Murillo describe the state of generalized terror that descended on the region: "The dead turned up in empty lots, roads, and ditches; they floated down the river like logs. At some point no one was willing to go identify the bodies for fear that they would be next. People were afraid to claim their dead, and only the next of kin came to the wakes and funerals. There were instances of funerals attended by two people. The bodies could not be counted in this tempest of death. We lived through weekends of thirty deaths" (Murillo et al. 1994, 167). The armed violence and brutal dispute between paramilitaries and guerrillas over territory, wealth, and civilian "support" had tremendous impact on civilians. From 1990 to 2001, attacks on civilians made up 66 percent of all armed violence in the region. Only 34 percent of armed violence targeted armed groups (Vásquez 2006, 346). The paramilitary, responsible for 45.7 percent of all attacks against civilians in Magdalena Medio between 1990 and 2002, are clearly the primary culprit in attacks on unarmed communities. The second most culpable group is ELN, responsible for 27.4 percent of all attacks against civilians, and the responsibility for the remaining attacks is shared by the Colombian armed forces (12.8 percent), FARC (7.4 percent), and other guerrillas (6.6 percent) (Vásquez 2006, 349). According to De Roux, the war costs Magdalena Medio 15 million dollars a month (De Roux 1999, 20).

Traveling in Magdalena Medio feels very different from traveling in Montes de María or Caquetá, as in these latter places evidence abounds of a territory in dispute. The landscapes are not as militarized in Magdalena Medio; army checkpoints are not as common; and there are no barricades on bridges or around police stations in towns and cities. Though the military presence is less overt, I am able to see and feel the degree of paramilitary control in the contained dress and behavior of the young people. I hear *vallenatos* or *corridos* played incessantly on the radio and peoples' home stereos, while other music genres, including salsa, rock, and hip-hop, are scarce. In conversation, when people discuss paramilitaries, they eliminate any specific subject from their sentence construction, as in *"they* were here." Locals refer to paramilitaries as *ellos* (them). Some of Magdalena Medio's character of dissent has persisted through the paramilitary presence, as I see in the huge billboards set up by the Organización Femenina Popular [Popular Feminine Organization] displaying its messages: "women don't have sons and daughters for war" and "ideas are stronger than weapons."

Women don't have sons and daughters for war. Photograph courtesy of Organización Femenina Popular.

Territory and Development

In 1995, in an attempt to curb the mounting armed violence and social unrest in Magdalena Medio, several institutions, including ECOPE-TROL, the Diocese of Barrancabermeja, and CINEP developed the PDPMM (see http://www.pdpmm.org.co/), a comprehensive development project for the region. The PDPMM is an experiment in regional development, attempting to tackle all the needs and hopes of local communities simultaneously. Inspired in part by the economic theories of Amartya Sen (De Roux 1999, 34), the PDPMM shelters three hundred initiatives that stimulate local economies; strengthen civic participation and consensus building in local and regional decision-making processes; rebuild transportation, energy, health, and education infrastructures; encourage local cultures; and nurture pluralism, diversity, and tolerance.[15] A program document reads: "The long-term objective of the PDPMM is to increase social capital and empower citizens, leading to a significant reduction in poverty and an increase in peaceful coexistence in the Magdalena Medio region" (World Bank 2004, 4).

As mentioned above, Magdalena Medio has no official territorial status. The territory known as Magdalena Medio comprises municipalities from four different departments—and sometimes five or six, depending on who is defining the region. In setting the boundaries for this regional development program, the PDPMM played a significant role in demarcating territorial boundaries and consolidating the Magdalena Medio as a region with its own map and its own identity (Rodríguez and Cadavid 2007). In the 1960s, long before PDPMM became a presence in the region, the Colombian armed forces coined the term Magdalena Medio to label this region that was already prone to social and political unrest (Murillo 1999, 43). Later, the Catholic Church created the Diocese of Barrancabermeja in an effort to strengthen its presence in the territories on the margin of the existing central dioceses. The Diocese of Barrancabermeja, like Magdalena Medio, comprises municipalities from four different departments (see also Cadavid 1996, 9, for Diocese of Barrancabermeja and Magdalena Medio origin). Colombian historian Fernán González argues that Magdalena Medio exists as a region only because the armed forces, the Catholic Church, and the PDPMM have set the boundaries, created maps, and normalized the use of the term "Magdalena Medio" (F. González 2006, 512).

The PDPMM completed a comprehensive diagnosis of the region's problems in 1996. The group made strengthening civil society, the public sphere, and democratic participation in local and regional decision-making processes among the top priorities for the region (De Roux 1996, 102). The theoretical underpinnings of the PDPMM are firmly rooted in a strong critique of theories of development understood merely as economic growth. The PDPMM insisted, in contrast to economic-growth-only theories, on the need to address ethical and cultural values as part of its mandate. Thus, since its inception, the PDPMM defined one of its goals as the need "to strengthen a shared sense of belonging, and produce cultural symbols that can unify" (Cadavid 1996, 13). In an effort to address the need for an ethical education in the region, the PDPMM insisted that citizens had to define a set of rights and responsibilities to be applied to all community members and be backed by law. The definition and implementation of these rights and responsibilities would protect the common good and end private control of public resources (by economic and political elites as well as armed groups), reinstating direct participation of citizens in resource-management decision making (Romero 1999, 67). "Either we all participate in the collective construction of the region or the Magdalena Medio will be destroyed" (De Roux 1999, 36), were the dramatic words used by Francisco De Roux, critical economist, Jesuit priest, and director of the PDPMM from its founding until 2008. With this statement he sought to emphasize the urgency of creating a diverse civil society that is open to dialogue and committed to the "complete sovereignty of the public sphere." De Roux saw this as the only hope for ending armed conflict and poverty (De Roux 1999). Over the years, the PDPMM has become integrated into the complex social fabric of Magdalena Medio. At the time of writing, it is difficult to accurately assess the work of the program. On one hand, the PDPMM succeeded in carving out an alternative social, political, and cultural sphere centered on peaceful coexistence, sustainable development, and local participatory democracies. On the other hand, armed violence, intimidation, and terror still run rampant in the region. In 2003 a PDPMM report to the World Bank (one of its funding agencies) mentioned the assassination of twenty individuals associated with the program (World Bank 2004, 11). In April 2008, the Black Eagles, a paramilitary group, threatened the PDPMM, warning that the program's personnel would be "exterminated one by one" (AREDMAG 2008).

Five nascent community radio stations were included in the PDPMM's 1996 inventory of Magdalena Medio's resources.[16] The Ministry of Communications had granted community broadcasting licenses to the Catholic parish of each municipality. The close alliance between the PDPMM and the Diocese led then-bishop Jaime Prieto Amaya to encourage these radio stations to serve the communication and grassroots participation goals of the PDPMM (Durán, Quijano and Gómez Ditta in press), more than religious proselytism. Local priests also played key roles in shifting the identities of the stations from religious radio to true community communication. A Puerto Wilches priest said, "I intend to empower this community so that they take ownership over the radio station. I want to give the station back to the people, so that if one day I have to leave, the people will be able to take over this project" (Durán, Quijano, and Gómez Ditta in press).

The Leading Characters of Magdalena Medio's Citizens' Radio

In the twelve years since 1995, the PDPMM adopted Magdalena Medio's community radio stations as one of the program's primary communication and culture initiatives. The stations, numbering fifteen today,[17] have received funding, training, equipment, and other types of support from the PDPMM through development grants. Although each station operates autonomously, together the radio stations form the network known as AREDMAG. Apart from the fifteen participating community radio stations, AREDMAG also includes seven school radio stations and eleven production collectives.[18] In keeping with the PDPMM's goals of peacebuilding and poverty reduction in Magdalena Medio, AREDMAG's radio stations developed what they call an "ethical pact." In their own words, AREDMAG's radio producers declare that "even though media are mere tools, they can be used to promote new visions, narratives, languages, sensibilities, and modes of being and thinking, toward new ways to shape our region" (Durán, Quijano, and Gómez Ditta in press).

In 2006 Omaira Arrieta and Julio Hoyos were my hosts in Puerto Wilches, a port town and home of Puerto Wilches Estéreo, one of AREDMAG's oldest community radio stations. They have been married for many years, have three kids, and juggle a busy schedule of

Radio is part of everyday life in Magdalena Medio. Photograph courtesy of Daniel León, 2008.

parenting responsibilities, participation in community development activities (part of the PDPMM), and their roles as community radio producers. In 2004, during my fieldwork in Magdalena Medio, Omaira was the director of Puerto Wilches Estéreo and Julio was the president of AREDMAG's board of directors. From the time he was a teenager, Julio was a fan of ham radio, and he later made a living as an electronic technician. It was his involvement in local politics, however, that drew him into community radio. When the PDPMM began implementing its program to support community communication, Julio was a member of Puerto Wilches' Municipal Council. As a result of his affinity for electronics and information technology, Julio was invited to one of the initial meetings the PDPMM held in each of the five municipalities (at that time, around 1996) with a community radio station (Hoyos 2004). Since then, his involvement and commitment to community radio has only grown.

Omaira told me how she entered the world of community radio:

> Since I was a little girl I wondered about radio. While my mother listened to her radio soaps, I wondered, "How do they do it?" I got a degree in something that has nothing to do with media: biology . . . then I got married and Julio was already involved with radio and things like that. He was a ham

radio aficionado. Later, he got involved with the community radio station here and one day he told me they were beginning to broadcast. I was intrigued, but I didn't have the courage to go see for myself until a week later. I decided to go to the station and they asked me to speak, and I really liked it. I realized there were no women participating, so it became my own personal challenge to get women involved in all of AREDMAG's radio stations. (Arrieta 2004)

Like Omaira and Julio, Magdalena Medio's community radio producers, station directors, managers, administrators, and programmers come from all walks of life. They are biologists, electronic technicians, heavy machinery operators, watch repair experts, farmers, and fishermen. They gravitate toward community radio because they want to make a difference and shape their communities' future. When asked, "What brought you to the community radio station?" they respond in many ways: "what moves us is the people," "we want to feel connected to the community," "the drive to empathize with others," "the feeling of being one with the community," "the ability to express the community's needs and wants," "the feeling that I can create, create in order to change something, to shape, to correct something" (AREDMAG Radio Producers 2004).

Orley Durán, one of the youngest members of AREDMAG's board, recalls his transition from community theater to community radio:

I have always felt that San Vicente de Chucurí is located in a very fortunate place because it includes three different altitudes, and thus three different climate zones. This diversity produces a vast variety of cultures, from the farmers of the highlands to the lowland fishing communities of the marshes. This means very different ways to feel life, including different customs, food, etc. When I came to the radio station, from the world of theater, I wanted to use radio to reflect everything we have here in Vicente de Chucurí . . . that was my initial proposal, to cultivate the cultural diversity and spaces of coexistence in San Vicente through art and culture. (Durán 2004)

Orley comes from a typical Magdalena Medio municipality, where a broken geography creates different lifestyles and cultural values. In places like San Vicente de Chucurí, it is common to hear lowland *Chucureños* refer to their highland neighbors as "cloud-eaters." One of the challenges facing Magdalena Medio's community radio producers is that of cultivating among audiences an attitude of embracing the region's very different cultural identities as a way of creating a collective imaginary, a notion of an "us" that, despite geographic diversity and cultural heterogeneity, can draw from the region's incredible richness to build a more peaceful future.

Bright blue walls are a joyful backdrop to my conversation with Sofi Torrenegra, a teacher and leader of a children's radio initiative in Simití, on the eastern bank of the Magdalena River. Sofi's house is painted a bright cobalt blue and filled with plants. Each bedroom offers an inviting hammock hanging over the bed. Sofi welcomed me into her house during my fieldwork in Simití in 2005 and she told me about the ways in which her life and her deep commitment to her students intersect with community radio. The radio programs produced by Sofi and her elementary school–age students are a combination of local music and discourses from kids about everything that affects them, from popular culture to the war around. Sofi describes the first time she witnessed children's metamorphoses provoked by their participation in the local community radio station. Having written a book about the subject, I know well what she is talking about (Rodríguez 2001).

When I question her about how and where her team produces the radio programs, she invites me to her bedroom and opens a well-secured cabinet. Here she shows me several digital recorders, professional-looking microphones, and earphones, along with all the small cables and widgets radio producers always carry with them. I am surprised that she keeps this equipment locked in her house and not at the community radio station; Sofi responds that if she left it at the radio station, it would be stolen in a flash. Through grants and a lot of hard work, she acquired the necessary technology for her kids to produce their programming; and she is not willing to see it disappear. This example of theft in the community radio station emphasizes something I mentioned in the book's introduction: though they generally possess noble goals, citizens' media projects can't be romanticized. AREDMAG's stations are plagued by negative and corrosive dynamics. Participants abuse their access to equipment, CDs, and other project resources, and the stations are frequently off the air for days and even weeks because technology fails and the funds reserved for maintenance have "disappeared." Not only Magdalena Medio's but most Colombian community media can easily see a revolving door of volunteer radio producers who never get off the ground and quickly burn out. Sometimes community media have highly creative radio producers and terrible administrators, and other times they have highly efficient administrators and boring media producers. Community media are rarely financially sustainable. They are sometimes coopted by local religious or political figures who use them as proselytizing tools, and some become for-profit initiatives behind a community communication facade.

Although I am well aware of the problematic, negative features of community media, three elements drive me to focus my research on the positives: first, the literature on alternative/community/citizens' media has already compiled more than enough evidence of community radio's problems, challenges, and barriers (Downing et al. 2001; Geertz, Van Oeyen, and Villamayor 2004; Gumucio Dagron 2001; Howley 2005; Langlois and Dubois 2005; Lewis 1984; O'Connor 2004; Opel and Pompper 2003; Rodríguez 2001); second, even with all of these problems, the stations frequently facilitate, cultivate, or nurture social and cultural processes with great potential for unarmed civilian communities under siege by armed groups; and third, while we know so much about the barriers and liabilities of citizens' media, we understand very little about the roles that these media can play in contexts of armed conflict.

Radio for Peacebuilding

Magdalena Medio provides an excellent laboratory in which to witness what anthropologist of war and famine Paul Richards says about armed conflict: "War is about casting social restraint to the winds" (Richards 1992, 4). The social fabric of Magdalena Medio has been devastatingly unraveled by more than fifty years of continuous government neglect and political violence. Despite a tremendous potential for wealth, public resources are managed by private interests, leaving a disempowered majority in poverty, while economic elites, leaders of armed groups, and corrupt government officials amass land and money, control political processes (local elections, municipal budgets, and municipal development programs), regulate social life (controlling public and private behavior), and impose cultural norms (values, popular culture, music, fashion, media) (Cubides, Olaya, and Ortiz 1998, 84). Echoing Carolyn Nordstrom's words, armed groups cultivate a social fabric that is "Illegal. Informal. Illicit. Gray-market. Brown-market. Extra-state. Extra-legal. Underground. Unregulated. Subterranean. Clandestine. Shadows" (Nordstrom 2004, 35).

Radio producers at La Original Estéreo, Simití. Photograph courtesy of Daniel León, 2008.

When people feel they can't trust local democratic institutions, they respond by seeking protection from a patron as the way to access at least a crumb of the region's resources. Amparo Cadavid goes so far as to say that in Magdalena Medio, "patron–client relationships are the only known type of relationship between individuals and the state" (Cadavid 1996, 97). According to De Roux, the number one element contributing to the high level of violence in the region is generalized legal impunity. He writes that "common criminality is not penalized. The armed groups are not either. Neither guerrillas, nor paramilitaries nor the military are controlled by the judicial system. Thus, taking justice in one's own hands is a normalized mode of operation" (De Roux 1996, 101). The normalization of arms and militarized, violent regulation of social life permeates Magdalena Medio even at the core of civilian, unarmed communities (F. González 2006, 564). A local testimony cited by Ingrid Bolívar aptly describes this state of affairs: "Here, if someone is not clearly in power, everyone acts his own way and there's too much fighting. Now [with the paramilitary] there are no fights, because if you don't do what they tell you to, you'll suffer the consequences. It has to be this way with people, because people don't understand and they do as they please. . . . [N]o one follows any rules. Here everything has to be done through force [*a las malas*]" (Bolívar 2006, 449). Drawing from her fieldwork in Sri Lanka's war zones, Nordstrom found a similar knowledge system, which one of her informants expressed in the following terms: "I tell you, the only way to solve these problems is to be the strongest, the most forceful" (Nordstrom 1992, 269).

AREDMAG's main success story has been its erosion of this type of perverse "social contract." Through my fieldwork in Magdalena Medio, I learned to identify several ways in which AREDMAG's radio stations disrupt the complex negative influence war has had on the social and cultural fabric of communities, with particularly interesting results in the realm of local governance and citizen political participation. Sandwiched between a social and political context of armed violence, impunity, and corruption on one side, and the PDPMM's framework of participation and accountability on the other, these citizens' radio stations put their energy toward strengthening good governance, government transparency and accountability, citizen participation in local decision-making processes, strong public spheres, and processes of mediation.

I also learned to identify the areas the stations acknowledge lie beyond their mandate, which include journalistic coverage of armed conflict and peace agreements among armed groups. AREDMAG's radio producers know that information about regional and national armed conflict is a minefield. Any news program mentioning one of the armed groups in the region can turn the station and everyone working there into a military target. Anything said about armed conflict or armed groups can be reinterpreted, misconstrued, and so forth; thus, Magdalena Medio's community radio stations avoid armed conflict journalistic coverage, news, and information. Even though most of AREDMAG's stations' programming grids include news programs, armed conflict coverage is almost nonexistent. Instead, journalistic programs focus on the everyday life in the communities that goes on *despite* armed conflict. Instead of traditional "war reporting," the stations focus on the consequences of war on the lives of civilians. For example, programming will chronicle the lives of forcefully displaced families, rather than reporting on the parties in conflict that cause the displacement. Navigating this ephemeral boundary between what they can and cannot "get away with" on the air is the sole way the radio stations ensure their survival. In chapter 4 I will further explore the question of how Colombian citizens' media manage to maintain their autonomy from armed groups. In the case of AREDMAG, radio stations learned that news and information about armed conflict does not exhaust their role in Magdalena Medio. Citizens' media leaders know well there are other and perhaps more significant functions for a community radio station in a context of armed conflict.

Even though the stations frequently act as mediators in community conflicts, they do not attempt to mediate between armed groups. As in most citizens' media cases examined in this book, AREDMAG's leaders know that the place of the stations is among unarmed civilians. Mediating among armed groups, brokering peace negotiations between the state and the guerrillas, or between the government and the paramilitaries, is not one of AREDMAG's goals. Instead, these citizens' media pioneers have decided that the stations should be at the service of those who have no weapons. They use technology to buffer civilian communities from the impacts of war and protect a social space where everyday conflicts are solved in nonviolent ways. They seek to cultivate a social fabric led by ethical principles of inclusion, participation, and empowerment, in which difference is embraced.

Radio for the people, not for the armed groups. Photograph courtesy of Daniel León, 2008.

In Magdalena Medio, community radio is not used to confront directly violence and war; instead, AREDMAG's stations "steal" a social and political space from war. This alternate space exists alongside war-permeated social, cultural, and political processes, producing what can be described as a "parallel reality." Thus, in the same municipality, social dynamics dictated by violence, impunity, corruption, and exclusion live next to social processes driven by accountability, transparency, participation, and inclusion. Day after day, the stations' directors, programmers, and administrators struggle to expand their sphere of influence a little more. In this continuous push and pull, public spaces, social processes, people (especially youth and children), and cultural practices are stolen from war in one moment and lost again to war in another.

In 2004 I collaborated on an evaluation study of AREDMAG. One of the study's methodologies asked respondents to draw how they experience their participation in their local community radio station. When asked why the visual representation of her lived experience as a community radio producer did not include any images of war, radio producer Sofi Torrenegra, from Simití, among the most violent municipalities in Magdalena Medio, responded: "I did not come here to talk about war, but about radio, something very peaceful, very beautiful . . . and I don't know about others, but what I experience when I'm working with radio is life, not death. It's the joy, and that's what I represented in my drawing" (Torrenegra 2004).

AREDMAG's community radio producers build strong cultural identities and solid public spheres for collective expression of a shared vision for the future, which can be realized through generalized political participation at the local level. According to a regional study, in Magdalena Medio people respond to armed violence with strategies that range from survival (keeping a low profile and continuing with everyday life the best you can), to resistance (organizing to reject the presence of armed groups in communities), to denial (blaming the media for the "bad image" it gives the region), to fear (hiding in isolation and mistrusting everyone), to support (legitimizing violence as the only way to protect rights and property), and to finding alternatives (Vásquez 2006). This last one, found most popular in the Magdalena Medio region, describes the attitude of those behind AREDMAG's radio stations: "The insatiable search to resolve conflict through dialogue, regional identity, democratic citizen participation, strong democratic institutions, and solid ethics centered on human dignity and people's ability and right to shape their own future" (Vásquez 2006, 360).

The emergence of this "ethics of citizenship," this feeling that a participatory democracy is the only light at the end of the tunnel, is partly the result, according to political scientist Mauricio Romero, of the powerful presence of radicalized social justice movements in the region: "Radical movements have contributed to the development of a citizenship ethics that is secular, linked to the middle classes, and with notions of citizenship that are more open and participatory than those espoused by [traditional bipartisan] liberal/conservative ones" (Romero 1998, 67).

In the following pages I present more specific instances of how AREDMAG's community radio stations seek to achieve these ends. Throughout my fieldwork in Magdalena Medio I witnessed many instances similar to the ones highlighted here; for the sake of conciseness, I focus only on a few salient examples.

Cultivating Good Governance, Transparency, and Local Accountability

On a hot day in October 2004, I hang out at Puerto Wilches Estéreo. Omaira, Julio, and Leonel are busy packing up microphones, earphones, and cables. They are preparing the transmission of what is known in Magdalena Medio as a Rendición de Cuentas (loosely translated as "presentation of the books"). The Rendición de Cuentas is a public event in which local authorities, led by the mayor, explain how they have spent the municipal budget over the past six months.

Once the equipment is ready, we walk outside, flag moto-taxis (motorcycles that function as local taxis), and speed through the sticky streets to a nearby school. I do my best to pitch in and help set up cables and microphones. Puerto Wilches Estéreo's mobile unit is under a large tree on the school's central patio. I can see a long cable snaking far behind a wall, and the console rests on a cement bench. Omaira and Julio share the microphone as they introduce listeners to what is about to begin. The national anthem starts playing, and we all stand up and look formal. Next, the departmental anthem of Santander plays, followed by the anthem of Puerto Wilches. About a dozen local government authorities sit around a long table on a stage with the mayor sitting in the middle. The scene reminds me of the popular paintings of the Last Supper that are frequently found in Colombian living rooms. The table faces an audience of approximately three hundred people, who have come to listen to the mayor's explanation of his fiscal management over the last half year.

Rendiciones de Cuentas have become common events throughout Magdalena Medio. The PDPMM defines two of its goals as increasing the influence of citizens in local and regional development and cultivating responsiveness and accountability in local institutions (World Bank 2004, 4). To achieve these goals, the PDPMM attempts to implement a strong participatory democracy as an alternative to the traditional system of representative democracy that is so plagued by corruption, bribery, and impunity. In 2004, twenty-six of the twenty-nine municipalities in the region had a Núcleo de Pobladores, or Citizens' Council, open to everyone in the community and responsible for designing a municipal development agenda (World Bank 2004, 8). It is the Núcleos that pressure municipal governments to hold town hall meetings and present the results of the government plans in public view. In 2003 "six municipal governments held such town hall meetings; none had done so previously" (World Bank 2004, 8).

Puerto Wilches Estéreo amplifies the town hall meeting to the entire municipality. Farmers in their fields, fishermen on their boats, health practitioners, teachers, and mothers caring for their children can listen to the mayor and his cabinet. Omaira, Julio, Leonel, and everyone else at Puerto Wilches Estéreo share the PDPMM's vision of local citizens actively engaged in the public administration and management of local resources. The radio station functions in the service of this emerging participatory democratic process.[19]

Later during the night of the Rendición de Cuentas, over dinner and a beer, Julio tells me that when the mayor procrastinates and does not call a timely Rendición de Cuentas, the radio station reminds him that it's time. Julio and his colleagues have selected an annoyingly high-pitched crow-like cry to mark these calls for attention. Every time listeners hear the crow, they know that Puerto Wilches Estéreo is slapping the hand of the mayor: "Mr. (or Ms) Mayor, it's time for a Rendición de Cuentas!"

I found several other instances in which AREDMAG's radio stations put pressure on local authorities, demanding transparency and accountability. Every day, at six in the morning, Simití Original Estéreo broadcasts *Chachareando* [Chatting], a program designed to encourage citizens' oversight of public services. The producer describes the program this way: "That's where people can ask those who are responsible why is it that only a year after an investment of 200 million pesos the new street pavement is already bursting" (Simití Radio Producer 2004). In Puerto Nare, a producer notes: "After a huge flood caused by a broken pipe, the people did not go to the mayor's office, they came to the radio station, so when the mayor saw that we were actually paying attention to people's complaints, he had to get moving with a solution" (Puerto Nare Radio Producer 2004). Several of AREDMAG's other stations have similar programs.

A recent study developed by the World Bank's Communication for Governance and Accountability in postconflict contexts found that nurturing positive relationships between citizens and the state is a key element of sustainable peace. The study affirms that "the nature of postconflict environments poses unique governance challenges. As a consequence of state abuse and exclusion, people have little or no trust in the fair functioning of state institutions and rely on personal networks: tribe, clan, family, religious groups. The fabric of society is torn by displacement and fighting, with non-state actors playing an important role in the absence of a functioning state" (Von Kalternborg-Stachau 2008, 5). With programs that focus and insist on local government

Citizens' journalism. Photograph courtesy of Daniel León, 2008.

officials' transparency and accountability, AREDMAG's stations contribute to improving trust and confidence of communities on their government.

Strengthening Local Participatory Democracies

In 1997 local elections became military targets for the ELN, who were trying to disrupt the democratic process. This guerrilla organization forbade people to vote and announced that anyone who voted would face negative consequences. At the same time, the ELN kidnapped close to fifteen candidates in electoral races for mayor or for municipal councils, intimidating several candidates into abandoning the race. In the Magdalena Medio municipality of San Pablo, the newly elected mayor was kidnapped by the ELN and pressured to resign. After he was freed, he continued to resist the guerrilla's intimidation in his role as mayor, only to be assassinated less than two years later (Madariaga 2006, 71). In 2000, during local and gubernatorial elections, twenty mayoral candidates were assassinated; according to the *Christian Science Monitor:* "facing threats from leftist guerrilla groups or the right-wing paramilitary forces, at least twenty-four mayoral candidates and sixty-four local council candidates—not to mention three candidates for governor of Colombian 'departments'—have pulled out of their races" (LaFranchi 2000). Gilberto Toro, director of the Colombian Federation of Municipalities stated that half of the 1,093 mayors faced real threats in 2000 (LaFranchi 2000). This type of violent takeover of local electoral processes was the result of a guerrilla military strategy in place since the late 1990s that seeks to sabotage regional and local electoral processes in order to erode any type of state or institutional presence in their areas of influence, thus consolidating a kind of "parallel power" (Vásquez 2006, 366).

In an attempt to reappropriate local elections from the control of armed groups, the PDPMM has implemented the Programmatic Vote, a type of work session in which mayoral candidates present their government platforms and make public commitments to their implementation if elected. In 2003 fifteen such sessions took place among mayoral candidates and their constituencies (World Bank 2004). In municipalities served by one of AREDMAG's community radio stations, this type of peacebuilding initiative was supported by the live transmission of the Programmatic Vote sessions. One election at a time, citizens' radio stations reinstate the legitimacy of the democratic process, and offer it up as an alternative to the normalized way of "getting things done" in the region through violence and/or corruption. Adamant about preventing violence and aggression from "stealing" their local elections, AREDMAG's radio producers commonly defuse conflict among political candidates as the following testimony from the municipality of Gamarra narrates:

> What I have drawn here is three political personalities, three candidates in the forthcoming election for mayor in our municipality; and every time they talked to each other, or met in a public space, they began insulting each other. I drew little red bombs under them because the situation was becoming a time bomb in our community. Seeing this, the youth collective at the radio station decided to organize what became known as the First Forum for Democracy in Gamarra. We wanted to find ways to enhance peaceful coexistence in the municipality; that is one of our objectives. The three candidates agreed to come to the station and the forum began at nine in the morning. It was supposed to end at ten, but the conversation was so exciting that the forum kept going until twelve thirty, and the three candidates, who had insulted each other just ten minutes before the forum started, left the station arm in arm. Here [in my drawing] you can see them draped in the yellow, green, and white of Gamarra's flag. How did we accomplish this? Well, as the dialogue began, we realized that the three candidates had all gone to high school together, so they began remembering all their escapades, like when they skipped school together to go to the river, or to play pool; this changed the mood of the conversation. They felt at ease with each other, they began looking at each other as human beings, and not just as rivals in a political race. We managed to lower the violent tone among them and cultivate a more fraternal relationship. A woman, and schoolteacher is the director of this program. She works with the radio production youth collective, and the way she conducted the interview was key to our success. (Gamarra Radio Producer 2004)[20]

In this case, the woman who directed the program made impromptu decisions as the program was developing. Originally, the station's youth collective was supposed to begin interviewing the three candidates with soft questions, to then pass the baton to senior producers responsible for asking more serious questions about the candidates' political platforms. However, once the director detected how the candidates were finding common ground around their responses to the soft questions, she decided to let the young interviewers continue conducting the entire program. The senior producers never came on the air. The director used her communication competence to assess that the threads of peacebuilding and rehumanizing the other emerging among the antagonized candidates were more important at that moment than a thorough explanation of their government agendas. This example is illustrative of one of my key findings; Magdalena Medio's community radio producers have moved beyond predesigned formulas for implementing peacebuilding communication strategies. Instead, they develop communication competencies and skills used to defuse conflict, and to "steal" public spaces and social/political processes from the realm of aggression and violence, moving them to the realm of discourse.

Throughout my fieldwork I have seen instances in which community media are used to strengthen local democratic processes by facilitating communication and dialogue between local government officials and their constituencies. One afternoon in August 2005, I witnessed Radio Andaquí's facilitation of an all-afternoon discussion between the mayor and local citizens. That morning, *El Tiempo,* the national daily, published the list of the best and worst municipalities in the country, according to fiscal management indicators. The municipality of Belén fared pretty badly, ranking sixteenth from the bottom on a list of 1,010 municipalities. Radio Andaquí invited the mayor to explain the ranking to his constituency. Walking down the streets that afternoon I was able to follow the entire dialogue by listening to the sound of peoples' radios coming out of their homes to reach me in the middle of the street, via open windows and doors. Everyone's dial seemed to be set on Radio Andaquí; the mayor tried to make his case to numerous callers, who kept asking him probing questions. Then, in one of those moments that only ethnographic research makes possible, I stood in front of the house of an irate caller, and through his open door I could see his distorted, sweaty face, arms waving, speaking in a loud voice as he argued on the phone that the municipal fiscal problems had been inherited from the previous administration. I could hear his real voice, and at the same time I could hear his arguments transmitted live by Radio Andaquí. When I arrived at the station the debate kept going; listeners kept calling and the mayor continued trying to clarify things. The forum ended with the mayor committing to hold an open forum with the appropriate authorities in front of the community in the near future.

As I sat outside the radio station listening to the forum, a large SUV arrived and parked nearby. Three men got out of the SUV and made sure we could see the guns tucked under their T-shirts. I soon learned that one of them was the mayor from a neighboring municipality and his two bodyguards, looking for Belén's mayor. After realizing that his colleague was unavailable, he signaled the bodyguards to get back in the car and said to whoever was listening: "I don't let anyone fuck with me like this!" (*"A mi si no me joden la vida así"*).

Later that evening, as I interviewed the mayor, he articulated how the debate on Radio Andaquí had contributed to peacebuilding in his municipality: "This was a grain of sand, a small but still significant contribution to peace, because for some days we were living a mood of rumors, comments coming and going; today we were able to bring much needed clarification to the community. With Radio Andaquí and this type of discussion, the community gains so much, because there's so much people do not know, like how the budget is managed, what kind of actions my administration is taking, etc." (Castro 2005).

In Colombian contexts where weapons, violence, corruption, and impunity have replaced communication and dialogue between local governments and their people, citizens' media can help reestablish two-way direct interaction between local mayors and other government officials and their communities. Progressively, this type of participatory democracy can improve people's trust in the democratic process and ultimately legitimize the rule of law against the use of force or patron–client modes (Kalathil, Langlois, and Kaplan 2008).

In Magdalena Medio the PDPMM and AREDMAG's community radio stations labor hand in hand to open, maintain, and expand more and more local occurrences of participatory democracy. As I traveled from one municipality to another on the Magdalena River, I too became familiar with a new vocabulary for these participatory democracy experiences. During my interviews, around lunch and dinner tables, and at the radio stations, everyone's talk was peppered by terms such as Rendición de Cuentas, Municipal Planning Council (citizens' council responsible for planning community development programs), Development and Peace Municipal Proposal (citizen-designed set of municipal public policies), Social Policy Council (citizens' council responsible for oversight of local social policies), Citizens' Nucleus (large citizens' council, open to anyone in the community, responsible for designing the Development and Peace Municipal Proposal), Youth Municipal Council (formed by local youth, defines needs and development initiatives by and for local youth), Territorial Planning Council (consolidates Municipal Development and Peace Proposals into regional development programs), Trocha Ciudadana (assembly-type meeting where citizens decide on a Public Agenda for Peace and Development that prioritizes needs and policies citizens want implemented in their municipality; this agenda is given to each mayoral candidate who is supposed to translate it into his or her government program; the idea is that citizens should vote for those mayoral candidates that better translate the citizens' designed agenda into a government program), and Veedurías Ciudadanas (citizen oversight mechanisms responsible for monitoring municipal budgets, contracts, elections, etc.). In the words of AREDMAG's leader Julio Hoyos: "All this very technical jargon has become part of everyday life; people in Magdalena Medio understand that their community's future depends on their participation in these spaces, making decisions in the public sphere" (Ministerio de Cultura 2004).[21]

Hanging out with Magdalena Medio's community radio producers puts me at the very center of those people who believe that these types of projects are the only way to overcome armed violence. According to Hoyos, AREDMAG's community radio stations are active participants in all these newly developed public decision-making spaces. Each station has a representative in at least the Citizens' Nucleus, the Municipal Planning Council, and the Municipal Council for Culture; Hoyos states: "Wherever public policies are being debated, that's precisely where our media are, proposing agendas" (Ministerio de Cultura 2004). In some cases I feel as if I have crossed a boundary, leaving behind the traditional Colombian democratic system so plagued by patron–client relationships, corruption, and bribery to enter a new "nation" in which everyone attends numerous daily meetings as part of their involvement with local decision-making processes. These new participatory spaces have strong legitimacy in the region; in the words of Julio Hoyos: "Nowadays, to be a member of one of these councils in Magdalena Medio is a symbol of power; not of individual power, but of public power" (Ministerio de Cultura 2004).

Everyone around me knows so much about water systems, garbage collection, local environmental issues, and management of public spaces such as parks, public schools, and health centers. In Colombian contexts like Magdalena Medio, where people are trying to find a way out of armed violence via participatory democracy, social processes that feed citizens' participation in local politics have been labeled *cultura ciudadana* (culture of citizenship, explained further in chapter 4). By now I am used to the paradoxes common to Colombian contexts of armed conflict: Magdalena Medio, perhaps one of the worst regions in the country in terms of armed violence indicators, is precisely where local participatory democracies thrive. Clearly, the region's traditional culture of dissent and more recently the PDPMM are the main root-causes behind Magdalena Medio's thriving participatory democracies.[22]

Apart from sending their own representatives to participate in these public forums, AREDMAG's stations give the groups visibility and legitimacy. The stations explain, through news, features, and informational programs, what each of the public forums do; they monitor ongoing decision-making processes, invite citizens to participate, and perhaps most importantly, offer information and analysis of local economic, social, and environmental issues so that citizens can be better informed when debating local needs and policies for their municipalities.

Belonging and Sense of Place Become Catalysts for Peace

Leonardo and Don Isidoro, both committed radio producers in their community radio station, pick me up in Barrancabermeja and take me to San Vicente de Chucurí to visit the town and their station. A friend who owns a four-wheel-drive SUV has agreed to come with them to fetch me. We leave Barrancabermeja behind and drive for two and half hours on a bad dirt road on which the SUV cannot go faster than twenty miles an hour. It's been dry, but I can see how the four-wheel drive becomes necessary on rainy days—the road surely becomes "a bar of wet soap," as my dad would say. Today the road is deserted; we pass only a couple buses and trucks. Our destination, San Vicente de Chucurí, is the birthplace of the ELN, one of the main guerrilla organizations operating in the region; I think, "There's no way I could have done this before the paramilitary takeover." I don't resent the slow pace of the drive; the scenery is spectacular, with the overpowering Andean mountains lying as the background to rolling hills and valleys traversed by pristine creeks and rivers. The vegetation that surrounds me is opulent; wildflowers and thick forests are interspersed with a variety of agricultural plots.

Later, at my desk in Oklahoma, memories of these images are easily triggered as I listen to AREDMAG's radio programs. Not all, but many of the programs are accurate mirrors of the land and its people. Throughout news features, chronicles, interviews, and variety shows, the programs make vivid and frequent references to fruits and vegetables familiar in farmers' everyday lives: pineapples, tangerines, lemons, oranges, *badea,* green beans, sugarcane, plantain, cacao, corn, manioc, coffee, blackberries. The programs are peppered with sounds of local birds, traditional drumming, and sounds from the river, used as special effects. The stories and histories, cultural identities and ways of life of the people of Magdalena Medio are showcased on the programs alongside the region's natural features. Local heroes are spotlighted on the programs, as in the case of bus driver Vicente González, who, every day, at five in the morning, braves the bad conditions of the only dirt road connecting Galápagos, a ten-house village, to the main highway. If it weren't for Don Vicente, Galápagos would be entirely isolated from the rest of Magdalena Medio; the fare he charges, explains the six-minute radio chronicle, is one thousand pesos per passenger (approximately fifty U.S. cents) (AREDMAG 2004d).

Central to AREDMAG's mandate is the belief that identity, expression, and collective political action are closely interconnected. Like other Colombian peacebuilding initiatives, including the Communications Collective of Montes de María (see chapter 2) and Radio Andaquí and EAIBA in Caquetá (see chapter 1), AREDMAG's community radio leaders gamble on the power of cultural identities to rescue communities from war. Unlike other cases of intranational armed conflict, such as Rwanda, Sri Lanka, or South Africa, armed violence in Colombia is not related to cultural, ethnic, or religious differences. In this sense, culture is a "safe" sphere that has the potential to engender social cohesion. AREDMAG's community radio practitioners seek to foment a common, peace-driven vision of the future by cultivating a sense of belonging to the shared geography, history, ways of life, and ethical cultural values of the Magdalena Medio region.

The radio stations consolidate strong public spheres to be used by a wide variety of local voices to express this sense of belonging and shared experience. In the words of a radio producer from Puerto Wilches: "What keeps me coming back [to the station] is that we get to weave words, we get to weave experiences" (Puerto Wilches Radio Producer 2004). In a context in which war and armed groups impose a sense of harsh individuality and "survival of the fittest," radio producers recognize the potential of a sense of collective: "In a region such

as ours, where armed conflict has left deep scars like a lack of trust . . .
you don't know if the person you are talking to is a paramilitary, or
who is it that you are talking with? . . . This provokes fear, suspicion,
mistrust, so how can you build a common future? This makes collective work even more valuable" (AREDMAG Radio Producers 2004).
On this basis, AREDMAG's stations are used to strengthen, empower,
and amplify anything that can contribute to a sense of an "us," of "we
are in this together," and "we need to build a future together." Thus
cultural identity, understood as the sense of belonging to Magdalena
Medio, the sense of feeling emotionally and historically attached to the
river's landscapes, to the kaleidoscopic collection of regional cultures,
to specific ways of speaking, cooking, socializing, moving in the world,
is privileged raw material in AREDMAG's programming. Citizens'
media leaders cultivate a sense of belonging to Magdalena Medio as a
way to weave threads of community and cohesion in a social fabric so
torn into shreds of individualism and antagonism.

Some programs feature local laborers, such as the embalmer of
Rio Negro, who explains that in order to overcome fear of the dead
he walks over the corpse twice, making a cross. Another program
focused on Oscar Fernando Rueda, Jose Luis González, and Michael
Machuca García, three boys between eleven and fourteen years old
who "proudly call themselves 'shoe beauticians'"; the kids charge one
thousand pesos (US$0.50) for a shoe-shine, fifteen hundred (US$0.75)
for an American shoe-shine, and two thousand for a *pintada,* which
includes leather dyes. Their day starts at six in the morning and normally goes until nine in the evening, unless it's market day, when they
can work longer to take advantage of the larger clientele. In response
to AREDMAG's interviewer, the kids explain:

   —on market days we can make from eight to ten thousand pesos; during
      weekdays we make maybe four thousand;
   —I take a thousand and I give my mom the rest;
   —and what do you spend those thousand on?—asks the interviewer.
   —eating stuff;
   —I save it week by week and spend it all at Christmas time, on new shoes
      and clothes;
   —and what do you want to do when you grow up?
   —I want to join the army;
   —Me too, so that I can be a professional;
   —I want to be a lawyer;
   —I want to be a judge. (AREDMAG 2004d)

The radio segment ends saying that Colombian law prohibits child labor, as a violation of children's rights; however, the law is the last thing in these children's minds (AREDMAG 2004d).

Local histories are also featured, as heard in a series of chronicles about the first pre-Columbian communities in Yuma (the indigenous name of what is now known as Magdalena River), and the subsequent waves of migrants that came to settle in the region, bringing different ethnic groups and cultures (AREDMAG 2004c). Other programs feature Simití's church, which displays a colonial painting of the Virgin Mary that was found in a nearby farmer's house in 1767 (AREDMAG 2004a); the traditional architecture of local train stations in river ports such as Gamarra, Puerto Wilches, Puerto Berrío, and Barrancabermeja (AREDMAG 2004b); the history and origin of local nicknames assigned to all the members of certain extended families in the region (ARED-MAG 2004d); or the history of La Calle del Crimen [Crime Street], which in the 1960s was lined with hole-in-the-wall bars, settings of frequent shoot outs where *"eso parecía el oeste, bala iba, bala venía"* (it was like the old West, bullets coming and bullets going) (AREDMAG 2004d). Local legends, ghosts, and superstitions have their place too, as in a humorous program about the love triangle between local ghosts such as La Llorona (a weeping female ghost), El Diablo (the devil), and La Máncara (a long-haired, one breasted female phantasm) (San Vicente Estéreo 2004a); or a chronicle about the haunted lake of San Jorge (AREDMAG 2004d).

In their attempt to create true mirrors of local life, AREDMAG's stations deal with thorny community issues, such as the common disputes between rural neighbors over someone leaving a gate open, allowing cattle and other farm animals to escape (San Vicente Estéreo 2004d); or chronicles of adults' complaints about local youth being scattered and easily manipulated, juxtaposed against youngsters' complaints about adults' judgmental attitudes toward fashion and piercings (San Vicente Estéreo 2004b). Another program tries to mediate between angry adults and frustrated youth. Adults are aggravated by the rowdy midnight singing and guitar-playing gatherings of teens in the town's central plaza, while the teens feel it's a public space and it is their right to use it for late-night musical gatherings (San Vicente Estéreo 2004b).

Programming is closely linked to local languages through liberal use of local colloquialisms and ways of speaking. One sex education spot says *"no me arriesgo a que el gusto se me convierta en susto"* (a joking pun merging the joy of sex and the fear of unwanted pregnancy) (San Vicente Estéreo 2004c).

AREDMAG's radio producers frequently express a sense of pride and accomplishment when they recall how their technical know-how managed to capture the cultural identities of the Magdalena Medio. AREDMAG's leadership explains that the network's goal is "to open spaces to communicate, reflect and dialogue about the different ways in which people feel, narrate, create, and conceive Magdalena Medio" (Durán, Quijano, and Gómez Ditta in press). During an assessment workshop in 2004, a radio producer said that his station "smells like the region" (AREDMAG Radio Producers 2004). The insistence on grounding radio programming in local cultural imaginaries, identities, aesthetics, histories, stories, and languages is part of AREDMAG's political agenda as one of the main building blocks for peacebuilding. Rooted in the notion that identity, expression, and political action go hand in hand, these citizens' radio pioneers use technology to strengthen people's sense of place. AREDMAG believes that love for the region, its natural features, cultural identities, and lifestyles will nurture a shared vision for the future and trigger the necessary political action to move toward this change.

AREDMAG's Stations Move Conflict from Violence to Discourse

In other coauthored studies, I have analyzed the role that AREDMAG's community radio stations play as mediators of conflict (Rodríguez and Cadavid 2007). Without much training in conflict resolution or mediation, many Magdalena Medio radio producers have learned to use the stations to de-escalate conflict between community groups, the community and local authorities, and local political figures. Since 1995 the stations have developed communication competencies that allow them to move community conflict from the realm of weapons and violence to the realm of discourse, argument, and nonviolent resolution (see Rodríguez and Cadavid 2007 for complete analysis).

Mediating Intercommunal Conflict

Mediating among groups when everyday quarrels emerge and diffusing conflicts that can easily escalate into aggression and violence,

AREDMAG's radio stations serve as peacebuilders in the region. In all communities, conflict is an unavoidable element of everyday life. However, in communities such as those of Magdalena Medio, where the violent resolution of quotidian conflicts has been legitimized and normalized for generations, simple disagreements can easily end in bloodshed. Tensions over the use of public space, or land tenure, or a community celebration, can easily turn into violent episodes. In the narratives cited below we can see how AREDMAG's community radio stations were used as tools to mediate and help resolve differences among local parties:

> I have drawn a lot that a government agency assigned to some people. . . . But the owners completely neglected it, no one did anything with it for five or six years, until the radio station started a campaign against neglected vacant premises in the community, because they'd become a nuisance, invaded with tall weeds, a refuge for burglars, a place where people congregate to do drugs . . . and all of a sudden, a bunch of houses appeared on the lot that had been vacant for so long. So a conflict emerged between the owners of the lot and the owners of the houses: lot owners wanting to vacate homeowners and homeowners refusing to leave the premise. This issue was brought to the radio station, and each party presented their arguments in front of the microphone, to the entire community. Meanwhile, the conflict escalated to such a level, that at one point the two parties went at each other with machetes and sticks. So the radio station became involved as a mediator. What did the station do? We invited both parties again, to explain the entire case and their arguments in front of the microphones, and the station pleaded both parties to find a negotiated resolution while call-in listeners proposed nonviolent ways to resolve the conflict. Finally, the homeowners agreed to pay the lot owners for the land, but later the problem started again because the homeowners were not paying the appropriate price, so the mayor had to be brought in. He decided to assign a new lot to the lot owners and to allow the homeowners to keep the land where they had built their homes. (Magdalena Medio Community Radio Producer 2004)

> I am going to talk about a situation that happened in our municipality that had to do with the use of a public space. At the time, our town's main park resembled more a Persian market than a park; little by little it filled with street vendors and their booths; the park was nothing more than clothes hanging, trinkets everywhere . . . a hullabaloo. So that when people arrived by boat to Puerto Wilches, they really could not see that we had a park, all they could see was multicolored ropes from which dozens of clothes for sale hung. That's when the conflict began, because we [the station] began a campaign to recover the park as a public space; so we began talking to the

municipal authorities and also to negotiate between the two parties. One party was the people who used the park to make a living selling stuff, and they have the right to work. The other party was the people of the community who wanted to reclaim the park as a public space. So we looked at all that, and started promoting a dialogue among all the parties involved and today I can say with pride that we have a proper park in Puerto Wilches. The park has been reappropriated by the community, and today it's totally different, rebuilt . . . this was a very significant moment for us at the station because we triggered the whole thing, we worked very close with the vendors, trying to raise their awareness of the need for public spaces, and then we began working with the municipal authorities trying to find a solution to the problem. The solution came when the vendors were able to remodel an old building into their own commercial center; the municipal government gave them a facility and together they reconditioned it and now all of us in Puerto Wilches can say that we have a public space for our leisure and enjoyment. (Puerto Wilches Radio Producer 2004)

The first narrative shows the radio station's impact on this local community's social fabric. The station created a communication space that operated as a public sphere accessible to the parties in conflict. The station cultivated a space for nonviolent conflict resolution and encouraged the parties in conflict and the listeners to find a nonviolent way to resolve the conflict. In this case the station had enough legitimacy within the community to be accepted as a mediator; both lot owners and homeowners agreed to allow the station to intervene; both parties accepted the station's invitation to explain their positions in front of the microphones and in front of their opponent; members of the community called in to offer their opinions and to propose conflict resolution strategies. The technology itself played a significant role, because it forced the parties in conflict to face not only their opponent, but also the entire community. Issues of public face and public legitimacy become salient when personal arguments have to be defended in a public arena as opposed to a private realm. When what I say can be heard by the entire community, my identity and social image is at stake. Anything I say will be used by my community to construct their image of who I am; in this sense, I have to be much more careful about what I say. This technology-mediated communication space allows subjects to engage in a process of self-reflection about the social image they want to cultivate, thus keeping impulsive, hot tempers in check.

Nevertheless, the station was not able to come up with a definitive solution to the conflict; local authorities still had to be brought in.

In this sense, the station is putting pressure on public authorities to assume their responsibility to protect and defend citizens' rights, and to help resolve community conflicts. However, if local authorities do not follow through with the commitments assumed on the radio, the station could ultimately lose its legitimacy in the community.

The second narrative shows two different ways in which this communication space influences the local social fabric. First, the radio station transformed everyday life in Puerto Wilches as the park was reappropriated and is now used as a public space where people meet and interact. Thanks to the station, the park was recovered from market interests and made available to public ones—strengthening the local commons and thus the public sphere. Second, participating in this citizens' communication initiative is transforming this radio producer into a visionary with clear ideas about the importance of public spaces in building relationships based on interaction, solidarity, and familiarity among community members.

Although, as stated earlier, the stations do not explicitly target armed conflict or armed groups with their actions of mediation, during my fieldwork I found some instances in which the stations could not avoid dealing with armed groups. After all, the region's civilians and their community radio stations are surrounded (and frequently under siege) by armed groups, so staying away is not always an option. At the risk of sounding as if I am recycling material published elsewhere, I would like to quote extensively from the analysis Cadavid and I developed about the role the stations play in supporting civilian communities' responses to the presence of armed groups (Rodríguez and Cadavid 2007). The cases bear repeating for their impressive evidence of courage and competence in using radio technologies to resist the impact of armed groups. In the following narratives we begin to understand the complex role(s) that citizens' media can play in contexts of armed conflict. The first narrative says:

> Five years ago I had a horrible experience; our station director, José Botella, was kidnapped by the ELN. They took him to the Serranía de San Lucas, fifteen hours away from downtown Santa Rosa. No one knew what had happened until a farmer who witnessed the kidnapping came to the station and told us. At the station we discussed what to do, because to say something on the air could make the station a military target of the guerrillas. But, still, we decided to broadcast a press release demanding that the captors respect his life and well-being as a civilian. As soon as we aired the press release,

messages, letters, and official press releases from hundreds of local grassroots organizations and citizens began pouring in the station, all with similar demands and words of support for José. In all we received more than a thousand letters, some of which we read on the air, and over two thousand signatures in a document that was sent to the president and also to the ELN. As messages continued to pour in, we shifted to a sad musical selection as an expression of protest. The ELN responded with a challenge to the community: if we wanted José back, if it was true that the community loved him so much, the community had to go get him. Immediately the station began communicating this new demand, and in six hours we had 480 people willing to travel more than ten hours to the place known as Micoahumado, way high in the mountains. We gathered in more than forty cars and trucks. There were women, children, and men, all carrying white flags. We left at night, and got there by seven in the morning. We passed a guerrilla checkpoint on the road close to where José had been kidnapped. At first the *guerrilleros* at the checkpoint began shooting in the air, saying we could not go through, but then they called their superiors and told them that the road was totally covered with people and cars and they were only six guys. Finally, they were given orders to let us go through, though they warned us that the rest of the way was mined. Still, we insisted and continued toward the guerrilla camp. It looked like a snake of cars and trucks going up the mountain! The guerrilla camp looked like a small town. We got to the central plaza and asked to speak with the *comandante*. The guerrillas told us he wasn't there and we would have to wait, so in no time we set up tents and began lighting fires. We brought pots and pans, potatoes, cassava, and bought a steer at the camps. We proceeded to feed everybody 'cause we were not going to leave until we reached a resolution.

The next morning the so-called *comandante* showed up, and we told him we needed José back, and not just his family but also the entire community were making the demand, as he could see. The *comandante* didn't know what to do, so he called his superior who told him to just make us wait, that we would surely give up and leave; when the superiors realized we were not leaving and that we had formed a negotiating commission, they freed José Botello. From beginning to end it was seven days of horror and seven days of hope. . . . [W]hen we came back to Santa Rosa with José we had two days of festivities, with everybody in the central plaza, celebrating. The station also transmitted the celebration live, from the streets, thanks to our mobile unit. (Santa Rosa Radio Producer 2004)

The next testimony, recorded during AREDMAG's evaluation study, addresses the recent phenomenon of blacklists. As in other regions, in Magdalena Medio right-wing paramilitary groups intimidate young men and women by imposing strict codes on fashion, hairstyles, body piercing, and everyday life practices and behaviors. Blacklists with the names of young people who defied paramilitary codes were posted in visible public places, and if the questionable behavior continued, these marked youth often ended up dead or disappeared:

> Our communities are cornered by the terror imposed by armed groups. There was a moment in San Vicente where the blacklists began multiplying, especially targeting those youth who wanted to be themselves. So one day I'm listening to the station and I hear a short message that addressed the issue of blacklists. All you heard was someone taking attendance and a second voice responding:
> —so and so
> —present!
> —so and so—present!
> —so and so
> And then, complete silence . . .
> he is not here. He is on a different list!
> The message was so strong! What I am expressing in my drawing is how the community is cornered, and in the middle of all this the station is trying to open a communication space to play, to sing, to love, and also to scream, because we are all terrified, but at the same time we are listening to these different proposals coming from the station. The station is playing an important role, especially for young people, who are the ones more affected by the war, and at the same time, they are the ones with different life options, alternative proposals, including their music. They are using the station to put forward their voice and their proposals in the middle of the generalized terror and death. (San Vicente de Chucurí Radio Producer 2004)

These two testimonies, from Santa Rosa del Sur and San Vicente del Chucurí, describe different ways citizens' media can contribute to collective action and peaceful conflict resolution. In the case of José Botello's kidnapping the station mediated between the ELN and the community. The station decided to make the kidnapping a public event, not just a private tragedy affecting the family and friends of the victim. The station addressed the entire community as a victim of the ELN and the community responded as a collective subject with strong agency. As in the cases of the guerrilla attack of Belén de los Andaquíes (see chapter 1) and the street-film project in Montes de María (see chapter 2), the medium triggered a collective action that left the community with a sense of "we are not completely helpless when threatened by armed groups." Assured by the strong response, the station decided to go one step further and engage the guerrilla group in a process of negotiation. In this case, thanks to the station, the community was able to galvanize forces and to act collectively and peacefully to confront the guerrilla group. In Santa Rosa, the community radio station operates as a communication space that can be used by the community on an ad hoc basis. Peaceful conflict resolution emerged from communication and interaction, not in the form of pre-designed messages or communication "strategies," but rather as the result of the communication competencies the citizens' media leaders learned, used in a moment of crisis.

The role of the radio station in the blacklists testimony is of a different nature. In a case of bravery (which could easily be suicidal), the young radio producers in San Vicente de Chucurí produced a well-designed, high-impact message protesting the blacklists posted by paramilitary groups in their municipality. They protested the demonization of difference and the pressure to conform imposed on local youth. This community radio station embraced angry local youth to express their feelings and their rejection of paramilitary impositions on their everyday lives.

Instead of using community radio to distribute messages *about* mediation and conflict resolution, AREDMAG's radio producers open communication spaces *to be used to mediate* with and/or respond to armed groups. As opposed to most media for peace initiatives, these Colombian radio stations are directly mediating conflicts themselves, instead of disseminating messages about the need to mediate conflict in nonviolent ways. The communication competencies of these citizens' media producers are not being used to design messages *to persuade* listeners of the need for peaceful coexistence; rather, the stations *perform* peaceful coexistence through communication. In chapter 5 I will further develop a theoretical analysis of citizens' media and performative communication for peace.

Conclusion

Community radio stations in Magdalena Medio understand "social and political violence as complex phenomena that emerge at the intersection of various factors, including unequal distribution of resources, weak state presence, corrupt government officials, legal impunity, and strong presence of illegal economies. Together, these factors erode the social fabric of local communities and normalize a culture of strong individuality, disbelief in the rule of law, fear, isolation, exclusion of difference, and lack of solidarity among individuals" (Rodríguez 2004).

In these contexts of violence, AREDMAG's citizens' radio stations and their producers open communication spaces in which citizens can weave a different social fabric and resist the impacts of war and the presence of armed groups on their everyday lives, their social and political processes, and their cultural identities.

4 MEDIA PIONEERS RESPOND TO ARMED CONFLICT

> Anything you do in that type of context is a miracle.
>
> —Phillipe Gaillard, *responsible for*
> *Red Cross operations in Rwanda in 1994*

EVERY MORNING IN BOGOTÁ after sending my daughter to school, I take a taxi through the crowded streets. I ask the driver to take La Circunvalar, a narrow avenue that, perched on the city's eastern Andean mountains, circumnavigates the worst traffic with a series of brutal curves. Toward the end of the dizzying journey, we go down Eleventh Street at the height of Egipto, one of Bogotá's oldest neighborhoods, with quaint tiny colonial houses and cobbled streets. Coming down from Egipto always feels like going down a rollercoaster, and every day I hope the taxi has good brakes. I get off at Fifth Avenue, but before I start my workday I cannot resist stopping for a *caldo de costilla* (rib soup) in a hole-in-the-wall restaurant nearby; the steaming soup, full of beef protein and the scent of cilantro, is the best antidote to the damp cold of the city morning.

My destination during several months in 2004 was always the same: the basement of the Ministry of Culture's Media Division. Here, I have been given access to a gold mine of data on the evolution of Colombian community media over the last ten years. I bury myself here every day for months, listening to the voices of community media pioneers, recorded on hundreds of cassette tapes stored in this basement. This amazing collection of audio recordings documents the work of the Media Division's Unidad de Radio [Radio Unit], which has been led by cultural anthropologist Jeanine El Gazi since 1995.

In this chapter I present my own analysis of what community media pioneers say in these recordings about the role(s) of their community media initiatives in Colombia's complex contexts of marginalization and armed conflict. I will begin by providing a history of the Radio Unit and the role of El Gazi's brilliant leadership of the project in sharpening the vision and wisdom of Colombian citizens' media pioneers. I believe this history deserves attention because state initiatives truly committed to supporting citizens' media are, in my experience, rare. The rest of the chapter explores the influence of these media pioneers on a new generation of community media that is driven by notions of *cultura ciudadana* (culture of citizenship), strong public spheres, and participatory democracy.[1] Drifting away from older models of community media as spaces for militancy and political mobilization, this new generation of Colombian community media responds to contexts of armed conflict and marginality by creating communication spaces for citizens to begin repairing the torn social and cultural fabric of their communities.

The Exception to the Rule: The Profound Contributions of the Ministry of Culture's Radio Unit

In Colombia, causality is frequently difficult to establish. This is the case of Colombian citizens' media. Trying to understand the causes behind an exceptional generation of community media leads to a layered intersection of multiplicities. Different, and sometimes even contradictory historical events, personalities, and institutions that, for complex and sometimes random reasons, intersect at specific moments, generate novel ways to use media technologies in conflicted scenarios.

At the time of writing, Colombia's Ministry of Communications has granted 651 community radio broadcasting licenses, 553 community television licenses, and 26 indigenous radio station licenses.[2] As stated in this book's introduction, not all these community media initiatives justify the writing of a book; in fact, a great majority of community radio and television ventures simply replicate commercial broadcasting models or are used for sectarian political or religious agendas. In a significant exception to this trend, however, there are a number of Colombian community media outlets that have developed an exceptionally sophisticated vision of their role(s) at the local level and are successfully putting these visions into practice. Most countries produce only a few cases of outstanding citizens' media,[3] which makes Colombia, with dozens of community media initiatives acting as citizens' media, truly exceptional. The question, then, is, what happened in Colombia that is unique? A familiarity with several historical processes helps explain the solid vision and practice of Colombian citizens' media. First, a long history of dissent and grassroots critical thinking galvanized around social movements frames media activism (El Gazi 2001). As can be seen in all previous chapters, labor, peasant, indigenous, and women's social movements have been active participants in shaping Colombia's social, political, and cultural landscapes. The strength of social movements explains both the need collectives feel to have their own voice, and also the struggle of media activists to democratize the airwaves. By placing continuous pressure on the Colombian state, these activists managed to get a favorable, although not perfect, community broadcasting legislation enacted in the mid-1990s.[4]

Second, since the mid-1980s, Colombia has been rapidly decentralizing in terms of political and economic power. Since 1986 municipal mayors are elected instead of appointed by departmental governors, and local governments determine municipal budgets. Municipalities have gained autonomy, visibility, presence, and the power to design and implement their own economic and social policies. Also, more and more Colombians have begun to understand that our country is "a country of regions," meaning that each region has its own culture(s), idiosyncrasies, languages, political processes, modes of armed conflict, and more. Within this regional framework, it makes sense for each municipality to develop its own community radio and television stations.

Third, Colombian community media have evolved without much help from international donors. This is explained in part by the fact that the country falls between the cracks: Colombia isn't poor enough for many poverty alleviation NGOs because poverty rates are much worse in other countries. On the other hand, many war-related NGOs (i.e., organizations that focus on refugee aid, fragile or failed states, or transitional nations) don't have a presence in Colombia because the country has never been officially declared at war. As a result, Colombian citizens' media initiatives have grown without the frequent toxic dependence from international funding so common in other regions of the world (Von Kalternborg-Stachau 2008, 20).[5] In Colombia, citizens' media are home grown, led by local community leaders, and shaped by local wisdom and vision. Finally, as I demonstrate in the following pages, a specific state intervention, unique to Colombia, has created the conditions for an exceptionally rich citizens' mediascape.

The following story has four protagonists, all working within the walls of state institutions: Jeanine El Gazi, Javier Espitia, and Tatiana Duplat from the Ministry of Culture, and Esmeralda Ortiz from the Ministry of Communications. El Gazi, a Colombian cultural anthropologist, discovered the power of media in the early 1990s while working at the Instituto Colombiano de Antropología e Historia (ICANH) [Colombian Institute of Anthropology and History]: "I was working with local youth in San Agustín and Tierra Adentro [southern Colombia]. During production workshops at the local radio station, producing programs on the conservation of archeological patrimony, I could see the youngsters' passion for radio work. At the time there were no community radio stations and no citizens' radio; only traditional commercial radio stations" (El Gazi 2004).

In 1994 El Gazi took a new position as the director of the Ministry of Culture's Unidad de Radio [Radio Unit], which, until then, had been responsible for producing high-brow radio programming for the so called "cultural" public radio stations (i.e., classical music programs, or programs about national intellectual events). El Gazi redirected the entire work of the Radio Unit, redefining "cultural" radio. The word "culture," formerly understood as elite culture, became "culture" understood as local culture, a mosaic of the diverse regional and local lifeworlds of millions of Colombian women, men, and children. As part of this groundbreaking redirection, El Gazi proposed to support the country's nascent community radio initiatives: "I proposed that our work should contribute to community radio, so that the new constitution's Article 20 could become a reality. I wanted to begin assisting those behind the community radio initiatives, offering training in legal matters, management, and programming so that they were the ones producing programs, not us" (El Gazi 2004).[6] At exactly the same time in 1994 that El Gazi began working in the Ministry of Culture, the Ministry of Communications began to process the first five hundred bids for community radio broadcasting licenses. El Gazi knew this was the right moment to put the Radio Unit to work for community radio. She organized her community radio initiative around three components: training, programming, and networking.

Training and Programming

Immediately after their licenses were approved, Colombian community radio broadcasters needed to know how to manage a station, how to abide by brand-new laws and decrees, and how to secure community participation. El Gazi responded with 120 "Seed Workshops" [Talleres Semilla] held throughout the country. Approximately fifty people attended each workshop, meaning that a total of six thousand community radio producers were trained in these Seed Workshops. El Gazi remembers, "Those first workshops lasted six days each and participants had to work on every aspect of community radio, from the legal framework to the communication goals behind a community radio station. They learned how to organize a team, manage a radio station, and form a programming committee" (El Gazi 2004).

One of the toughest challenges the new stations faced was that of finding appropriate programming to fill the hours and hours of daily broadcast time. In response to this challenge, El Gazi's Radio Unit began producing a series of high-quality radio programs, especially designed for Colombian community radio stations. Each program was distributed to the stations in the form of mailed CDs, at no cost to the stations themselves. During these first years, the unit produced seven radio series with ten programs each, focused on topics of profound relevance to the community radio stations isolated in distant Colombian municipalities.

For example, one series focused on the history of social movements, with programs about the Vietnam war, the Cuban revolution, women's movements, and the origin of Colombian labor movements; another series, titled *Relatos de a Pie* (Narratives on Foot), chronicled the journey of an anthropologist traveling through the country and documenting different forms of armed conflict in each region. "We had programs on forced migration due to violence in the 1950s, the war around emerald mafias in Boyacá, and the history of the Yanaconas, an indigenous community that resuscitated its traditions after 1991 when the new constitution legitimized indigenous cultures," Pablo Mora reported (cited in Márquez 2003). A series titled *Historias Recientes para Gente Actual* (Recent Histories for Contemporary People) recreated recent historical phenomena like "U.S. hippies" or Perestroika, in an effort to "link the everyday lives of young people at those times with today's youth, emphasizing that young men and women have always made history," Isabel Uribe noted (quoted in Márquez 2003).

A series called *De Qué Hablamos cuando Hablamos de Violencia* (What We Talk about When We Talk about Violence) explores the ways different forms of violence and armed conflict mark the Colombian collective imaginary. A series about Colombian music included Bach, making connections between Colombian culture and other world cultures, and a series about world music featured Lucho Bermúdez, a well known Caribbean Colombian musician. The unit produced *Amor y Literatura* (Love and Literature), "showing that Colombian literature speaks about who we are without any type of nationalism," in Maria Elena Rueda's words (quoted in Márquez 2003), and *Historias y Aventuras del Cine* (Cinema's Histories and Adventures), where "the goal was to seduce listeners to open up to interesting films," reported Hugo Chaparro (quoted in Márquez 2003).

After completing a doctoral degree in Peace Studies, young historian Tatiana Duplat joined El Gazi's team at the Radio Unit. Together, El Gazi and Duplat took on new challenges. According to the legislation, community radio stations need to produce at least 12 percent of their own programming,[7] an overwhelming number of hours for people without much experience in radio production. Duplat explains: "Jeanine decided that merely providing programming would not do. We began incorporating a pedagogical component, explaining how the program was produced, into each program we sent out. These series were sent in small boxes containing the CDs and a booklet explaining how the research was done, how many people were interviewed, how the music was selected and edited, and how the topic was chosen. The goal was to show how much research and effort is needed to produce programs of this quality" (Duplat 2004).

Between 1995 and 2003, El Gazi's Radio Unit produced 3,920 hours of radio programs especially designed for Colombian community radio stations. Toward the end of El Gazi's tenure at the ministry (she left in 2006), radio production dwindled under the belief that by then, radio producers had accumulated enough competence to produce their own programs.

In 1998 El Gazi and her team organized a series of training events called Talleres de Formación de Formadores [Training for Trainers Workshops], designed for those community radio and television producers who began emerging as passionate leaders (approximately 130 people participated). These men and women would eventually become the people I refer to as Colombia's citizens' media pioneers.

In May 2000, El Gazi and Saskia Lockhart organized the First International Congress of Indigenous Radio in the Americas. Twenty-eight Colombian indigenous media leaders attended this event, joined by an Ecuadorian Shuar, a Chilean Mapuche, and a Hopi leader from the United States, each of whom presented their own peoples' experiences with citizens' media. This event opened an unprecedented space for discussion among Colombian indigenous leaders about the pros and cons of embracing media technologies.[8]

In 2000, five years after the first community radio and television licenses had been granted, El Gazi and her team analyzed the community media scenario and found that some of these initiatives—not all of them, but certainly the pioneers—were shaping up as true citizens' media. The stations were emerging as actors with enough power to enact change in their municipalities, demanding transparency from local officials, encouraging grassroots participation in local governance, and strengthening local cultures. On the basis of these findings, the unit developed a new, two-step line of action; first, the unit would help community media leaders organize approximately fifty *cabildos* (town hall meetings) in which the stations would bring together local community organizations, collectives, and citizens in general. These meetings were intended to encourage dialogue between the medium and its audience, in order to improve citizen participation and allow the stations to better respond to community information and communication needs. The town hall meetings were followed by the second step of the unit's plans: seven regional and two national Citizens' Communication Round Tables [Mesas de Comunicación Ciudadana] to be held in different parts of the country. The Round Tables were intense discussions of the goals, purposes, and roles of citizens' media. Approximately ninety citizens' radio and television pioneers attended each of these events, for a total of approximately eighteen hundred participants. Duplat remembers:

> at the time, the Ministry of Communications was closing down many of the community radio stations because they had lost direction and begun unsuccessfully copying commercial radio. They didn't have the right music, or the appropriate programming, or the producers. So many community radio stations began to resemble bad copies of commercial radio. When this happened, no one would listen, the station could not sustain itself, and it would be closed down. In the meantime, some other stations found a new direction, realizing that they had to produce a different type of radio, one

distinct from commercial radio. People began to realize, "a commercial radio station does not mention my neighborhood, my county *[vereda]*, or the problems in my water system, nor would it feature my neighbor talking on air." I don't know how many made this realization at the time, maybe no more than ten. What I do know is that when one of these ten told their story to others, those others started to change the way they produced radio. (Duplat 2004)

The roundtables were designed precisely to facilitate dialogue and discussions between the citizens' media pioneers who were finding exciting ways to use radio and television technologies in their communities and many other community media producers, directors, and managers.

Between 1999 and 2002, El Gazi and Javier Espitia organized three advanced seminars *(Diplomados)* for approximately 150 citizens' media pioneers (each *Diplomado* included 50 participants). In two weeks of daily grueling sessions of ten to twelve hours each, participants read, listened to presentations by experts, and discussed issues such as media and democracy, media and armed conflict, community participation in media, and more. The same year, Esmeralda Ortiz, one of the media activists who had pressured the Colombian state for media reform in the early 1990s, and who now worked within the walls of the Ministry of Communications, collaborated with El Gazi and her team. Together, they organized meetings in which citizens' media pioneers discussed and designed codes of ethics and style manuals for community media. In Duplat's words, "In these four-day meetings [community media pioneers] discussed what to do or not to do about armed conflict; how to avoid falling into the trap of moralizing and how to keep programming focused on citizenship, rights and duties, and away from moralistic judgment" (Duplat 2004).

In 2004, almost ten years after the first community radio and television stations began broadcasting, El Gazi and Duplat gathered a larger team and launched what would be their last initiative before they left the ministry. The new initiative, known as Radios Ciudadanas, Espacios para la Democracia [Citizens' Radio Stations: Spaces for Democracy], focused on news, analysis, and public opinion, topics that El Gazi and Duplat considered weaknesses of the community broadcasters' offerings. A unit document articulates the project's goal in the following terms: "The project's goal is to broaden local public spheres by encouraging public reflection and debate on public interest issues, with pluralistic participation. By encouraging diverse expression, community radio stations can create open spaces for deliberation in which different cultural groups, social sectors, and public institutions can meet to envision and enact the construction of realities that respond to the plurality of visions and interests in each context" (Unidad de Radio—Grupo de Políticas e Investigación 2006).

Radios Ciudadanas trained teams of citizens' journalists in thirty-eight community radio stations across the country. These teams were responsible for producing thirty-minute news and public opinion programs four days a week, focusing on important issues in their respective municipalities. The fifth day, all participating radio stations broadcast the same national interest program, produced in Bogotá by El Gazi and Duplat's office.[9] In the words of El Gazi, "this back and forth between local and national programs was intended to spark dialogue between local and national approaches to the same issues" (El Gazi 2006). Issues addressed in the national programs included forceful displacement, gender equity, voting, and youth identity. In its pilot phase, Radios Ciudadanas offered thirty-five training workshops for citizens' journalists, providing instruction in areas such as reporting, audience analysis, codes of ethics, radio production of public opinion, political analysis, and journalistic genres.[10] From 2004 to 2006 Radios Ciudadanas produced more than eight thousand half-hour news and public opinion citizens' journalism programs in thirty-eight municipalities throughout Colombia. In 2006, two of those programs, Mujeres Que Paren Sueños [Women Who Birth Dreams], about regional and national women's movements, and Memorias del Desplazamiento Forzado en Barrancabermeja [Memories of Forceful Displacement in Barrancabermeja], received journalism awards in competitions that included professional journalists. In 2006, at which time El Gazi left the Ministry of Culture, the second phase of Radios Ciudadanas was about to begin training another batch of 250 citizens' journalism teams.

How can this complex and unique relationship between a state institution (the Ministry of Culture) and citizens' media be explained? In my view, there are frequent fissures in the Colombian state, which can be seized by individuals like El Gazi, Espitia, Duplat, and García to set and achieve goals rarely sought by governments with the characteristics of Colombia's. Duplat articulates the relationship between the unit and citizens' media in these terms: "A democratic state must allow and encourage dissent—dissent via peaceful means. So we, the ministry, as a state institution, are responsible to give people the freedom and platform to disagree with the state without fearing that their opinions will get them killed. In the specific case of our unit, everything we do is for these community radio stations to become precisely those channels of dissent, because that is precisely the reason for which they were created" (Duplat 2004).

El Gazi tape-recorded every workshop, seminar, and roundtable. The resulting tapes are the ones stored in the basement of the Ministry of Culture on Eleventh Street. These tapes constitute the gold mine El Gazi made available to me, and the data they contain supports this chapter.

A note for the academic reader: clearly, I could pepper this chapter with citations from Habermas's theories of public sphere, Fraser's counter-publics, Foucault's subjugated knowledges, Mouffe's agonist politics and radical democracy, or Galtung's peacebuilding. However, Colombian citizens' media pioneers have developed their wisdom through reflection and debate on their media praxis, not by studying academic theories. To translate their ideas into academic jargon would be not only arrogant, but also unfair, so I will present the theories of these citizens' media pioneers without academic interference.

Networking

From 1998 to 2006, citizens' media pioneers profited twofold from El Gazi's initiatives; first, they received many hours of training in the form of seminars, roundtables, and workshops. Renowned media and cultural studies scholars frequently led these events, including Jesús Martín Barbero and Germán Rey, as well as telecommunication lawyers and political scientists specializing in participatory democracy and citizens' political action. Workshops were held on the topics of citizens' journalism, participatory communication, management and accounting, sustainability and financing, and media production, among others.

Secondly, since 1998, El Gazi's training events began to be more regional and national than local, and as a result, citizens' media pioneers from northern Colombia had the opportunity to meet those from the South, the East, and the West. I cannot overstate the significance of these networking opportunities. How else would Soraya Bayuelo, living in El Carmen de Bolívar on the Colombian Caribbean, meet Alirio González from Belén de los Andaquíes in southern Colombia?[11]

How else could Soraya and Alirio both meet Guillermo Pérez, a brilliant teacher and director of a community radio station in Inírida, a town on the Colombia–Venezuela border? Traveling from El Carmen de Bolívar to Belén de los Andaquíes requires more than twenty hours by bus or at least two expensive plane tickets. Inírida is not reachable by car or bus, only by air through a few airlines at exorbitant cost. Despite never having visited one another's geographic locations, by the time I met Alirio, Soraya, and Guillermo in 2004, they knew one another well. Since meeting at the first Seed Workshop in 1994, these three citizens' media leaders had accumulated ten years of dialogue, cross-fertilization, and discussion, all facilitated and financed by the Ministry of Culture's Radio Unit under El Gazi's leadership.[12] As an example of the importance of these networking opportunities, in one of the *Diplomados* a Pijao indigenous media producer stated:

As an Indian, one has few opportunities to travel beyond one's own territory, but here [in the *Diplomado*] I've had the opportunity to meet and share knowledge with people from different parts of the country. . . . I came

Soraya Bayuelo (in the white shirt) and Alirio González (with headphones around his neck) producing a radio program in the cemetery of the city of Mompox, during the OURMedia Regional Meeting, 2005. Photograph by Clemencia Rodríguez.

hesitantly, knowing that I was to interact with people from contexts very different from mine, one comes with five hundred years of colonialism under the skin, but the time we have shared here has been like therapy, and now I feel like part of a family, the Colombian family, a very diverse family. (Unidad de Radio—Diplomado Cartagena 2002)

After each event, citizens' media pioneers returned to their media projects to field test the new ideas, visions, and theories from the collective discussions during El Gazi's training events. Clearly, the producers tested and experimented with not only what they heard from experts, but also what their peers were doing on the other side of the country. This going back and forth between discussion, reflection, and experimentation explains, in part, the acute know-how of Colombian citizens' media pioneers. Duplat agrees: "I left to do my doctorate in 1997. I returned in 2000, and when I attended my first roundtable I was so impressed with how, in such a short time, the discourse of the citizens' media pioneers had become so sophisticated" (Duplat 2004).

The recordings I listened to in the unit's basement document how experimenting led to growing communication competence. For example, in one roundtable discussion a producer at a community radio station called Radio Rumbo Estéreo recounts a long process of trial and error finally producing a satisfactory news program:

Our station is in Soacha, a city of nine hundred thousand people, most of whom are migrants from other parts of the country. We realized that, despite being so close to the capital city, Soacha is a completely uninformed community. We noticed that unless events in our community involve incidents of public unrest, they don't make it into our local media, so we knew the main element of our programming had to be information.

Currently we have a two-and-a-half-hour daily news program that runs from six to nine thirty in the morning. The program, which covers mostly local information, is produced by a team of twenty-two community reporters who comb Soacha inch by inch, neighborhood by neighborhood. These reporters don't receive a salary; they do this work out of their own commitment to their city and what they want their neighborhoods to be; they work from a commitment with their life project.

Learning how to produce this show required a lengthy process of trial and error. We began by making a public call for people with an interest in becoming community reporters; in response, people called to complain about stuff, but no one was willing to truly become a reporter. Next, we made arrangements with three local schools, so that one of the mandatory social service areas for students in their last year could be community reporting. This didn't work either, because the participation was mandatory, and these young people were not interested in journalism or the issues they had to cover. One day, assuming that the lack of willing participants meant that our news program was not what our people needed, we discontinued it without telling anyone. Complaints began pouring in; people wanted to know, why had we stopped the news program? That response prompted us to take things seriously: we raised funds, recruited people, and locked the whole group of volunteers up for forty-five days, Monday through Friday, in order to truly train a team. We offered basic journalism training and also training on topics like participation and the ethics of information management. We felt it was important to offer training on a broad range of topics, because we understand that each of the participants, apart from being community leaders, plays a role in a political game of interests to which no one is foreign. We emphasized the importance of differentiating between information and personal interests, and we have seen the results. Not to say that everything has been rose petals, but these community reporters have made tremendous improvements. Two weeks after the training ended, they independently decided to form a watchdog committee among themselves, to guarantee the project's success.

Currently we have a weakness, which is that we have not been able to establish a youth information and public opinion program. What we have learned so far is that you cannot call youth "community reporters." Young people dislike the term "reporter," and they are even more averse to the term "community" . . . we're still working on this. (Unidad de Radio—Mesa Regional Cauca, Putumayo, Nariño 2000)

Workshops and meetings frequently triggered lively discussions in which citizens' media pioneers competed to see who had the best participation or diversity. For example, in one roundtable plenary, Jeanine asked about the diversity of musical genres played by each station. The question led to a discussion in which community radio producers tried to demonstrate that their station's music was more diverse than their neighbor's. The following dialogue among participants reflects their drive to have the best record in terms of music diversity:

—in Boyacá, community radios are playing *vallenato, ranchera,* and ballads;
—we do *champeta* too;
—we also play ethnic music;
—we do hip-hop, rap, reggae, jazz, *metallica;*
—please include *guasca,* if not, you're really stepping on my callus;[13]

—we do instrumental;

—in Cristal Estéreo in Aquitania, we do classical music;

—in our station in Arauca we have a program on Sundays about folklore of the Llanos, our regional music. (Unidad de Radio—Mesa Regional Boyacá, Arauca, Casanare 2001)

It is not surprising that, after participating in these kinds of discussions for ten years, citizens' media pioneers actively cultivate diversity in their media at the level of musical genres, types of programming, community voices, and formats.

The formulation of an ethics of citizens' media is another constant theme in the pioneers' discussions. They argue, "We need to bet on imagination, on going against the current. If the municipality's mayor is corrupt and the people are corrupt, the radio station does not need to be corrupt; it has to swim up-stream. We need to make the radio station an alternative life option" (Unidad de Radio—Mesa Regional Cauca, Putamayo, Nariño 2000). One of El Gazi's roundtable proceedings concludes: "Our stations need to be able to question everything that has been taken for granted, so that new communicative options can flourish. Community radio, television and print media will be able to survive only when they can transgress and reconstitute the current orders of things" (Unidad de Radio—Memorias Mesa Regional Antioquia 2000).

Ultimately, twelve years of collective discussions, reflection, dialogue, and experimentation allowed citizens' media pioneers to articulate a unique and steady vision. In the following pages I document this vision.

In no way do I intend to romanticize Colombian community and citizens' media. Indeed, I could write an entire book about their vulnerabilities, weaknesses, blind spots, and questionable practices. Of nearly one thousand radio and television community broadcasting stations operating in the country, perhaps one hundred can be thought of as citizens' media. In a recent analysis by El Gazi, dozens of weaknesses were identified in the areas of community participation, quality of programming, audience analysis, evaluation, connectivity and technologies, financial sustainability, accounting, and management.[14] Yet, as I said before, community/alternative/citizens'/radical media literature extensively documents these numerous Achilles' heels (Atton 2002; Downing et al. 2001; González and Rodríguez 2008; Gumucio Dagron 2001; Howley 2005; Lewis 1984; O'Connor 2004; Opel and Pompper 2003; Rennie 2006; Rodríguez 2001). On that basis, I choose to focus on what we don't yet know or understand about the role(s) these media can play in complex and difficult contexts, such as those found in Colombia.

Using Media to Respond to War

Taking Sides with Unarmed Civilians

In the late 1990s, in an attempt to keep armed groups at bay and lessen war's negative impact on people and social life, several Colombian communities declared themselves "territories of peace" (Castellanos 2001). A community that declares itself a "territory of peace" (also known as "peace community") demands that all armed groups respect its unwillingness to be involved in armed conflict (Sanford 2004). This status demands that armed groups do not trespass community boundaries, recruit people from the community (especially youngsters and children) to be soldiers or civilian informants, and do not ask the community for logistical support including food, shelter, medicine, right of way, and so forth.[15] In November 2000, one hundred citizens' media pioneers sat at one of El Gazi's roundtables to vote on and approve an unprecedented statement declaring their media "territories of peace." The declaration reads:

> Antioquia, San Pedro de los Milagros, November 3, 2000.
> The delegates at the Antioquia Regional Roundtable on Community and Citizens' Communication held in San Pedro de los Milagros, between October 31 and November 4. Based on their autonomy and considering:
> • That community media are located throughout the entire Antioquia territory, in regions strongly affected by violence and the presence of antagonistic armed groups.
> • That community media are spaces for community participation in social, economic, and cultural local processes.
> • That community media promote the wide expression of diverse interests, needs, and accomplishments of various community groups and individuals.
> • That some of these media have been targets of armed groups' attacks or pressures, and that some media producers or their relatives have been assassinated.
> Agree:
> 1- To reaffirm the goals and criteria driving the foundation of these media as community media.
> 2- To recognize and promote community media as tools to strengthen public spheres where different community groups and sectors can discuss, reflect, and state their ideas about issues concerning collective interests.

3- To maintain community media's independence from all political or ideological parties, and from all armed groups.

4- To declare:

A) COMMUNITY MEDIA AS PEACE TERRITORIES/SPACES AT A LOCAL, DEPARTMENTAL, NATIONAL, AND INTERNATIONAL LEVEL.

B) Community media as institutions that have made, are making, and will make great efforts toward peace, a negotiated resolution of conflict, and peaceful coexistence.

5- To send this declaration to all media and to all local, departmental, national, and international institutions working toward human rights and freedom of expression. Signed by all those in attendance, San Pedro de los Milagros, Antioquia, November 3, 2000. (Unidad de Radio—Mesa Regional Antioquia 2000)

The lucidity evident in this response to the complexities of a context of armed conflict is truly exceptional. Generally, the path is not so clear. In this section I attempt to illustrate the give and take in which Colombian citizens' media pioneers engage, debating different angles, arguments, and perspectives on the actions their radio stations, community television stations, or print media should take when paramilitaries, guerrillas, drug traffickers, and/or the Colombian armed forces have a strong presence in their communities, often pushing unarmed civilians into the center of a cruel cross fire.

Most Colombians are not involved in armed conflict. In fact, the number of armed Colombians directly involved in waging war is very small (Pécaut 2001, 19). The following statement, voiced at one of El Gazi's seed workshops in Magdalena Medio, expresses this realization: "The armed groups, all together, represent a few hundred thousand people, but they hold 40 million under threat *[en jaque]* . . . so we need to realize that those of us who want to live in peace are many more than those who threaten us" (Unidad de Radio—Taller AREDMAG 1998). This statistical reality raises a significant question in discussions about the mission of citizens' media: should these media be at the service of the armed minority, or the unarmed majority? We can hear this question echoed in the words of the citizens' media pioneers recorded at one of the unit's events:

—I think the medium's role is to promote peaceful coexistence *[convivencia pacífica]*, not to voice the role of violence as a protagonist in daily life;

—in certain contexts, the situation of unrest is so severe, it's impossible to promote any kind of dialogue among different armed actors—militaries, paramilitaries, drug traffickers—it's impossible to promote nonviolence among them;

—someone was saying that in his region the station could not transmit public service announcements: even a message about domestic violence could be interpreted [by one of the armed groups] in certain ways that would make the medium a target;

—these media should open spaces for the different armed actors to engage in dialogue because these radio stations are public spheres for everyone;

—we are all in agreement that these media should become spaces for dialogue; what we don't agree on is if armed actors, those directly involved in armed conflict, should be included in such dialogue;

—in our group we agreed that we should not give more visibility to violence as a protagonist in community life, but that we cannot ignore it either. We believe that the role of these media is to show the possibility of a life based on dialogue and peace and not on the use of force;

—we have three arguments on the table: one, that all the different armed actors have the right to express themselves using these media, which are supposed to be public sphere spaces. Two, that community media should absolutely not give visibility to armed actors; if we allow armed actors to use our media, they are going to use them for their own purposes and goals. A third position promotes neither putting violence at the center nor ignoring it; this means establishing a pedagogy of peace that, without naming specific armed groups, addresses violence as a problem related to citizenship and public spheres. (Unidad de Radio—Mesa Regional Boyacá, Arauca, Casanare 2001)

Indeed, even in contexts of armed conflict in which vast numbers of people engage in violence, there are those who opt out. In the words of peace studies expert Jean Paul Lederach, "I have not experienced any situation of conflict, no matter how protracted or severe, from Central America to the Philippines to the Horn of Africa, where there have not been people who had a vision for peace, emerging often from their own experience of pain. Far too often, however, these same people are overlooked and disempowered either because they do not represent 'official' power, whether on the side of government or the various militias, or because they are written off as biased and too personally affected by the conflict" (Lederach 1997, 94; cited in Lynch and McGoldrick 2005, 255).

Citizens' Media in Crisis Situations

In the above discussion, I see the beginnings of the best practices later developed by many Colombian citizens' media in contexts of armed conflict. In these early discussions I can hear the awareness that music is as important as, if not more important than, given its weight in the stations' programming, other content. There is also evidence of an awareness of the need for programming committees that would be responsible for designing programming policies, and the realization that citizens' media can be better used to trigger processes of cultural change than to persuade audiences.

In situations of crisis, when unarmed civilians become trapped between embattled armed groups, citizens' media redirect all their energy toward meeting the information and communication needs of families trapped in the cross fire. The following example illustrates well this use of citizens' media:

> In 2000, during the three-month-long *paro armado* protesting the fumiga-
> tions in Putumayo,[16] everything stopped from September to December;
> phone lines were cut, there was no transportation, and communication
> between families from the North and the South became impossible. Twenty
> days into the *paro,* the situation became truly dramatic; there was no food,
> because no trucks were allowed to move, and fear took over because the
> crisis was lasting such a long time;[17] people started traveling on foot, 'cause
> there was no transportation, and no gas.
>
> The stations began asking, "What do we do?" one of the directors told
> me that he thought, "our stations have to do something because our commu-
> nities, the communities we belong to, are suffering." So the stations' leaders
> found a way to link community radio stations from the south, middle, and
> north of Putumayo. There are ten community radio stations in the region,
> and five of these linked themselves together in daily broadcastings. So we,
> the listeners, started hearing messages like, "Mom, stay calm, I'm OK. I'm
> in Puerto Asis, but do not worry, I am fine." The daily shared broadcasts
> from the linked radio stations became crucial for communication between
> families spread throughout the region. (Espitia 2004)

In addition to facilitating communication between families, the linked broadcasts provided a public sphere used by unarmed civilians to discuss how to address the situation. Javier Espitia, long-time community radio leader living at the time in Putumayo, explained:

> Teachers began using the linked broadcasts to discuss what to do. Listeners
> might hear someone on air say, "The teachers from Orito have talked about
> what to do, and we agree that we should start the holiday break now"; and
> the teachers from another municipality would reply, "In our case we will
> try to continue classes because we are not going to let them intimidate us."
> The entire debate happened on air, through the radio stations. The linked

broadcasts were so successful that one of the stations in La Hormiga was the target of machine gun fire by the guerrillas because the guerrillas interpreted these broadcasts as resistance. We are being accused not only for what we say, but for what we say without saying it; these radio stations were not saying, "we are doing these linked broadcasts because we are against armed conflict." No! They did it to serve the families. (Espitia 2004)

Liberman Renjifo, director of Radio Ocaina Estéreo, a community radio station in Putumayo, described his station's actions during a guerrilla-mandated *paro armado* in 1998:

After several weeks without any food, gas, or electricity in the region, the radio station joined forces with several other community organizations, especially some women's collectives, to decide how to confront the situation; what emerged was a very beautiful action, because at the time, the station didn't have its own generator, so any time the electricity was cut, the station went off the air. At the meeting, it was decided that the community radio station was the most important medium to keep people informed, so the decision was made to pull together funds from all the different organizations and to raise more funds among the community, in order to buy a generator for the station. This would keep people informed, not only in Puerto Caicedo, but also in Mocoa, which is the capital city.

That was when we saw the community really begin to value their community radio station. At that time the guerrillas had a strong presence in town, and they convened meetings. Sometimes we had to attend those meetings, but when the guerrillas saw that the community was getting really organized around the station, they realized they could not intimidate us anymore. Before the community began to organize around the station, people didn't leave the municipality to get food because the guerrillas didn't allow it. Once people began to mobilize, we started going to other municipalities for food. Food came by plane to Puerto Asís, a municipality about an hour away, and we had to sneak out in a horse cart to bring back food and gas. The station helped in all this, and we also helped by keeping people in far away rural areas, who were not allowed to come to town, informed about the food shipments. We monitored how much local stores were charging for food, because sometimes they tended to hike the prices, arguing that food was more expensive because it was coming by plane. (Renjifo 2004)

Pressures from Armed Groups

In some instances, the debate comes down to the specific pressures citizens' media pioneers feel from the armed groups in their regions. It is important to note here that the Ministry of Communications prioritized isolated regions in allocating community broadcasting licenses, on the premise that regions with less access to media were more in need of access. As a result of this prioritization, many of the oldest community radio stations operate in isolated regions, including some of the same regions where democratic institutions are weaker and armed groups are stronger. Citizens' media pioneers from the southern regions explain how they experience armed groups' pressure:

—I have a question for all present. What would you do if the paramilitaries were to come to your station's studio and give you a CD or a piece of paper with a communiqué? What would you do? Would you transmit it?

—let me try to answer that; in our station we had something like that happening to us. They asked us to help them distribute information to advance their goals, and we had to tell them: "Our community radio station does not allow us to do that; if we do it, the army, or any of the other groups will be after us, and it will mean the complete disappearance of our media project, so it's up to you whether or not you force us to do it." So far, they have respected our decision as a community radio station, that's where we stand so far;

—sometimes transmitting their messages is inevitable because these are groups beyond the law and we don't have any type of institution behind us, backing us. We don't have any type of safeguard. We, too, went through a similar experience. We have to do it [transmit their messages], because look, that time the station's director said "no" and they responded immediately by declaring that by six PM all of the station's staff and producers better be gone from [the department of] Casanare. We just cannot say no; and thank God, the communiqué was not against one of the other groups, they only wanted us to inform the community that some people were doing awful things in the area while impersonating members of their group, that's all the communiqué said. On that occasion the National Police helped us and we managed to avoid horrendous consequences, but there's no way to prevent them forcing us to help them;

—the idea of having regulation prohibiting armed groups to use community media may be appropriate for regions such as Boyacá or Cundinamarca, where there's not much violence. In those regions, when someone comes to the station with a message to transmit, you can simply say "no." But I know there are regions where conflict is rampant, where four armies are present: paramilitaries, guerrillas, common delinquents, and on the other side, the country's armed forces, so there's horrendous conflict. What happens in those regions? The stations aren't allowing illegal groups to have a voice and participate, but if someone comes pointing a machine gun at your head and saying "you have to transmit this," well, you have to do it, because no regulation is going to help you then; you have to do it!

—I say, life above all! When confronted with a machine gun, a weapon, a threat, you have to think twice, and if it's unavoidable, you have to do it!

—but if they put a machine gun against my head and they tell me to transmit a communiqué, or a forbidden *corrido*,[18] something that goes against my principles, and he says "life above all," I ask, what type of life? A life of kneeling down? A life without dignity? A life with violence? The future depends on us! But it's not about getting yourself shot, it's about negotiating;

—but any type of resistance will get you [killed]!

—and as for negotiating, their hands don't shake when it's about killing you! I say "no," and PUM [sound of gun shot], at once!

—the question is if, as a collective [of all citizens' and community media] we are going to let them corner us; what are we to do as a collective?

Based on the sound of his voice, the next speaker appears to be a child of about twelve years old:

—I want to propose that we ask the Ministry of Communications to place these stations under a special regimen, so that if we have to transmit those messages, then they don't blame us for it;

—but the ministry cannot guarantee our safety. Who will prevent the other group from coming the next day to screw us? Or, tomorrow, the other group will come and say, "You transmitted the message for the other group, so now you have to transmit our message too." (Unidad de Radio—Mesa Regional Boyacá, Arauca, Casanare 2001)

Through discussions such as this one, citizens' media pioneers gradually formulated methods of responding to armed conflict. They learned that each situation and each context is different, that formulas do not work and neither does legislation. The group discussions began to value collective actions, they became aware of the tenuousness of their situations. If their radio or television station is left alone by armed actors one day, the next they may have to deal with dangerous pressures from guerrillas, paramilitaries, mafias, or the armed forces. Because of the war, each citizens' medium has to find its own "safe place" where it can still contribute but without becoming a target of armed groups. In some cases, citizens' media have had to learn the hard way; for example, in Magdalena Medio two community radio producers were assassinated in 1999 (Cadavid 2000, 4). As a result, Magdalena Medio community radios initiated a continuous process of reflexivity where at each step of the way they set the boundaries of a safe place, define the themes and issues that can be talked about and those that can not.

Addressing War (or Not)

A recurring topic in these discussions is how stations can mention armed violence on the air without becoming a target of armed groups. Participants at a Seed Workshop in Caquetá said: "I think, that here in Caquetá, to speak about that which everyone is afraid to mention: coca, and guerrillas . . . the question is how to speak about everything that is happening to peasants, all their suffering" (Unidad de Radio—Taller Belén 1997). Citizens' media pioneers have developed creative tactics that may indirectly allow them to carve a space for expression. In one of these tactics, radio stations feature on-air discussions of how armed violence affects a distant region, avoiding mentioning specific, identifiable actors or actions that might be threatening to local armed groups. For example, a Seed Workshop participant and media leader from Caquetá said:

> The program about armed violence in Boyacá we just heard explores the issues raised by the exploitation of emeralds and the emerald mafias. It makes me think that maybe we could do the same here with coca, discussing how it is planted and harvested. Taking such programs to other regions, to Boyacá for example, could be interesting. They could listen to our problems involving violence and coca and we could listen to their problems involving emerald exploitation . . . two different contexts that involve, on one side, violence, and on the other, wealth. (Unidad de Radio—Taller Belén de los Andaquíes 1997)

Other media pioneers implement strategies in which the medium attempts to reach out to armed groups with subtle messages, as explained by participants at a roundtable in Boyacá:

> In Paz del Aripuro, Casanare, we address the issue of conflict and violence in an indirect manner. For example, we bring together different religious groups to discuss the causes of violence, why armed conflict is happening in our area, and what can we do to stop it. This type of programming tries to strengthen values of peace among those not involved in armed conflict, so that they stay away [from armed groups]. We also try to reach those who are involved and who we know listen to the station, in a very indirect, subtle way [por debajo de cuerda], so that they realize that we, unarmed civilians, are not to blame for what they are going through. (Unidad de Radio—Mesa Regional Boyacá, Arauca, Casanare 2001)

Other alternative tactics involve children's programming: "In some places the medium addresses issues of armed violence through the children; because children can talk about many issues that adults cannot even mention" (Unidad de Radio—Mesa Regional Boyacá, Arauca, Casanare 2001). In still other cases, radio stations transmit programs about armed conflict that are clearly authored by external, and preferably international, organizations, such as the United Nations Development Program: "We can do conferences, or presentations, but not dialogue, because dialogue implies feedback; instead, experts come and lecture, and their words reach the listener, and end of story" (Unidad de Radio—Mesa Regional Boyacá, Arauca, Casanare 2001).

One pioneer explained how these media use what Jeanine El Gazi calls circumlocution, defined as "addressing in an indirect and tangential way how the violence and abuse of armed actors is affecting people" (El Gazi 2001, 3):

> I'd like to make it clear that human rights are not only violated when someone is murdered, but also when a child is denied an education, or a woman is not allowed to realize her potential as a human being. From this perspective, because we live in a region immersed in armed conflict, we cannot talk about the violation of human rights in the forms of death, silence, or selective massacres, but we can have these discussions from the point of view of children, women, or youth, and what they think about their rights being violated. These perspectives are denunciations of human rights violations that go beyond denouncing the number of dead, which is a narrow definition of human rights anyway. (Unidad de Radio—Mesa Regional Magdalena Medio and Santanderes 2000)

Some citizens' media have developed programs specifically focused on peace initiatives:

> There's a guy named Henry Holguin, and he's the driving force behind the peace pacts among barrio gangs; he has secured fifty-seven pacts in different neighborhoods in Medellín, very controversial work, but very important for the city. He produced a program for our television station in which he told people where the next meeting would take place, what happened in the last meeting among the Cañada gang and the Silla gang, and how things were going between the gang of 29 and Los Calvos, that type of thing. (Unidad de Radio—Mesa Regional Magdalena Medio and Santanderes 2000)

The question of what to do about *corridos prohibidos* (forbidden *corridos*) sparked complex arguments among citizens' media pioneers. The *corrido* is a Mexican musical genre that usually tells the story of a popular hero. Composed as long troubadour-type songs, *corridos* recount their hero's origin, personal biography, victories, and defeats. Traditionally, Colombians are passionate fans of Mexican music in general, including *corridos*. During the late 1980s, a new type of *corrido*, known as *corridos prohibidos*, began circulating in the country. These songs told stories of guerrilla, paramilitary warriors, or drug traffickers in terms glorifying their personal histories, violent acts, illicit enrichment, and violation of the law. Among citizens' media pioneers, these songs pose specific and complex dilemmas, as I heard in this discussion:

—we have heard two different positions. The first position suggests that addressing armed conflict means giving a voice to the armed ones *[los armados];*[19] those are the stations playing *corridos prohibidos.* The other position argues, "No! I don't want to give armed violence any visibility," and so *corridos prohibidos* will never have a place on the programming grid of these community radio stations;

—others say, "the phenomenon of *corridos prohibidos* is part of our identity, so it is important to document it, be critical of it, and propose some kind of value judgment on it." Here is my first proposal: *Corridos prohibidos* are clearly not music for music's sake, so we must ask, "what do we say about the music?" In this case we could have a radio station that decides to do a program about *corridos prohibidos,* playing the songs, but including analysis and criticism of what these songs are all about;

—but that music is just promoting illicit drugs and violence!

—in our station, two of the youngsters that helped us in the initial phase loved *corridos prohibidos,* and they are the reason I had the chance to listen to the lyrics; the content truly incites violence, drug consumption, and drug cultivation. In one of the songs I heard, when the guys in the red truck [drug traffickers] were annihilated by the police, the traffickers were glorified as victims and martyrs. As far as possible, it is best to avoid playing that stuff, and avoid the glorification of violence and drugs, even if you add analysis and criticism. I believe that for many people hearing these songs makes them curious to become involved in those kinds of things;

—I believe our role is to question people about why they like that type of stuff. Is it the theme? Or is it the rhythm? Or the marketing done to sell this type of music? Plus, it's not only *corridos prohibidos,* there are many other types of music that transmit questionable values. I ask you to reflect on *vallenatos,*[20] or the music that the armed forces are distributing for free station to station, the *vallenato* band of the army . . . that, too, is sectarian, it transmits questionable values;

—there is another type of *corrido,* using the same rhythm and the same genre, but with lyrics about people who *were* involved in drug trafficking but now discourage it;

—the problem is not the music! What matters is not the rhythm but what the lyrics incite; here we are, completely focused on how horrible *corridos prohibidos* are, but they are *not* the problem! The problem is that we must determine how to use the medium of radio to change the culture, and ourselves because with these media one can truly have an influence. We make people cry, we make people laugh;

—we know that more than 70 percent of the content transmitted by community radio stations is music, so we do have to consider the criteria used to select the music. I believe that when we establish criteria to define our programming, priority should be given to the criteria for music programs. The problem is not the *corridos prohibidos,* the *rancheras* that talk so badly about women, the *carranguera,* or the *champeta* with its erotic dance movements; the problem is how well prepared we are as community radio producers and popular communicators to transmit these kinds of music, whether they are foreign or national. Let's not lie to ourselves, rarely do we ask ourselves these questions when we are designing the programming; the criteria to select the music is the most neglected aspect of our programming. We say loudly that we will not transmit a program about witches because that type of content threatens our communities, but we do transmit lyrics that harass women and children, and other vulnerable social groups. I believe that we need to reflect on the types of music we are transmitting, and determine our music selections by carefully considering each regional, local context. Do *vallenatos* make sense in my region? Do *rancheras?* What music should be made relevant according to our local context?

—the problem is that in many of our community stations, the announcer selects the music, and whatever music he likes is what gets played. We should advocate for each station to create a programming committee specifically responsible for selecting the music, so this matter is not simply left to the announcers;

—what we could do is to produce peace-oriented programs about the *corridos prohibidos,* such as the ones the ministry produced;[21] we could take all those *corridos prohibidos* and produce peace pedagogy programs. We should not turn into media with music blacklists, like the Catholic Church did in the past with books, because that would be terrible! (Unidad de Radio—Mesa Regional Boyacá, Arauca, Casanare 2001)

Commonly, citizens' media pioneers find a compromise in contexts of armed conflict by focusing their programming on analysis of armed conflict while staying away from burning news and information. A neighborhood newspaper editor explained:

San Antonio de Prado is among the most peaceful districts in the [Medellín] area. We don't have the common delinquency of the city here. Neither do we have violence in the form of guerrillas taking over of towns, nor in the form of *pesca milagrosa*,[22] but all that stuff does happen in our vicinity, and that's what makes us part of the armed conflict. We receive waves of displaced people fleeing the violence in nearby municipalities to come here. Not long ago, there was a guerrilla attack on a paramilitary group in the vicinity, and because that neighborhood doesn't have its own newspaper, people looked to our newspaper—the closest to the events—to cover it. People bought our newspaper to see how we showed the dead bodies, but we didn't publish that, so people complained. We waited until the next edition, a month later, and published a long analysis, complete with interviews with armed conflict experts and proposals to consolidate Popular Peace Committees, all with the goal of starting a dialogue with the community about how to maintain the climate of peace which has more or less survived here in San Antonio. (Unidad de Radio—Mesa Regional Magdalena Medio and Santanderes 2000)

Another common option to deal with armed conflict is to stay away from news programs altogether, so as to completely avoid mentioning armed conflict. The following excerpts attest to this:

We have paid a high price lately, due to the situation of unrest in our region. We haven't been able to realize our dream of producing a news program. As you saw in my presentation, for obvious reasons we don't have any news programs; we don't want to get in trouble or risk the safety of the kids that work with us. (Unidad de Radio—Mesa Regional Boyacá, Arauca, Casanare 2001)

In truth, on our community radio station we rarely say anything about armed conflict because doing so would provoke much trouble and we are afraid one day they will get us and disappear us, which is so easy for them. We don't have a news program because they [the armed groups] prevent us from doing so. We transmit the national news program from SIPAZ;[23] but not our own local news; we don't want to risk the lives of those leading the community radio station in San Vicente de Chucurí, a situation we share with many other community radio stations in Colombia. (Unidad de Radio—Mesa Regional Magdalena Medio and Santanderes 2000)

With reference to conflict and violence? We cannot address those issues directly. We cannot address either conflict or violence; we have to address only peace. The question is not if we want to address those themes or not. Simply we can't. It's the same for Arauca and Casanare and some regions of Boyacá. (Unidad de Radio—Mesa Regional Boyacá, Arauca, Casanare 2001)

War Is Not All We Are

Elsewhere I explained one of the most significant findings of my fieldwork among Colombian citizens' media pioneers: "War does not exhaust it all. War has a tremendous negative impact on the social and cultural fabric of unarmed civilian communities; armed conflict touches and permeates everything, appropriates social and cultural processes, public spaces, and people's ways of relating and interacting. Yet, people, their everyday lives, and creativity are not entirely engulfed by war" (Rodríguez 2008, 9). Apart from their direct responses to armed conflict, Colombian citizens' media play another significant role—sometimes I think the most significant role—in giving visibility to what remains beyond the reach of war. Citizens' media pioneers make a conscious decision to focus their microphones and their television and video cameras on social and cultural spaces where people loudly confirm that they are living lives outside of the armed conflict afflicting their communities, and that war has not become the main protagonist in their lives. Communities acknowledge the presence of armed conflict in their lives and territories but also make it very clear that war does not exhaust who they are. In regions of armed conflict, what people say and do, and how they live their lives and spend their days encompasses much more than their actions to resist, survive, or stop war. The discussions of citizens' media pioneers frequently express this perspective: "Without a doubt, the great majority of Colombians are peaceful people. Here in the south, we resist being labeled 'violent departments' because the truth is that most of us are contributing to a social fabric of peace. We resent being visible only when there's war news in our territory" (Unidad de Radio—Mesa Regional Huila 2001). Based on her fieldwork in different parts of the world, Carolyn Nordstrom finds that most people living in war zones will not engage in violent behavior; instead, "people stop war by creating peace, not by fighting war better or harder or meaner" (Nordstrom 2004, 179). Other citizens' media pioneers' discussions brought up a similar point:

> Without ignoring the fact that we live in a region of armed conflict, or the fear and suspicion that invade us every day, we prefer to talk about life. Talking about life does not mean suspending all talk about war; to talk about life means talking about our girls and boys and the farmers that work here, and it is also to question and interrogate the word "war," which for us goes way beyond the conflict between paramilitaries and any other group. (Unidad de Radio—Mesa Regional Magdalena Medio and Santanderes 2000)

> The idea behind the SIPAZ news programs is to give visibility to all those processes that communities generate which are invisible in the commercial

media; it's about getting to know the other face of the region, the municipalities, and the people. As we know well, there are many more of us building spaces for peace than destroying what we have. We try to provide information useful for peace building, based on peoples' narratives and the cultural diversity of the regions. We cover real processes that strengthen a peaceful social fabric, processes authored by kids, youth, and mothers. . . .

For example, does anyone here know of a place called San Pablo, south of Bolívar? All you hear about is that it's a region of guerrillas, drug trafficking, and goldmines, and that the government is planning to make it a demilitarized zone as part of peace dialogues with the ELN. Who would have thought that in that same place, in the middle of the forest, there's a women's collective running a poultry commercial venture! We showcased it in our community radio network, in a program called *Tejiendo la Red* [Weaving the Net], where each municipality has three minutes to talk about their projects. It's interesting that all they needed was a small recorder to produce this story, which was heard in the entire region. Before the show, no one had any idea that in San Pablo, where it's all about armed conflict, war, dollars, and coca, there are also these women and their children, with such proposals. (Unidad de Radio—Mesa Regional Boyacá, Arauca, Casanare 2001)

Silenced Does Not Mean Silence

Colombia's armed conflict is the oldest in the Western hemisphere. As I explained in this book's introduction and first three chapters, violence permeates and attempts to dictate the social and cultural fabric of unarmed civilian communities that have to coexist with armed groups. This is well known to citizens' media pioneers who have witnessed the normalizing of the use of force in resolving everyday life conflicts with neighbors. The pioneers are very familiar with the ways violence has come to permeate communal interactions, and thus use media as tools to resist this invasion. Believing their media to be invaluable in activating processes of cultural transformation, the pioneers welcome the challenging task of using community media as tools for cultural resistance against the normalization of violence in everyday life. Citizens' media target local cultures—all the social processes by which communities make sense of who they are (identity), and how they should interact with others (communication). Inch by inch, these media attempt to reappropriate every thread of social and cultural fabric that has been eroded by war and conflict. These pioneers see their media as tools for opening communication spaces in which the aggressive culture of armed conflict can be interrogated and proposals for more peaceful cultures can become viable, appealing alternatives.

In her study of reconciliation in Alto Ariari, Tatiana Duplat found that communities engaged in similar processes that attempted to "delegitimize violence as a way of interacting and as political action" (Duplat 2003, 338).

Colombian citizens' media introduce new identities, new ways for people to interact with one another and with the environment, and new ways to manage and sometimes resolve conflict. A media pioneer from Magdalena Medio explains:

> The community radio station is part of a wider cultural project we have been working on for nine or ten years in San Vicente de Chucurí. In this place where war has unfortunately damaged so much, where we have learned to disregard each other as human beings, where we cannot approach each other without hurting each other, we have found culture to be the formula for learning again to get close to each other and be able to touch each other without harming each other *[nos ha permitido acercarnos y tocarnos sin hacernos daño]*. Drawing from our own aesthetics, and also from our anger and all the rancor locked in our hearts, the community radio station has allowed people to envision new ways of feeling, seeing, and listening, both within our community and in the wider region of Magdalena Medio. The station's central element is culture, but not culture understood merely as artistic expression. Here culture means all the imaginable possibilities that can contribute to regional development. (Unidad de Radio—Mesa Regional Magdalena Medio and Santanderes 2000)

Similarly, another citizens' media pioneer said:

> We need to work with the power of civil society to use language and expression to find alternatives to violence and coercion, based on cultural diversity. We need to find these alternatives in each of our municipalities, otherwise we are contributing to the same patterns of disregarding the other. Here, the other—understood as whoever is different from us—has always been our enemy, the one we need to push aside, and the one we don't have to take into consideration. The idea is for our community radio stations, founded as projects supporting life, to respond to this situation of generalized violence and exclusion of the other.
>
> Our toughest challenge is to make the community radio stations into the best possible settings for dialogue, coexistence, and peace. . . . [W]e need to assume that in our role as citizens' media, we can contribute to the construction of this type of setting; otherwise, we are contributing to deepening conflict in this country. (Unidad de Radio—Mesa Regional Cauca, Putumayo, Nariño 2000)

Finalizing a roundtable plenary, participants decided that their citizens' media should:

address themes related to conflict in everyday life, so that communities can approach the resolution of conflict in a negotiated way, and see that conflicts can be managed in nonviolent ways. This reinforces the idea that peaceful conflict resolution is one way these media can strengthen public spheres and citizenship, ultimately contributing to peace. Rather than dealing directly with armed conflict, community radio stations focus on the peaceful resolution of everyday life conflicts, opening spaces where those conflicts are dealt with and talked about. These media need to engage in a kind of pedagogy of conflict in the community. They need to promote attitudes of respect and peaceful coexistence. (Unidad de Radio—Mesa Regional Boyacá, Arauca, Casanare 2001)

Citizens' media pioneers meet the challenge of peacebuilding by working toward a culture of citizenship (*cultura ciudadana*) and strong public spheres.[24] In the Colombian context, the term *cultura ciudadana* refers to a cultural fabric woven from numerous social processes that contribute to peaceful coexistence, among which the main ones include strengthening public spheres for dialogue about public policy (as opposed to individual interests controlling public resources); recognizing different identities as legitimate subjects with equal rights to access public spheres and voice their interests, goals, and dreams; normalizing nonviolent conflict management and resolution (as opposed to using force to annihilate any "other"); the right and responsibility of citizens to oversee public institutions and their representatives; and transparency and accountability on the part of public institutions and public officials.

From the perspective of the discourse of *cultura ciudadana*, Colombian citizens' media pioneers clearly articulate how their media can contribute to strengthening public spheres, dialogue, and participation, nurturing a cultural fabric that embraces difference, and improving good governance. In what remains of this chapter I attempt to present the pioneers' ideas about citizens' media and *cultura ciudadana*.

Using Citizens' Media to Nurture *Cultura Ciudadana*

As citizens' media pioneers debated how to use radio, video, television, and other communication technologies in complex contexts of armed conflict, their vision of an ideal community medium began to crystallize. The following discussions among several community media leaders reflect how this ideal takes shape:

—Why do we want a community radio station?
—to be used as a space of encounter *[espacio de encuentro]*;
—to educate the type of citizen we want;
—the programming grid should emerge from our dialogue with the community, so we need to offer training workshops to help the community learn to produce radio, and audiences learn to be critical;
—we want the community to lead this process . . . in three years, the community should be able to take over the station;
—the community should have direct participation in the station, representatives are not enough. (Unidad de Radio—Mesa Regional Huila 2001)

The ideal community radio station would play important roles in the community, strengthening a sense of belonging, activating public life, allowing the community to look at itself from the inside, helping the community build a life project, improving the quality of life, and addressing public services. The station should have power to lobby the municipal government, and should also be an active participant in municipal development plans. (Unidad de Radio—Mesa Regional Cauca, Putumayo, Nariño 2000)

In contrast to the previous, more militant generation of community media, these pioneers envision their media as peace tools and catalysts for processes that strengthen participatory democracies, rather than as tools for mobilization in alliance with specific social movements:

—The way to build this nation is through dialogue around the meaning of citizenship, the cultural richness so alive despite armed conflict, and the local spaces of peaceful coexistence, which should be all of our declared cultural patrimony;
—embracing diversity and difference has to be the foundation upon which we build this nation;
—acknowledging the other and recognizing our self-worth should be the starting point from which we build this nation. (Unidad de Radio—Diplomado Cartagena 2002)

For decades these community leaders have witnessed conflict and the presence of armed groups, the normalization of violating citizens' rights, the legitimization of corruption, bribery, and illicit drug economies eroding their communities' social fabric. In these contexts, violence and aggression in everyday interactions become the norm. The core belief of citizens' media pioneers is that their communication projects can reduce this type of violence. As the previous sections in this chapter explain, the violence provoked by armed groups is usually beyond the scope of local citizens' media.[25] Also, citizens' media pioneers know that, in the end, all armed groups feed off of their local communities; guerrillas, paramilitaries, and mafias comprise Colombian men and women who have given up on peaceful ways of building a decent life. The pioneers place their bets on the creation of an alternative culture, driven by empowered yet unarmed citizens able to transform their loud voices and views into public policies that shape their municipalities. Tatiana Duplat explains this gamble in more eloquent words: "The dark forces ruling these local contexts are so numerous, and so strong, the armed ones *[los armados]* are so horrifying, that the citizenship option, of strengthening *cultura ciudadana* becomes the only option to confront this, to do something at the local level" (Duplat 2004).

An intimidating, inquisitive gaze and quick satirical wit have made Guillermo Pérez a well-known character in the world of Colombian community media. Among the most brilliant people I have ever met, Pérez is a high school teacher, and also the founder and director of Custodia Estéreo 101.2, a community radio station that operates out of the school where he teaches. Custodia Estéreo is located in Inírida, the urban capital of the department of Guainía, on the Colombian border with Venezuela. Among the youngest and most isolated and marginalized departments in the country, Guainía is an exemplar of the variables that erode social fabrics: state neglect, presence of armed groups, illicit drug economies, and official corruption that create a survival-of-the-fittest type of mentality. In his school, Pérez is witness to the normalization of violence seeping through his students' interactions. He experiments with communication processes as interventions to disrupt the violence:

In 1995 parents and teachers began to discuss the school curriculum. We [the teachers] asked parents: "Why do you want to educate your child?" We provoked them [parents], telling them we should just close the schools, and instead set up *empanada*-vending carts,[26] or coca plots, or some shit like that, because the only thing we are giving the region is *raspachines* [coca leaf pickers] with high school diplomas, nothing else. Why? Because we don't have a well-thought-out education project for the region.

People questioned the youngsters' participation in these discussions, saying that the kids didn't have anything to say, they were nothing but an intellectual cemetery. But I thought, "Of course the kids have a lot to say, the thing is that they are saying it in different languages, like the music they listen to, cussing in class, and drawing penises ejaculating on the walls of the girls' bathrooms . . . those kids are saying something!" But others [other teachers], in the same school argued, "Those sons-of-bitches kids! Can you see how they have damaged the school's walls?" Precisely! If they are filling the walls with drawings, it's because they are trying to say something! As we examined this more carefully, we discovered that it was the boys who drew penises in the girls' bathroom, not the girls. And so I asked them, "Why?" Because, you know me, I tend to see the other side of everything, so I thought, if it's the girls filling the blackboards and the walls with drawings of ejaculating penises, well, that's great! They are expressing their sexual desires. But why the boys? We found out it's the aggressive way in which the boys tell the girls they love them! So we created a strategy, and presented the boys with a challenge. I asked them, "So you're telling me you're not capable of getting a woman in bed through poetry and words? You're incapable of seducing a woman by talking to her? *A punta de labia?* All you can do is push her and cuss?"

We created a love letter contest and 176 students subscribed! The idea was to tell them: "Hey bro, why don't you interact with the girls in a different way? Do you want her? Well, can you ask her in a different way? Let's see what you can do, tell her, in a different way," instead of labeling them perverts and hitting them with long moralistic lectures. We got sponsors and organized the First Love Letter Contest. This year we are doing the fifth contest. We got a jury to judge the letters, which cannot be anonymous, we need name and grade. We ask them if they want to read their letter or if we should get someone to read it for them, and all the letters are read in public at the school, so the Love Letters initiative becomes a recital, and it's always packed. The Love Letters Contest was the mother of the radio station . . . because when we got the kids in a public space, in front of a microphone and loudspeakers where they could express themselves, what we found out is that they have tons of stuff to say, but they were saying it in their own distinct ways. The question became, "Where is the space where these kids can speak?" We saw the need to create spaces for expression. We created the Love Letter Contest, the Wall of Graffiti, and the Book of Complaints, and things improved, the interaction among them is so cool now. (Pérez 2004)

These initial experiments and their successes prompted Pérez to consider a community radio station as the next step. Pérez submitted a request for a community radio license and Custodia Estéreo, his school's nonprofit radio station, entirely run by the students with help from teachers, began broadcasting in March of 1998.

Again and again, I hear the citizens' media pioneers discuss the need to transform their media into communication spaces for local citizens' voices. In the words of Magdalena Medio community radio leader Orley Durán:

Our oldest program is *Imagining My World: The Planet of Boys and Girls,* where kids come together, all kinds of kids, peasant kids, poor kids, school kids, and explore their opinions about issues that affect them, their dreams, and their fantasies. This program gives the kids a voice that can be heard by adults, and now adults have a little more respect for the opinions of kids. I used to be the director of the program, but now I have lost my role as director; I have lost everything because the kids do everything! They do it all, even the controls. We leave them alone to produce the show, and sometimes they do crazy stuff, but that's the idea, that they express themselves, and if they want to invite an adult to the program, they'll do it . . . they haven't invited us in a long time. These are the type of communication spaces that the radio station opens. (Unidad de Radio—Mesa Regional Magdalena Medio and Santanderes 2000)[27]

In a documentary about Magdalena Medio's community radio stations produced by Alfonso Gumucio Dagron and Amparo Cadavid, a girl and radio producer describes the feeling of recognition she received from her community: "In my neighborhood there's a lady that, every time our program airs, takes her entire sound system out on the sidewalk and amplifies the broadcasting for all the neighbors to listen. And I feel so happy when I walk by, because everyone congratulates me!" (Gumucio Dagron and Cadavid 2006). In Sierra Leone, Search for Common Ground (SFCG), a nongovernmental international organization working with media for peacebuilding, experimented with similar uses of media produced by children. Facilitated by SFCG, Golden Kids News is a weekly news feature radio program produced by a team of about sixty children about children's lives. Frequently affected by a decade-long brutal armed conflict, children narrate their experiences as abducted fighters in rebel guerrillas or as sex slaves; they recount how war has separated them from their families, how rebel groups use them on the front lines ("because it is believed that children are fearless fighters") (Rolt 2005). Ten FM radio stations in different regions of the country broadcast the programs.[28]

In the context of trying to figure out how to use community media in situations where the use of force has become normal and difference is regarded with contempt, Colombian citizens' media pioneers find in *cultura ciudadana* an ideal social model that encourages "everyone to understand difference. We understand that we are all different but that there's room for everyone: that is how you build citizenship" (Unidad de Radio—Mesa Regional Boyacá, Arauca, Casanare 2001).

Cultura Ciudadana *and Peacebuilding*

As I said before, citizens' media pioneers bet on the creation of *cultura ciudadana* as a way, perhaps the only way, their media can intervene in local contexts of conflict and violence. These pioneers evidently believe in a causal relationship between *cultura ciudadana* and violence, in which an increase in *cultura ciudadana* is followed by a decrease in violence. Of all of the ideas expressed by the citizens' media pioneers, this is perhaps the most difficult to articulate. How does *cultura ciudadana* reduce violence in an isolated Colombian municipality? Again, we can find answers in the refined insight of Guillermo Pérez:

> In radio, the process of strengthening public spheres has so much potential, because many stupid people change after they begin producing radio. Why? Because being a radio producer allows them to immerse themselves in the daily life of their communities in ways they couldn't see before, so they start to see things differently. They start feeling that they belong to something, belong from the inside, instead of just seeing things from the outside.
>
> Let me tell you about one case. [Inírida], just thirty-six years old, is the youngest municipality in the country, and a frontier region full of religious missions. Their idea of a mission, however, is so crude . . . the more shit they eat, the prettier they feel . . . and the churches compete for parishioners, so the pulpits become sordid spaces of violence and self-serving monologues. This brings negative consequences, especially in schools, because after all, the schools in a region like this are social spaces of convergence. In these towns, schools are often the only shared social space where everyone converges. Kids from every faith, and every church come together, and in the school classroom we can feel the aggression between kids of different faiths. The aggression is also evident in the neighborhoods, and even within families, because maybe you are Adventist but your daughter wants to be a Baptist. The problems of violence and aggression are visible everywhere.
>
> So when the radio station became a solid presence in the municipality, I called leaders of the different churches and told them "I have a proposal for you. You are all very interesting, so there will be a daily program on the station for all of you." We carved out a five minute spot every day, from six to six-o-five; Monday was for Catholics, Tuesday for the Movimiento Misionero Mundial [World Mission Movement], Wednesday for Adventists, Thursday for Gran Sion de Amor [Great Sion of Love], and Fridays for Jehovah's Witnesses. . . . But, we told them, "You cannot attack the others. Neither can you, for example, use the radio station to promote the Catholic Holy Week."

The idea is that the station's programming grid is a reflection of the town, and as we are not all Catholics, the station cannot promote one over the others. The medium guarantees equity to all religious communities. Because they behaved well, we extended the program to fifteen minutes and titled it *En el Cuarto con Dios* [A Quarter with God].[29] Today, this program is three years old, and full of beautiful things . . . because we told them, "Listen, at the pulpit, you can say that the others [from different faiths] are idolaters. At the pulpit, if that's what you want, you can sink your teeth into each other to the death, but not here! This is a different medium; here you cannot attack each other, because this medium, this little gadget intrudes everywhere, in people's bathrooms, in the kitchen, in the car, the plot, the *conuco*.[30] In other words, radio is like the crazy aunt *[la loca de la casa]* that goes everywhere, so we cannot use it to attack others."

So the religious representatives themselves came up with three rules. The first rule is the "Right to Annunciation," meaning that the program is to be used to explain beliefs, but not for religious proselytism. For example, if your faith preaches that alcoholism and drug addiction are faith problems, then, sure, come here and explain that, but you cannot come to the station and tell all the heroin addicts, the marijuana addicts, and the cocaine addicts that they will be saved by simply embracing your faith; that's not allowed. The second rule is the "Right to Denunciation." Four years ago, the entire departmental administration belonged to the World Missionary Movement, but their political actions totally contradicted the way they describe their faith, so the program can be used to denounce religious hypocrisy in public life. The third rule is "Brothers in Christ," meaning that, after all, all of the groups are Christians and should therefore respect one another. So the groups began listening to one another, and the more they listened to the others, the smarter they became, because now when they talk, they have to consider what the other said yesterday. Listen, I give a shit about religion, but this here is really amazing! It's such a good example of peaceful coexistence. You don't see the atrocious levels of aggression that we used to see before. I believe that the fact that it's a daily program, week after week, helps people get the idea and makes them ask themselves, "What's the problem with listening to someone who is very different from me? Someone who sings songs that I don't sing?" (Pérez 2004)

Pérez carefully designs communication spaces in which local groups, collectives, and even individuals can voice their identities. Programs, formats, production routines, regulations, and procedures at Custodia Estéreo are meticulously designed to trigger respectful dialogue among the various identities in the municipality. In different corners of the world, community leaders find similar uses of citizens' media to promote peace. For example, DXUP-FM, a community radio station operating in Upi, on the Mindanao Islands, Philippines, maintains a communication space where local ethnic groups, including the indigenous Tedurays, Muslims, and Christians, among others, are in continuous dialogue about their religious identities. In this region, engulfed for decades in armed conflict between Muslim guerrillas and government forces, radio programs that promote interreligious dialogue play a significant role in de-escalating potential conflict. A local imam says: "We hear programmes about Islam and Christianity done by our own people. So we learn about each other's way of life and we learn to live in peace. . . . [Listeners] hear discussions on religious ideas and the way you live and they begin to respect the other. . . . Sometimes people ask me, 'in your Koran, I heard in the radio that this is like this, very similar to our Bible.' . . . That shows how community radio creates peace" (Seneviratne 2008).

Dozens of other Colombian citizens' media attempt, like Custodia Estéreo does in Inírida, to transform daily interactions among Colombians from aggression and violence to civil dissent. By disrupting violence the stations work toward stopping the erosion of the social fabrics of local communities that has been caused by more than half a century of normalized and legitimized violence and aggression. As they disrupt violence, the stations interject communication models in which different identities have legitimate access to public spheres, and where "different" does not mean "enemy." In Pérez's words:

> Ideas of community like, "we are all little brothers and sisters and we are going to hold hands?" Forget it! Now, on the other hand, there is the idea that because we are different we are going to snatch each other's heads and fill each other with bullets. Well, no! I believe that coexistence, responsible coexistence, implies that I can say "no" to you. It implies that I can say to you, "I don't like that; I am 'allergic' to that, but I can understand that there are people that do like it. So if you like it, go for it." (Pérez 2004)

Pérez's notions resonate with Jesús Martín Barbero's understanding of diversity:

> The idea of diversity has lost its value, because it's understood as "everyone is allowed to exist, as long as the other doesn't have anything to do with me, does not question me, and doesn't mess with me and my stability." I believe that there's true diversity in a country not when the biological fact that we are all different is established, because that's undeniable, but when we can

believe the notion that no one has a complete truth and we acknowledge that a great deal of being permitted to be who we are depends on being able to accept what others are. Diversity is not just there, it has to be constructed as we become interlocutors, when we seriously listen to others, even if doing so means risking our own certainties. (Ministerio de Cultura 2004)

Will citizens' media pioneers succeed in curbing the nation's violence? My outlook remains skeptical. I am encouraged by the fact that citizens' media initiatives, driven by goals of achieving a *cultura ciudadana* and peaceful coexistence, are mirrored by numerous other peacebuilding initiatives in schools, municipal governments, environmental organizations, public libraries, women's collectives, and associations of displaced people (Samper 2002). Just as citizens' media use communication, these projects use art, education, reading, writing, grassroots political participation, gender equity discussions, and environmental education to advance *cultura ciudadana*.[31] Historian Daniel Pécaut observed that "coexistence initiatives, regional development and peace programs, and the efforts of so many communities to self-organize and stay away from armed violence constitute a testimony to how vast social sectors resist war" (Pécaut 2001, 19). Colombia is simultaneously engulfed in armed conflict, and home to concentrations of people who share a profound ethos of respect for the other and an immutable trust in public dialogue as a means to manage conflict and avoid aggression.

I am skeptical, however, because these peacebuilding pockets exist almost exclusively among Colombian working classes. To this day, the only *cultura ciudadana* initiative I have encountered among Colombia's elite is a required course on citizenship competencies taught in private schools and mandated by the Ministry of Education to all schools in the country. I am wary of how economic and political power groups will respond to the strong voices of empowered citizens. Will they respect those who are different? Will the elites share the public sphere? The nation's resources and opportunities? The responsibility for nation-building? Or will they respond with repression and violence built on stigmatization and demonization of difference?[32] Pécaut's statement resonates with my skepticism, when he says that the missing element is the elites' willingness to recognize the urgent need to fortify national and regional democratic institutions (Pécaut 2001, 19).

One promising trend toward *cultura ciudadana* in Colombia is an idea known as Responsabilidad Social Empresarial [Corporate Social

Responsibility]. In subscribing to this idea, corporations commit to improving the quality of life in the communities where they operate. In my view, if properly executed, Responsabilidad Social can be an enactment of *cultura ciudadana,* taken on by a corporation instead of individuals and communities. An option that would involve not only the working classes, but professionals, corporate executives, traditional economic elites. A recent study, however, found that only four out of ten Colombian corporate executives even know what Responsabilidad Social Empresarial means (El Tiempo 2007). Will power elites rise to the challenges of *cultura ciudadana?*

Using Media to Strengthen Democratic Institutions

Although rarely stated explicitly by community leaders and NGOs, the close affiliation between *cultura ciudadana* and participatory democracy is clear. Indeed, citizen involvement in politics is an important component of *cultura ciudadana.* In the Colombian context, this involvement most often happens in municipal-level politics rather than at the regional or national level. *Cultura ciudadana* discourages practices such as selling your vote or establishing patron–client relationships with local politicians. *Cultura ciudadana* encourages citizens to be well informed about municipal political affairs, vote responsibly, oversee local politicians' actions and omissions, demand transparency and accountability, and get involved in municipal development planning committees and in municipal health, education, and cultural commissions.

Citizens' media pioneers have committed themselves to the challenge of making their media effective tools for the creation of *cultura ciudadana,* good governance, and accountability. As I explore thoroughly in chapter 3, the simple act of holding a microphone or television camera in front of mayors and other local government officials changes the dynamics of municipal politics:

> After the first time we put the television cameras in front of the Municipal Council and transmitted the session live, people asked the council members, "Hey, why did I vote for you if you don't even talk during the council's sessions?" A constituent told one representative, "You are not doing a good job; you don't even dress properly!" At the next session, we saw how the representatives changed in response to this feedback. They showed up in ties and long-sleeve shirts, with their proposals written and well prepared. We don't even have a journalist doing any type of coverage; we simply turn on

the cameras and let people see what the council representatives are doing. People make their own assessments about how they voted; we don't get involved beyond that. (Unidad de Radio—Mesa Regional Cauca 2000)

Our department doesn't have a university, there's no sewage system or potable water system, we only have electricity six, sometimes eight hours a day, and so what are we playing here? The radio station has to be like a window display where we show everything and anything that affects the community's everyday life, where we debate everything there is to debate. If things get worse, well, we lost, but at least we told it like it was. So, our two representatives to the Senate have a program where they have to sit in front of a microphone and tell the people, whether they like it or not, about legislative acts and discussions in the Senate. The show airs every Friday, from eight to nine in the morning, and the representatives have to submit their scripts to me in advance, so that they don't try to score a goal [trick me]. Why do they agree to do it? This region is still the type of place where politicians conceive of the political process as an opportunity to profit from any situation, to make yourself look better than your opponent, see? And if one of them is talking on the radio and the other one is not, well, the one not on the radio won't have anything to show . . . but, the station is registered at the press offices of the Senate and the House, so every week they send us the legislative agenda via e-mail. By the time the representatives come to do their program, we already know what the agenda was, what was discussed, who talked and what they said . . . so they cannot bullshit us. Once, one of them tried to say that thanks to his maneuvering, a vocational school was coming to Inírida, but we knew that it was a Senate decision that had nothing to do with him! So after he spoke, I pressed and probed. I don't know how democratic that is, but I figure, it's a citizenship responsibility! (Pérez 2004)

The use of media to improve governance, accountability, and transparency in contexts where armed violence and corruption have replaced the rule of law is still uncharted territory. International peacebuilding organizations such as SFCG are contributing with promising projects. For example, in Sierra Leone, this organization helped develop an information network to ensure prompt information about the May 2002 election results. Being the first election after a violent civil war, it was important to avoid manipulation of results, typically delayed for weeks in this country. A project report states:

For the day of the elections the Network begged, rented and borrowed fourteen satellite phones, sixty-two cell phones, four landlines, and two vehicles, and deployed 120 people—everyone from journalists to office assistants—across the country to gather the election results at each polling centre as they were counted. Each person was given five polling stations to cover, and from there they phoned the results to either Bo or to Freetown (as there are two cell phone networks). The results were collated in those two cities, phoned out to the radio stations, and a few minutes later broadcast—all the same day. A first for Sierra Leone, where election results are not usually announced for two or three weeks. . . . By the end of the day the state-run radio station was taking the results off the air from the partner FM stations and rebroadcasting the same results themselves. And the National Election Commission was itself phoning the Network coordinators to get the results. . . . This whole massive effort cost a little less than $25,000; it is credited by many for ensuring the peaceful outcome to the elections, and received national acclaim. (Rolt 2009)

Colombian citizens' media cultivate participatory democracy by prompting different citizens' committees to have their own radio or television programs. For example, on Asoparabólica, a community television in Cali:

We have a program called *Todos Planificamos la Comuna* [We All Plan the Community] produced by the Territorial Planning Committee, who is responsible for deciding about social investments. Another program is called *Siguiendo el Rastro* [Tracing the Tracks], produced by the Citizens' Monitoring Committee, who are responsible for overseeing how public resources are spent. The Community Action Boards [Juntas de Acción Comunal] have a program called *Célula Básica* [Basic Cell] and the local health centers have two programs called *Vida Sana* [Healthy Life] and *Salud Dando* [Providing Health]. (Unidad de Radio—Mesa Regional Cauca, Putumayo, Nariño 2000)

Government officials often believe that the only role of municipal community media is to serve as a loudspeaker broadcasting the current administration's benevolent actions. A common complaint among citizen journalists is that local mayors call them on the phone to tell them, "Get over here now, I need to be interviewed!" Citizens' media pioneers have had to demonstrate to their communities and local administrations that their role is to maintain well-informed citizens and trigger debate, discussion, and dialogue about public policies. A pioneer from TeleMedellín, a community television station, recounts her experience:

One day, the mayor took me aside and said, "Hey, come here and listen! What is it that you are doing with that television station? We helped sponsor your television station, and now I already have five complaints from different government officials who say that you send your people to cover their events and your people don't even say hi to them. What do you think you're doing?" So we started a long struggle, with the mayor, the Administrative Councils, the Secretariats, and the entire administration. In the end, though, they understood that if TeleMedellín is covering news about how CORVIDE [the government institution responsible for low-income housing] recently allocated two thousand homes to poor families, it's better, prettier, more effective, and ethical to tell the story of Doña Rosita, who saved the profits of her sewing business for fifteen years until she had enough for a down payment on her new home, than to simply present an interview with a public official saying, "We delivered what we promised!" So now, after years of showing these government officials videos contrasting our coverage with that of the traditional TV news, we finally have credibility among them. (Unidad de Radio—Mesa Regional Magdalena Medio and Santanderes 2000)

The discussion over whether or not to allow paid political ads is an exemplar of how citizens' media pioneers have gained remarkable practical insight into the role their media should play in local political elections and electoral campaigns. In the words of community media leaders speaking at one of El Gazi's roundtables:

I don't think we have realized the immense influence and legitimacy citizens' media have earned in our communities. Our communities appreciate their radio stations and they believe in their radio stations. We risk that [legitimacy] if people end up voting for a candidate who can pay for more political ads. For this reason, we need to completely avoid paid political ads. I don't believe in equitable paid political advertisements; they are never truly equitable; they have never been equitable anywhere. What we need to focus on is the power of citizens' and community media to strengthen democratic processes in our communities.

We don't allow any paid political ads. We don't believe in it and on top of that, the Ministry of Communications itself states that community media cannot be used for political campaigns. So does that mean that there's no room for politics on our station? Absolutely not. We would do much damage to the community if we deny them the opportunity to get to know the proposals of the two candidates competing in the election for mayor, or the ten candidates in the election for Municipal Council representatives. We go talk to the two candidates for mayor, and if they are both willing, we do a program about both their proposals. If one of the candidates doesn't agree, well, sorry, but then we cannot do anything about either of them.

Our radio station called all candidates for mayor and Municipal Council to a meeting. On one side of the room were the candidates for mayor and on the other side, the candidates for the council. We told them how important it was for them each to present their proposals on the radio station. They agreed, and among themselves they decided how much they each could pay so they would be assured of having exactly the same number of hours of airtime. The mayoral candidates told us, "We each are able to pay one hundred thousand pesos for four hours [US$50] of programming." The council candidates said, "We can pay fifty thousand pesos each [US$25] for our spots." Then, the station produced the programs, but not in a "vote for this candidate" kind of format. Instead, we told people, "Listen to this candidate's proposal, he's going to be on the air on such and such date at such and such time." I think this is the best we can do.

In our station we did political spots, but we didn't say, "Vote for this or that candidate." We told the citizens, the people, "Vote for the best one." We told them, "Open your eyes wide, be aware of who you are voting for." (Unidad de Radio—Mesa Regional Boyacá, Arauca, Casanare 2001)

Citizens' Media Mirror Communities

For many reasons, including pressure from armed groups, this new generation of citizens' media has gravitated away from militancy and social mobilization to pursue different goals that have different measures of success. Older, militant community media measured their success by the number of people they were able to mobilize behind a specific movement. In contrast, the Colombian citizens' media pioneers featured here measure their success by how well they are able to make their media mirror their communities. Their goal is to open communication spaces for dialogue between different voices and identities, in which these disparate groups are able to negotiate the community's future, discuss local policies, monitor local government officials and institutions, and manage community conflicts in nonviolent ways. To achieve these goals, the medium must prioritize the inclusion of all the voices and identities represented in the community. Frequently, citizens' media pioneers express this priority in a phrase that has become kind of a motto among them: "To what extent does your programming grid reflect your community?" In the words of Guillermo Pérez: "My department is very large, with very low population density. We are number one in hepatitis B, malaria, coca, and all that stuff. To live here is to experience major issues around land tenure and land use, border problems, and armed conflict. In a region like this, what I worry about most is my programming grid; is my programming grid truly reflecting this terrible mess [*todo este mierdero*]? Is it obscuring it? Is the grid looking away, in a different direction, neither reflecting nor concealing this mess?" (Pérez 2004).

At a roundtable discussion, long-time citizens' media leader Francisco Betancourt explained:

> We need to produce cultural maps of our communities. We need to ask ourselves who are the cultural actors, the social actors, and the political actors in our communities and place them on the map. This should orient the direction of our programming. Our programming should emerge from the community's interests, understood in a very inclusive way. We should reflect the interests of our neighborhoods, our counties, and our *cabildos*. The cultural map has to show us who our interlocutors will be and it has to show us the direction of our communication project. It's not about *my* communication project, but rather a project that embraces the expectations, dreams, and interests of my whole community, and we're talking about people of flesh and bone and their community organizations. So, to the extent that my cultural map is clear, the medium's contents will be clear. To the extent that I am clear on my municipality's environmental problems, I'll be clear in the content of my environmental programs. To the extent that I am clear on what our health problems are, our needs in terms of infrastructure . . . the first thing is the cultural map to demarcate the protagonists, and from there I need to define their challenges, and ask myself how can a radio station respond to those challenges. The medium's contents need to emerge from a dialogue with our audiences. The minute we can get that dialogue going between the medium, the audiences, and the local environment, we will find the medium's content. It's not about telling people that they should participate; it's more about dialoguing with different identities and people's needs and dreams. The station is about locally driven designs for format and content; it's the only way these media will respond to each context. (Unidad de Radio—Mesa Regional Cauca 2000)

When the goal is developing programming grids truly reflective of the community's diverse identities, getting people to participate becomes the number-one challenge. As one way of responding to this challenge, citizens' media have conscientiously provided a number of different training opportunities to get people involved with media production. In the words of citizens' media pioneers from Magdalena Medio and Huila:

> These media are not born as community media; we have to make them into community media, and this is a long and arduous process . . . at our station we believe that neither the stations' directors, announcers, nor programming committee should be the producers of radio programs. Different sectors of the community should be the ones producing programs. A real community radio station should include the entire community; to this end, our station offers training workshops for people, where they can ask the

question: "Why a radio station? What's the sense of producing radio in this place? What's the use of a radio station for me as a teacher? As a farmer?" Through our training programs, we create processes through which people can approach the station. Some say that people do not participate because they are lazy, but we think that it is up to the medium to facilitate the process by letting people see what's in it for them. (Unidad de Radio—Mesa Regional Magdalena Medio and Santanderes 2000)

In Colombia we are all talking about participation and citizenship, but citizens are not prepared to participate. If we tell the community, those that have nothing to do with the radio station, that by law, they have the right to participate in community media, we'll find that they don't even know what community media are, or what the right to participate is, and most likely they won't even care about all this. So we need to develop training processes. We need to improve the production skills of people involved with the medium, but we also need workshops on citizenship and participation, so that citizens know that this is their station, and that they can count on it. Most of our training is not for the people involved with the medium—who, after all, are already involved—but for groups who have never approached the medium, such as community mothers.[33] Motivating community participation is easier said than done, so we need to offer training on participation in general, where people can see how participation *is* political action. We need to help people find the answer to the question, "Why should I participate? For what purpose?" (Unidad de Radio—Mesa Regional Huila 2001)

It's a learning process. The phenomenon of community media is not very old, and people are only just getting started, speaking in front of a mic, saying, "I am here, and I have something to say about my street, my park, our water system; I have a proposal." (Ministerio de Cultura 2004)

Motivated by what he witnessed in Inírida, Guillermo Pérez conceptualizes these processes as a circle. According to Pérez, the medium triggers processes that affect the social fabric, and the social fabric created through these processes in turn impacts the medium. During our interview, he gave me several examples:

[In Inírida] there's a very cool old guy, from Boyacá, an elderly lawyer, who's a teacher too, and the guy all of a sudden decided that the station was good for nothing because it didn't have any programming on poetry. So I told him, "Brother, precisely now we are making a call for new programs; what do you say? Are you capable of producing a poetry program? Would you go for it? Are you brave enough?" I told him, "All I have is Mondays from four to five in the afternoon," thinking, there's no way he'll say yes. But the old bastard said, "Yes!" Can you imagine? Monday afternoons, in a frontier town where people only want to listen to *vallenato* and the man is talking about poetry? To make matters worse, the guy did not just read the poems: he was truly passionate about poetry, so he declaimed them! I swear sometimes he forgot half the poem. He was so into it, he would close his eyes and be completely spaced out and he would forget! So, he just made up the verses, I swear! But of course, no one could confront him on this, because in those latitudes, who would know these poets? Carlos Castro Saavedra? People began calling us to say, "Listen Guillermo, the station is doing great! But please, get that guy out of there! Poetry at four in the afternoon? No, please!" The program was called *Raudales de Poesía* [Torrents of Poetry]. We are interested in this kind of programs.

The station tells people, "If you have something to say, this is your place; the station will support you, we believe that what you have to say is very important, even if you don't have a large audience. Audience size is not our game! The fact that you are one of our citizens and you have something to say is important for the station, so we are going to help you and support you." So I said to the old man, "Orlandito, we need to do something, maybe we need to change the program's schedule, maybe we need to publicize the program, something," and he told me, "I am on top of it. I have designed an Expectations Campaign." The guy went school by school and told the kids, "*M'ijo,* I am going to be here every day from ten to eleven, to meet with whoever is interested in reading poetry, writing poetry, and talking about poetry." Poetry Circles, he called these meetings. Soon, the guy had groups of about a dozen youngsters in six local schools. These kids were his guests during the program, so their mothers and fathers would listen to the program, and then their teachers and classmates became listeners too. The Poetry Circles became stronger, and later the kids started organizing a School Poetry Festival, so poetry really took off.

Can you see the circle? Having the medium for the medium's sake is nonsense. The medium should trigger social processes, and these processes in turn should impact what goes on at the station. For these media to truly be citizens' media, they need to place their bets on triggering social processes that start with the medium then travel to the social fabric, and back to the medium. (Pérez 2004)

In another example, Pérez further articulates his theory of the media–social fabric circle:

In an attempt to promote gender equity at the station I was trying to steer us away from the kinds of *vallenato* songs that have titles like, "My Girlfriend is for Sale," or "I Won't Take a Second Turn, Because Another Guy Already Had You." Then, because I was avoiding these songs, a rumor started circulating in the school, saying that teacher Guillermo had forbidden *vallenatos* at the station. I don't like *vallenato*. The music is so crybaby, so hyper-sentimental, *tan piroba*, but I did not forbid it. What I actually said was, "We need to find a way to make *vallenato* programming meaningful because if we don't, we're going to end up endorsing the same type of perverse gender relationships we're trying to change." We decided to educate people about *vallenato*, using *vallenato* itself by getting people on air, to talk about *vallenato!*

The first one to respond was the station technician's mother, Doña Deinisia, who arrived at the station with a bag of thirty cassettes, saying, "I love Otto Serge." So she went on the air and played Serge's classics. Let me explain the idea behind the program. The *vallenato* program doesn't have an owner; it's a place for getting to know others in your community, a space for dialogue. Again, we're dealing with the issue of opening spaces for dialogue. So this week's speaker was Doña Deinisia, and people loved the show. But then next week, someone else will do the show: a neighbor from the town, or someone from the countryside. The station opens the space and all the *vallenato* lovers, those who are really passionate about *vallenato* sign in and have a turn to play their own favorites. That's how we got the name of the program, *"Amantes del Vallenato"* [*Vallenato* Lovers]. Each week, the host of the week talks about how they fell in love with a particular song, how this other song reminds them of their first girlfriend, or how another song makes them cry and why, so the show becomes a document about their life. It airs Fridays from five to six, and we're never short of people wanting to host. Sometimes we even have to divide the show, thirty minutes for you and thirty minutes for you! And, listen to this, 'cause we stumbled upon something really cool! We gave half an hour to these kids who wanted to play kid *vallenato* groups, groups called Los Pirulitos or Los Diablitos, bands made up of children who sing *vallenatos*. We gave the other half hour of the show to older people. And what happened that day was spectacular, an entire intergenerational dialogue around *vallenato!* Now we are thinking about how to design more of those spaces, where older guys with drug problems can speak with younger ones, or where three grandmothers and three pregnant teens can come together and talk. The station should be useful, and trigger those types of dialogues. (Pérez 2004)

According to Pérez, sometimes the starting point of the circle is the medium, as in the case of Orlando's poetry programs. In other cases, the "circle" process starts at the level of the social fabric, and from there it jumps to the medium. An example of this, according to Pérez, is the newly formed Departmental Anti-Corruption Committee. Created to comply with a national government mandate, Guainía's Anti-Corruption Committee seemed as though it could be just another bureaucratic piece of paper. However, Custodia Estéreo pressured the committee into having its own program on the station to tell listeners about its actions against corruption. Perez recounts, "We had to force the committee to do it, and they have absolutely no way to say no, 'cause they would have to come out and publicly say that they refuse to report their actions, and well, we would tell everybody on the radio" (Pérez 2004).

Conclusion

Since the late 1990s, a new genre of citizens' media has emerged in Colombia. Several historical forces converged to create the conditions for this new phenomenon. First, pressures from armed groups in regions of war and violent conflict forced citizens' media leaders to rethink the role of their medium. To continue in the traditional, militant style of media loudly denouncing social injustice became suicidal. These Colombian media leaders, however, were not willing to remain silent. In response, they redirected their energy, away from denunciation and mobilization, and toward nurturing communication spaces for dialogue.

Second, although the citizens' media pioneers were scattered in every corner of the national territory, a decade of continuous meeting opportunities, facilitated by the Ministry of Culture's Radio Unit, allowed citizens' media leaders to meet and exchange ideas, skills, lessons learned, ways to meet specific challenges, and more. These skills were then tried in the field, and accumulated, allowing the stations to reach higher and higher levels of competency. It is not surprising that twelve years after these leaders first met, they have highly sophisticated understandings of the role(s) their media fill in complex contexts of marginality, corruption, apathy, and armed conflict.

Although Jesús Martín Barbero has not written extensively about citizens' media, he articulated this new Colombian trend while speaking as a guest on a radio program about community radio in 2004:

> The emergence of these citizens' radio stations is tied to a change in the political culture. The pioneers of the 1950s, such as the miners' radio stations in Bolivia, called themselves "alternative radio," or "popular radio," and conveyed a strong sense of marginality. They identified with that which was done on the margins of power, very much to the side of the mainstream. I believe that the current shift toward calling these media "citizens' radio" means that more and more social groups are coming to see radio as a way to participate in the decisions that shape the nation. This type of radio is no longer about giving marginalized groups a minimal voice and opportunity for expression. These stations are now about making every voice count in

decisions about the nation's policies on culture, development, and health. The difference is in whom these radio stations are now addressing. The 1950s alternative radio stations only talked to themselves. I believe that "citizens' radio," the name and the concept, is changing that. This new horizon I see (with some utopianism, because, as Serrat says, "without utopia, breathing in this country becomes impossible"), tells me that the new nation we want to build will be strongly linked to these citizens' media. This will be a nation based on diversity and participation taken seriously, not on the simulacrum of these things; a nation linked to the ways citizens' media are shaping the future in every corner of the country, naming the world as seen through the eyes of Indigenous worldviews, the perspectives of peasant communities and urban barrios. (Ministerio de Cultura 2004)

Among the most significant lessons to be learned from Colombian citizens' media pioneers is that we must recognize the complexity and nuance of the experiences of unarmed civilian communities in contexts of armed conflict. From the outside, it is easy to think that war permeates the entire range of experience for civilians under siege by armed groups. I have attempted here to demonstrate that the everyday lives of people in contexts of armed conflict are not subsumed by violence and war. In these communities, identities, daily interactions, and experiences exist beyond war, by the side of war, and parallel to war. Colombian citizens' media are really not about war. These courageous community radio and television stations accompany their communities through an enormous range of human experience. These stations are there, witnessing and supporting laughter and parties at local festivals, children's play, the planning sessions of community associations, harvests from organic collective gardens, and teachers teaching, even when armed groups are waging war nearby.

The option to focus not on armed violence but on what happens despite war resonates with Joanne Rappaport's ethnography of Colombian indigenous social movements. Rappaport found that indigenous public intellectuals and social movement leaders were more interested in talking about their community initiatives and bilingual education projects than about armed conflict: "They want to be seen as actors, not as victims. And because they are unarmed, their agency emerges through their dreams and plans, not through military action" (Rappaport 2005, 10).

To say that unarmed civilian communities are immune to the presence of armed groups would be naïve and simplistic. Colombian citizens' media pioneers know very well how their communities' social and cultural fabric is continuously permeated and torn by armed groups and their militaristic logic. Armed groups recruit the children of these communities and inject massive doses of mistrust, individualism, fear, suspicion, and uncertainty into the people's lives. Tanks invade public spaces, sand trenches are built, and armed men patrol parks and plazas, severely restricting freedom and mobility. The fashion styles and flirting of young people are closely monitored, and worst of all, weapons and aggression are normalized. Citizens' media pioneers have learned that, in order to operate and effect change in these contexts, their power to deal with armed actors is limited. To expect a community radio station, isolated in southern Colombia, operating on a shoestring budget, to cover armed conflict news, facilitate dialogue with or among armed groups, or denounce armed groups' human rights violations is, in itself, naïve and ill informed. Other actors, including national and international responsible media, international human rights organizations, and the United Nations, can more effectively perform these overtly political actions. Yet, citizens' media are not left empty-handed. In their contexts of permanent flux, Colombian citizens' media find ways to respond to the negative impacts of war and the presence of armed groups in the everyday lives of their communities. By facilitating complex communication processes, designing new uses for media practice, and weaving information and communication technologies into quotidian life, Colombian citizens' media pioneers disrupt violence and repair the broken threads of their communities' social fabric.

5 THE DOING IS EVERYTHING!

Toward a Theory of
Citizens' Media in Contexts of War

Ring the bell that still can ring,
forget your perfect offering,
there is a crack, a crack in everything.
That's how the light gets in.

—Leonard Cohen

IN OCTOBER OF 2008 I was invited to present my work at a seminar on media and violence in Hermosillo, Sonora, a northern Mexican state on the border with the United States. I still cringe at the memory of what I witnessed on the second day of the seminar, when a human rights expert led a workshop among local reporters and media producers. During the three-hour workshop, she went through detailed explanations of all kinds of legislative tools, procedures, and institutions available to confront the rising violence against journalists and media practitioners in Mexico. Participants asked numerous questions about how to deal with violent attacks, illegal detentions, torture, disappearance, and assassinations of journalists and reporters. The seminar was organized as a response to Mexico's increasing violence emerging from drug trafficking cartels and their strong alliances with municipal, regional, and federal politicians and security forces. Increasing numbers of journalists and reporters trying to denounce these perverse dealings have fallen prey to violent attacks. In 2008 Mexico became one of the most dangerous places to practice journalism.

What made me cringe, however, was the fact that a significant number of seminar participants were young reporters and radio producers working at a community radio station called Radio Bemba. I thought about how shaky it might be to expect a handful of young community radio reporters to cover and denounce the actions of powerful Mexican drug mafias and corrupt politicians, police, and militaries. As I listened to step-by-step explanations of what to do in case one is detained by a corrupt police force, I asked myself how wise it was to expect Radio Bemba's reporters, these volunteer youngsters in their black T-shirts, tattoos, and long ponytails, to cover and denounce the violent disintegration of Mexican society. It scared me that Radio Bemba itself has assumed this suicidal challenge. However, Radio Bemba radio producers are determined in their goal of maintaining excellent journalistic coverage of the increasing lawlessness, corruption, and human rights violations in northern Mexico.

In this chapter I intend to demonstrate that frequent assumptions about the role of a community medium operating in a violent context may limit the potential of these media. For instance, traditional journalistic news coverage does not have to be the main undertaking of a community medium. In fact, as I learned from the pioneers of Colombian citizens' media, journalists reporting on armed violence are frequently the first casualties in situations where powerful armed groups impose the use of force over the rule of law. If it is difficult for well-funded, well-connected, and well-known national and international media to maintain responsible journalistic practices, it is unfair and somewhat irresponsible to expect vulnerable, isolated local community media to meet this challenge. In violent situations, news coverage requires powerful media organizations to call upon all of their legal and financial might to protect their journalists as they attempt to cover and denounce human rights violations, illicit economies, and corrupt politics. In exceptional cases, when alternative, volunteer-run media can count on strong backing from international communities, they do cover armed conflict. Benjamin Ferron found that if the Alternative Information Center can cover the Palestine–Israel conflict and the Centro de Medios Libres can offer alternative news about the Chiapas conflict in southern Mexico, it's partly because these media are part of complex and dynamic transnational networks of alternative media, social justice organizations, and activists (Ferron 2009). It's naïve to expect isolated, local community media operating on shoestring budgets and staffed by young volunteers to act as watchdogs of vicious heavily armed groups. And yet, it is frequently, and dangerously, assumed that the role of citizens' media in contexts of armed violence and corruption should be to provide comprehensive journalistic coverage. The lesson I learned from Colombia is that when operating in contexts in which unarmed civilians are under siege by armed forces, the role of citizens' media is to go beyond journalistic coverage and to focus on the communication needs and daily realities of the people in their communities.

Bill Siemering reveals a second perspective, which can also limit the role of citizens' media. In his work with community media in Africa and Mongolia, he found that peacebuilding organizations tend to perceive community media as "loudspeakers for public service announcements" (Siemering 2008). This "loudspeaker" role doesn't allow for the rich potential of community-produced media in violent contexts to mature. These perspectives on the role of community media in situations of armed conflict—whether as producers of news and information, or as transmitters of pro-peace PSAs—both suffer from the same type of myopia: they understand communication technologies to be tools of persuasion and one-way dissemination of information.

We need to rethink the functions of media in terms of communities' communication and information needs in order to understand the complex and multidimensional roles citizens' media can have in contexts of armed violence. Instead of conceiving of a medium exclusively as a tool for information or persuasion, we need to uncover and consider each of the varied communication needs of a community cornered by armed violence, and how a community medium can meet those needs. Of course, news and information must be included, but by no means do they constitute the community's only or primary communication need. Detecting and understanding the complex communication needs of real communities in these contexts reveals all the potential of media technologies as tools to foster horizontal communication and interaction, grassroots leaders' communication competence, dialogue between citizens and local governments, networking, and endless opportunities to resignify life worlds. The presence of armed groups and the proximity of armed violence and war have a tremendous impact on a community's daily life, social fabric, local political and economic processes, and intercommunal relationships and interactions. I believe we need to thoroughly examine the different ways war affects a community if we want to understand how citizens' media can counter these impacts, helping communities resist armed violence's devastation. In the following pages I draw heavily from ethnographers and anthropologists of armed violence to illuminate the specific ways in which armed conflict erodes the social and cultural fabric of unarmed communities. Drawing from my fieldwork in Colombia (presented in chapters 1 to 4), I propose various ways in which citizens' media can disrupt such erosion.

Contemporary anthropologists and ethnographers of war have departed from traditional studies of armed conflict, which were mostly focused on politico-military protagonists, actions, and issues. These scholars have refocused the study of armed conflict on the centrality of unarmed civilians' experiences of war. In the introduction to *Fieldwork under Fire*, Robben and Nordstrom claim that the study of violence has "fallen through the meshwork of the institutional analyses of war" (Nordstrom and Robben 1995, 10). According to Robben and Nordstrom, we need studies that represent the lived experience of violence in all its complexity and ambiguity. These lived experiences frequently involve absurdity and contradiction, situations where creativity and oppression, and the ordinary and the exceptional live side by side. Armed violence and war forcefully intrude upon and erode communal life in a myriad of complex ways; unarmed civilians respond, resist, and survive with equally complex, clever, and subtle practices and actions.

Ethnographer Carolyn Nordstrom, whose research agenda focuses on the central position of unarmed civilians, writes: "I want to explore the phenomenon of sociopolitical violence as experienced by average citizens, to examine . . . lives and life-worlds of civilians who find themselves on the frontlines of today's dirty wars, wars they did not start and do not control" (Nordstrom 1992, 260–61). Nordstrom's studies of war zones in several countries demonstrate that today's intrastate wars seek to control territories and populations, using terror as the primary weapon to reach this goal. Military victories over enemy soldiers are not the main focus of armed violence in these wars, instead, "civilians are the tactical targets, and fear, brutality and murder are the foundation on which control is constructed" (Nordstrom 1992, 261). Some of the impact of war is obvious, taking the form of visible injury and destruction; however, less visible effects can be even more devastating. Nordstrom calls these effects "maimed culture," including the demolition of routines of daily life, the undermining of socially constructed life worlds, and the dismantling of essential knowledge frameworks and social institutions. These consequences of violence "are equally powerful realities and their destruction may have a much more enduring and serious impact than the more obvious and gruesome casualties of war" (Nordstrom 1992, 261). Traditional studies of war by experts, politicians, and military officials perceive and analyze armed conflict in strategic and political terms that "barely scratch the surface of the actual personal engagement of individuals in the violence that enmeshes them" (Keppley Mahmood 2000, 74). Unarmed civilians' experiences of violence have a "nonstrategic and nonpolitical quality . . . which often prompts a similarly nonstrategic and nonpolitical resistance" (Keppley Mahmood 2000, 74). How do citizens' media contribute to such practices of resistance?

Community Media and Daily Life in Times of Violence

Reappropriating War-Ravaged Public Spaces

Local public spheres are among the first casualties when unarmed communities are caught in the fighting of warring groups. People witness their streets, plazas, and markets being invaded by heavily armed uniformed groups. During my fieldwork I frequently passed sandbag barricades that had been erected to protect local police stations, banks, or government buildings. In this kind of war, local geographies become sites of surveillance, in some cases via the "massive importation of advanced surveillance technologies" (Feldman 1991, 87), and sometimes through informants recruited by armed groups from the local population. When public places are permeated by suspicion, surveillance, and threats, people desert them and retreat to their private spaces; the result is what Suárez-Orozco calls "centrifugal isolationism" (Suárez-Orozco 1992, 242).

How many processes of social cohesion, conversations, social bonds, new friendships, instances of "getting to know someone," keeping up with someone's life, agreeing or disagreeing with someone, are thwarted when people abandon local public spaces? When this isolation starts to occur, citizens' media have a vital and unique role to play. By triggering communication processes that draw people back into their local public spaces, citizens' media can help communities reappropriate their spaces from the logic of war. Creative uses of communication technologies, as seen in the Christmas decorating contest in Belén de los Andaquíes (chapter 1) or the street-film project in Montes de María (chapter 2), bring people back to their streets and

their parks, nurturing a sense of togetherness and collective identity—
a sense of "we." Preventing war from stealing people's places and
imposing total isolation is in itself a form of resistance. Colombian citizens' media pioneers clearly understand how armed conflict progressively pushes people out of public places and into private spheres.
Using media technologies, these pioneers counter isolation by designing communication processes that draw people out of the private into
the public sphere. Since their goal is to generate communication and
interaction among their audiences rather than simply transmit messages, citizens' media privilege collective spaces of encounter, as
opposed to sites of individual reception. Toward this end, the street-
film project triggers people to gather at the central plaza, and the
Christmas contest encourages collective neighborhood decorations of
one's block, instead of individuals or families decorating their own
homes' façades.

As I write this, I recoil at the thought that what I've written could
be interpreted as a prescriptive formula. In no way do I believe that
the uses of citizens' media in contexts of armed conflict can be formulaic, predesigned, or taken from one context and applied to another.
In fact, it could prove lethal to interpret the following pages as a sum-
mary of static, replicable tools for strategic communication that will
ease the lived experience of armed conflict. If not set in motion organically, with the local context as a guide, using community radio to
encourage people to go back out into a militarized public space could
result in a massacre. Also, the notion itself of participation is context
specific. In places such as Colombia, participatory media evolved in
contexts where social movements have normalized grassroots participation in political and economic decision-making processes for almost
a century. Expecting community media to flourish in contexts where
social movements and participation are foreign may be improbable.
Rather than prescribing communication and media interventions à
la edutainment,[1] my goal here is to encourage all of us to learn to
detect and understand instances in which unarmed civilians use their
media to resist the impact of armed conflict on their everyday lives
and social fabric.

Resignifying the Landscapes of Memory

When waged in the local geographies in which people live their lives,
armed violence leaves scars on streets, farming fields, and plazas. Pilar

Riaño-Alcalá's work on memory and violence in Medellín describes young survivors of urban violence who have mental maps of their neighborhoods on which streets and corners are remembered as the place where their buddy was killed, or the spot where the trace of his blood sat for days (Riaño-Alcalá 2006). With their ability to permeate things with meaning, citizens' media can help structure people's personal narratives by recodifying the meanings that violence leaves behind. As tools designed precisely to produce meaning, media technologies can help people resignify their memories of violence.[2] The following words, spoken by a Colombian man after seeing a film deliberately shown on the same spot where a bomb had exploded some years before, reveal how citizens' media can help resignify the memory of a violent attack: "And to think that this same place brings such conflicted memories. Ever since the bomb [exploded], people were afraid to come here; or worse, people ran for cover in their houses if they heard the noise of a car they did not recognize. With the film and the music I felt that people recovered not only trust, but also joy. We had lost the joy in this town. [This film project] is so that life can be reborn here in Chalán" (Vega and Bayuelo 2008, 60).

Defying Fear and Isolation

According to Sluka, a "culture of terror" emerges from "the permanent, massive, and systematic use or threat of violence and intimidation" (Sluka 2000b, 22). In a culture of terror, unarmed civilians live with the knowledge that at any moment their sense of normalcy could shatter. Even in times between violent attacks, people share a collective feeling of fear, established by the culture of terror "as a brutal means of social control" (Sluka 2000b, 22). Sluka describes how collective fear erodes the social fabric:

> In such a system, there is an ever present threat of repression, torture, and ultimately death for anyone who is actively critical of the status quo: "Rumors of death lists and denunciations, gossip, and innuendos create a climate of suspicion. No one can be sure who is who. The spectacle of torture and death, of massacres and disappearances . . . became deeply inscribed in individuals and in the collective imagination through a constant sense of threat." . . . When fear becomes a way of life, as it did in Argentina and Guatemala, a culture of terror has emerged. (Sluka 2000b, 22–23)

Armed groups move in and out of communities; at times their presence is felt in the form of violent attacks, massacres, assassinations, rapes, and shoot-outs. When armed groups aim to control a population through brutality and terror, death is used as a weapon and a symbolic message: "The reappearance of highly mutilated corpses in public spaces instills fear of the known, rather than of the unknown" (Afflitto 2000, 118). Drawing from her fieldwork in Guatemala, Kay Warren writes: "Characteristically [death squads] leave evidence of their activities in the form of tortured bodies or bloody survivors, as messages that convey the brute power of the state" (Warren 2000, 227). *Combat,* a magazine published by the Ulster Defense Association, an Irish paramilitary organization, states: "There is only one way to control an area of ghetto that harbors terrorists and insurgents and that is to reduce its population to fear by inflicting upon them all the horror of terrorist warfare. Where these means cannot, for whatever reason be used, the war is lost" (Sluka 2000a, 135).

Collective fear and generalized isolation are key tactics used by armed groups to control unarmed civilians. Using this kind of terrorism, an armed minority can oppress an unarmed majority into hopelessness and powerlessness, even if the numbers are not on their side. In Colombia, people frequently described to me how, during a moment of collective terror, the simple act of moving from isolation to togetherness felt like a powerful force. No one could clearly explain exactly why, but feelings of togetherness effectively countered feelings of powerlessness. When people told me of their experiences of terror, as in the stories I heard about the small town in Caquetá under attack by the guerrillas (chapter 1), the Caribbean city under siege by guerrillas and paramilitaries, the two towns broken apart by friend/foe stigmatization in Alto Ariari (chapter 2), or the general paralysis brought by a guerrilla mandated *paro armado* in Putumayo (chapter 4), moments of collective solidarity stood out as empowering forces. In these instances, citizens' media can trigger communication processes between community members that promote communal interaction in moments of crisis. Also, and perhaps more significantly, citizens' media can strengthen, amplify, and support instances of collective solidarity and togetherness as these emerge in the community. Here, the competence of local citizens' media communicators is critical, as they are the only actors able to detect when and where those moments are materializing, and focus their cameras, microphones, and other media technologies on those situations, however precarious they may be.

As mentioned in previous chapters, it is imperative that the boundaries between safety and danger in a situation of armed violence are continuously reexamined. For communities under siege by armed groups, the line demarcating what is and is not safe changes from moment to moment. Although my experience is limited to the Colombian case, the time I've spent in contexts of armed violence has taught me that local community leaders are generally well positioned to determine where the boundaries of safety lie on any given day. Though they are by no means infallible, local leaders are generally able to read the subtle environmental signs that signal whether armed groups are leaving a community alone for a while or moving in with further violence, recruitment, or surveillance.

As unarmed civilians navigate these complexities, Colombian citizens' media creatively design modes of expression to bypass the restrictive presence of armed groups. In previous chapters I explained how the Montes de María Communications Collective devises subtle ways to open communication spaces in which men and women can express their experiences and feelings while under siege by armed groups (chapter 2). In chapter 4 I described various discursive practices used by citizens' media pioneers in different parts of Colombia to articulate community members' lived experiences of human rights violations and other modes of victimization by armed groups. As mentioned in chapter 2, researchers seeking insight into the lives of people whose lives are affected by armed violence analyze "hidden transcripts," the camouflaged messages people use to communicate their experiences without alerting armed groups (Nordstrom 2004; Ramírez 2001; Scott 1992). My fieldwork in Colombia allowed me to see first-hand how citizens' media can carefully and safely move these hidden transcripts from private spheres to public ones, where feelings of shared experience can grow.

Wise local community media leaders with strong connections to their communities are a key factor in realizing these media's potential in contexts of armed violence. In light of their essential role, supporting local community media leaders with training, opportunities to meet and interact with others, and access to forums where experiences, challenges, and successes can be collectively shared and examined seems much safer, wiser, and more effective than keeping community media's know-how and decision-making power locked in the hands of international donors, NGOs, or international peacebuilding organizations.

Countering Uncertainty

Armed groups often impose curfews (Werbner 1991, 16) and engage in "surveillance, spatial immobilization, and periodic subtraction of subjects from homes and communities . . . the routinization of house raids, [and] the frequent arrest of males of military age" (Feldman 1991, 87). The unpredictability of events in daily life, and the resulting uncertainty and paralysis, are some of the most common elements identified by anthropologists in studies of war zones and unarmed communities' lived experiences of armed violence. In her study of terror in Spain, Aretxaga demonstrates that while collective fear can be produced by violent actions, it is also produced through discursive practices such as gossip, jokes, rumor spreading, and saga-like stories about potential violent actions (Aretxaga 2000). The unpredictable nature of victimization causes "Belfast nerves": "Sweeps of neighborhoods occur suddenly, often at night, people are dragged off to police stations and interrogation centers in their night clothes. One house will be hit; another spared . . . civilians are virtually prisoners, awaiting the knock on the door, the siren at the end of the street. . . . Whether one is spared or not is more a matter of luck than of innocence" (Keppley Mahmood 2000, 76). Suárez-Orozco reveals how one anonymous phone call could become lethal during Argentina's years of terror: "The randomness characterizing the dirty war became a key to the establishment of social control through collective terror" (Suárez-Orozco 1992, 237). In Colombia, armed groups descend into a community with a list itemizing which individuals will be victimized. It is widely known that names frequently end up on these lists as a result of an acquaintance or neighbor seeking revenge for a personal slight, discrepancy over land boundaries, because of a love triangle, and so forth (Maria Victoria Uribe 2007). Meertens notes that in Colombia "terror is therefore imposed as a selective but arbitrary act of exemplification: erratic, intermittent and absolutely *unpredictable*" (Meertens 2001, 136). Nordstrom documents a Tamil woman in Sri Lanka's conflict region who said, "I never know what will happen from one day to the next" (Nordstrom 1992, 262). Based on her work in Guatemalan communities cornered between guerrillas and state security forces, Kay Warren concludes:

> Another dimension of anguish is represented as the arbitrariness of power be it the military that largely controlled this region or the guerrillas when they were most active. Uncertainty and anxiety weighed heavily on *Trixanos*.

There was no way of knowing if one might become a target of surveillance, when one might be singled out for detention and torture, and what may be considered evidence of subversive or collaborationist intentions. One would not know what would trigger the wrath of the *judiciales,* whether guerrillas were moving from strategies of recruitment to punitive actions, whether one's name may be on a list or which list it might be on, or whether a trip to the fields or the market would result in being caught in someone's sweep. (Warren 1993, 48)

Can citizens' media play a role in counteracting the arbitrariness experienced by unarmed civilians when cornered by armed violence? I hesitate to state a definite conclusion, but when the Colombian citizens' media pioneers insist on focusing their communication initiatives on the normal everyday lives of their communities rather than on the experience of war, I believe they are seeking precisely this type of impact. I learned from these community leaders that, even when engulfed by the chaos of armed conflict, some aspects of community life remain "normal," and these aspects become key sources of strength for people.

Here I need to emphasize some of the crucial differences between armed conflict in Colombia and other types of armed conflict such as the genocide in Rwanda, or the brutality of military regimes in Guatemala. In more than fifty years of armed conflict in Colombia, the state has never ceased to function, and communities are rarely entirely obliterated, as they often were in Africa or Central America. Also, war in Colombia has never involved massive numbers of citizens taking up arms. Instead, Colombia's violence is the work of organized minorities who form guerrilla groups, paramilitaries, militias, mafias, and the armed forces, all of which terrorize unarmed civilians. Thus, armed conflict in the country is experienced as low-intensity warfare, with armed groups coming in and out of communities. In contrast to the constant low-level warfare of Colombia, in other contexts massive numbers of people become victims and victimizers, and "normal" life actually disappears as communities are wiped out.

In Colombia, where "normal" life coexists with uncertainty and fear, citizens' media can focus their cameras and microphones on those aspects of everyday life that continue beyond the reach of war. The media images produced by Montes de María's Communications Collective, the audiovisual school in Belén de los Andaquíes, and the community radio stations in Magdalena Medio are cases in point. For example, the image of two boys riding their bicycle around a refugee neighborhood's empty soccer field reminds us that, despite all the chaos of forced displacement, kids still play their games (Colectivo de Comunicaciones 2006a). Similarly, the images of *El Guarapo*, a *foto-video* produced by children in Belén de los Andaquíes, focus on a lemonade vendor whose stand sits a few feet from the barricaded police station of a small town in southern Colombia (García, Góngora, and Silva 2006). The children opted to focus their camera on the refreshing lemonade they enjoy daily, "erasing" the scary images of nearby sandbag barricades invading their local landscape. While some critics might suggest that these media images merely romanticize contexts of armed conflict, I interpret these images as efforts to balance the weight of the ubiquitous images of war, and the feelings of anxiety, chaos, and uncertainty associated with those images, in these contexts. If it is true that armed violence and "normal" life are experienced as parallel realities (Das 2007; Lewin 2002; Nordstrom 2004; Nordstrom and Martin 1992; Nordstrom and Robben 1995), we know all too well that most mainstream media privilege the reality of war images. Citizens' media can step in and produce the images and sounds that make the other reality more visible in public spheres.

Reconstructing Life Worlds

Armed conflict erodes people's sense of normalcy and upsets everyday life, dislocating what Carolyn Nordstrom calls people's life worlds. According to Desjarlais and Kleinman, "some of the most important repercussions of this kind of violence are social. . . . [T]he psychosocial dynamics of ethnic violence often pivot on a lack of control, a lack of certitude, and a reversal in moral and social orders as previously understood" (Desjarlais and Kleinman 1994, 10). Violence undermines cultural notions of meaning and purpose, and "the dissolution of these rather ordinary notions can apparently have a profoundly disturbing effect on the way people go about their lives and relate to one another" (Desjarlais and Kleinman 1994, 11).

In the chaos of terror, that which is normally inside moves outside and that which is outside moves inside. Feldman describes the time in Northern Ireland when political activism had to recede to the most intimate spheres of trust, moving politics from public to private spheres. At the same time, surveillance became so insidious that people's private spheres were permanently exposed to the foreign gaze of security forces. In reference to video cameras mounted on street corners, a Belfast resident stated: "They know the patterns of your wall paper and the color of your underwear!" (Feldman 2000, 47).

As I explained in the previous chapters, Colombian citizens' media spend enormous amounts of time, energy, and resources on strengthening local cultural imaginaries. In southern Colombia, where coca economies and the war between FARC and the Colombian armed forces erode local social and cultural fabrics, Radio Andaquí creates the concept of Territorio Andaquí, thus giving a name to the life worlds of all the men, women, and children in the region who have not embraced weapons and violence. Every hour, the radio station reminds people: "It is nine A.M. in our Territorio Andaquí." "It is twelve noon in our Territorio Andaquí." "It is six P.M. in our Territorio Andaquí" (see chapter 1). In Magdalena Medio, AREDMAG's community radio stations devote a significant portion of their programming to local histories, lifestyles, ways of life, expressions, landmarks, cuisines, and even ghosts (see chapter 3). Videos and television programs in Montes de María, and radio series in Inírida, on the Colombian border with Venezuela, feature the cultural practices, local landscapes, youth cultures, and local personal/family/regional histories of those who have refused to take up arms (see chapters 2 and 4). Local cultural identities, languages, aesthetics, and characters—all the elements that make up the life world of a community—are privileged material for these citizens' media.

In some cases the rivers, mountains, and bird songs of the natural landscape become protagonists. This is particularly true in the community radio stations of Magdalena Medio, where the Magdalena River emerges frequently in the stations' programming as a marker of cultural identity (chapter 3). Nature becomes a main character again for Radio Andaquí and the children's audiovisual school in Caquetá, where local geographies are featured prominently (chapter 1). By producing and listening to programs that recreate the sounds of the river, the songs of local birds, or the wisdom of the community's farmers interacting with their land, media producers and their audiences continuously interact with the beauty, uniqueness, diversity, and potential of their place.

In my view, citizens' media programs focused on local cultural identities and geographies act to counter armed violence in two ways. First, these programs remind people that their life worlds have not been obliterated by war. Second, the programs encourage children and youth to be "seduced" by their natural and cultural environment, potentially reducing the attraction of the promises of a life as a warrior and/or drug trafficker. Youth in love with their local environments may be immunized against the lure of armed groups that prey on the youth of communities endangered by state neglect and marginalization. In the same way that citizens' media reappropriate public places from war, they can also help recover children and youth from the grip of armed groups.

Building Trust

The traumatic uncertainty and chaos that war brings into everyday life "breach the attachments of family, friendship, love, and community. They shatter the construction of self that is formed and sustained in relation to others. They undermine the belief systems that give meaning to human experience. They violate the victim's faith in a natural or divine order and cast the victim into a state of existential crisis" (Orr 2002, 119, citing Judith Herman).

In times of armed conflict, survivors often violate the moral principles that govern their everyday interactions in times of peace. Werbner describes behaviors that emerge in contexts of war: "How could one manage to share food? How could one join in burying others? How could one avoid betraying others to the enemy, when the betrayal meant protecting oneself and one's own immediate kin?" (Werbner 1991, 172). Warren's fieldwork in Guatemala resonates with Werbner's research in Africa: "Individuals become complicit by informing on the activities and putative alliances of their neighbors. Whether coerced, offered in exchange for personal gain, or solicited to enhance one's power at the expense of others, these complicities involve betrayals that splinter family and community. The aggravation of existing divisions becomes an enduring cost of this mode of conflict as trust among family members and neighbors erodes in the face of secretive alliances" (Warren 2000, 229).

As they compete for control and the allegiance of local populations, armed antagonist groups recruit informants and allies inside local communities. The boundaries between "armed" and "unarmed" blur. Distrust and suspicion creep into relationships among neighbors, friends, and even extended families. Based on her anthropological research in Alto Ariari, Colombia, Tatiana Duplat states that "distrust makes its appearance and breaks the remaining threads sustaining a weakened and fragile social fabric" (Duplat 2003, 163). Also writing about armed conflict in Colombia, Iván Orozco states: "Looking for a way to survive, many become collaborators and informants, but the situation reaches a point at which collaborating and informing no longer protect. Paranoia reigns. The only way out is forceful displacement" (Orozco 2002, 85). Allen Feldman records a local testimony of a Belfast resident during the Troubles: "When you lived in a Protestant area after '69 and you went into a shop, all the people would be having their heads together and whispering, and when you entered they stopped and there was dead silence. And nobody spoke a word till you went out. (Catholic housewife, St. James)" (Feldman 1991, 25). Suárez-Orozco mentions the paralysis and lack of trust resulting from the circulation of rumors during Argentina's dirty war. These rumors informed people that if they acted, their disappeared relative would be badly hurt: "A massive and unparalleled social centrifugal force was set in motion. People no longer trusted one another, not even close friends. The terror induced silence and perhaps more importantly, social isolation" (Suárez-Orozco 1992, 234). Suspicion spread like a virus: "The relatives of *desaparecidos* soon found themselves abandoned by many friends and even relatives afraid of being associated with them. It was as if a plague had hit Argentina. The centrifugal forces set in motion by the terror were overwhelming" (Suárez-Orozco 1992, 241).

Allen Feldman's work in Northern Ireland and Kay Warren's work in Guatemala found that ghost stories multiply when communities are suffocated by feelings of anxiety, uncertainty, and the randomness of violence (Feldman 1991, 67; Warren 2002). Kay Warren uncovered Maya narratives of "rajav a'a," or men and women who are normal people by day and animals by night, that emerged as militarized Mayan communities dealt with not being able to trust anyone (Warren 1993).

Postconflict reconciliation experts agree that in these contexts, "community projects and initiatives are needed in societies coming out of conflict to facilitate reconstruction of interpersonal relationships" (Hamber and Gráinne 2005, 13). In 2005 Paul Murphy, the secretary of Northern Ireland, spoke about the urgency of rebuilding trust in everyday interactions as a condition for overcoming a troubled past: "In my view the absence of trust will set back both economic and social development; we will fail to realize the talents of our more diverse society" (quoted in Hamber and Gráinne 2005, 33).

When used as genuine participatory media, community media can be used to reestablish interaction, communication, and trust among people. In previous chapters we saw how the Communications Collective of Montes de María builds an alternative ethos that surrounds program participants with trusting relationships. Every interaction within the walls of the Collective, including trusting children with expensive audiovisual equipment or allowing teenagers to make important decisions, is designed to intensify the lived experience of being trusted and trusting others (chapter 2). In this sense, Collective participants are not told about the virtues of trust and peaceful coexistence; instead, they are allowed to feel what it is like to trust and be trusted, with the hope that they will develop a strong commitment to protecting these feelings and the social processes that make them possible.

In cases where citizens' media are used to reappropriate public places and reclaim public spheres for intercommunity interaction, trust can be reestablished among neighbors, friends, and extended families. The building blocks of trusting relationships, the acts of getting to know, and communicating with others, are established when the Purple Rose of Cairo Itinerant Street-Film Project reclaims the central plaza of El Carmen de Bolívar for the people to gather every Friday night (chapter 2); or when using a Christmas decorating contest as a pretext, Radio Andaquí reclaims the warmth of evening visits with neighbors (chapter 1); or when, using a Love Letter Contest, Custodia Estéreo reclaims a school's patio for gentle interactions among young men and women (chapter 4).

De-escalation and Mediation of Violent Conflict

In a different way, Radio Andaquí was also able to build trust during the *cocalero* demonstrations of 1996. *Cocalero* demonstrators and local citizens used the Sun Stage, a communication space set up by Radio Andaquí during this complex mobilization, to find common ground and question stigmatized visions they held of one another (chapter 1). In this instance, the community radio station found a way to use communication technologies to de-escalate conflict and overcome friend/foe frameworks. Initially, local residents viewed the *cocalero* demonstrators through the lens imposed by the mainstream media, seeing them as "terrorists manipulated by the guerrillas." After a week of gatherings in front of the radio stations' microphones, local residents found that the *cocaleros* were agricultural families, just like themselves. This citizens' medium created the conditions necessary for these two potentially conflicted groups to find common ground, empathy, and trust (Mouffe 2006).

In the case of Montes de María, the Communications Collective functions as a peacebuilding school where hundreds of children, youth, and others from displaced communities are exposed to alternative modes of human interaction. While armed groups and the violence they bring make aggression a basic ingredient of family and intercommunity interactions, the Collective cultivates a social fabric where participants leave aggression at the door.

Citizens' media projects have ripple effects throughout their host communities. Media producers are influenced by their experiences of participation and the opportunities they have to speak, name the world, and express their own version of the world in their own terms (Rodríguez 2001). The impacts of citizens' media spread out in waves of concentric circles, beginning with those most closely involved with the projects and extending outward (Tacchi, Slater, and Lewis 2003). Media producers' parents, spouses, and siblings are among the first to feel the effects. Nonaggressive interactions travel from the medium to the family home. Teachers and classmates also feel the impacts, as a different type of nonaggressive interaction moves from the medium to the playground and the classroom. In small isolated communities, such as El Carmen de Bolívar (chapter 2), Belén de los Andaquíes (chapter 1), Magdalena Medio's small towns (chapter 3), and Inírida (chapter 4), a couple hundred direct participants (media producers) can trigger nonaggressive communication processes that influence many more people, ultimately influencing a significant proportion of the local population.

In the hands of local leaders committed to peacebuilding, citizens' media can help foster processes of mediation and nonviolent conflict resolution. In chapter 3 I presented several cases in which Magdalena Medio's citizens' radio stations were used to mediate among community groups in conflict (see also Rodríguez 2010). In these cases, community radio producers were able to shift disputes over the use of a park and the rights of property owners from a state of aggression and violence toward one of civil dissent. The stations opened a public sphere for civil debate, and positioned the issue of conflict at the center of community discussions.

The radio stations also pressured local government authorities to fulfill their responsibilities and clearly define the rights and duties of the different parties in conflict according to the rule of law. In situations of community conflict, communication between citizens and local governments is crucial (Bloh and Rolt 2007). As Von Kalternborg-Stachau states, communication among citizens and governments has to be approached in all its complexity (Von Kalternborg-Stachau 2008). In local contexts, community media, audiences, and local government officials are enmeshed in a continuous and interconnected conversation. When the medium facilitates dialogue with the community about public issues, local government officials listen. When a local mayor opens dialogue with his or her constituency, the medium listens. Rich interactions among media, government, and local residents are all elements of a peaceful public sphere.

I found some exceptional cases where community radio stations mediated between a community and the armed groups with local presence (chapter 3). In Magdalena Medio, community radio producers told me their stations played key roles protecting the community from victimization by armed groups. In Santa Rosa, the radio station helped resolve the case of a community leader who was kidnapped by the guerrilla. In Carmen del Chucurí, the local community radio station facilitated dialogue between two different paramilitary groups; in this case, both groups agreed to leave the community alone. In San Vicente del Chucurí, the station allowed angry youth to vent their grievances against the oppression of paramilitary groups.

The potential of citizens' media to serve as tools for mediation and nonviolent conflict resolution depends on the ability of local communicators to detect moments and situations ripe for de-escalation of conflict. Examples presented in chapter 3 about community radio stations in Magdalena Medio demonstrate how community radio producers improvised decisions on the go and galvanized an entire community around a rescue effort; in another example, a program director wove together the common threads emerging from her program's interviewees (chapter 3). Both of these examples provide evidence of nonviolent conflict resolution requiring excellent communication competences from local communicators. Moments in which a potentially violent process can be transformed into a peaceful transaction are not predictable, nor even very visible to those outside the community. However, local communicators well acquainted with the potential of community media to cultivate dialogue and interaction can detect such moments and use their communication skills to nurture peacebuilding processes wherever they discover these opportunities.

To this day I am amazed by the Magdalena Medio radio producers' nonchalant attitudes as they recounted the cases of mediation presented in chapter 3. I found it hard to believe that these heroic tales of small community media in isolated regions of Colombia successfully confronting vicious armed groups had never been told before. When I voiced my disbelief, my interviewees responded: "No one asked us before!" How many similar situations, in which citizens' media buffer unarmed communities from armed violence, are we missing in different parts of the world? Unfortunately, traditional community media evaluation and assessment methodologies miss these cases because the questions asked do not encourage local media producers to consider instances of peacebuilding as significant accomplishments.[3] Community media experts and evaluators (those who design assessment methodologies and evaluation questionnaires) come from the ranks of development communication or communication for social change, usually lacking a background in the study of peacebuilding. On the other hand, peacebuilding experts frequently see media exclusively in terms of information and persuasion tools. Those of us operating at the intersection between community media and peacebuilding are scarce, but it is only at this intersection that the full spectrum of questions can be asked.

The Intangible Dimension of Peacebuilding

Duplat identifies several key elements in her analysis of a successful reconciliation initiative between two adversarial towns in Alto Ariari, Colombia (2003).[4] Together with economic and political participation policies, Duplat explains, in this reconciliation initiative, community leaders purposefully addressed the "intangible" dimension of conflict resolution (or what Nordstrom calls "maimed culture" [Nordstrom 1992]). Duplat explains that the towns' leaders "worked hard at resignifying collective imaginaries" (Duplat 2003, 271). The leaders showcased by Duplat displayed a series of community initiatives that reestablished social relationships of friendship and solidarity, generated trust, built a sense of "us" that embraced differences, and allowed people to meet those from the antagonist camp with a fresh perspective. These initiatives encouraged people to overcome the notion of the other-as-enemy, to learn to acknowledge the legitimacy of the other's collective imaginary, to reclaim and retell stories of their past in which the communities lived in peace side by side. People were reminded that, even during times of conflict, many competencies and practices of peaceful coexistence had survived (for example, instances of continuous trading throughout conflict). People went back to calling individuals by their names, instead of using war-imposed identities such as, "friend of the guerrilla," "victim," or "displaced person." The boundaries between armed groups and unarmed civilians were redrawn in bold lines. People were invited to resignify the concept of "the town's warriors" to mean the courageous and hardworking people who founded the towns, rather than those most heavily armed (Duplat 2003).

Interestingly, every single one of the elements Duplat identifies as part of "the intangible" requires communication processes. It is precisely these communication processes that citizens' media can help activate, maintain, and multiply.

Citizens' Media in Dislocated Democracies

As is the case with numerous other intrastate wars today, the Colombian conflict is inextricable from the presence of state institutions in rural areas otherwise isolated from capital centers. In some cases, absent, weak, or corrupt judicial systems and/or local governments undermine the rule of law and engender social contracts based on military might and wealth. Drawing on their research in Africa and Eastern Europe, Desjarlais and Kleinman write that weak nation states are "often marked by violence, dislocation, civil strife, the breakdown of food and health systems, and widespread human rights violations that affect the residents of these and other states. . . . Evoking the Oedipal-like ghost of state repression, thus contribut[ing] little in a place like Sierra Leone, where villagers are troubled more by lack, rather than an excess of state control" (Desjarlais and Kleinman 1994, 10). In other cases, repressive state institutions, such as armed forces, the police, and/or their paramilitary allies terrorize the communities they are supposed to protect and defend.

Absent, weak, or corrupt state institutions generate what Carolyn Nordstrom calls "the shadows"—a set of economic and political arrangements that exist outside legal systems. The shadows facilitate the "smuggling of everything from everywhere to everywhere, including radioactive material, human organs, and illegal immigrants; prostitution; gambling; loan-sharking; kidnapping; racketeering and extortion; counterfeiting of goods, bank notes, financial documents, credit cards, and identity cards; killers for hire, traffic of sensitive information, technology, or art objects; international sales of stolen goods; or even dumping garbage illegally from one country to another" (Nordstrom 2004, 111, citing Manuel Castells). Shadow economies and political systems constrict legal and moral frameworks. To survive and make a living under these systems, otherwise decent men, women, and children are pushed toward breaking their own moral codes:

> At the front lines, where the resources are extracted and the weapons fired, smuggling is what the powerful and the elite do; the rest is survival. It is here a woman trades an assault rifle for a chicken to feed her family. It is here a man works in the mines (or logging timber, processing drugs, poaching game, or working in the sex industry) under dangerous and harsh conditions, either because he is forced to by military or business officials who need the proceeds, or because he hopes to make enough to improve his own lot in life. Without the poor and the powerless doing this work, neither the official nor the illicit system can be maintained. (Nordstrom 2004, 128)

One of Nordstrom's informants eloquently describes how shadow economies corner people between poverty, crime, and violence: "My options? Get shot, starve, or do this work. . . . What would you choose?" (Nordstrom 2004, 128).

In these contexts, citizens' media can be useful in strengthening participatory democracies, the rule of law, good governance, and accountability and transparency in local state institutions and government authorities. In chapters 3 and 4 I examined how citizens' media have pressured local mayors to inform their constituencies about fiscal management and local development plans; how community media are used to monitor local elections, prompt voters to vote responsibly, and inform voters about candidates' government programs. In some cases, such as that of Puerto Wilches Estéreo in Magdalena Medio, and Custodia Estéreo in Inírida, community media subject local authorities to strong, consistent public pressure, demanding increased transparency. Citizens' media also encourage all residents to become involved in local decision-making processes, monitor their local mayors and other government officials, and keep an eye on public works, municipal budgets, and local governments' actions and omissions.

In some cases, an individual takes on a profound commitment to the rights and responsibilities of residents and government officials in small communities. These individuals can become self-proclaimed community watchdogs, the type of person who devotes much of his or her free time to monitoring how well others follow the rules. When community media open up to these self-appointed community watchdogs, their monitoring talent can become an asset for the whole community. Programs such as *Chachareando* (Chatting) in Magdalena Medio (chapter 3) and *La Cantaleta* (The Tirade) in Caquetá (chapter 1) strengthen the rule of law and the notion that peaceful coexistence is strongly linked to citizens' participation in decision-making processes, good governance, accountability, and transparency on the part of local governments. Clearly, good communication between governments and the people they govern is the primary condition for peacebuilding (Von Kalternborg-Stachau 2008).

The case of AREDMAG's radio stations in Magdalena Medio demonstrates the synergy that can emerge from peacebuilding initiatives working hand in hand with citizens' media. In this Colombian region the Magdalena Medio Peace and Development Program funds hundreds of initiatives working to strengthen citizen participation and good governance. AREDMAG's fifteen community radio stations, with close ties to these funded initiatives, welcome citizens' committees to have their own programs, announce new participation opportunities, and participate in regional and local decision-making committees and councils.

In sum, my fieldwork in Colombia revealed the complex and varied roles citizens' media play as they disrupt the impact of violence on the lives of unarmed communities. First, when communities are victimized by armed groups, citizens' media can help create a buffer around the community in several ways: by prompting collective actions and reasons to interact and repopulate public spheres, thus decreasing extreme isolationism; by creating communication spaces that trigger a sense of togetherness to fight collective fear and feelings of powerlessness.

Second, as war affects the social and cultural fabric of a community even when people are not under direct attack, the functions of citizens' media grow to fill the needs created in the community. The continuous presence of armed groups roaming around, in and out of people's communal and public spaces, permeates social and cultural fabrics with epistemologies of force. The presence of these groups normalizes aggression as a way to manage conflict, dissent, and difference; infuses personal, family, and communal relationships with violent interactions; and displays models of success and power based on violent behavior that influences the life choices of youth and children. Citizens' media step in to remind people of who they used to be. Programming emphasizing local cultural imaginaries, languages, life worlds, and culturally grounded ways of interacting can counter the corrosive influences of armed groups and militaristic frameworks.

Citizens' media have a third function, intervening when violence disturbs life worlds, traditional epistemologies and moralities, and a sense of normalcy. War imposes a foreign reality in which action is motivated by fear and the primal desire to survive and to protect one's kin. The lived experience of war invades a community and coexists with the lived experience of peace. As Johan Galtung states, war and peace are frequently not lived as either/or (Galtung 1993), as mutually exclusive, binary realities. Instead, unarmed communities cornered by warring factions experience violence and peace simultaneously (Duplat 2003), as competing realities. War threatens to take over more and more aspects of normal life, while people attempt to resist this invasion. Paul Richards states that part of armed violence's impact on a community is that "habitus (to use Bourdieu's term) has been torn up and defiled" (Richards 1992, 5).

In these situations, broadcasting a weekly community television program about local organic gardening and how to manage pests, or a radio transmission of the local soccer tournament are actions of resistance. In performing these types of actions, citizens' media strengthen the notion that the community's normal life world has not been entirely obliterated by war, and that habitus still survives. Citizens' media serve as loudspeakers for those realities that still exist out of the reach of armed violence, situations not yet permeated by logics of war and aggression. Throughout the previous chapters I have tried to demonstrate the ways in which communities have refused to allow armed groups to completely invade their everyday lives and life worlds. All media, and perhaps especially community media, need to make these peace-in-the-midst-of-war spaces visible and shareable— part of the community's and the nation's cultural capital. Irish historian F. S. L. Lyons implored, referring to media coverage of Northern Ireland, "show us the place as it really is, show it to us in all its human ordinariness, its quirky humour, its stubborn contrariness, its integrity. Show it to us, above all, as a place inhabited not only by evil men . . . but also by decent human beings" (quoted in Parish, Hamber, and Price 2006, 3). Citizens' media are strongly connected to the everyday lives of their communities, so they are in a privileged position from which they can focus their microphones, cameras, and other communication technologies on those dimensions of people's lives that exist beyond the reach of armed violence. From this privileged close range, citizens' media can provide access to a television cooking show in Montes de María (chapter 2), a radio chronicle of the women's poultry micro-enterprise in Magdalena Medio (chapter 4), or a *foto-video* about the toy boats made by children in southern Colombia (chapter 1). Seen through the lens of citizens' media, these are all practices of resistance against the destructive impact of armed violence on the social fabric of unarmed civilian communities. Broadcast images of a grandmother who wakes every morning to make *arepas* serve as a reminder that not everything has been invaded by chaos and uncertainty.[5] Citizens' media create the conditions that allow people to experience what remains of their peaceful life worlds.

From Learning about Peace to Experiencing Peace

Johan Galtung defines "culture of violence" as a set of relationships and discursive practices that legitimize violence or make violence seem an acceptable means of responding to conflict (Galtung 1991, 1998). The continuous presence of armed groups in civilian communities normalizes weapons, military uniforms, aggressive ways of dealing with conflict, and friend/foe frameworks. Children and youth begin to perceive armed warriors as role models. Young women begin to see warriors as good suitors as they see how armed men in uniform are feared, have power and money, and can make things happen.

In these contexts, citizens' media can help stimulate social and cultural scenarios where people can experience the normalization of nonviolence. Instead of sending messages describing nonviolence or trying to persuade people to live nonviolently, the great potential of citizens' media is in their ability to allow people to have a lived experience of nonviolent ways to manage conflict, deal with difference, and interact with one another. Thus, citizens' media carve out spaces where, even in the midst of armed conflict, people can experience a way of being that neutralizes friend/foe frameworks, promotes peaceful deliberation, and "provides reasons that make nonviolent conflict management legitimate and reasonable" (Duplat 2003, 9). Citizens' media can "subject people" to a culture of peace understood as a set of discursive practices and relationships that legitimize respect and inclusion, celebrate difference, and opt for dialogue rather than force (Brand-Jabobsen 2002, 19–20).

Here I would like to introduce the core ideas of communication as performance theory (Bell 2008; Conquergood 1995, 1998; Madison 2005; V. Turner 1988). According to these theories, performance engages all the senses of participants, allowing them to embody and feel communication. In performance, messages are communicated through smell, taste, sight, sound, and touch; performance participants are enveloped in a holistic experience that engages all of their senses. Performance scholar Edward M. Bruner emphasizes the centrality of experience in performance: "Lived experience, then, as thought and desire, word and image, is the primary reality" (quoted in Madison 2005, 151). Performance emerges at the intersection of experience and expression, in the form of expressed experience, or as experience shaped into meaningful expression (Madison 2005, 152). In performance, the constitutive potential of language over reality is salient; performance is language that has the power to "do something in the world" (Madison 2005, 161). In his theorization of performance, J. L. Austin explained that language is not only constative (statements about reality), but performative, whereby language creates reality (Austin 1975).

More than simply listening to a message or seeing a message, performance participants experience a multiplicity of messages in a multiplicity of sensorial events. From the concept of communication as performance, I want to propose the idea that citizens' media create a performance of peacebuilding. Instead of transmitting messages about peacebuilding to audiences, Colombian citizens' media involve audiences in, and subject audiences to, the felt, embodied experience of peace. For example, the cases examined in chapter 3, in which Magdalena Medio's citizens' radio stations involved the community in processes of mediation, can be examined as examples of performances of mediation. In these cases, the medium did not try to persuade people of the value of mediation, nor transmit mediation skills. Instead, the medium created communication spaces where media producers, participants, and their audiences could actually experience mediation. In the case of peaceful conflict-resolution among the Montes de María Communications Collective participants, children and youth were able to experience what peaceful resolution of conflict feels like. Collective participants are "subjected" to peace, and made to feel peace, rather than being told about the virtues of peace. The words of a community radio leader from Magdalena Medio echo the idea of citizens' media as performance of peacebuilding: "The community radio station *allows people to envision new ways of feeling, seeing, and listening*, both within our community and in the wider region of Magdalena Medio. The station's central focus is culture, but not just artistic expression. Here, culture means all the magical possibilities for regional development" (Unidad de Radio—Mesa Regional Magdalena Medio and Santanderes 2000; my emphasis). The performance spaces that "subject" people to peacebuilding are crucial, because, as one of Carolyn Nordstrom's informants says: "So is the war really over? Is the violence of war gone suddenly with declarations of peace? No, violence lives in the belly of the person and ruins society, unless peace is taught to the violent. And peace must be taught just like violence is, *by subjecting people to it*, by showing them peaceful ways to respond to life and living, to daily needs and necessities, to political and personal challenges" (Nordstrom 2004, 179–80; my emphasis).

Unhinged Realities

Performance is dynamic and generative (Bell 2008, 17). As a communicative process, performance is a transactional communication event that involves speakers and listeners as active participants (Pelias 1992, 15). Performance triggers communication processes that constitute meaning, affirm certain cultural values (Stern and Henderson 1993, 3), and engender transformative processes (Bell 2008, 17). Performance tends to favor boundary-crossing experiences and the transformative over the normative (Conquergood 1995, 1998). Central to social and cultural life, a performance allows a collectivity to look at itself as in a "hall of mirrors" (V. Turner 1982, 105). Madison describes the self-reflexive potential of performance: "When we perform and witness cultural performances, we often come to realize truths about ourselves and our world that we cannot realize in our day-to-day existence" (Madison 2005, 154). Moreover, performance can trigger processes of change and transformation among participants: "Cultural performances are not only a reflection of what we are, they also shape and

direct who we are and what we can become" (Madison 2005, 154).
Through performance we can become something we currently are not;
performance is "the experience of becoming" (Conquergood 1998).
Performance scholar Victor Turner theorized the idea of *liminality,* a
moment triggered by performance when social conventions and structures are suspended opening the potentiality for new alternatives:
"a realm of pure possibility, a temporary breach of structure whereby
the familiar may be stripped of certitude and the normative unhinged,
an interlude wherein conventional social, economic, and political life
may be transcended" (St John 2008, 5).

Various aspects of Colombian citizens' media can be examined as
performances in that they facilitate collective communication processes that disrupt established cultural codes and allow participants to
reconstitute alternative codes. As active participants of these media
performances, unarmed communities can overcome fear and uncertainty, and resist the disintegration of public spaces and life worlds.
Citizens' media trigger communication performances that encourage
people to transform the way they go about their lives and to place
their bets on building relationships of trust, resignifying public spaces,
and committing to democratic participation.

When citizens' media insist on the permanence, beauty, and force
inherent in people's life worlds, unarmed communities can inhabit
identities and ways of being outside of ascribed war identities. When
men, women, and children bring their chairs out to the street and sit
together in front of a large screen to watch a two-minute video about
a boy and his grandma, people enter a communication performance.
The performance subjects people to experiences that remind them
that their identities are not exhausted by war and that their life worlds
have not been entirely eroded by the values and codes imposed by
armed groups.

I profoundly agree with Carolyn Nordstrom when she states that
getting a mental image of what peace feels like, and being reminded
that one's world already contains the seeds of peace, is necessary for
communities to begin processes of peacebuilding. In other words,
imagined peace, embodied peace are needed before it is possible to
start working toward sustainable peaceful communities. Peace scholar
Paul Richards cites a study on famine done through an analysis of
the songs composed by African women survivors of famine: "Perhaps Megan Vaughan's focus on famine as expressed through song

was even more apposite than her readers realized at the time, because it may be that overcoming the effects of famine (and war) requires the ability to dance to a new tune" (Richards 1992, 5). From this angle, citizens' media can be seen as sites of cultural resistance (Bell 2008, 17) or, as explained by peace scholars, as communication processes that trigger "the performative abilities through which human groups improvise fresh beginnings" (Richards 1992, 5).

Performance theorists explain that during certain type of performances, a sense of "communitas" emerges among participants (Bell 2008; E. Turner 2005; V. Turner 1988). Edith Turner describes "communitas" as "a sense of sharing an intimacy . . . the gift of togetherness . . . unity, seamless unity" (E. Turner 2005, 97–98). Madison describes it as "a moment of utopian unity [where] individual identities come together in a direct and immediate manner" (Madison 2005, 159). Performances that provoke "communitas" galvanize collectivity and diminish individuality. The experience of being part of a group, being a "we" intensifies and overwhelms the sense of being an "I." Based on Victor Turner's anthropological work on performance, Richard Schechner defines "spontaneous communitas" as "the dissolution of boundaries shutting people off from each other" (Schechner 2003, 156). During these exceptional moments when a gathering of people experience "communitas" triggered by performance, the groups' rules and everyday life codes are suspended, and the group experiences a moment when "everything and anything" can happen (Bell 2008). New rules, new ways to do things can emerge, as performance triggers a moment of "unprecedented potency" (Matthews 2008, 177). In this sense, performance is spontaneous, unscripted, a sudden empty space of freedom to start new beginnings, to figure out, collectively, new ways to respond to the surrounding conditions.

During my fieldwork I found at least four instances in which Colombian citizens' media triggered collective communication-as-performance events that spiraled into the experience of "communitas." First, during the guerrilla attack on the small town of Belén de los Andaquíes in 2001, community radio helped hundreds of unarmed civilians break away from collective terror and extreme isolation provoked by the invasion of heavily armed *guerrilleros* (chapter 1). In response to the community radio station's broadcast of Colombian Christmas carols and a gathering in the town's central park, men, women, and children defied terror and came out of their houses to be with one another. Once at the park, accompanied by their priest, their radio station, and their Christmas songs, these brave Colombians overcame the sense of hopelessness and powerlessness imposed by armed groups and engaged in collective action that restored their sense of agency. When I asked Alirio González what exactly allowed them to overcome the feeling of fear in that moment, he responded: "I don't know; just the feeling of being together made the fear subside" (A. González 2006).

The second case of citizens' media inspired "communitas" is Radio Andaquí's response to the 1996 *cocalero* mobilization in southern Colombia (chapter 1). Radicalized by the Samper administration's indiscriminate fumigations of their agricultural plots under pressure from the United States, coca growers rose in protest. Known as the *"cocalero* demonstrations," in these protests, thousands of Colombian farmers embarked on long marches from southern Colombia toward Florencia and Mocoa, the largest cities in the region. *Cocalero* demonstrators demanded that officials replace chemical fumigations with manual eradication of coca plots. They also called for social investment, regional development programs, and economic alternatives for coca-growing families. The demonstrators insisted that coca growers were neither terrorists nor delinquents, but agricultural families in such conditions of marginality that growing coca was their only alternative.

In September 1996 approximately twenty thousand *cocalero* demonstrators arrived in the small town of Belén de los Andaquíes in Caquetá. They stayed for three days before continuing on their pilgrimage toward the region's capital city of Florencia. The people of Belén hesitantly welcomed these thousands of newcomers, who had been labeled "criminals," "terrorists," "drug traffickers," and "guerrillas" by the national and regional mainstream media. However, thanks to Radio Andaquí, the local community radio station, *cocalero* demonstrators and their local hosts found they had much more in common than anyone could have predicted. Radio Andaquí set up an outdoor stage and put its microphones at the service of these two groups. During the following week, this outdoor stage became a performance involving demonstrators and local residents. The performance triggered a multiplicity of sensory messages that subjected participants to experiences of empathy, collective solidarity, and nonviolent ways to coexist with others who are different. Soon, *cocaleros* and the people of Belén were sharing songs, poems, and personal and local stories that allowed them to perceive their commonalities as struggling agricultural communities dealing with marginality and a neglectful government. The tension lessened as the feeling of "us" and common ground solidified.

The third case is the inaugural session of the Purple Rose of Cairo Itinerant Street-Film Project in 2000 (chapter 2). By this time, the region of Montes de María had endured five years of extreme armed violence between guerrillas, paramilitaries, and the Colombian armed forces. Unarmed civilian communities in the region were becoming targets of paramilitary violence, and victims of some of the worst massacres in the country. Communities lived under siege as guerrillas, paramilitaries, and armed forces competed for control of the territory and its people. In the middle of this experience of collective terror, a youth group designed a new use of communication technologies to try to bring people out of fear and isolation, and back into a public space of togetherness. Here, I believe that the simplicity of the performance is brilliant. The performance consisted of a white wall serving as a screen, a table on the street, a DVD player, a projector, a sound system, and *Central Station,* a Brazilian film. Invited by the Communications Collective of Montes de María to come to the central park and watch a film, hundreds of men, women, and children came out of their homes and their terror and gathered around the screen. The feeling of "communitas" that emerged among the people of El Carmen is echoed in Wilgen Peñaloza's eloquent description of the night:

> I remember the smiling faces of children, entire families sitting together watching the film, moms with their babies, teens on their bicycles, men on their motorcycles, couples in love sharing a broken bench on the plaza. This was like a human fusion of shared smiles, as if trying to say, "We are all still here." That night was a turning point for many of us, myself included. I never imagined that in the middle of the terror of war you could find ways to reach out to each other, so that you do not end up all alone in the middle of the war. That night I learned that we have the necessary skills to build peace, we are not entirely powerless in the face of war, and that we can transform public spaces from sites of fear and isolation to scenes for sharing experiences and life. (Peñaloza 2004)

The fourth case I want to mention is that of the collective rescue mission coordinated by Santa Rosa Estéreo, the community radio station in a small community in Magdalena Medio (chapter 3). In 1999 the ELN, the second largest guerrilla organization in the country, kidnapped José Botello, a long-time community leader, educator, and director of Santa Rosa Estéreo, the local community radio station. The station's producers decided on the spot to make this kidnapping a public event, not just a terrible tragedy happening to Botello's family and friends. After all, they reasoned, the technology necessary to make the kidnapping a collective concern was at their fingertips. In a matter of minutes they redesigned that day's programming and redirected the station's broadcasting to announce José Botello's kidnapping. The community responded by expressing their willingness to engage in anything necessary to rescue their valued community leader. By the end of the day, a caravan of almost five hundred people, coordinated by the station, snaked up the Andes toward the guerrilla camp. Once at the guerrilla camp, these brave unarmed Colombians demanded the release of their leader. Three days later, the guerrilla's *comandantes* realized that the civilians would not leave their camp unless Botello was released. They decided that losing Botello was better than dealing with five hundred men, women, and children settling into their encampment's central square, cooking on improvised bonfires, and sleeping in makeshift tents. Seven days after Botello was kidnapped, the caravan came back to Santa Rosa, exhausted but reunited with their leader. Step by step, local communicators used radio technologies to generate an amazing chain of collective experiences. Each communication process activated by Santa Rosa Estéreo is more in line with the notion of performance than with communication as transmission of information or persuasion. The station was used to subject people to collective experiences, not to transmit messages. To this day, the people of Santa Rosa share a strong appreciation for their community radio station. In a documentary about community radio in Magdalena Medio, José Botello says, "No one, not even the armed groups, mess with Santa Rosa Estéreo. They all know that to mess with our community radio station is to mess with our entire town" (Gumucio Dagron and Cadavid 2006).

In these four examples, citizens' media triggered performances that instilled in unarmed civilians under siege a feeling of "communitas." More importantly, the experience of "communitas" made it possible for these men, women, and children to recover their sense of collective agency in the face of armed violence.

Using Communication Technologies in Contexts of War

In contexts where communities are cornered by armed groups, communication technologies reach far beyond the role of tools for transmitting content. I hope this is sufficiently conveyed in the previous chapters. Colombian citizens' media pioneers use communication technologies in fluid ways, responding to each war situation. The impact of armed conflict on a community's cultural fabric and everyday life is complex, multifaceted, and unpredictable. In response, the pioneers featured in this book employ media technologies, in all their plasticity and fluidity, to imagine and design new ways to help communities resist violence. I cannot overemphasize that my goal is not to encourage the replication of these specific media implementations in other contexts of armed violence. Instead, I believe our role as alternative/community/citizens' media scholars is to document, analyze, and share these uses when we find them, making them part of the cultural capital of all those attempting to use media technologies for peacebuilding. There is no formula!

More important than setting up community media for the sake of community media is to nurture communication know-how at the local level. Once communication competencies are developed, communities can put them to use in times of crisis. A recent World Bank study corroborates my own findings; the independent/community media system set up in Sri Lanka to strengthen peacebuilding goals was immediately redirected toward relief efforts during the 2004 tsunami (Kalathil, Langlois, and Kaplan 2008, 20): local communicators knew how to use the technologies, and they could quickly put their skills and competence to use when disaster struck.

Communication and information skills and competencies learned in times of peace can be used by a community to keep armed groups at bay; resist the normalization of cultures of death, weapons, aggression, and violence; strengthen dimensions of life not permeated by war; reconnect families and communities separated by war; negotiate and mediate with armed groups; assist refugees and forcefully displaced families; and coordinate food distribution and other logistics.

It is almost impossible to predict when a community will need its own media to respond to armed conflict, war, or natural or human disasters; however, if the communication expertise is present in the community, it will be put to use in times of need, whenever that need arises. It is urgent, therefore, to strengthen community media legislation, sustainability, training opportunities, and other elements that bolster community media's legitimacy. Peace studies scholars suggest that of all elements that precipitate armed violence, "cultural violence is the hardest to change, it is the deep-rooted constant which legitimates structural and direct violence, especially when there is a reaction (violent or not) against the structural violence by those who are victims of it" (Graf, Kramer, and Nicolescou 2007, 131). Moreover, Johan Galtung and other peace experts insist that peace agreements signed between leaders and/or elites are not enough to secure long-term, sustainable peace (Galtung 2002; Graf, Kramer, and Nicolescou 2007). In the hands of those who opt for nonviolence even in the middle of war, media technologies can be used to dismantle cultures of violence and to build sustainable and peaceful social fabrics at the community level, beyond peace pacts among elites.

Too often in the fields of development and peacebuilding, communication is falsely equated with public relations. This narrow approach to communication limits the use of media to publicizing development and peacebuilding programs and institutions, and maintaining good information flows between different program agents and offices. In this paradigm, communication and media are perceived as tools to publicize and promote development and peacebuilding programs, but not as central components of the programs (Gumucio Dagron and Rodríguez 2006; Kalathil, Langlois, and Kaplan 2008). A "communication initiative" to help a United Nations peacekeeping program is one thing; a United Nations peacekeeping program that includes various communication initiatives designed to enable communication among local communities is quite a different thing. The first is public relations, the latter is communication for peacebuilding. The public relations approach to media and communication is instrumental, narrow, and terribly wasteful; the tremendous potential of media and communication to nurture peaceful social fabrics, support active civil societies, empower citizens to take ownership of their communities' destinies, and strengthen good governance, accountability and transparency are lost when media are only employed as public relations tools.

Conclusion

In his memoir about the 1993 siege of Sarajevo, Dzevad Karahasan tells of a moment when, despite the past year of destruction, lack of electricity, heat, food, or medicine, his theater students put together a stage play. Karahasan describes the hands of a young woman playing the leading female role on opening night. Ripping branches from trees to use as fuel for baking had shredded her hands to pieces. The lack of water made basic hygiene impossible, and the extreme cold ruined her skin. The script called for a young male actor to kiss her hand, and when he did, all the actors on stage and their audiences gasped, suspended in a moment of intense emotion. In the way the young man kissed the young woman, he honored the beauty and dignity of her hands, which had been destroyed by war. Karahasan writes: "The internal truth of the work of art is reached only when art raises over everything else to show the lived realities of people, and people's need to live as beings of culture, demonstrating how the need for culture is also an existential need" (Karahasan 2005, 58).

Felicja Karay reveals the significance of cultural practices in some of the most extreme conditions of armed violence, such as a Nazi slave labor camp for women in the 1940s. Based on a series of prisoner testimonies and her own experience as a prisoner, Karay writes, "They sang another Hanukkah song of joy and happiness but there was no joy and happiness. Still, it was better to sing together than to curl up in a corner and cry. . . . We wanted to maintain the sense that we were cultured people whatever the cost, because the conditions we lived in were created to break our spirit. There was no way we could change the physical situation, so at least we fought for our souls" (Karay 2002, 183–207).

In Carolyn Nordstrom's account of her visit to a city drain that had been transformed into a home by internally displaced street children in Angola in 1998, we can clearly see everyday people, refusing to let war break their spirits, using cultural practices as resistance:

> Without taking time to think, I squeezed down the drain after the child. In my mind's eye, when I had heard about children living in the drains under the streets, I had visualized decaying, dirt-encrusted tunnels with children huddled in dismal conditions amid stagnant water and rats. Everyone I knew held the same idea. But when I entered the drain, I felt the world stop, existentially, for a moment—and my view of the human condition, in its most profound sense, expanded. In this drain the children had created a home and a community. It was spotlessly clean. I remember being surprised that there was no smell. The children had lined the walls with pictures from magazines. An old inner tube of a tire served as a chair. . . . [S]ome meters down

the drain they had fashioned a wall, and at the end they had constructed shelves that held the few possessions they had managed to acquire. . . . [T]hey pulled me over to show me a sleeping boy wrapped up in a blanket, and began to gently pull the blanket from him. I whispered not to wake the boy, but that was not their intent. They lifted up the blanket to show me that wrapped up and sleeping with the boy were four plump, healthy and very happy puppies. Clearly, the children had shared what little food they could manage with the puppies' mother. They treated these puppies with a tenderness they themselves might never have known, and were obviously proud of their family-like community. (Nordstrom 2004, 177)

We must recognize the ways armed violence disrupts the cultural fabric of communities, and how civilians use culture, communication, and art to overcome this violence. Media technologies play key roles, strengthening people's actions of cultural resistance against armed violence. I would like to end with Nordstrom's words: "Without the arts and literature and media that set up belief systems of resolution over conflict, without a sense of the future, peace cannot emerge. No peace accords brokered at elite levels will work if these bases are not there to build upon. 'The doing is everything'" (Nordstrom 2004, 184).

ACKNOWLEDGMENTS

So many people in so many places made this book possible. First and foremost, so many thanks to all the citizens' media pioneers for allowing me into their lives, their communities, and their media initiatives. In Montes de María, Soraya Bayuelo Castellar, Beatriz Ochoa, Modesta Muñoz, la Chichi, Wilgen Peñaloza, and Leonarda de la Ossa each taught me that, even when hit by tragedy and surrounded by war, we need to make time for a gentle embrace or a Caribbean dance. In Magdalena Medio, where I found people in love with their homeland, trying so hard to rescue their region from the recent history of brutality; people like Orley Durán, Manfry Gómez Ditta, Julio Hoyos, Omaira Arrieta, Amparo Murillo, and Melba Quijano. In Simití, Sofi Torrenegra and Fidel Castro took time to show me around. Exhausted, I took one of the best naps in my life in one of the hammocks in Sofi's home, and she fed me a scrumptious breakfast the following morning. In San Vicente de Chucurí, Leonardo Amaya, Don Isidoro Caballero, Sonia Durán, and Jorge Correa opened every door for me and spent so many hours explaining their region and the role(s) of San Vicente Estéreo. On one occasion they even took my daughter to market so that I could focus on my interviews. When they returned, she had a new pet: Charquito de Colombia, a white bunny that later hopped from room to room in our apartment in Bogotá. In Santa Rosa, Pacho Urbiñez told me countless stories about the gold mines nearby and his own experiences with the guerrillas. I could write an entire chapter about Pacho, who was at the time director of Santa Rosa Estéreo. In Belén de los Andaquíes, Doña Marta Calderón, Blanco Alirio, Raul Sotelo, Mariana García, and Mariana's mom and dad all went out of their way to welcome me into their homes and their lives. I felt so welcomed so many times I did not want to board that plane from Florencia back to Bogotá. Alirio González, the man who understands so well the comings and goings of tides, my unconditional *parcero,* taught me entirely new ways of seeing and understanding my own country, my own people.

I also want to thank Guillermo Pérez for the most fascinating interview I've ever done, and Benjamín Casadiego for so many ideas essential to understanding the connections between citizens' media and schools. Jeanine El Gazi showed me endless generosity in allowing me to explore the Ministry of Culture's Unidad de Radio archives, in her thorough readings of everything I sent her, and in giving me the context I needed to make sense of so many issues. Other key people at the Ministry of Culture include Javier Espitia and Tatiana Duplat. Esmeralda Ortiz at the Ministry of Communications explained so many issues related to community media legislation and the history of media activism in Colombia. My academic colleagues in Colombia, Jair Vega at Universidad del Norte and Amparo Cadavid at Uniminuto, were critical allies in several citizens' media projects. To Adelaida Trujillo, at Citurna, thanks so much for organizing a luncheon where Jeanine and I could meet; that single event set in motion an endless chain of wonderful outcomes, including chapter 4 in this book. So many thanks to Jesús Martín Barbero, for more than twenty-five years of continuous mentoring and support. Remedios Fajardo, Nat Nat Iguarán, and Jeremías Tunubalá helped me understand Colombian indigenous media history and issues. Omar Rincón at the Centro de Competencias en Comunicación para América Latina (Fundación Friedrich Ebert) was an unconditional supporter of my citizens' media projects, as were Jaime Abello at the Fundación para un Nuevo Periodismo Iberoamericano, and Camilo Tamayo at CINEP. Thanks so much to Rafael Obregón and Jesús Arroyave, also my colleagues at Universidad del Norte. Rafa and Jair made it possible for me to spend a semester in 2004 at Universidad del Norte as a visiting professor—that's where and when it all started. My students at the Maestría en Comunicación, Cultura y Cambio Social at Universidad del Norte, especially the first class, were essential to early stages of the project. Many of them, familiar with complex regional contexts of armed conflict, responded with enthusiasm when I began talking about the roles of community media in communities cornered by armed groups. It was their enthusiasm that allowed me to envision the project's potential.

So many hours of dialogue and exchange with others allowed me to articulate the ideas in this book. Thanks to Maria Emma Wills Obregón at Universidad de los Andes; Pilar Riaño-Alcalá at University of British Columbia; Susana Kaiser and Dorothy Kidd at the University of San Francisco; Robert Huesca at Trinity University; John Downing at Southern Illinois University; Nick Couldry at Goldsmiths, University of London; Jill Irvine at the Center for Women's and Gender Studies at the University of Oklahoma; Peter Lemish at Sapir College in Israel; Salvatore Scifo at Marmara University in Turkey; Liz Miller at Concordia University in Montreal; Laura Stein at the University of Texas; Antoni Castells i Talens at Universidad Veracruzana; Claudia Magallanes-Blanco at Universidad Iberoamericana Puebla; Jose Manuel Ramos at Universidad Autónoma de Puebla; Mario Murillo at Hofstra University; Yeidi Rivero at the University of Michigan; Francis Rolt at Radio for Peace Building; Bill Siemering at Development Radio Partners; Sheldon Himelfarb at the Center of Innovation for Media, Conflict, and Peacebuilding; Vladimir Bratic at Hollins University; Juan Salazar at the University of Western Sydney; Bejamin Ferron at the Université de Rennes; and Shane Moreman at California State University at Fresno. Thanks to Alfonso Gumucio Dagron and all my friends and colleagues at the global network OURMedia/NuestrosMedios—such a supportive and enthusiastic community. So many thanks to Faye Ginsburg and George Yúdice, early believers in this book.

And finally Sarah VanGundy, my friend, *parcera, coya,* ally in faraway journeys to the other side of the moon. Sarah, my editor who knows exactly what I mean and rescues my ideas again and again from the tangles of my second language.

ABBREVIATIONS

ACCU   Autodefensas Campesinas de Córdoba y Urabá
            (Peasant Self-Defense Forces of Córdoba and Urabá)

ALER   Asociación Latinoamericana de Educación
            Radiofónica (Latin American Association of Radio
            Education)

ANAPO   Alianza Nacional Popular (National Popular
            Alliance)

ANUC   Asociación Nacional de Usuarios Campesinos
            (National Association of Peasants)

AREDMAG   Asociación Red de Emisoras Comunitarias del
            Magdalena Medio (Magdalena Medio's Community
            Radio Stations' Network)

ASOCIPAZ   Asociación Cívica para la Paz (Civic Association for
            Peace)

AUSAC   Autodefensas de Santander y del Sur del Cesar (Self-
            Defense Forces of Santander and the South of Cesar)

CIESPAL   Centro Internacional de Estudios Superiores de
            Comunicación para América Latina (International
            Center for Higher Studies of Communication in
            Latin America)

CINEP   Centro de Investigación y Educación Popular
            (Center for Popular Research and Education)

CODECAL   Corporación Integral para el Desarrollo Cultural y
            Social (Integral Corporation for Social and Cultural
            Development)

CRS	Corriente de Renovación Socialista (Socialist Renovation Line)
EAIBA	Escuela Audiovisual Infantil de Belén de los Andaquíes (Belén de los Andaquíes Children's Audiovisual School)
ECOPETROL	Empresa Colombiana de Petróleo (Colombian Petroleum Company)
ELN	Ejército de Liberación Nacional (National Liberation Army)
ENDA	Environment and Development Action
EPL	Ejército Popular de Liberación (Popular Liberation Army)
FARC	Fuerzas Armadas Revolucionarias de Colombia (Revolutionary Armed Forces of Colombia)
GDP	gross domestic product
GTZ	Gesellschaft für Technische Zusammenarbeit
ICANH	Instituto Colombiano de Antropología e Historia (Colombian Institute of Anthropology and History)
ICT	information and communication technologies
INCORA	Instituto Colombiano de Reforma Agraria (Colombian Institute of Agrarian Reform)
JAC	Junta de Acción Comunal (Community Action Board)
M-19	Movimiento 19 de Abril (April 19 Movement)
MAS	Muerte a Secuestradores (Death to Kidnappers)
MORENA	Movimiento de Restauración Nacional (National Restoration Movement)
NGO	nongovernmental organization
PDP	Programa de Desarrollo y Paz (Development and Peace Program)
PDPMM	Programa de Desarrollo y Paz del Magdalena Medio (Peace and Development Program for Magdalena Medio)
PNUD	Programa de las Naciones Unidas para el Desarrollo (United Nations Development Program)

PSA	public service announcement
RCN	Radio Cadena Nacional (National Radio Network)
SENA	Servicio Nacional de Aprendizaje (National Learning Service)
SFCG	Search for Common Ground
SIPAZ	Sistema de Información para la Paz (Information for Peace System)
UNESCO	United Nations Educational, Scientific and Cultural Organization
UNICEF	United Nations Children's Fund
USAID	United States Agency for International Development
USIP	United States Institute of Peace
USO	Unión Sindical Obrera (Workers' Union)

NOTES

Life at the Crossfire

1. All translations from Spanish originals (publications and interviews) are my own.

2. The Huitoto are one of Colombia's indigenous peoples.

3. One of the first laws of the National Front, Law 14 of 1958, started JACs; these were initially formed as rural neighborhood committees with the idea that JACs would bring peace by involving community members in local decision-making processes; by 1966 nine thousand JACs had been formed in the country (Zamosc 1986, 38). According to Jaramillo et al., the concept of JACs came from three sociologists: Camilo Torres, Orlando Fals Borda, and Andrew Pearse (Jaramillo, Mora, and Cubides 1986, 255).

4. For decades, the weak presence of state institutions has been blamed for the absence of the rule of law and the use of armed violence as a way to rule social life. To this day in Colombia, there are more than twelve hundred urban centers where there is not one police officer, and approximately 20 percent of the country's municipalities have no state institutional presence (García Villegas and de Sousa dos Santos 2004, 54).

5. For more on Colombian women in the guerrillas, see Hodgson 2000; Lara 2000; Vásquez Perdomo 2005.

6. In some regions, guerrilla organizations became the de facto state. Another testimony narrates the life of a Magdalena Medio woman so badly battered by her husband that around 1984 the guerrillas advised her to leave the region; later, the same organization helped her get the title to the land she had lived on, forced her husband off the land, and invited her to come back to take over the farm and live in peace with her children (Arenas Obregón 1998, 54).

7. Money paid to guerrillas in exchange for protection from their violence.

8. It is not only hacienda owners who had dealings with the paramilitaries. Other national and international corporate sectors used or backed paramilitaries to fend off guerrillas; in May 2008, Chiquita Brands International was fined for payments made to paramilitaries over several years. Other international corporations,

such as Drummond, Nestlé, and Coca-Cola, are being investigated (Brodzinsky 2007).

9. Even during the worst years of armed violence between Sendero Luminoso (the Shining Path), the self-defense groups known as Rondas Campesinas, and the Peruvian armed forces, the homicide rate per hundred thousand inhabitants in Peru was eight to ten times lower than the Colombian rate (Romero 2003, 27).

10. In Rincón del Mar, a small fishing village on the Caribbean coast, someone told me that the paramilitaries forbade villagers to make love on the beach at night, a traditional practice for couples unable to find privacy anywhere else, due to the cramped conditions in their small houses and large families. For first-person narratives of civilian life among opposing armed groups see "Le tengo anotado el parte," Desde Adentro, http://www.desdeadentro.info/index.php?option=com_con tent&task=view&id=51&Itemid=14.

11. *Norteño* and *vallenato* music are preferred by paramilitaries.

12. The lists of behaviors imposed and prohibited by paramilitaries changes from one region to another.

13. Profiting from stolen gasoline is common, especially among paramilitaries in Magdalena Medio (Vásquez 2006, 319).

14. Colombian journalist and filmmaker Mady Samper documents some of the most salient cases of civilian resistance to armed conflict. See Samper 2002.

15. The study was conducted under the auspices of the U.S. Institute of Peace (http://www.usip.org) and was carried out by Vlado Bratic (Hollins University), Ian Larsen (USIP), and Lisa Schirch (Eastern Mennonite University). Scholars have recently defined the term "peacebuilding" as "the effort to rebuild social fabrics and relationships torn by armed conflict." The term "peace making" refers more specifically to the signing of peace agreements, cease-fires, etc. While peacebuilding involves everyone affected by armed conflict, peace making generally involves only elites, military leaders, and diplomats (Lederach 1997; Wolfsfeld, Alimi, and Kailani 2008, 375).

16. Without a doubt, the world's main protagonist in this camp is Search for Common Ground (see http://www.sfcg.org/programmes/cgp/programmes_cgp.html).

17. Benjamin Ferron compiled terms, including alternative, radical, citizens', marginal, participatory, counter-information, parallel, community, underground, popular, libres, dissident, resistance, pirate, clandestine, independent, new, young, micro (Ferron 2006, 1). For a thorough list see Alternative Media Global Project, "Naming and Qualifying Alternative Media," available at http://www.ourmedia network.org/wiki/introduction:defining_alternative_media:naming.

18. Decree 1446 of 1991 regulates the airwaves and defines these three categories for radio broadcasting. See Ministerio de Comunicaciones, "Radio y Pluralismo: Política de Radiodifusión Sonora Comunitaria," November 2007, available at http://archivo.mintic.gov.co/mincom/documents/portal/documents/root/Radio difusion%20Sonora/Archivos%20PDF/POLITICA%20PUBLICA%20DEL%20 SERVICIO%20COMUNITARIO%20DE%20RADIODIFUSION%20SONORA. pdf.

19. *Cabildo* is an indigenous government with legislative and jurisdictional autonomy.

20. Given the ambiguous definition of the term "community organization," numerous community broadcasting licenses were assigned to nonprofit organizations that do not nurture community participation. To remedy this problem, in 2003 the Ministry of Communications passed decree 1981 that mandates that each community radio station form a programming committee, responsible for shaping the station into a truly participatory medium. Programming committees are supposed to include a wide diversity of community representatives.

21. Two national public radio networks, four departmental government radio stations, five navy radio stations, seven school radios stations, twenty-two indigenous stations, twenty-four university stations, twenty-four army radio stations, twenty-eight police radio stations, and fifty-one municipal government radio stations. See Ministerio de Comunicaciones, "Radio y Pluralismo: Política de Radiodifusión Sonora Comunitaria," November 2007, available at http://archivo.mintic. gov.co/mincom/documents/portal/documents/root/Radiodifusion%20Sonora/Arch ivos%20PDF/POLITICA%20PUBLICA%20DEL%20SERVICIO%20COMU NITARIO%20DE%20RADIODIFUSION%20SONORA.pdf.

22. Key NGOs during the late 1980s included Centro de Investigación y Educación Popular (CINEP) [Center for Popular Research and Education], Corporación Integral para el Desarrollo Cultural y Social (CODECAL) [Integral Corporation for Social and Cultural Development], Servicio Colombiano de Comunicación Social [Social Communication Colombian Service], and Dimensión Educativa [Educational Dimension].

23. From 1984 to 1988 I worked at CINEP, one of these NGOs. In 1986 and 1987 I was one of the primary organizers of the First and Second Alternative and Popular Communication Festivals held in Bogotá.

24. Several international organizations, including the United Nations Children's Fund (UNICEF) and the government of Holland, supported these initiatives (Gómez and Quintero 2002, 26).

25. Aires del Pacífico was endorsed and supported by the Universidad del Valle, the Ministry of Education, SENA, UNICEF, and Holland's international aid (Gómez and Quintero 2002, 26).

26. La Voz del Barrio was endorsed and supported by SENA, the Ministry of Health, the Universidad Autónoma de Bucaramanga, and UNICEF (Gómez and Quintero 2002, 29).

27. La Fiesta de la Palabra was endorsed and supported by SENA, the Ministries of Culture and the Interior, Bogotá's City Government, ENDA, and Fundación Social (Gómez and Quintero 2002, 31–32).

28. The original Spanish states: "Se garantiza a toda persona la libertad de expresar y difundir su pensamiento y opiniones, la de informar y recibir información veraz e imparcial, y la de fundar medios masivos de comunicación. Estos son libres y tienen responsabilidad social. Se garantiza el derecho a la rectificación en condiciones de equidad. No habrá censura" (Constitución política de Colombia

1991, available at http://www.alcaldiabogota.gov.co/sisjur/normas/Normal.jsp?i=
4125).

29. For example, approximately 35 percent of all community radio licenses
were assigned to the Catholic Church (El Gazi 2008, 7).

30. Although community media are defined as nonprofit ventures, Colombian
legislation allows community radio and television to sell advertising (fifteen minutes per hour in the case of community radio). The legislation states that all profits
should be reinvested in the media initiative.

1. Drugs, Violence, and the Media of the People

1. This state of affairs describes the situation during the first half of the 2000s.
Armed conflict in Colombia is permanently in flux from region to region and from
one year to the next, thus readers should not assume that the militarization of
Belén is still the same at the time of reading.

2. Cinchona tree extraction in Caquetá reached its peak between 1870 and
1881. By 1883 cinchona tree extraction was dwindling (Arcila Niño et al. 2000,
33) due to the establishment of cinchona tree plantations in Asia, where South
American seeds were exported. The boom in rubber extraction took place between
1903 and 1920 (Ramírez 2001, 33; Jaramillo, Mora, and Cubides 1986, 5–6). One
of the earliest routes into Caquetá was the corridor established for cinchona tree
extraction between southern Huila and Belén de los Andaquíes (Arcila Niño et al.
2000, 34).

3. In 1951 the population in Belén de los Andaquíes was 6,512 (Arcila Niño et
al. 2000, 48).

4. The colonization of the Caquetá coordinated from the central government
began in 1958. In the areas of Maguaré (forest), La Mono (east of Belén), and Val-
paraíso (on the Pescado River), 698,000 hectares were assigned to the Caja Agraria
by the Ministry of Agriculture for distribution among homestead families coming
from other regions (Jaramillo, Mora, and Cubides 1986, 15). In 1961 INCORA was
created with the charge of coordinating government sponsored colonization processes on the agricultural frontiers of the eastern savannas (Los Llanos) and the
southern region of Caquetá (García Montes and Santanilla 1994, 110).

5. According to Jaramillo and his colleagues, twenty thousand families came
and only 15 percent were embraced by this government initiative (Jaramillo, Mora,
and Cubides 1986, 17).

6. *Panela* is sugarcane syrup solidified into brick-size blocks. Colombians eat
panela as a source of carbohydrates.

7. *Colono* is the Colombian word for homesteader.

8. In 1993, 35 percent of people living in Caquetá came from other regions,
primarily Huila (33 percent), Tolima (19 percent), and Valle (10 percent) (SINCHI
2000, 25). According to a study carried out by the German geographer Wolfgang
Brücher in 1974, 48 percent of people from Belén de los Andaquíes originally came
from Huila (cited in Jaramillo, Mora, and Cubides 1986, 14).

9. Typical participants include Tolima Grande (Huila and Tolima), paisa (Antioquia, Caldas, Risaralda, and Quindío), cundiboyacense (Cundinamarca and Boyacá), costeña (Costa Atlantica), and Valle del Cauca region (Valle, Cauca, and Nariño) (García Montes and Santanilla 1994, 113).

10. For example, during the state-led colonization initiative known as Caquetá I, one of the conditions to obtain government loans was to have at least twelve acres of pasture (Arcila Niño et al. 2000, 135).

11. In 1997 Nestlé was buying 42.8 percent of all the milk produced in Caquetá (Arcila Niño et al. 2000, 130).

12. According to Arcila Niño and his colleagues, the land in Caquetá can only sustain 0.98 cows per hectare per year (in Belén it is 0.90); also, while the average for milk production in Latin America is 1,177 kilograms per cow per year, the average in Caquetá does not even reach the national average of 1,000 kilos per cow per year (Arcila Niño et al. 2000, 127).

13. *Rancheras* is a Mexican musical genre; in Colombia, this genre is associated with cattle ranching, cowboys, etc.

14. ANUC was created and promoted by the state under the administration of President Carlos Lleras Restrepo (1966–70), as part of his agenda to support poor agricultural families (Zamosc 1997, 106).

15. For example, Marco Antonio Chalitas was a well-known M-19 *comandante* from Belén de los Andaquíes.

16. According to an interview conducted by García Montes and Santanilla with a retired army official and member of the army's psychological team, thirty-four army officials received three years of training by military personnel from the United States who, based on their own experiences in Vietnam, insisted that the war for the hearts and minds had to be waged parallel to the war of weapons (García Montes and Santanilla 1994, 153).

17. For example, only one kilo of salt and one pound of rice per family were allowed.

18. In 1998 FARC charged buyers COP$20,000/kilo (US$ 8.50) for each kilo of coca paste and sellers COP$50,000 (US$ 20.80) (Ramírez 2001, 86). FARC also charged 1 million pesos (US$416.60) for the right to set up a cocaine lab (Ramírez 2001, 87). The group also charged between ten and twenty dollars per hectare of coca every forty-five to sixty days (equivalent to a coca crop cycle). FARC forbade paying laborers in coca paste (*bazuco* or crack) in an attempt to decrease local coca paste addiction (Ramírez 2001, 74).

19. Croydon is a popular Colombian shoe brand-name.

20. Twelve kilos of coca leaf produce between eighteen and twenty grams of coca paste (Arcila Niño et al. 2000, 150).

21. Jaramillo, Mora, and Cubides mention how, during a coca boom, the population of prostitutes reached four hundred in a town that had no more than five hundred homes (Jaramillo, Mora, and Cubides 1986, 63). Although this is not the case of Belén de los Andaquíes, several authors describe how in some areas, the coca rush brought hordes of eccentric characters to settlements way beyond the

agricultural frontier, from urban college students to mid-level mafiosi. They came to coca regions, "giving origin to towns and settlements that, like ghosts, appeared and disappeared with every coca boom and twist" (Arcila Niño et al. 2000, 159). Molano describes how his imagined vision of a forest trail, where the deep silence is only interrupted by sounds of water running down the creeks and birds chirping, was shattered during his travels to Calamar (a town undergoing a coca boom in the 1980s), where the rain forest trail more closely resembled a Persian market (Molano 1987, 89–90).

22. Casas de la Cultura are municipal government institutions responsible for developing initiatives to cultivate culture at the local level, such as orchestras and bands, theater, dance, concerts, festivals, etc.

23. Radio Andaquí is administered by a local nonprofit organization called Comunarte, which is responsible for submitting proposals and administering the funds secured.

24. EAIBA's new headquarters were built with funds from Tomando Conciencia, a Catalonian nonprofit organization that supports communication projects in the Global South.

25. *Villancios* are traditional Colombian Christmas carols.

26. Since the early 1990s Colombia has received significant military aid to fight "the war on drugs." In 1998 this aid package solidified in what is known as Plan Colombia, making this country the recipient of the second-most military aid from the United States, after Israel. On June 29, 2000, the United States Senate approved US$1.3 billion in aid for Colombia's war on drugs. This aid package included eighteen Blackhawk and forty-two Huey II helicopters to transport army personnel to Putumayo and Caquetá, which were designated as the first two departments where the war against illicit crops and insurgency would be waged during the first two years (Ramírez 2001, 292). On May 16, 2001, George W. Bush presented the Andean Regional Initiative, an 880-million-dollar aid package intended to reduce coca production in Andean countries by 40 percent before 2007 and to reduce Colombian coca production by 30 percent before 2002 (Ramírez 2001, 329). The United Nations Office of Drugs and Crime reported that Colombia had 443,500 acres of coca in 2006, 32,000 acres more than the same office reported in 2005 (United Nations Office of Drugs and Crime 2007). While 86 percent of antidrug aid coming from the United States to Peru is for alternative development projects (Ramírez 2001, 62), in 2000 less than 10 percent of the aid for Colombia had this type of use (U.S. Department of State 2000) and 14.5 percent in 2010 (U.S. Department of State Bureau of International Narcotics and Law Enforcement Affairs 2011).

27. Civic strike is a form of protest widely used by social movements in Colombia. During a civic strike, all social movements and progressive grassroots organizations hold a coordinated protest that paralyzes the locality for a few days. Teachers' associations, unions, peasant organizations, women's organizations, and others join forces, stop traffic and take over the streets with massive demonstrations, disabling normal operations in the area.

28. Contrary to the popular myth that perceives Caquetá as *tierra de nadie* (no man's land), Jaramillo et al. find a strong network of civic and grassroots organizations that perform many of the functions generally carried out by the state (Jaramillo, Mora, and Cubides 1986). As early as the 1960s, homesteading families had already formed JACs as elected bodies in charge of regulating land claims, carrying out police functions, seeking funds from state agencies, and planning and implementing community development initiatives. JACs operate by *vereda,* the smallest unit used to organize rural areas in the country. In part JACs are public institutions since they are backed by the central state, but in reality they operate more as self-organized grassroots entities. Although JACs are found throughout the national territory, they have developed differently region by region, and thus have to be described and understood in each of their local incarnations. In Caquetá, JACs have definitely been a strong regional protagonist since the 1960s. In 1993, 1,427 JACs with 44,476 members operated in Caquetá (SINCHI 2000, 19). All political actors in the region including the central government, the Colombian army, the guerrillas, and even the coca entrepreneurs have had to learn to negotiate with JACs. Nothing happens in Caquetá without negotiation with local JACs. Jaramillo and his colleagues explain how JACs regulated colonization and land appropriation processes, negotiated boundaries with FARC, and welcomed coca growing as a survival strategy. These same authors also observed how, a few years later, as JAC leaders began seeing the negative consequences coca had brought to the region, they began an organic process of turning away from coca and toward other economic development options (Jaramillo, Mora, and Cubides 1986, 255–67). The reason Caquetá and other regions are perceived as "barbarian" regions where the rule of law has no role and where civil society has been high jacked by armed groups is that JACs and other civil society organizations and social movements are invisible to the rest of the country. Also, political actors that do not fall in alignment with political elites and traditional parties become targets of state persecution. Thus, JACs, organic labor organizations, and neighborhood associations have had to maintain low profiles.

29. Later, the Samper administration was found to have accepted funds from drug cartels to finance the presidential campaign. The U.S. government canceled Samper's visa, his main financial advisor was jailed, and in a shady process known as Proceso 8000, Samper was indicted by the Colombian national Congress.

30. Cement was demonized as one of the substances needed to process coca leaves into coca paste. The Consejo Nacional de Estupefacientes resolution 0001 of 1996 tightened the control of all substances needed for coca processing (Ramírez 2001, 134).

31. Established by Decreto 0871 of the army (Ramírez 2001, 135).

32. *Narcoguerrilla* is a term coined in Colombia and used by various military, government, and media spokespersons to refer to a so-called merger of guerrilla and drug trafficking organizations. In truth, the term *narcoguerrillas* is nothing but a shortcut that obscures complex relationships between these two very different types of organizations.

33. On August 2, 1996, *La Nación,* a national newspaper, reported ten thousand peasants marching into Santuario, Caquetá (*La Nación,* August 2, 1996, 10, cited in Ramírez 2001, 141).

34. In some areas FARC has become so overwhelmed trying to solve a myriad of daily conflicts that it has promoted the formation of "reconciliation committees for conflict resolution" in each county *(vereda).* These committees are instructed to try to solve local conflicts on their own. There is a clear message that citizens are *not* to seek out FARC help until everything else has been exhausted (Ramírez 2001, 159).

35. For example in one *vereda* twelve people stayed behind. Everyone else stored valuables in the school and left. The twelve who stayed were responsible for guarding valuables, watching over crops and animals, and sending food to the demonstrators representing their *vereda.* They had all their meals together (Ramírez 2001, 162–63).

36. Gradual eradication means that agricultural families progressively decrease plots of illegal crops while increasing legal ones. Some crops take longer to yield a profit. Rubber trees require seven years to see returns, while others such as corn produce a profit in only eight months.

37. Common graffiti and slogans during the *cocalero* demonstrations stated, "We, too, are Colombian!"; "We are sons and daughters of Colombia!"; and "We, too, have a Colombian *cédula de ciudadanía* [Colombian citizenship identity card]" (Ramírez 2001).

2. Nation Building, One Voice at a Time

1. Montes de María includes seventeen municipalities spread over 2,677 square kilometers over the departments of Sucre and Bolívar in the northern region of the Colombian Caribbean. Approximately four hundred thousand people inhabit the region (PNUD, Corporación Territorios, and Universidad de Cartagena 2004). The municipalities of Montes de María include Carmen de Bolívar, Marialabaja, San Juan Nepomuceno, San Jacinto, Córdoba, El Guamo, and Zambrano in the department of Bolívar, and Ovejas, Chalán, Colosó, Morroa, Los Palmitos, San Onofre, San Antonio de Palmito, and Tolúviejo in Sucre (for more information and maps see http://www.fmontesdemaria.org/nregion.asp).

2. The National Peace Award is granted to the Colombian initiative that, according to a jury, has the most significant accomplishment in terms of peacebuilding in the country that year. On December 10, 2003, the National Peace Award was given to the Communications Collective of Montes de María for "its contribution to reconciliation and peaceful coexistence through a communication project that strengthens the social fabric of the region" (FESCOL 2003). The National Peace Award is sponsored by the German foundation Friedrich Ebert and several national media groups (Caracol Radio, Caracol Televisión, Semana, El Tiempo, El Colombiano, and El Espectador).

3. The militarization of areas such as Montes de María is financed by Plan Colombia (more recently known as the Andean Initiative. See chapter 1 for more detailed information on Plan Colombia).

4. By the end of the nineteenth century, tobacco had become the main product in Montes de María. Toward the end of the century, "Adolf Held and other German immigrants, who had settled in El Carmen, initiated a direct export industry of tobacco to Germany. Held himself became a cattle rancher and established one of the most modern haciendas of the region" (Escobar 1998, 19). In 1848 a tobacco-processing plant was established in Montes de María (Escobar 1998, 19).

5. Peasant mobilizations were particularly intense (in number and strength) in 1970 and 1983 (Escobar 1998; Zamosc 1986).

6. In fact, according to Cristina Escobar, for most of the nineteenth and twentieth centuries the region shared a nonviolent ethos: "It is very important to emphasize that in comparison to other regions, the people of the coast were much more reluctant to participate in confrontations. The weak presence of the state and the Catholic church, the heterogeneity of the population and the relaxed character of the social relations in the area, are all mentioned as elements contributing to the people's non-violent ethos" (Escobar 1998, 49).

7. Violent actions include: armed combat, sabotage, armed attacks, armed checkpoints, attacks to infrastructures, armed attacks on villages or towns, ambushes, armed attacks on state institutions (banks, police stations, etc.), armed attacks on private property.

8. As a result of armed conflict there are more than 2 million internally displaced persons (IDPs) throughout the national Colombian territory. Because IDPs do not cross international borders, they are not entitled to the rights of war refugees; thus, they have no formal system of legal rights and no international agency responsible for delivering aid or solutions.

9. When the people of El Salado arrived to El Carmen de Bolívar in a state of shock and terror, the children and teens of the Collective decided to postpone all their planned programming and to focus on helping the displaced community. Joining forces with local radio stations, an extensive live fund-raising broadcasting was organized in a matter of hours.

10. The capital for the satellite dish came from an alliance with a local tobacco grower (Colectivo de Comunicaciones 2000, 2).

11. Along with the income from cable subscriptions, the Collective obtains funding from national and international donors such as the Programa de las Naciones Unidas para el Desarrollo (PNUD) [United Nations Development Program], Alto Comisionado para la Paz, Ministerio de Cultura, Red de Solidaridad, Fondo Mixto, Fondo de Educación de Alto Riesgo en Bolívar, Entidades de prevención de uso de estupefacientes, Observatorio del Caribe, Red de Gestores Sociales, Presidencia, GTZ, and Fondo de Cultura de Bolívar.

12. In the Colombian context the term *"cultura ciudadana"* (a culture of citizenship) is used frequently. Although the country has been a democracy since the nineteenth century, in everyday life, democratic practice is rare. Instead, rights and responsibilities are regulated via patron–client relationships, bribes, connections, influence, or by violent means. A culture of citizenship refers to a social fabric in which individuals respect the rule of law and the state guarantees civil rights; also, state actions are driven by community (and not individual) needs and interests.

13. In Spanish *"cinta"* refers to ribbon but also to the type of film used in cinema.

14. During the U.S. invasion of Iraq, Mohammed Khodier, a well-known Iraqi novelist, used a similar image of a turtle to describe his people's ability to survive the war (Dagher 2007).

15. The Plataforma Colombiana de Derechos Humanos, Democracia y Desarrollo, author of the report, is an umbrella organization of 121 grassroots organizations and social movements that includes some of the largest and most legitimate indigenous, labor, women's, teachers, and peasant organizations in the country (see list of members at http://www.plataforma-colombiana.org/integrantes.htm).

16. The concept of *cultura ciudadana* (culture of citizenship) will be thoroughly analyzed in chapters 3 and 4.

17. According to Rubio (cited in García and Uprimny 1999, 40) out of one hundred crimes committed in Colombia, only thirty-one are denounced, ten are investigated, three reach a court, and only one of two cases reach sentences.

18. I have to thank my friend and colleague Jair Vega for articulating the sound bite that describes well what citizens' media are accomplishing in terms of peacebuilding in Colombia: moving conflict from violence to discourse.

19. Benkos is the legendary African slave who led the seventeenth-century flight.

20. Montes de María is home to several different cultural groups: Afro-Colombian cultures in Palenque and Marialabaja; indigenous communities in San Jacinto, El Carmen de Bolívar, and San Juan Nepomuceno; and communities of riverine culture in Zambrano (Magdalena River) and San Estanislao (Canal del Dique).

21. Armed conflict in the region of Montes de María is the cause of the exodus of approximately 37,238 people who fled to nearby Cartagena, 32,544 people to Barranquilla, 6,339 to Marialabaja, and 26,973 to El Carmen de Bolívar (Sarmiento 2005). Between 2003 and 2007, the number of displaced people in Montes de María was 49,937 (Programa de Desarrollo y Paz de Montes de María 2009, 4). In 2002 El Carmen de Bolívar was the Colombian municipality with the highest number of displaced people in the country (PNUD 2004).

22. *Bullerengue* is a local traditional Afro-Colombian dance.

23. Grants came from Acción Social and the Fundación Red Desarrollo y Paz de los Montes de María.

24. *Coche-taxi* is a cycle rickshaw used in northern Colombia; these vehicles, operated by young men, take passengers around town for a fee.

25. *Gaita* is a folk pipe always present in local music in Montes de María. Pipes come in female and male versions.

3. Radio, Resistance, and War

1. Between 1997 and 2002 the homicide rate in Magdalena Medio was 200 per 100,000 people, while the homicide rate in Colombia as a whole (one of the highest in the world) was 66 per 100,000 and in the United States was 5.7 per 100,000.

2. Colombian historians and policy makers in Bogotá are especially responsible for this conception of the river.

3. "Magdalena Medio produces 75 percent of all Colombia's oil, which is significant since the nation is the fifth largest producer in South America" (Rodríguez and Cadavid 2007, 315).

4. In June 2003 ECOPETROL S.A. became a public stock-holding corporation, organized as an Anonymous Society under the Ministry of Mines and Energy.

5. In 2009 Colombia had the fifth largest reserve of crude oil in South America (Energy Information Administration 2009).

6. Only 40 percent of school-aged children and youth have access to education (CINEP 2001, 62).

7. In 1870 Bucaramanga's economic elite (to the east of Magdalena Medio) decided to build a railway as a gateway for goods to travel to the Magdalena River. The railroad was finalized in 1940 connecting Bucaramanga to Puerto Wilches, one of the main ports in Magdalena Medio (Cadavid 1996, 20; Murillo 1994, 100). In 1874 the elite in the coffee region to the west of Magdalena Medio decided to build a railway to facilitate the transport of coffee to national and international markets (Cadavid 1996, 19). The railroad, completed in 1929 (Murillo 1994, 145), linked Medellín with Puerto Berrío.

8. Socialist ideas have circulated in Magdalena Medio since the 1920s. In 1929 a group of socialists led what is known as the "the Bolshevik insurrection" in San Vicente de Chucurí, in which townspeople confronted local authorities and the police (Murillo 1999, 52). In 1948, during the aftermath of popular leader Jorge Eliécer Gaitán's assassination, Magdalena Medio's Liberal Party leaders instigated what has become known as the Ten Days of Popular Power—a nonviolent takeover of local municipal governments. For ten days Liberals set up autonomous governments in several Magdalena Medio municipalities, and negotiations with the Conservative central government in Bogotá brought this revolutionary local government to an end (Madariaga 2006, 49). However, the central government never delivered on its part of the agreement. In response, Liberal leaders formed La Colorada, one of the first Liberal armed guerrilla organizations, led by Rafael Rangel (Cubides, Olaya, and Ortiz 1998, 80; Murillo 1999, 54).

9. Since 1972 the Asociación Nacional de Usuarios Campesinos (ANUC) [National Association of Peasants] has supported organizations of peasants and small farmers in their struggles to acquire land, legalize land titles, gain government support for the marketing of agricultural products, take over unused land holdings of large hacienda owners, and end the militarization of the region (Murillo 1999, 57).

10. "Here, acting within the law, the army subsidized, promoted, and encouraged the creation and presence of self-defense groups, which later, with the arrival of drug traffickers, became the ill-named paramilitary groups" (Murillo et al. 1994, 166), testimony by General Herrera Luna, commander of the XIV Army Brigade about his brigade's role in Puerto Berrío in 1983.

11. One of the main targets of the paramilitaries has been the Organización Femenina Popular [Popular Feminine Organization], the primary women's organization

in Magdalena Medio (Martha Cecilia García 2006, 299). The Autodefensas Unidas de Colombia, one of the largest paramilitary groups, publicly rejected what they call "the politization of women in Magdalena Medio" because "woman should remain distant from the public world, the world of politics, she needs to return to the home, where she can realize her traditional roles as mother, wife, as the one who cares for others and as the one in charge of raising the children" (Martha Cecilia García 2006, 298).

12. Paramilitary organizations frequently target local government officials. After murdering, threatening, and/or forcing local mayors and other key government officials into exile, paramilitary groups replace elected officials with their own candidates, thus taking control over development programs, contracts, and municipal budgets (generally taking an annual percentage for their own uses) (CREDHOS 2002, 12; OPPDHDIH 2002, 93).

13. *Vallenato* is a Colombian Caribbean musical genre, known as one of the paramilitaries' favorites.

14. This is a staggering rate given that the homicide rate per 100,000 in Colombia was 80 in 1990, four times as high as in the rest of Latin America (Romero 2003, 27).

15. Funded by the European Union, PEACE I and PEACE II are similar multiproject peace programs implemented in Northern Ireland between 1995 and 2004. Approximately 17,600 projects were implemented through PEACE I and PEACE II (Hamber and Gráinne 2005).

16. In the municipalities of San Vicente de Chucurí, Sabana de Torres, Betulia, Puerto Nare, and Puerto Wilches (Durán, Quijano, and Gómez Ditta in press).

17. The stations are San Martín de Tours in San Martín and Campo Serrano Radio in Aguachica (in Cesar Department); Simití Original Estéreo in Simití, Santa Rosa Estéreo in Santa Rosa del Sur, San Sebastián Estéreo in Morales, Ecos de Tiquisio in Tiquisio, La Negrita de Arenal in Arenal, and Cantagallo Estéreo in Cantagallo (in Bolívar Department); San Vicente Estéreo in San Vicente de Chucurí, Betuliana Estéreo in Betulia, Puerto Wilches Estéro in Puerto Wilches, La Voz de la Inmaculada in Rionegro, Bolivariana Estéreo in Bolívar, La Voz de Landázuri in Landázuri, and La Voz del Carare in Puerto Parra (in Santander Department).

18. The school radio stations are in Gamarra, Aguachica, Barrancabermeja, Puerto Wilches, and San Vicente de Chucurí. For radio production collectives, in some cases they consist of a group of people with a radio production studio but no radio station. In general, these collectives ultimately aspire to receive a community broadcasting license from the Ministry of Communications and have their own radio station.

19. See Bloh and Rolt 2007 for similar initiatives in Liberia, where community media are used to improve communication between government and citizens as part of the postconflict reconstruction effort.

20. Some of the interviews are part of an evaluation study conducted by Jair Vega, Amparo Cadavid, AREDMAG, and I about the radio stations' accomplishments in

the region. Respondents were asked to illustrate their response visually and then to narrate what they had drawn.

21. At the time of my fieldwork in Magdalena Medio, Julio Hoyos was president of AREDMAG's board of directors.

22. The model of the PDPMM has been adapted to other conflict-ridden regions in Colombia. In 2005 seventeen Development and Peace Projects (PDPs) covered approximately 50 percent of the national territory and the worst conflict-ridden regions. All PDPs work in coordination under a coordinating body called REDPRODEPAZ.

4. Media Pioneers Respond to Armed Conflict

1. I use the term "community media" to refer to media that have been granted a community broadcasting license by the Ministry of Communications. I reserve the term "citizens' media" to refer to community media that actually use media technologies to trigger social and cultural processes of social change at the local level (see the introduction for a thorough discussion of these terms).

2. At the time of writing 651 community radio stations were operating on a regular basis. Fifty-two community radio stations had been approved by the Ministry but were not operating yet. Also, four of the five capital cities requesting community broadcasting licenses are being considered (Tunja, Quibdó, Riohacha, and Mitú; Puerto Carreño was not approved). The twenty-six indigenous radio station licenses cover 82 percent of all Colombian indigenous territories (http://www.mincomunicaciones.gov.co/mincom/src/user_docs/Noticias/DocPolitica RadioPluralismo.pdf, p. 12). See Rodríguez and El Gazi 2007 for more on indigenous radio in Colombia. For information on the community television licenses, see http://www.mincomunicaciones.gov.co/mincom/src/user_docs/Noticias/Doc PoliticaRadioPluralismo.pdf. See entire list of community televisions at http://www.cntv.org.co/cntv%5Fbop/servicio_cober/tarifas/2_trimestre_08.pdf.

3. Bush Radio in South Africa, La Tribu in Argentina, Radio Bemba in Mexico, TV-Viva in Brazil, Radio Latacunga in Ecuador, Calandria in Peru, Inuit media in Canada, Aboriginal media in Australia, Mapuche media in Chile (Bosch 2010; Ginsburg 2002; Molner and Meadows 2001; Morris and Meadows 2001; Roth 2005; Salazar 2002, 2003, 2007) are some other internationally renowned examples. For a more complete picture of international citizens' media see Rodríguez, Kidd, and Stein 2010.

4. See Ministerio de Comunicaciones 2007, 62–72, for the full text of the community broadcasting legislation.

5. See Radio Netherlands 2008 for numerous African community radio stations that failed as soon as international donors terminated funding, and Von Kalternborg-Stachau 2008, 24, for failed cases in Timor Leste.

6. Decades of struggle by social movements led to constitutional reform in the late 1980s. The new constitution, in place since 1991, includes Article 20, which states: "The state guarantees that every person has the freedom to express and

disseminate his/her thoughts and opinions, to inform and to receive accurate and impartial information, and to found his/her own mass media" (see entire constitution at http://www.cna.gov.co/cont/documentos/legislacion/constitucion.pdf). In 1995 the administration of President Ernesto Samper approved Decree 1447, which gave a green light to the approval of community broadcasting licenses. In 1999 the administration of Andrés Pastrana approved Acuerdo 006, which regulates community television broadcasting and made the first community television licenses a reality.

7. The law states that community television stations have to produce fourteen hours per week of original local programs (see "Estación Local sin Animo de Lucro," at Comisión Nacional de Televisión (CNTV) Web site, http://www.cntv.org .co/cntv%5Fbop/servicio_cober/modalidades/index.html).

8. See Rodríguez and El Gazi 2007 and Unidad de Radio 2000 for more on this subject.

9. Radios Ciudadanas was an ambitious and expensive project. El Gazi and Duplat sought and secured most of the project's funding from national and international agencies, including PNUD, USAID, Organización Internacional de Migraciones, Agencia Rural para el Desarrollo, and Parques Nacionales. More than 90 percent of the project's total cost of 2 billion pesos (about 2 million dollars) was funded by these agencies.

10. This last one was supported by the Fundación Nuevo Periodismo Iberoamericano, the journalism foundation established by Gabriel García Márquez to encourage excellence in Latin American journalism (see http://www.fnpi.org).

11. Soraya Bayuelo is founder and executive director of a television, video, and radio production collective (see chapter 2); Alirio González is founder of a community radio station and a children audiovisual school (see chapter 1).

12. Although El Gazi's Radio Unit focuses on radio, she generally invited pioneers from other types of citizens' media initiatives, such as television, video, and print media, to the unit's roundtables and workshops.

13. *Me está pisando los callos* is an expression that means "rubbing me the wrong way."

14. See Ministerio de Comunicaciones 2007, 16–24.

15. In 2005, fifty-two communities had become "territories of peace," with mixed results. San José de Apartadó and Carare are famous examples; although these communities have been awarded national and international peace awards, they have also been victimized by armed groups (see Amnesty International 2008, 60–64).

16. *Paro armado* is a type of demonstration in which guerrilla organizations order people to stay home, thus stopping all activities and bringing paralysis to local economies.

17. *Paros* typically last only a couple of days.

18. Forbidden *corridos* are songs that glorify the lives and deeds of drug traffickers, guerrillas, and paramilitary warriors; a more thorough explanation appears below.

19. *Los armados* is a term frequently used in Colombia to refer to *all* armed groups, including guerrillas, paramilitaries, drug traffickers, emerald (and other) mafias, and the Colombian armed forces and police.

20. *Vallenato* is a Colombian musical genre from the northern Caribbean. Although traditional *vallenatos* narrate all types of stories, modern, commercial *vallenatos* tend to be strongly misogynist and conservative.

21. Reference to one of the Ministry of Culture's radio series *De Qué Hablamos Cuando Hablamos de Violencia* (What We Talk about When We Are Talking about Violence), which focused on *corridos prohibidos* in one of its programs.

22. Known as *pesca milagrosa* (miraculous fishing), guerrilla organizations establish checkpoints on major highways, detaining hundreds of cars and trucks. Using laptops, guerrillas check drivers' and passengers' identity documents against information databases. Those unfortunate enough to show as property owners, members of high tax brackets, or other evidence of wealth are then kidnapped for ransom.

23. Sistema de Información para la Paz (SIPAZ) [Information for Peace System] is an online network of community media that jointly produce information programs about peace actions, projects, and events (see http://www.sipaz.net).

24. In no way can I claim credit for the generalized use of "citizenship" or "citizens' media" among Colombian community media leaders. That I use the same terminology in my book *Fissures in the Mediascape* (Rodríguez 2001), published exclusively in English in 2001, is merely a happy coincidence.

25. In exceptional and heroic cases, Colombian citizens' media have helped communities resist armed groups (see chapters 1 and 3 for a couple of cases).

26. *Empanada* is a Colombian turnover made of corn.

27. For similar peacebuilding initiatives that use youth media see Stubbs 1997.

28. SFGC produces other youth radio programs in contexts of armed conflict, such as *Sisi Watoto* [We, the Children] in Democratic Republic of Congo (see Shipler 2006).

29. *En el Cuarto con Dios* uses the Spanish pun where *cuarto* means both room and a quarter of an hour.

30. *Conuco* is an indigenous family dwelling. Pérez mentions it because Guainía is a department with only one municipality; the rest of the department is made of indigenous *resguardos,* thus Custodia Estéreo has a large indigenous audience.

31. See El Callejón con Salida for a database of peacebuilding initiatives compiled by the UNDP–Colombia at http://www.saliendodelcallejon.pnud.org.co/index.shtml.

32. Interestingly, at the time of writing, indigenous movements have complained that President Uribe and his ministers label indigenous rights as an abused privilege: "He insists on presenting these rights as undeserved or abused privileges, with the objective of generating resentment against us [indigenous communities], and promoting conflict with other social sectors. We are calling attention to these attitudes and policies, which continue to generate discrimination and promote prejudice" (Plataforma Colombiana de Derechos Humanos 2008).

33. Community mothers (*madres comunitarias*) are women who organize cooperative-like day care centers in low-income neighborhoods.

5. The Doing Is Everything!

1. For the reader unfamiliar with communication for social change, edutainment, or entertainment-education, is a communication for social change approach based on using entertainment media programming to persuade target audiences to adopt proposed social behaviors or attitudes (see Rodríguez 2005a; Singhal and Rogers 2003).

2. Susana Kaiser's work on memory and violence in Argentina shows how war memories remain alive for a long time—and even transfer to new generations that did not have a direct experience with the violence (Kaiser 2005).

3. For a new methodological proposal to evaluate citizens' media see Rodríguez 2010.

4. During the 1990s one of the towns became known as a "friend of the guerrillas," while its neighbor town became known as a "friend of the paramilitaries." Violence escalated between the two towns, to the point that people from one town could not set foot in the other town (see chapter 2 for more detail).

5. *Arepas* are traditional Colombian cornmeal cakes cooked for breakfast.

BIBLIOGRAPHY

Acevedo, Darío. 1995. *La Mentalidad de las Élites Sobre la Violencia en Colombia, 1936–1949*. Bogotá: IEPRI and El Áncora Editores.

Acosta, Diana Marcela. 2007. *Cómo Habla Ralph*. Video. Belén de los Andaquíes: Escuela Audiovisual Infantil de Belén de los Andaquíes.

Afflitto, Frank M. 2000. "The Homogenizing Effects of State-Sponsored Terrorism." In *Death Squad: The Anthropology of State Terror*, ed. Jeffrey A. Sluka, 114–26. Philadelphia: University of Pennsylvania Press.

Allen, Tim, and Jean Seaton. 1999. *The Media of Conflict: War Reporting and Representations of Ethnic Violence*. London: Zed Books.

Amnesty International. 1997. *Colombia: Hacienda Bellacruz: Land, Power and Paramilitary Power*. Report 23/006/1997; identifier 305598883. Available at http://repository.forcedmigration.org/show_metadata.jsp?pid=fmo:3922.

———. 2008. *'Leave Us in Peace'. Targeting Civilians in Colombia's Internal Armed Conflict*. Report 23/002/2009. Available at http://www.amnesty.org/en/library/asset/AMR23/023/2008/en/65b11bee-a04b-11dd-81c4-792550e655ec/amr230232008eng.pdf.

Angulo Novoa, Alejandro, and Jairo Arboleda. 2003. "La Dimensión de Fe en el Programa de Desarrollo y Paz del Magdalena Medio." *Controversia* 181:127–39.

Appadurai, Arjun. 1996. *Modernity at Large*. Minneapolis: University of Minnesota Press.

———. 2006. *Fear of Small Numbers: An Essay on the Geography of Anger*. Durham: Duke University Press.

Arango Rendón, German, Camilo Pérez Quintero, Mónica Pérez Marín, and Jair Vega Casanova. 2008. "Pasolini en Medellín: Apuntes para una Etnografía Visual sobre la Periferia, Cuatro Años de Experiencia con Jóvenes Realizadores." Paper presented at the OURMedia VII Conference: Identity, Inclusion, and Innovation in a Globalized World, Accra, Ghana, August 11–15.

Archila, Mauricio. 2006. "Las Identidades en el Magdalena Medio." In *Conflictos, Poderes e Identidades en el Magdalena Medio 1990–2001*, ed. Mauricio Archila and Ingrid Bolívar, 467–508. Bogotá: CINEP.

Archila, Mauricio, and Ingrid Bolívar, eds. 2006. *Conflictos, Poderes e Identidades en el Magdalena Medio 1990–2001.* Bogotá: CINEP.

Arcila Niño, Oscar, Gloria González, Franz Gutiérrez, Adriana Rodríguez, and Carlos Ariel Salazar. 2000. *Caquetá: Construcción de un Territorio Amazónico en el Siglo XX.* Bogotá: Instituto Amazónico de Investigaciones Científicas, SINCHI.

AREDMAG. 2004a. *La Ermita de la Virgen de la Original.* Radio program. Barrancabermeja, Colombia.

———. 2004b. *Las Estaciones del Ferrocarril.* Radio program. Barrancabermeja, Colombia.

———. 2004c. *Los Primeros Pobladores.* Radio program. Barrancabermeja, Colombia.

———. 2004d. *Noti Rio.* Radio program. Barrancabermeja, Colombia.

———. 2008. "Aredmag Rechaza Amenazas en Contra del PDPMM y los Pobladores." Press release. April 16.

AREDMAG Radio Producers. 2004. Interview by author at Memory Workshop. Tape recording. Bucaramanga, Colombia. August 15–18.

Arenas Obregón, Martha. 1998. *Historias del Magdalena Medio.* Bogotá: PDPMM.

Arendt, Hannah. 1966. *The Origins of Totalitarianism.* New York: Harcourt, Brace and World.

Aretxaga, Begoña. 2000. "A Fictional Reality: Paramilitary Death Squads and the Construction of State Terror in Spain." In *Death Squad: The Anthropology of State Terror,* ed. Jeffrey A. Sluka, 46–69. Philadelphia: University of Pennsylvania Press.

Arrieta, Omaria. 2004. Interview by author. Tape recording. Bucaramanga, Colombia. October 2.

Atton, Chris. 2002. *Alternative Media.* London: Sage.

Austin, J. L. 1975. *How to Do Things with Words.* Cambridge, Mass.: Harvard University Press.

Balabanova, Ekaterina. 2007. *Media, Wars and Politics: Comparing the Incomparable in Western and Eastern Europe.* Aldershot: Ashgate.

Bayuelo, Soraya. 2000. "El Colectivo de Comunicaciones de los Montes de María." In *Mesa Regional Cauca, Nariño, Putumayo. Unidad de Radio. Ministerio de Cultura.* Audio recording. Pasto, Colombia. May 7.

———. 2004. Interview by author. Tape recording. Barranquilla, Colombia. August 11.

———. 2005. Interview by author. Tape recording. El Carmen de Bolívar, Colombia. December 8.

———. 2009. Interview by author. Tape recording. San Basilio de Palenque, Colombia. August 7.

Bell, Elizabeth. 2008. *Theories of Performance.* Thousand Oaks, Calif.: Sage.

Bennett, W. Lance, Regina G. Lawrence, and Steven Livingston. 2007. *When the Press Fails: Political Power and the News Media from Iraq to Katrina.* Chicago: University of Chicago Press.

Bloh, Oscar, and Francis Rolt. 2007. "Media Sector Mapping in Liberia." Unpublished paper. Washington, D.C.: Search for Common Ground/Talking Drum Studio Liberia.

Bolívar, Ingrid. 2006. "Transformaciones de la Política: Movilización Social, Atribución Causal y Configuración del Estado en el Magdalena Medio 1990–2001." In *Conflictos, Poderes e Identidades en el Magdalena Medio 1990–2001,* ed. Mauricio Archila and Ingrid Bolívar, 373–466. Bogotá: CINEP.

Bosch, Tana E. 2010. "Theorizing Citizens' Media: A Rhizomatic Approach." In *Making Our Media: Global Initiatives toward a Democratic Public Sphere.* Vol. 1: *Creating New Communication Spaces.* Ed. Clemencia Rodríguez, Dorothy Kidd, and Laura Stein, 71–87. Creskill, N.J.: Hampton Press.

Bouchard, Gérard. 2005. *L'Analyse Pragmatique des Figures et Mythes des Amériques: Proposition d'une demarche.* Available at http://www.uqac.ca/~bouchard/chaire_doc_e.html.

Brand-Jabobsen, Kai F. 2002. "Peace: The Goal and the Way." In *Searching for Peace: The Road to TRANSCEND,* ed. Johan Galtung, Carl G. Jacobsen, and Kai F. Brand-Jacobsen, 16–24. London: Pluto Press and TRANSCEND.

Brodzinsky, Sibylla. 2007. "Terrorism and Bananas in Colombia." *Time,* May 7.

Cadavid, Amparo. 1996. "El Magdalena Medio: Una Región que se Construye por el Río." Unpublished Report. Bogotá: Programa de Desarrollo y Paz del Magdalena Medio–Unidad de Región, Sujetos y Redes Sociales.

———. 2000. "How Do We Remain Alive, Participative and Happy in the Midst of a War?" Paper presented at 5th annual Grassroots Radio Conference. Madison, Wisconsin, July 21.

———. 2005. "Cómo Entregarle las Llaves al Ladrón." Unpublished report. Colectivo de Comunicaciones de los Montes de María Linea 21. Estudio de Caso. Bogotá: Banco Interamericano de Desarrollo.

Calderón, Marta. 2005. Interview by author. Tape recording. Belén de los Andaquíes, Colombia. August 7.

Castellanos, Camilo. 2001. "Comunidad y Resistencia." In *Éxodo, Patrimonio e Identidad, V Cátedra Anual de Historia, 2001,* ed. Ministerio de Cultura–Museo Nacional de Colombia, 255–61. Bogotá: Museo Nacional de Colombia y Ministerio de Cultura.

Castro, Jesús E. 2005. Interview by author. Tape recording. Belén de los Andaquíes, Colombia. August 8.

Centro de Estudios Regionales. 2008. Observatorio de Coyuntura Socioeconómica del Magdalena Medio. Barrancabermeja: Centro de Estudios Regionales.

Chalk, Frank. 1999. "Radio Broadcasting in the Incitement and Interdiction of Gross Violations of Human Rights Including Genocide." In *Genocide: Essays toward Understanding, Early-Warning, and Prevention,* ed. Roger W. Smith, 185–203. Williamsburg, Va.: Association of Genocide Scholars.

CINEP. 2001. *Informe Final de Sistematización: Hacia una Metodología para Construir Comunidad en Situaciones de Conflicto.* Bogotá: CINEP.

Colectivo de Comunicaciones de Montes de María Línea 21. 1999. "Productores de Sueños: Itinerario de una Televisión Local." Unpublished document. El Carmen de Bolívar: Colectivo de Comunicaciones de Montes de María Línea 21.

———. 2000. "Una Apuesta a la Vida desde la Comunicación Participativa." Unpublished document. El Carmen de Bolívar, Colombia.

———. 2003. "Colectivo de Comunicaciones Montes de María Línea 21." Premio Nacional de Paz. Unpublished document. El Carmen de Bolívar, Colombia.

———. 2004. *Voces de Colores.* Radio program. El Carmen de Bolívar, Colombia.

———. 2006a. *Ciclistas en el Atradecer.* Video. El Carmen de Bolívar, Colombia.

———. 2006b. *Cinta de Sueños: Un Sueño Hecho Realidad.* Video. El Carmen de Bolívar, Colombia.

Colectivo de Comunicación Popular. 1988. *El Sonido: Una Alternativa. Memorias del II Festival de Comunicación Popular Alternativo.* Bogotá: CINEP.

Collective Participant. 2004. Group interview with Colectivo de Comunicaciones de Montes de María Línea 21 participants by author. Tape recording. El Carmen de Bolívar. October 18.

Colson, Elizabeth. 1992. "Conflict and Violence." In *The Paths to Domination, Resistance, and Terror,* ed. Carolyn Nordstrom and Jo Martin, 277–83. Berkeley: University of California Press.

Comisión Nacional de Televisión. 2006. "Informe Sectorial de Televisión." Report. Bogotá. Available at http://www.cntv.org.co/cntv%5Fbop/estudios/in_sectorial.pdf.

Conquergood, Dwight. 1995. "Of Caravans and Carnivals: Performance Studies in Motion." *TDR: The Drama Review* 39 (4): 137–41.

———. 1998. "Beyond the Text: Toward a Performative Cultural Politics." In *Future of Performance Studies,* ed. Sheron Daily, 25–36. Annandale, Va.: National Communication Association.

CREDHOS. 2002. *Situación Regional de DH y DIH—Magdalena Medio, Colombia Diciembre 2001 a Junio 2002.* Bogotá: CREDHOS.

Cubides, Fernando, Ana Cecilia Olaya, and Carlos Manuel Ortiz. 1998. *La Violencia y el Municipio Colombiano 1980–1997.* Bogotá: Centro de Estudios Sociales and Universidad Nacional.

Cuéllar, Fabián, Juan Carlos Romero, Luis Alfredo Capera, and Yeison Capera. 2007. *Raspachines.* Video. Belén de los Andaquíes: Escuela Audiovisual Infantil de Belén de los Andaquíes.

Dagher, Sam. 2007. "Arbil Arts Festival: Iraq Is More than Blood." *Christian Science Monitor,* May 29, 4.

Das, Veena. 2000. *Violence and Subjectivity.* Berkeley: University of California Press.

———. 2001. *Remaking a World: Violence, Social Suffering, and Recovery.* Berkeley: University of California Press.

———. 2007. *Life and Words: Violence and the Descent into the Ordinary.* Berkeley: University of California Press.

Deas, Malcolm. 1995. "Canjes Violentos: Reflexiones sobre la Violencia Política en Colombia." In *Dos Ensayos sobre la Violencia Política en Colombia*, ed. Malcolm Deas and Fernando Gaitán, 2–88. Bogotá: Fonade–DNP.

Delgado, Alvaro. 2006. "El Conflicto Laboral en el Magdalena Medio." In *Conflictos, Poderes e Identidades en el Magdalena Medio 1990–2001*, ed. Mauricio Archila and Ingrid Bolívar, 85–164. Bogotá: CINEP.

Delgado, Sebastián. 2009. Interview by author. Tape recording. San Basilio de Palenque, Colombia. August 7.

Department for International Development. 2000. *Working with the Media in Conflicts and Other Emergencies*. London. Available at http://www.dfid.gov.uk/pubs/files/chad-media.pdf.

De Roux, Francisco. 1996. Documento Central de Diagnóstico, Conclusiones y Recomendaciones. Bogotá: PDPMM—Consorcio SEAP-CINEP. Unpublished Report.

———. 1999. "El Magdalena Medio en el Centro del Conflicto y la Esperanza." *Controversia* 174:14–37.

Desjarlais, Robert, and Arthur Kleinman. 1994. "Violence and Demoralization in the New World Disorder." *Anthropology Today* 10 (5): 9–12.

de Sousa Santos, Boaventura, and Mauricio García Villegas. 2004. *Emancipación Social y Violencia en Colombia*. Bogotá: Norma.

Downing, John, Tamara Villarreal Ford, Genève Gil, and Laura Stein. 2001. *Radical Media: Rebellious Communication and Social Movements*. Thousand Oaks, Calif.: Sage.

Duplat, Tatiana. 2003. "Paz en la Guerra: Experiencias Comunitarias por la Paz y Construcción de Democracia en Colombia; El Proceso de Reconciliación y Convivencia del Alto Ariari." PhD diss., Universidad de Granada, Granada, Spain.

———. 2004. Interview by author. Tape recording. Bogotá. September 20.

Durán, Orley. 2004. Interview by author. Tape recording. Bucaramanga, Colombia. October 16.

Durán, Orley, Melba Quijano, and Manfry Gómez Ditta. In press. "Cuando el Río Suena, AREDMAG Está al Aire." In *Evaluación Participativa de Medios Ciudadanos: El Caso de la Red de Radios Comunitarias del Magdalena Medio en Colombia*, ed. Jair Vega. Barranquilla: Universidad del Norte.

El Gazi, Jeanine. 2001. "La Experiencia de los Medios Ciudadanos y Comunitarios Frente al Conflicto Armado." Paper presented at the Mesa de Trabajo Cultura y Medios de Comunicación, Mompox, Colombia, November 30–December 2.

———. 2004. Interview by author. Tape recording. Bogotá, Colombia. September 25.

———. 2006. "Radios Ciudadanas, Relatos y Construcción de Democracia desde lo Local." Paper presented at the Conferencia de la Federación Latinoamericana de Facultades de Comunicación (FELAFACS), Bogotá, September 25–28.

———. 2008. "Políticas Públicas de Radiodifusión y Procesos Sociales: La Radio Comunitaria y Ciudadana en Colombia. Dos Décadas de Experiencias y Aprendizajes, el Diálogo entre Demandas Ciudadanas y Legislación Estatal."

Paper presented at the International Conference on Community Radio, La Paz, Bolivia, November 18–20.

El Tiempo. 2007. "Responsabilidad Social S.A." August 21. Available at http://www.eltiempo.com/archivo/documento/MAM-2625624.

Energy Information Administration. 2009. "Colombia Oil." Available at http://www.eia.doe.gov/emeu/cabs/Colombia/Oil.html.

Equipo de Producción Audiovisual de Marialabaja. 2007. *De Cochero a Piloto*. Video. El Carmen de Bolívar: Colectivo de Comunicaciones de Montes de María Línea 21.

Equipo de Producción Audiovisual de Ovejas. 2007. *El Niño Dios de Bombacho*. Video. El Carmen de Bolívar: Colectivo de Comunicaciones de Montes de María Línea 21.

Equipo de Producción Audiovisual de San Antonio de Palmito. 2007. *Son del Carángano*. Video. Carmen de Bolívar: Colectivo de Comunicaciones de Montes de María Línea 21.

Equipo de Producción Audiovisual de San Onofre. 2007. *Locuras de Adolecentes*. Video. El Carmen de Bolívar: Colectivo de Comunicaciones de Montes de María Línea 21.

Escobar, Cristina. 1998. "Clientelism, Mobilization, and Citizenship: Peasant Politics in Sucre, Colombia." PhD diss., University of California, San Diego.

Espitia, Javier. 2004. Interview by author. Tape recording. Bogotá. October 6.

Feldman, Allen. 1991. *Formations of Violence: Narratives of the Body and Political Terror in Northern Ireland*. Chicago: University of Chicago Press.

———. 2000. "Violence and Vision: The Prosthetics and Aesthetics of Terror." In *Violence and Subjectivity,* ed. Veena Das, Arthur Kleinman, Mamphela Ramphele, and Pamela Reynolds, 46–78. Berkeley: University of California Press.

Ferreira, Leonardo, and Joseph Straubhaar. 1988. "La Radio y la Nueva Colombia." *Journal of Popular Culture* 22 (1): 287–302.

Ferron, Benjamin. 2006. "Les Médias Alternatifs: 'Contre-Culture' ou 'Sous-culture'? Les Luttes de (Dé-)légitimation de la Communication Contestataire à Travers l'Etude de Publications Académiques et Militantes." Paper presented at the Actes du VIIIème colloque international Brésil France, in Echirolles, France, Septermber 29–30.

———. 2009. "Alternative Media in Palestine and Chiapas." Paper presented at the OURMedia VIII: Communication, Conflict and Coexistence, Individual and Collective Narratives, Rionegro, Colombia, July 26–31.

FESCOL. 2003. "Premio Nacional de Paz." Unpublished document. Bogotá: Fundación Friedrich Ebert–Colombia.

Foucault, Michel. 1972. *The Archaeology of Knowledge*. New York: Routledge.

———. 1980. *Power/Knowledge: Selected Interviews and Other Writings 1972–1977*. Brighton: Harvester Press.

Frohardt, Mark, and Jonatha Temin. 2003. "Use and Abuse of Media in Vulnerable Societies." Wahington, D.C.: United States Institute of Peace. Available at http://www.usip.org/pubs/specialreports/sr110.pdf.

Galtung, Johan. 1991. "Contribución Específica de la Irenología al Estudio de la Violencia y su Tipología." In *La Violencia y sus Causas*, ed. UNESCO, 91–106. Paris: UNESCO.

———. 1993. "Los Fundamentos de los Estudios de Paz." In *Presupuestos Teóricos y Éticos sobre la Paz*, ed. Ana Rubio, 15–46. Granada: Universidad de Granada.

———. 1998. *Peace by Peaceful Means: Peace and Conflict, Development and Civilization*. Oslo: Sage and PRIO (International Peace Institute).

———. 2002. "TRANSCEND: 45 Years, 45 Conflicts." In *Searching for Peace: The Road to TRANSCEND*, ed. Johan Galtung, Carl G. Jacobsen, and Kai F. Brand-Jacobsen, 189–321. London: Pluto Press and TRANSCEND.

Gamarra Radio Producer. 2004. Interview by author at Memory Workshop. Tape recording. Bucaramanga, Colombia. August 15–18.

Garay Salamanca, Jorge Luis. 1999. "La Transición hacia la Construcción de Sociedad: Reflexiones en Torno a la Crisis Colombiana." In *Armar la Paz es Desarmar la Guerra*, ed. Alvaro Camacho Guizado and Francisco Leal Buitrago, 403–39. Bogotá: CEREC, IEPRI, and FESCOL.

García, Isabel, Daniel Góngora, and Nicolás Silva. 2006. *El Guarapo*. Video. Belén de los Andaquíes: Escuela Audiovisual Infantil de Belén de los Andaquíes.

García, Mariana. 2006. Interview by author. Tape recording. Belén de los Andaquíes, Colombia. May 15.

García, Martha Cecilia. 2006. "Barrancabermeja: Ciudad en Permanente Disputa." In *Conflictos, Poderes e Identidades en el Magdalena Medio 1990–2001*, ed. Mauricio Archila and Ingrid Bolívar, 243–311. Bogotá: CINEP.

García, Mauricio, and Rodrigo Uprimny. 1999. "El Nudo Gordiano de la Justicia y la Guerra en Colombia." In *Armar la Paz es Desarmar la Guerra*, ed. Alvaro Camacho and Francisco Leal, 33–72. Bogotá: CEREC, IEPRI, and FESCOL.

García Montes, Carlos Elias, and Eulise Santanilla. 1994. *Recuperación Histórica y Análisis Cultural: Belén de los Andaquíes*. Bogotá: CINDE–Universidad Pedagógica Nacional.

García Villegas, Mauricio, and Boaventura de Sousa dos Santos. 2004. "Estudio Preliminar: Colombia, el Grado Cero de la Emancipación Social? Entre los Fascismos Sociales y la Emancipación Social." In *Emancipación Social y Violencia en Colombia*, ed. Boaventura de Sousa dos Santos and Mauricio García Villegas, 31–69. Bogotá: Grupo Norma.

Geertz, Andres, Victor Van Oeyen, and Claudia Villamayor. 2004. *La Práctica Inspira: La Radio Popular y Comunitaria Frente al Nuevo Siglo*. Quito: ALER.

Ginsburg, Faye. 2002. "Screen Memories: Resignifying the Traditional in Indigenous Media." In *Media Worlds: Anthropology on New Terrain*, ed. Faye Ginsburg, Laila Abu-Lughod, and Brian Larkin, 39–57. Berkeley: University of California Press.

Gómez, Nelson. 2005. Interview by author. Tape recording. El Carmen de Bolívar, Colombia. December 12.

Gómez, Gabriel, and Juan Carlos Quintero. 2002. *Diagnóstico del Servicio Comunitario de Radiodifusión Sonora en Colombia.* Bogotá: Ministerio de Comunicaciones.

González, Alirio. 2004. Interview by author. Tape recording. Belén de los Andaquíes, Colombia. October 15.

——. 2005. Interview by author. Tape recording. Belén de los Andaquíes, Colombia. December 18.

——. 2006. Interview by author. Tape recording. Bogotá. March 1.

——. 2007. Interview by author. Tape recording. Belén de los Andaquíes, Colombia. October 10.

González, Alirio, and Clemencia Rodríguez. 2008. "Alas para tu Voz: Ejercicios de Ciudadanía desde una Emisora Comunitaria del Piedemonte Amazónico." In *Lo que le Vamos Quitando a la Guerra. Medios Ciudadanos en Contextos de Conflicto Armado en Colombia,* ed. Clemencia Rodríguez, 65–140. Bogotá: Centro de Competencias en Comunicación—Fundación Friedrich Ebert.

González, Fernán. 2006. "Conflicto Armado, Movilización Social y Construcción de Región en el Magdalena Medio." In *Conflictos, Poderes e Identidades en el Magdalena Medio 1990–2001,* ed. Mauricio Archila and Ingrid Bolívar, 509–69. Bogotá: CINEP.

González, Fernán, Ingrid J. Bolívar, and Teófilo Vásquez. 2003. *Violencia Política en Colombia: De la Nación Fragmentada a la Construcción del Estado.* Bogotá: CINEP.

González, Maikol Andrés. 2007. *El Barco.* Video. Belén de los Andaquíes: Escuela Audiovisual Infantil de Belén de los Andaquíes.

Graf, Wilfried, Gudrun Kramer, and Augustin Nicolescou. 2007. "Counselling and Training for Conflict Transformation and Peace-Building: The TRANSCEND Approach." In *Handbook of Peace and Conflict Studies,* ed. Charles Webel and Johan Galtung, 123–42. London: Sage.

Greenberg, Bradley S., and Walter Gantz. 1993. *Desert Storm and the Mass Media.* Creskill, N.J.: Hampton Press.

Grupo de Memoria Histórica. 2009. "La Masacre de El Salado: Esa Guerra no Era Nuestra." Report of the Grupo de Memoria Histórica de la Comisión Nacional de Reparación y Reconciliación (CNRR). Bogotá: CNRR. Available at http://memoriahistorica-cnrr.org.co/archivos/arc_docum/informe_la_masacre_de_el_salado.pdf.

Gumucio Dagron, Alfonso. 2001. *Haciendo Olas: Comunicación Participativa para el Cambio Social.* New York: Rockefeller Foundation.

——. 2003. "Arte de Equilibristas: La Sostenibilidad de los Medios de Comunicación Comunitarios." Paper presented at OURMedia III Conference, Barranquilla, Colombia, May 19–21.

Gumucio Dagron, Alfonso, and Amparo Cadavid. 2006. *Voces del Magdalena.* Video. Bogotá: Communication for Social Change Consortium.

Gumucio Dagron, Alfonso, and Clemencia Rodríguez. 2006. "Time to Call Things by Their Name." *Media Development* 3:9–16.

Hamber, Brandon, and Kelly Gráinne. 2005. *A Place for Reconciliation? Place and Locality in Northern Ireland*. Belfast: Democratic Dialogue.

Harbom, Lotta, Stina Högbladh, and Peter Wallensteen. 2006. "Armed Conflict and Peace Agreements." *Journal of Peace Research* 43 (5): 617–31.

Hess, Stephen, and Malvin Kalb. 2003. *The Media and the War on Terrorism*. Washington, D.C.: Brookings Institution.

Hiebert, Loretta. 2001. *Lifeline Media: Reaching Populations in Crisis: A Guide to Developing Media Projects in Conflict Situations*. Geneva: Media Action International.

Hodgson, Martin. 2000. "Girls Swap Diapers for Rebel Life." *Christian Science Monitor*, September 6.

Howard, Ross. 2002. *An Operational Framework for Media and Peacebuilding*. Vancouver: Institute for Media, Policy, and Civil Society (IMPACS).

———. 2003. *Conflict Sensitive Reporting: A Handbook*. Vancouver: International Media Support/IMPACS.

———. 2005. *Gender, Conflict and Journalism: A Handbook*. Paris: UNESCO.

Howley, Kevin. 2005. *Community Media: People, Places, and Communication Technologies*. Cambridge: Cambridge University Press.

Hoyos, Julio César. 2004. Interview by author. Tape recording. Bogotá. October 15.

Hudson, Miles, and John Stanier. 1998. *War and the Media: A Random Searchlight*. New York: New York University Press.

Jaramillo, Jaime E., Leonidas Mora, and Fernando Cubides. 1986. *Colonización, Coca y Guerrilla*. Bogotá: Alianza Editorial Colombiana.

Jeffords, Susan, and Lauren Rabinovitz. 1994. *Seeing through the Media: The Persian Gulf War*. New Brunswick: Rutgers University Press.

Kabanda, Marcel. 2005. "Rwanda: Control of the Media." In *Violence and Its Causes: A Stocktaking*, ed. Pierre Sané, 53–60. Paris: UNESCO.

Kaiser, Susana. 2005. *Postmemories of Terror*. New York: Palgrave Macmillan.

Kalathil, Shanthi, John Langlois, and Adam Kaplan. 2008. *A New Model: Media and Communication in Post-Conflict and Fragile States*. Washington, D.C.: International Bank for Reconstruction and Development/The World Bank Communication for Governance and Accountability Program (ComGAP). Available at http://siteresources.worldbank.org/EXTGOVACC/Resources/CommGAP MissingLinkWeb.pdf.

Kamalipour, Yahya R., and Nancy Snow. 2004. *War, Media, and Propaganda: A Global Perspective*. Lanham, Md.: Rowman and Littlefield.

Karahasan, Dzevad. 2005. *Sarajevo: Diario de un Éxodo*. Barcelona: Galaxia Gutenberg S.A.

Karay, Felicja. 2002. *Hasag-Leipzig Slave Labour Camp for Women: The Struggle for Survival Told by the Women and Their Poetry*. Portland: Vallentine Mitchell.

Kavoori, Anandam P., and Todd Fraley. 2006. *Media, Terrorism, and Theory: A Reader*. Lanham, Md.: Rowman and Littlefield.

Keppley Mahmood, Cynthia. 2000. "Dynamics of Terror in Punjab and Kashmir." In *Death Squad: The Anthropology of State Terror,* ed. Jeffrey A. Sluka, 70–90. Philadelphia: University of Pennsylvania Press.

Kidd, Dorothy, and Clemencia Rodríguez. 2010. Introduction to *Making Our Media: Global Initiatives toward a Democratic Public Sphere.* Vol. 1: *Creating New Communication Spaces,* ed. Clemencia Rodríguez, Dorothy Kidd, and Laura Stein, 1–22. Cresskill, N.J.: Hampton Press.

LaFranchi, Howard 2000. "Elected Office: A Post Too Perilous to Occupy." *Christian Science Monitor,* October 25.

Langlois, Andrea, and Frédéric Dubois. 2005. *Autonomous Media: Activating Resistance and Dissent.* Montreal: Cumulus Press.

Lara, Patricia. 2000. *Las Mujeres en la Guerra.* Bogotá: Editorial Planeta.

Lawrence, Patricia. 2000. "Violence, Suffering, Amman: The Work of Oracles in Sri Lanka's Eastern War Zones." In *Violence and Subjectivity,* ed. Veena Das, Arthur Kleinman, Memphele Ramphele, and Pamela Reynolds, 171–204. Berkeley: University of California Press.

Lederach, Jean Paul 1997. *Building Peace: Sustainable Reconciliation in Divided Societies.* Washington, D.C.: United States Institute of Peace Press.

Legrand, Catherine. 1986. *Frontier Expansion and Peasant Protest in Colombia, 1850–1936.* Albuquerque: University of New Mexico Press.

Lewin, Carroll. 2002. "Ghettos in the Holocaust: The Improvisation of Social Order in a Culture of Terror." In *Ethnography of Unstable Places: Everyday Lives in Contexts of Dramatic Political Change,* ed. Carol J. Greenhouse, Elizabeth Mertz, and Kay B. Warren, 37–60. Durham: Duke University Press.

Lewis, Peter. 1984. *Media for People in Cities: A Study of Community Media in the Urban Context.* Paris: UNESCO.

Loewenberg, Shira, and Bent Bonde. 2008. *Media in Conflict Prevention and Peacebuilding Strategies.* Bonn: Deutsche Welle. Available at http://dw-gmf.de/download/Media_In_Conflict_Prevention.pdf.

Lynch, Jake, and Annabel McGoldrick. 2005. *Peace Journalism.* Stroud: Hawthorn Pres.

Madariaga, Patricia. 2006. "Región, Actores y Conflicto: Los Episodios." In *Conflictos, Poderes e Identidades en el Magdalena Medio 1990–2001,* ed. Mauricio Archila and Ingrid Bolívar, 37–84. Bogotá: CINEP.

Madison, Soyini D. 2005. *Critical Ethnography: Method, Ethic, Performance.* Thousand Oaks, Calif.: Sage.

Magdalena Medio Community Radio Producer. 2004. Interview by author at Memory Workshop. Bucaramanga, Colombia. August 15–18.

Magnusson, Tomas. 1996. *From Saigon to Sarajevo: Mass Media in Times of War.* Stockholm: Swedish Peace Council; Geneva: International Peace Bureau.

Manoff, Robert Karl. 1996. "The Media's Role in Preventing and Moderating Conflict." Paper presented at the Colloquium on Science, Technology, and Government, New York University, New York. April 29.

Márquez, César. 2003. "La Unidad de Radio del Ministerio de Cultura: Un Proyecto de Comunicación-Cultura desde el Estado." Audio material in support of BA thesis, Universidad Externado de Colombia, Bogotá.

Mathews, Anie. 2008. "Backpacking as a Contemporary Rite of Passage: Victor Turner and Youth Travel Practices." In *Victor Turner and Contemporary Cultural Performance*, ed. Graham St John, 174–189. New York: Berghahn Books.

Meertens, Donny. 2001. "The Nostalgic Future. Terror, Displacement and Gender in Colombia." In *Victims, Perpetrators, or Actors? Gender, Armed Conflict and Political Violence*, ed. Caroline Moser and Fiona Clark, 133–48. New York: Zed Books.

Melone, Sandra, George Terzis, and Beleli Ozsel. 2002. "Using the Media for Conflict Transformation: The Common Ground Experience." In *The Berghof Handbook for Conflict Transformation*. Berlin: Berghof. Available at http://www.berghof-handbook.net/uploads/download/melone_hb.pdf.

Mesa de Trabajo en Mujer y Conflicto Armado. 2004. "Mujer y Conflicto Armado: Informe sobre Conflicto Armado contra Mujeres, Jóvenes y Niñas en Colombia." Bogotá: Mesa de Trabajo en Mujer y Conflicto Armado. Available at http://www.mujeryconflictoarmado.org.

Ministerio de Comunicaciones de Colombia. 2007. "Radio y Pluralismo. Política de Radiodifusión Sonora Comunitaria." Available at http://archivo.mintic.gov.co/mincom/documents/portal/documents/root/Radiodifusion%20Sonora/Archivos%20PDF/POLITICA%20PUBLICA%20DEL%20SERVICIO%20COMUNITARIO%20DE%20RADIODIFUSION%20SONORA.pdf. Accessed January 16, 2011.

Ministerio de Cultura de Colombia. 2004. *Radios Ciudadanas, Encuentro, Participación y Debate: Que Suene la Radio*. Radio program. October 7.

Moeller, Susan. 1999. *Compassion Fatigue: How the Media See Disease, Famine, War, and Death*. New York: Routledge.

Molano, Alfredo. 1987. *Selva Adentro: Una Historia Oral de la Colonización del Guaviare*. Bogotá: El Áncora Editores.

Molner, Helen, and Michael Meadows. 2001. *Songlines to Satellites: Indigenous Communication in Australia, the South Pacific, and Canada*. Leichhardt: Pluto Press.

Moreno, Jordan Alejandro 2007a. *Un Día con mi Abuela*. Video. Belén de los Andaquíes: Escuela Audiovisual Infantil de Belén de los Andaquíes.

———. 2007b. *Chulos*. Video. Belén de los Andaquíes: Escuela Audiovisual Infantil de Belén de los Andaquíes.

Morris, Christine, and Michael Meadows. 2001. *Into the New Millennium: Indigenous Media in Australia*. Final Report. Brisbane: Griffith University.

Mouffe, Chantal. 1988. "Hegemony and New Political Subjects: Towards a New Conception of Democracy." In *Marxism and the Interpretation of Culture*, ed. Larry Grossberg and Cary Nelson, 89–102. Urbana: University of Illinois Press.

———. 1992. *Dimensions of Radical Democracy: Pluralism, Citizenship, Community*. London: Verso.

————. 2006. "Las Identidades Colectivas Políticas en Juego." Paper presented at Conferencia de la Federación Latinoamericana de Facultades de Comunicación (FELAFACS), Bogotá, September 25–28.

Murillo, Amparo. 1999. "Historia y Sociedad en el Magdalena Medio." *Controversia* 174:41–61.

————. In press. "Historia, Cultura e Identidades en el Magdalena Medio." In *Evaluación Participativa de Medios Ciudadanos: El Caso de la Red de Radios Comunitarias del Magdalena Medio en Colombia,* ed. Jair Vega. Barranquilla: Universidad del Norte.

Murillo, Amparo, Maria Teresa Arcila, Manuel Alberto Alonso, Giovanni Restrepo, and Gloria Estella Bonilla. 1994. *Un Mundo que se Mueve como el Río: Historia Regional del Magdalena Medio.* Bogotá: ICANH.

Murillo, Mario. In press. *Voices of Resistance: Indigenous Mobilization, Community Radio and the Struggle for Social Justice in Colombia.* New York: South End Press.

Myers, M., Gordon Adam, and L. Lalanne. 1995. *The Effective Use of Radio for Mitigation of Drought in the Sahel.* Swindon: Disaster Preparedness Centre, Cranfield University.

Ndong'a, Otieno R. J. 2005. "Radio Kwizera a Tool for Community Development." Paper presented at the Radio Conference 2005: A Transnational Forum for Radio Scholars, Teachers, and Broadcasters, RMIT University City Campus, Melbourne, Australia, July 11–14.

Nordstrom, Carolyn. 1992. "The Backyard Front." In *The Paths to Domination, Resistance, and Terror,* ed. Carolyn Nordstrom and JoAnn Martin, 260–74. Berkeley: University of California Press.

————. 2003. "Public Bad, Public Good(s) and Private Realities." In *Political Transition: Politics and Cultures,* ed. Paul Gready, 212–24. London: Pluto Press.

————. 2004. *Shadows of War: Violence, Power, and International Profiteering in the Twenty-first Century.* Berkeley: University of California Press.

Nordstrom, Carolyn, and JoAnn Martin. 1992. "The Culture of Conflict: Field Reality and Theory." In *The Paths to Domination, Resistance, and Terror,* ed. Carolyn Nordstrom and JoAnn Martin, 3–17. Berkeley: University of California Press.

Nordstrom, Carolyn, and Antonius C. G. M. Robben. 1995. "The Anthropology and Ethnography of Violence and Sociopolitical Conflict." In *Fieldwork under Fire: Contemporary Studies of Violence and Survival,* ed. Antonius C. G. M. Robben and Carolyn Nordstrom, 1–24. Berkeley: University of California Press.

Norris, Pippa, Montague Kern, and Marion R. Just. 2003. *Framing Terrorism: The News Media, the Government, and the Public.* New York: Routledge.

Observatorio de Paz Integral. 2005. "Estadísticas Sobre Violaciones a los Derechos Humanos e Infracciones al Derecho Internacional Humanitario en el Magdalena Medio, 2002–2004." Compilación de Información de la Revista *Noche y Niebla.* Barrancabermeja: CINEP. Available at http://www.opi.org.co/docs/Violaciones_%20DH_Infracciones_DIH_MM_2002_2004.pdf.

Ochoa, Beatriz. 2004. Interview by author. Tape recording. Barranquilla, Colombia. June 6.

O'Connor, Alan. 2004. *Community Radio in Bolivia: The Miners' Radio Stations.* Lewiston, N.Y.: Edwin Mellen Press.

Opel, Andy, and Donnalyn Pompper. 2003. *Representing Resistance: Media, Civil Disobedience, and the Global Justice Movement.* Westport, Conn.: Praeger Press.

OPPDHDIH (Observatorio del Programa Presidencial de Derechos Humanos y Derecho Internacional Humanitario). 2001. *Panorama Actual de Barrancabermeja.* Bogotá: Vicepresidencia de la República de Colombia.

———. 2002. *Colombia: Conflicto Armado, Regiones, Derechos Humanos y DIH 1998–2002.* Bogotá: Vicepresidencia de la República de Colombia.

Orozco, Iván. 2002. "La Posguerra Colombiana: Divagaciones sobre la Venganza, la Justicia y la Reconciliación." *Análisis Político* 46:78–99.

Orr, Gregory. 2002. *Poetry of Survival.* Athens: University of Georgia Press.

Osses Rivera, Sandra Liliana. 2002. "Nuevos Sentidos de lo Comunitario: La Radio Comunitaria en Colombia." MA thesis, FLACSO, Mexico City, Mexico.

Parish, Erin, Brandon Hamber, and Megan Price. 2006. "The Media Are Not the Enemy: Victim/Survivor and Media Relations in Northern Ireland." Belfast: Democratic Dialogue.

Pécaut, Daniel. 1999. "Cofiguraciones del Espacio, el Tiempo y la Subjetividad en un Contexto de Terror: El Caso Colombiano." *Revista Colombiana de Antropología* 35:8–35.

———. 2001. *Guerra Contra la Sociedad.* Bogotá: Editorial Planeta.

———. 2003. *Violencia y Política en Colombia: Elementos de Reflexión.* Bogotá: Hombre Nuevo Editores.

Pelias, Ronald. 1992. *Performance Studies: The Interpretation of Aesthetic Texts.* New York: St. Martin's Press.

Peñaloza, Wilgen. 2004. Interview by author. Tape recording. Barranquilla, Colombia. June 6.

Perea, Carlos Mario. 1996. *Porque la Sangre es Espíritu.* Bogotá: IEPRI and Editorial Aguilar.

Pérez, Guillermo. 2004. Interview by author. Tape recording. Bogotá. October 28.

Plataforma Colombiana de Derechos Humanos, Democracia y Desarrollo. 2008. "Otra Versión sobre el Uso de Armas de Fuego Contra la Movilización Indígena del Cauca." October 25. Available at http://plataforma-colombiana.org.

PNUD (Programa de las Naciones Unidas para el Desarrollo), Corporación Territorios, and Universidad de Cartagena. 2004. "Programa de Desarrollo y Paz de los Montes de María." Unpublished report. Bogotá.

Programa de Desarrollo y Paz de Montes de María. 2009. "Seminario Derechos Humanos, Desplazamiento Forzado y Reparación a Víctimas en Montes de María." Available at http://www.observatoriomontesdemaria.org/userimages observatorio/file/Seminario_Derechos_Humanos.pdf.

Puerto Nare Radio Producer. 2004. Interview by author at Memory Workshop. Tape recording. Bucaramanga, Colombia. August 15–18.

Puerto Wilches Radio Producer. 2004. Interview by author at Memory Workshop. Tape recording. Bucaramanga, Colombia. August 15–18.

Radio Andaquí. 2003. *Promo—Bárbara Charanga*. Audio recording. Belén de los Andaquíes, Colombia.

Radio Netherlands. 2008. "Counteracting Hate Radio." Online dossier available at http://www.radionetherlands.nl/features/media/dossiers/hateintro.html.

Ramírez, Maria Clemencia. 2001. *Entre el Estado y la Guerrilla: Identidad y Ciudadanía en el Movimiento de los Campesinos Cocaleros del Putumayo*. Bogotá: ICAHN.

Rappaport, Joanne. 2005. *Intercultural Utopias: Public Intellectuals, Cultural Experimentation, and Ethnic Pluralism in Colombia*. Durham: Duke University Press.

Red de Gestores Sociales. 2004. "Colectivo Montes de María Línea 21: Una Comunidad Unida para la Comunicación y la Paz." *Red de Gestores Sociales*, November, p. 18.

Renjifo, Liberman. 2004. Interview by author. Tape recording. Bogotá. October 7.

Rennie, Ellie. 2006. *Community Media: A Global Introduction*. Boulder, Colo.: Rowman and Littlefield.

Reyes, Alejandro. 1999. "La Cuestión Agraria en la Guerra y la Paz." In *Armar la Paz es Desarmar la Guerra*, ed. Alvaro Camacho and Francisco Leal, 205–26. Bogotá: CEREC, IEPRI, FESCOL.

Riaño-Alcalá, Pilar. 2006. *Dwellers of Memory: Youth and Violence in Medellín, Colombia*. New Brunswick, N.J.: Transaction Publishers.

———. 2008. "Seeing the Past, Visions of the Future: Memory Workshops with Internally Displaced Persons in Colombia." In *Oral Histories and Public Memories*, ed. Paula Hamilton and Linda Shopes, 269–92. Philadelphia: Temple University Press.

Richards, Paul. 1992. "Famine (and War) in Africa: What Do Anthropologists Have to Say?" *Anthropology Today* 8 (6): 3–5.

Rodríguez, Clemencia. 2001. *Fissures in the Mediascape: An International Study of Citizens' Media*. Cresskill, N.J.: Hampton Press.

———. 2004. "Communication for Peace: Contrasting Approaches." *Drum Beat*, no. 278, December 6, http://www.comminit.com/drum_beat.html.

———. 2005a. "From the Sandinista Revolution to *Telenovelas*: The Case of Puntos de Encuentro, Nicaragua." In *Media and Global Change: Rethinking Communication for Development*, ed. Oscar Hemer and Thomas Tufte, 367–84. Sweden: NORDICOM, University of Göteburg.

———. 2005b. Field Diary.

———. 2008. Introduction to *Lo Que le Vamos Quitando a la Guerra: Medios Ciudadanos en Contextos de Conflicto Armado en Colombia*, ed. Clemencia Rodríguez, 9–14. Bogotá: Centro de Competencias en Comunicación—Fundación Friedrich Ebert.

———. 2010. "Knowledges in Dialogue: A Participatory Evaluation Study of Citizens' Radio Stations in Magdalena Medio, Colombia." In *Making Our Media:*

Global Initiatives toward a Democratic Public Sphere. Vol. 1: *Creating New Communication Spaces.* Ed. Clemencia Rodríguez, Dorothy Kidd, and Laura Stein, 131–54. Cresskill, N.J.: Hampton Press.

Rodríguez, Clemencia, and Amparo Cadavid. 2007. "From Violence to Discourse: Conflict and Citizens' Radio Stations in Colombia." In *The Cultures and Globalization Series.* Vol. 1: *Conflicts and Tensions,* ed. Raj Isar and Helmut Anheier, 313–27. Thousand Oaks, Calif.: Sage.

Rodríguez, Clemencia, and Jeanine El Gazi. 2007. "The Poetics of Indigenous Radio in Colombia." *Media, Culture, and Society* 29 (3): 449–68.

Rodríguez, Clemencia, Dorothy Kidd, and Laura Stein, eds. 2010. *Making Our Media: Global Initiatives toward a Democratic Public Sphere.* Vol. 1: *Creating New Communication Spaces.* Cresskill, N.J.: Hampton Press.

Rodríguez, Clemencia, and Patricia Téllez. 1989. *La Telenovela en Colombia: Mucho más que Amor y Lágrimas.* Bogotá: CINEP.

Rolston, Bill, and David Miller. 1996. *War and Words: The Northern Ireland Media Reader.* Belfast: Beyond the Pale Publications.

Rolt, Francis. 2005. "Golden Kids News: Our Story." E-mail communication. May 26.

———. 2009. "Media and Peacebuilding around Elections: Sierra Leone 2002." E-mail communication. January 9.

Romero, Mauricio. 1998. "Identidades Políticas y Conflicto Armado en Colombia: El Caso del Departamento de Córdoba." In *Conflictos Regionales—Atlántico y Pacífico,* ed. FESCOL and IEPRI, 59–92. Bogotá: FESCOL–IEPRI.

———. 1999. "El PDPMM: Desarrollo y Paz 'En Caliente.'" *Controversia* 174: 63–71.

———. 2003. *Paramilitares y Autodefensas.* Bogotá: IEPRI and Editorial Planeta.

Rotberg, Robert I., and Thomas G. Weiss. 1996. *From Massacres to Genocide: The Media, Public Policy, and Humanitarian Crises.* Washington, D.C.: Brookings Institution; Cambridge, Mass.: World Peace Foundation.

Roth, Lorna. 2005. *Something New in the Air: The Story of First Peoples Television Broadcasting in Canada.* Montreal: McGill-Queen's University Press.

Rothman, Jay, and Marie L. Olson. 2001. "From Interests to Identities: Towards a New Emphasis in Interactive Conflict Resolution." *Journal of Peace Research* 38 (3): 289–303.

Salazar, Juan F. 2002. "Activismo Indígena en América Latina: Estrategias para una Construcción Cultural de Tecnologías de Información y Comunicación." *Journal of Iberian and Latin American Studies* 8 (2): 61–79.

———. 2003. "Articulating an Activist Imaginary: Internet as Counter Public Sphere in the Mapuche Movement, 1997–2000." *Media International Australia Incorporating Culture and Policy* 107:19–30.

———. 2007. "Indigenous Peoples and the Cultural Constructions of Information and Communication Technology in Latin America." In *Indigenous People and Information Technology,* ed. Lauren E. Dyson, Max Hendriks, and Stephen Grant, 14–26. Hershey, Pa.: Idea Book Publishing.

Salazar Arenas, Oscar Ivan. 1988. "Notas Para Iniciar una Historia de las Radios Comunitarias en Colombia." Unpublished document. Bogotá.

Salgado, Alvaro. 2004. Interview by author. Tape recording. Bogotá. August 12.

Samper, Mady. 2002. *Una Colombia Posible: Historias de Resistencia Civil Frente a la Guerra*. Bogotá: Norma.

Sandoval Merchan, Efrain Danilo. 2009. Researcher at the Centro de Estudios Regionales del Magdalena Medio. E-mail communication, November 10.

Sanford, Victoria. 2004. "Contesting Displacement in Colombia: Citizenship and State Sovereignty at the Margins." In *Anthropology in the Margins of the State*, ed. Veena Das and Deborah Poole, 253–77. Santa Fe, N.M.: School of the Americas Research Press.

Santa Rosa Radio Producer. 2004. Interview by author at Memory Workshop. Bucaramanga, Colombia. August 15–18.

San Vicente de Chucurí Radio Producer. 2004. Interview by author at Memory Workshop. Bucaramanga, Colombia. August 15–18.

San Vicente Estéreo. 2004a. *Coplas de los Abuelos—Espantos*. Radio program. San Vicente de Chucurí.

———. 2004b. *Spot Adultos Vs Jóvenes*. Radio program. San Vicente de Chucurí.

———. 2004c. *Spot Anticonceptivos*. Radio program. San Vicente de Chucurí.

———. 2004d. *Spot Cerrar Cercas*. Radio program. San Vicente de Chucurí.

Sarmiento, Joyce. 2005. "Sistematización de la Implementación de los Medios Comunitarios del Proyecto de Formación de Niños como Actores Sociales al Interior del Colectivo Infantil Montes de María Línea 21, a Partir de la Experiencia de los Actores." BA thesis, Universidad del Norte, Barranquilla, Colombia.

Schechner, Richard. 2003. *Performance Theory*. London: Routledge.

Scott, James. 1992. "Domination, Acting and Fantasy." In *The Paths of Domination, Resistance and Terror*, ed. Carolyn Nordstrom and JoAnn Martin, 55–84. Berkeley: University of California Press.

Semana. 2003. "La Ira Presidencial: El Discurso de Alvaro Uribe contra las ONG Indica que la Línea más Dura Gana Espacio en el Gobierno." September 9, http://www.semana.com/wf_InfoArticulo.aspx?IdArt=73121.

———. 2008. "Colombia Tiene Triste Liderazgo Mundial en Ataques a Defensores de Derechos Humanos." June 20, http://www.semana.com/wf_InfoArticulo .aspx?IdArt=112841.

———. 2010. "La Tierra Prometida." September 4, http://www.semana.com/noti cias-nacion/tierra-prometida/144024.aspx.

Seneviratne, Kalinga. 2008. "Community Radio—Balm in Troubled Areas." *IPS*, September 2, http://ipsnews.net/news.asp?idnews=43756.

Shamas, Kristin. 2011. "Lebanese Subjectivities and Media Use. Post/Global Contexts." Phd diss., University of Oklahoma.

Shipler, Michael. 2006. *Youth Radio for Peacebuilding: A Guide*. Brussels: Search for Common Ground. Available at http://www.radiopeaceafrica.org/assets/texts/ pdf/manual_03_EN_color.pdf.

Siemering, Bill. 2008. E-mail communication. October 8.

Silva, Maira Juliana. 2007. *La Finca de mi Abuelo*. Video. Belén de los Andaquíes: Escuela Audiovisual Infantil de Belén de los Andaquíes.

———. 2008. *Celulares*. Video. Belén de los Andaquíes: Escuela Audiovisual Infantil de Belén de los Andaquíes.

Simití Radio Producer. 2004. Interview by author at Memory Workshop. Tape recording. Bucaramanga, Colombia. August 15–18.

SINCHI, Instituto. 2000. *Caquetá: Dinámica de un Proceso*. Bogotá: Instituto Amazónico de Investigaciones Científicas, SINCHI.

Singhal, Arvind, and Everett Rogers. 2003. *Entertainment-Education and Social Change: History, Research, and Practice*. Mahwah, N.J.: Lawrence Erlbaum.

Sluka, Jeffrey A. 1992. "The Politics of Painting: Political Murals in Northern Ireland." In *The Paths to Domination, Resistance and Terror*, ed. Carolyn Nordstrom and JoAnn Martin, 190–216. Berkeley: University of California Press.

———. 2000a. "'For God and Ulster': The Culture of Terror and Loyalist Death Squads in Northern Ireland." In *Death Squad: The Anthropology of State Terror*, ed. Jeffrey A. Sluka, 127–57. Philadelphia: University of Pennsylvania Press.

———. 2000b. "Introduction: State Terror and Anthropology." In *Death Squad: The Anthropology of State Terror*, ed. Jeffrey A. Sluka, 1–45. Philadelphia: University of Pennsylvania Press.

Smith, Hedrick 1992. *The Media and the Gulf War*. Washington, D.C.: Seven Locks Press.

Spitulnik, Debra. 2002. "Alternative Small Media and Communicative Spaces." In *Media and Democracy in Africa*, ed. Goran Hyden, Michael Leslie, and Folu F. Ogundimu, 177–206. New Brunswick, N.J.: Transaction Publishers.

Steiner, Claudia. 2000. "From the Rainforest to Heaven: Dead Infants and Angels." Paper presented at the Panel on Memory, Representation, and Narratives: Re-Thinking Violence in Colombia, XXII International Congress of the Latin American Studies Association, Miami, Florida, March 16–18.

———. 2005. "Memories of Violence, Narratives of History: Ethnographic Journeys in Colombia." PhD diss., University of California, Berkeley.

Stern, Carol Simpson, and Bruce Henderson. 1993. *Performance: Texts and Contexts*. New York: Longman.

St John, Graham. 2008. "Victor Turner and Contemporary Cultural Performance: An Introduction." In *Victor Turner and Contemporary Cultural Performance*, ed. Graham St John, 1–37. New York: Berghahn Books.

Stubbs, Paul. 1997. "Peace Building, Community Development and Cultural Change: Report on Conflict Resolution Catalysts' Work in Banja Luka, Bosnia-Herzegovina." Assessment report. Montpelier, Vt.: Conflict Resolution Catalysts. Available at http://www.crcvt.org/stubb.pdf.

Suárez-Orozco, Marcelo. 1992. "A Grammar of Terror: Psychocultural Response to State Terrorism in Dirty War and Post-War Argentina." In *The Paths of Domination, Resistance, and Terror*, ed. Carolyn Nordstrom and JoAnn Martin, 219–59. Berkeley: University of California Press.

Tacchi, Jo, David Slater, and Peter Lewis. 2003. "Evaluating Community-Based Media Initiatives: An Ethnographic Action Research Approach." Paper presented at the OURMedia III Conference, Barranquilla, Colombia, May 19–21.

Téllez, Maria Patricia. 2003. *La Televisión Comunitaria en Colombia: Entre la Realidad y la Utopía.* Bogotá: Ministerio de Cultura and Comisión Nacional de Televisión.

Thumber, Howard, and Jerry Palmer. 2004. *Media at War: The Iraq Crisis.* Thousand Oaks, Calif.: Sage.

Tokatlián, Juan. 2000. *Globalización, Narcotráfico y Violencia: Siete Ensayos sobre Colombia.* Bogotá: Norma.

Torrenegra, Sofi. 2004. Interview by author. Tape recording. Bucaramanga, Colombia. August 16.

Turner, Edith. 2005. "Rites of Communitas." In *Encyclopedia of Religious Rites, Rituals and Festivals,* ed. Frank A. Salomone, 97–101. New York: Routledge.

Turner, Victor. 1982. *From Ritual to Theatre: The Human Seriousness of Play.* New York: Performing Arts.

———. 1988. *The Anthropology of Performance.* New York: PAJ.

Unidad de Radio. 2000. *Radios y Pueblos Indígenas: Memorias del Encuentro Internacional de Radios Indígenas de América.* Bogotá: Ministerio de Cultura.

Unidad de Radio–Diplomado Cartagena. 2002. Recorded session. Tape recording. Cartagena, Colombia.

Unidad de Radio–Grupo de Políticas e Investigación. 2006. "Radios Ciudadanas: Espacios para la Democracia. Fase II: 2006–2010." Unpublished document. Bogotá: Dirección de Comunicaciones, Ministerio de Cultura.

Unidad de Radio–Memorias Mesa Regional Nariño. 2000. Unpublished document. Bogotá: Unidad de Radio, Dirección de Comunicaciones, Ministerio de Cultura.

Unidad de Radio–Mesa Regional Antioquia. 2000. Recorded session. Tape recording. San Pedro de los Milagros, Colombia.

Unidad de Radio–Mesa Regional Boyacá, Arauca, Casanare. 2001. Recorded session. Tape recording. Aquitania, Colombia.

Unidad de Radio–Mesa Regional Cauca, Putumayo, Nariño. 2000. Recorded session. Tape recording. Pasto, Colombia.

Unidad de Radio–Mesa Regional Huila. 2001. Recorded session. Tape recording. Huila, Colombia.

Unidad de Radio–Mesa Regional Magdalena Medio and Santanderes. 2000. Recorded session. Tape recording. San Juan de Girón, Colombia.

Unidad de Radio–Taller AREDMAG. 1998. Recorded session. Tape recording. Barrancabermeja, Colombia.

Unidad de Radio–Taller Belén de los Andaquíes. 1997. Recorded session. Tape recording. Belén de los Andaquíes, Colombia.

United Nations Office of Drugs and Crime. 2007. "Coca Cultivation in the Andean Region: A Survey of Bolivia, Colombia and Peru." Available at http://www.unodc.org/pdf/andean/Andean_report_2007.pdf.

Uribe, Maria Teresa. 1991. *Matar, Rematar, Contramatar.* Bogotá: CINEP.

Uribe, Maria Victoria. 2007. *Antropología de la Inhumanidad: Un Ensayo Interpretativo sobre el Terror en Colombia.* Bogotá: Norma.

U.S. Department of State. 2000. "United States Support for Colombia." Fact sheet released by the Bureau of Western Hemisphere Affairs. March 28. Available at http://www.state.gov/www/regions/wha/colombia/fs_000328_plancolombia .html.

U.S. Department of State Bureau of International Narcotics and Law Enforcement Affairs. 2011. "Program and Budget Guide." Available at http://www .state.gov/p/inl/rls/rpt/pbg/fy2011/index.htm.

Vásquez, Teófilo. 2006. "Dinámicas, Tendencias e Interacciones de los Actores Armados en el Magdalena Medio 1990–2001." In *Conflictos, Poderes e Identidades en el Magdalena Medio 1990–2001,* ed. Mauricio Archila and Ingrid Bolívar, 313–72. Bogotá: CINEP.

Vásquez Perdomo, Maria Eugenia. 2005. *My Life as a Colombian Revolutionary: Reflections of a Former Guerrillera.* Philadelphia: Temple University Press.

Vega, Jair, and Soraya Bayuelo. 2008. "Ganándole Terreno al Miedo: Cine y Comunicación en Montes de María." In *Lo Que le Vamos Quitando a la Guerra: Medios Ciudadanos en Contextos de Conflicto Aramdo en Colombia,* ed. Clemencia Rodríguez, 53–63. Bogotá: Centro de Competencias de Comunicación— Fundación Friedrich Ebert.

Von Kalternborg-Stachau, Henriette. 2008. *The Missing Link: Fostering Positive Citizen-State Relations in Post-Conflict Environments.* Washington, D.C.: International Bank for Reconstruction and Development/World Bank Communication for Governance and Accountability Program (ComGAP). Available at http://siteresources.worldbank.org/EXTGOVACC/Resources/CommGAP MissingLinkWeb.pdf.

Wallensteen, Peter, and Margareta Sollenberg. 2000. "Armed Conflict, 1989–99." *Journal of Peace Research* 37 (5): 635–46.

Warren, Kay B. 1993. "Interpreting La Violencia in Guatemala: Shapes of Mayan Silence and Resistance." In *The Violence Within: Cultural and Political Opposition in Divided Nations,* ed. Kay Warren, 25–56. Boulder, Colo.: Westview Press.

———. 2000. "Death Squads and Wider Complicities: Dilemmas for the Anthropology of Violence." In *Death Squad: The Anthropology of State Terror,* ed. Jeffrey A. Sluka, 226–47. Philadelphia: University of Pennsylvania Press.

———. 2002. "Toward an Anthropology of Fragments, Instabilities, and Incomplete Transitions." In *Ethnography in Unstable Places: Everyday Lives in Contexts of Dramatic Political Change,* ed. Carol J. Greenhouse, Elizabeth Mertz, and Kay B. Warren, 379–92. Durham: Duke University Press.

Werbner, Richard. 1991. *Tears of the Death: The Social Biography of an African Family.* Washington, D.C.: Smithsonian Institution Press.

Wills Obregón, Maria Emma. 2000. "De la Nación Católica a la Nación Multicultural: Rupturas y Desafíos en la Constitución de 1991." In *Museo, Memoria y*

Nación: Memorias del Simposio Internacional y IV Cátedra Anual de Historia Ernesto Restrepo Tirado, 385–415. Bogotá: Ministerio de Cultura, Museo Nacional de Colombia, PNUD, ICANH, IEPRI-UN.

Wilson, Scott. 2001a. "Chronicle of a Massacre Foretold: Colombian Villagers Implicate Army in Paramilitary Strike." *Washington Post,* January 28.

———. 2001b. "Colombian Death Site Abandoned to Ghosts: Village Still Inspires Fear." *Washington Post,* December 30.

Wolfsfeld, Gadi, Eitan Y. Alimi, and Wasfi Kailani. 2008. "News Media and Peace Building in Asymmetrical Conflicts: The Flow of News between Jordan and Israel." *Political Studies* 56:374–98.

World Bank. 2004. *Implementation and Completion Report on a Learning and Innovation Loan in the Amount of U.S. $5 Million to Colombia for the Second Magdalena Medio Regional Development Project.* Report number 30271. Washington, D.C.: World Bank.

Zamosc, Leon. 1986. *The Agrarian Question and the Peasant Movement in Colombia, 1967–1981.* London: Cambridge University Press.

———. 1997. "Transformaciones Agrarias y Luchas Campesinas en Colombia: Un Balance Retrospectivo." In *Estructuras Agrarias y Movimientos Campesinos en America Latina (1950–1990),* ed. Leon Zamosc, Estela Martínez, and Manuel Chiriboga, 76–132. Madrid: Centro de Publicaciones, Ministerio de Agricultura, Serie Estudios.

INDEX

081 (paramilitary school), 145

Acción Social, 284n23

accountability, 2, 4, 8, 34, 160, 210, 219, 252; improving, 22, 161–64

ACCU. *See* Autodefensas Campesinas de Córdoba y Urabá

Acosta, Marcelino, 129

activism, 29, 183; community, 7–11; dissent and, 141–43; political, 242

Agencia Rural para el Desarrollo, 288n9

agency, 12, 19, 58–63, 82, 259

aggression, 119, 166, 208, 215, 217, 218, 230

agricultural families, 39, 45, 48, 139

Aires del Pacífico, 29, 277n25

ALER. *See* Asociación Latinoamericana de Educación Radiofónica

Alfaro, Rosa María, 30

Alianza Nacional Popular (ANAPO), 9

Alirio, Blanco, 38, 52

Alternative Information Center, 232

Alto Ariari, 132, 209, 238

Amantes del Vallenato, 227

Amor y Literatura, 186

ANAPO. *See* Alianza Nacional Popular

Andaquí Territory, 77; photo of, 77

Andean Regional Initiative, 280n26, 282n3

Anselmo, Don, 52, 83

Anti-Corruption Committee, 227

Antioquia, 42, 135, 195, 279n9

Antioquia Regional Roundtable on Community and Citizens' Communication, 195

ANUC. *See* Asociación Nacional de Usuarios Campesinos

Archila, Mauricio, 18, 136

Arcila Niño, 69, 279n12

AREDMAG. *See* Asociación Red de Emisoras Comunitarias del Magdalena Medio

Arendt, Hannah, 64

armed conflict, 2, 4, 5, 13, 19, 21, 56, 58, 64, 75, 76–77, 104, 106, 109, 113, 126, 130, 148, 150, 158, 160, 169, 176, 182, 196, 203, 204, 206, 210, 220, 228, 244, 260, 261, 262, 264; analyzing, 23, 232, 235; in Caquetá, 44–47; citizens' media and, 20, 34, 60, 156, 188, 201, 205, 207, 232–33, 241, 249, 253, 254–55; citizenship and, 211; collective imaginary and, 186; community and, 60, 234, 239; community radio stations and, 159, 199, 202; culture of, 208; economic elites and, 10–11; family life and,

CLEMENCIA RODRÍGUEZ is professor of communication at the University of Oklahoma. She has conducted research on citizens' media in Nicaragua, Colombia, Spain, and Chile, and among Latino communities in the United States. She is author of *Fissures in the Mediascape: An International Study of Citizens' Media*; coauthor (with Patricia Téllez) of *La Telenovela en Colombia: Mucho más que Amor y Lágrimas*; and editor of *Lo Que Le Vamos Quitando a la Guerra: Medios Ciudadanos en Contextos de Conflicto Armado en Colombia*.